PRIESTHOOD

A COMPARATIVE STUDY

STUDIES
IN THE HISTORY OF RELIGIONS

(SUPPLEMENTS TO *NUMEN*)

XXV

PRIESTHOOD
A COMPARATIVE STUDY

LEIDEN
E.J. BRILL
1973

PRIESTHOOD

A COMPARATIVE STUDY

BY

LEOPOLD SABOURIN, S.J.

LEIDEN
E.J. BRILL
1973

ISBN 90 04 03656 3

PRINTED IN BELGIUM

CONTENTS

FOREWORD

The writing of this book has been an arduous and difficult task, which required extensive reading on widely varying subjects, not all hitherto familiar to the present writer. Hopefully the overall result will appear as a satisfactory compendium of what is known about ancient priesthood and the priesthood of Christ. No attempt is made to present an exhaustive survey of the phenomenon of priesthood in comparative religion. On the other hand, great attention is paid, especially in chapters II and III, to the cultural and religious framework in which priesthood asserts itself. Thus will the particulars be seen in their proper perspective and the reader better introduced to fields of knowledge with which he might not be familiar, as, for example, the Indo-Iranian or the Mesopotamian cultural worlds.

Considering that priesthood displays varying physionomies even in a given milieu, it will often appear advisable to speak of priesthoods in the plural. No notion of priesthood can be found which could uniformly apply to the multifarious expressions of it in the religions of mankind. A peculiar case is the so-called "natural priesthood," that of the heads of families or of clans, often acknowledged also in kings as "royal priesthood". Without being priests in the strict sense these privileged persons exercised priestly functions in given circumstances, especially when or where no organized priesthood yet existed.

It is distinctive of the professional priest to be connected with a sanctuary or shrine, small or large, where he serves according to a traditional set of rites and customs. In this he differs from the ecstatic or the prophet, whose activity is exercised on an individual basis. There is, then, in the priest's profession, continuity and stability, often assured by hereditary succession. More specifically, the priest is the professional of worship, in a variety of forms. Among the primitives he is the specialist who regulated the rites of sacrifice in line with tradition, while in Mesopotamia and Egypt the priest's essential function centered on the statue which embodied the god of the temple. In Israel also the priest was the guardian of tradition, and he was, besides, consecrated to his office by the rites of tradition. The Israelite priest was, in addition, a presence among the people, to whom he offered guidance, especially as regarded ritual purity. But we shall see that in Levitical priesthood the emphasis shifted from the oracular and teaching functions to that concerned with the offering of sacrifice. A further attempt will be made in the general conclusion to determine what belongs to the generic notion of priesthood and what its specific features are, as it appears in the various societies studied.

We are concerned in this book with the priesthood of men or of women forming a distinct category in the society. So we prescind from the so-called "general priesthood" (*allgemeine Priestertum*) either of the laymen or of the community, a theory commonly associated with texts like Ex 19:6 and 1 Pet 2:5. Excepting the High Priesthood of Christ himself, we do not treat here of Christian priesthood or ministry. The present book ends fittingly with the priesthood of Christ, who alone fulfilled all that mankind expected from its representatives before God. Rather than the greatest priest, Christ is, in fact, the only Priest in the full sense of the term, the only perfect Mediator who by his unique sacrifice leads humanity to God.

The present writer is greatly indebted to several scholars who examined the first redaction of the work and suggested corrections and improvements. They are Fr. Joseph Goetz, S.J., of the Gregorian University (ch. 1), and my colleagues of the Pontifical Biblical Institute : Dr. Annelies Kammenhuber (Indo-Iranians and Hittites), Fr. Edouard des Places, S.J. (Ancient Greece), Rev. Dr. Jan van Dijk (Mesopotamia), Fr. Mitchell Dahood, S.J. (Canaanites), Fr. Adhémar Massart, S.J. (Egypt), Fr. Raimund Köbert, S.J. (ancient Arabs), Fr. Robert North, S.J. (ch. IV and V), Fr. Albert Vanhoye, S.J. (ch. VI). Needless to say that the responsibility for what is written remains entirely my own.

The footnotes contain mostly references to the authors quoted. Signs in the text, like* or +, indicate that substantive notes or further references on the matter can be found in the "booknotes" at the end of the book (page references in the margin). Cross-references have been avoided, but the index of subjects will serve a similar purpose. The abbreviations used are generally self-explanatory.

L. Sabourin, s.j.

CHAPTER ONE

PRIESTHOOD IN PRIMITIVE SOCIETIES

The term *primitive societies* is used here to refer to peoples who have not yet attained the cultural development proper to what is called civilization. Since no written and little monumental documentation is available on the original institutions of ancient preliterate races, any investigation of their priesthoods depends almost exclusively on direct observation of present-day "primitives" (for this reason we shall generally refer to them in the present tense). Such an investigation is not, however, an easy task. Fortunately, published reports of systematic inquiries made by ethnologists are available. Only one study, to my knowledge, has been published expressly on the subject of priesthood among primitive peoples. It is G. Landtman, *The Origin of Priesthood* (Ekenaes, Finland, 217 pp., hereafter cited as *LOP*). It is a synthesis, written *in camera*, of conclusions drawn from a large number of observations the author read in the library of the Britisch Museum. The article in Hastings, *ERE*, vol. 10, pp. 325-335, by the same author, is an outline of his previous, larger work. Numerous general histories of religions and particular studies published since then* offer new data and often changed perspectives. The data regarding priesthood, for example, are no longer explained and classified, as in Landtman's time, in terms of linear evolution : magic, animism, religion, monotheism. The distinctiveness of the priest as compared to other specialists, like the magician, the diviner, the medicine man, and the shaman is now being increasingly recognized. However, Landtman's work remains a good source book of facts and inferences.

A. The Origin of Priesthood

Although priesthood, understood in its proper sense, is a notion quite different from that of other professions which are also concerned with the invisible forces and supernatural beings, we include here references to magic, partly because clear-cut distinctions are not always evident in primitive religious behavior.

a) Religious Practitioners

The primitives feel, more than literate peoples, the presence of the invisible powers that surround them and with whom they have to coexist. The religious specialists are expected to offer guidance and assistance in the pertinent ways of dealing with these forces. One type of solution suggests dependence and is founded on religion, while another seeks to dominate the powers, with magic as its means. The need of specialists is felt particularly in specified areas of human wants : weather forecasting and control, propagation and preservation of life, food supply, knowledge of the future. It is common knowledge that the magician, the diviner, and the priest, among the primitives, are concerned with these problems, although they approach them with very distinctive viewpoints.

The universal conviction among the primitives that the whole of nature, as well as any prosperity in life, is governed by supernatural agencies has accentuated the need of specialists able to understand these agencies and, if possible, control them. One early manner of dealing with these powerful presences involved magic, which in the beginning everyone practiced as he could. There were practitioners who devoted more time than others to the art, and if they were skillful they gained in confidence, even becoming professional magicians. These gradually emerged as a distinct class, the specialists who dealt with the unknown powers present in nature.

b) The Requisites of Worship

Another form of specialization, a more religious way of dealing with the spirit-world, was provided by worship. This was meant to act directly on the personal forces through prayer, sacrifice, and the various means of pleasing or placating them. "There is every reason to believe that in the earliest history of the cult no proper priesthood existed. Although various kinds of priestly practitioners undoubtedly belong to a very early period of religious evolution, all conclusions point to the rule that originally everybody invoked the gods each for himself. Cult has therefore existed in some form or other before there were any professional men entrusted with the duty of conducting the different religious observances" (*LOP*, p. 53). The Thongas, for example, have no priestly caste. The right of officiating in religious ceremonies is strictly confined to the eldest brother through whom all offerings have to be made.[1] The need for guidance in worship, however, was felt very soon. The naturally religious primitives want to know what deities to worship and how to obtain their favor. The origin of priesthood is especially connected with the primitive forms of worship.

In the family cult the paterfamilias or another prominent member of the family circle conducts the service.* When tribal gods and ancestral gods appear on the mythological scene, the cult becomes properly worship and extends to the clan and even beyond it. The privilege of conducting worship may pass to one of the descendants of the gods. When "bloodrelationship" with the gods (e.g., in the totemic system) becomes obscured, the office is eventually held by the tribal chief or the national ruler. Not rarely, however, dynasties of sacerdotal kingship originate when a family of priests rises through accumulated power to national prominence and sovereignty. In some cases priests of great reputation accede to the spontaneous wish of the population and become both temporal and spiritual heads of their community. Some chiefs are known to have assumed the office of priest with a view to strengthening their personal power. But the king-priest institution tends to dissolve when temporal rulers can no longer perform adequately the ever increasingly complex duties of priesthood. This form of development, as understood by Landtman and others (see *LOP*, p. 67), undoubtedly applies in many cases, especially in the later phases of advanced societies. If among them a chief assumes the function of priest in his tribe, he does so as the father would in his own family.

Perhaps the following description of priesthood in ancient China can illustrate an original pattern also followed elsewhere. "In ancient times, though officers were appointed to guard the temples and prepare the temple sacrifices, they did not form a separate class, nor were they a sacrificial priesthood. The Emperor was the High Priest of Heaven for the whole nation, the Prince was the Prince-Priest in his domain, the chief was the priest for the clan, and the father priest for his household.[2]

c) *Other Specialists and Forerunners of Priests*

Recapitulating, it can be said that the primitives have been aware of unseen forces whose presence played an important role in man's

---

[1] H. Junod, *The Life of a South African Tribe*, v. 1 (2nd edit., London 1927) 411.

[2] W. Soothill, *The Tree Religions of China* (3rd edit., Oxford 1930) 142. See also H. Maspéro, *La Chine antique* (new edit., Paris 1955) 156-158 (the clergy), 131-146 (the gods), 146-155 (the ancestors).

earthly life and in the regulating of nature. The means of dealing with these powers, personal and impersonal, developed in two directions: worship was advocated by the priests; the technique of efficacious rites belonged to the magicians. The magicians were not, any more than the medicine men and the shamans, strictly speaking, forerunners of the priests, nor can they be considered as forming a sort of embryonic priesthood. It is true, however, that in various primitive societies, these other types of specialists, the medicine men especially, appeared before the priest, with whom they are also sometimes equated. The reason is that various specializations do in fact meet in the same individual or even in regional types of "priesthood".

It is natural enough that the origin of priesthood should in some way be connected with holy sites and with the origin of temples and other sanctuaries. Surveys of primitive societies show that the guardians of sacred places have in many regions pioneered the institution of priesthood. Since holy sites generally have been considered as being the abode of gods or spirits,* those having charge of them were often popularly promoted, rightly or wrongly, to the status of mediators with the supernatural (*LOP*, p. 72). The special function of the *Buyya* (priest), among the Saoras, for example, is to maintain the cult of the *sadru* shrines and to guard the village lands from the interference of hostile spirits and sorcerers.[3] In Mesopotamia and Egypt the priests' main function was the care of the god dwelling in his earthly image. For Plato, priests were mainly sacristans (*neôkoroi*) of the gods. It is true that the god's well-being conditioned, even produced, the prosperity of his worshippers or of the nation. Hence the important mediatorial role of the priest.

The ability to communicate with the divine has always been considered a prerogative of priests. This ability was in high esteem and demand, among the primitives, who could single out persons supposedly gifted in that respect, the ecstatics, individuals who, affected by convulsive fits, appeared to be outside of themselves and presumably possessed by a supernatural power. While in this state of "occasional inspiration," they could be interrogated on the will of the gods or on the future course of events. Because of their extraordinary instuitions of the divine these visionaries often were credited with priesthood. Priestly functions also were exercised occasionally by individuals who, because of their truly religious behavior, or because of their eccentric habits, were classed among the *holy men.* Those who performed wonders easily

---

[3] See V. Elvin, *The Religion of an Indian Tribe* (Oxford 1955) 129.

became the object of great veneration and were looked upon as divinely appointed mediators. Holy men were consulted on various occasions, and in this capacity of advisers they also can be numbered among the pioneers of priesthood.

B. The Differentiation of Priesthood

The subsequent chapters of the present study will show how priesthood developed in successive periods and in various milieux. The early differentiation of priesthood into a distinctive institution results from general factors which can be determined. These will now be examined, together with some features common to the priesthoods of primitive societies.

a) *Early Differentiation*

Some kind of social differentiation is quite inevitable in any given tribe or race. Yet ethnological observations of primitive societies seem to demonstrate that "arbitrarily divided classes are by no means universal among mankind" (*LOP*, p. 5). As a result of the natural process of differentiation, three main categories have eventually divided most human societies : the nobility, the commonalty, and the slave or servant class.

Of the more distinctive and lesser classes, ethnology also teaches, priesthood has generally been the first to appear. This fact warrants the conclusion : priesthood is found very early, among all peoples, even where other class distinction is wanting. Such early and general differentiation of priesthood seems partly due to the exceptionally broad basis of its origin as an answer to man's most fundamental problems. Another reason is the commitment of many of its members to several important areas. Professionals of worship, their essential concern, the priests often appropriated the function of other specialists, such as medicine men, diviners, and magicians. While the medicine men, generally the first religious specialists in time, do not form a class, the priests, coming later, constitute both a profession and a class, especially when the establishment of a state fosters group distinctions within a given society. The term *priest* writes E. Norbeck, "usually implies large societies with centralized authority, a fairly elaborate development of culture, [and] the existence of an organized cult with well-formulated doctrine and fixed rituals."[4] Norbeck concludes that, as the conceptions of religion and magic, although logically different, tend to be mixed, so also the priest often assumes the role of the medicine man, the diviner, and the shaman. J. Goetz believes that the notion of priesthood essentially implies a specific relation to one or to several divinities; and for J. Wach, "The popular authority of the priest... rests ultimately on his communion with the numen expressed in formalized cult." While the magician forces the deity or the spirits to obey him, the priest submits his will to the divine.[5]

b) *A very Distinctive Class*

The numerous features that have made of priesthood a very distinctive class from the beginning belong to two types: priests are above their fellow men, and they live apart from the community. What will be said under the present heading is primarily true of primitive societies, much less so of a sophisticated environment.

Several important factors contribute to elevate the priests above their fellow men. Generally more intelligent than the common folk, the priests often owe their vocation to their knowledge, which, however rudimentary, is a great asset in an illiterate society. This knowledge they jealously keep and possibly increase, both as individuals and as members of a class, transmitting to others the formulae and the secrets of the profession. As a point of fact, "the scanty learning of savage races is almost exclusively confined to the priesthood" (*LOP*, p. 125). Both as preservers of the tribal traditions and as initiators in the useful arts, the priests stand apart from their fellow tribesmen and beyond the narrow limitations of life in primitive conditions. Where the *taboo* laws also affect the sacred persons, priests stand farther away from the ordinary circles of society. "If it seems strange," H. Webster writes, "that sacred persons should be treated in much the same fashion as polluted persons, the explanation lies in the ambivalence of the conception of *taboo*. Primitive thought does not clearly distinguish sacredness from uncleanness.... The common characteristic of sacred persons and polluted persons is their mystic dangerousness."[6]

As we shall see shortly, priests willingly stress their exceptional ability and power. As mediators of the supernatural they are indeed expec-

---

4 E. Norbeck, *Religion in Primitive Society* (New York 1961) 103.

5 J. Wach, *Sociology of Religion* (London 1947) 371.

6 H. Webster, *Taboo. A Sociological Study* (Stanford, Calif., 1942) 261.

ted to stand apart and above their fellow men. Some willingly and consciously accentuate the distinctiveness of their profession in various ways. They like to be seen leading a very ascetic life, often made more conspicuous by eccentric habits, like growing long hair and studiously displaying a bizarre external appearance. They maintain and develop a strong *esprit de corps*, protecting one another and keeping the rule of exclusiveness in given areas. Another factor of separateness is the particular language, which the priests use in the divine service or to communicate with one another. American Indian magicans, for example, would give a flavor of *arcanum* to their formulas by using words of another dialect, unknown in the tribe. Great cults are known to have used languages long abandoned by the general public. In 1905, Landtman could cite Latin as the all-purpose language of the Roman Catholic clergy (*LOP*, p. 65). To further signify their separateness, priests in primitive societies often change their names, a custom also common, until recently, in several Catholic religious orders.

c) *Promoting Prominence*

The priests of primitive societies are not devoid of genuine superiority in many areas. The members of the corporation have access to a store of accumulated wisdom transmitted and augmented generation after generation. A sort of "weather-wisdom", for example, expresses itself in forecasting axioms based on long-term observation. Widespread experimentation and the combination of its data produce curing maxims, many of which are wise and practical.

It is often stated that priests in a primitive society are inclined to promote their own prominence by every means. They willingly propagate, it is said, popular belief in their exceptional learning and power. To safeguard their own interests they foster credulity among the people to make the practice of a thousand arts of deceiving easier. Superstition favors priestly domination. Made to believe, for instance, that sorcery has caused their illness, the sick obtain from the priests a liberating rite, well paid for. The awe-inspired attitude on the part of the people is deemed necessary to support sacerdotal prominence. It is encouraged in many ways : weird costumes (see *LOP*, p. 136), gloomy ceremonies, mysterious gestures, and other mystifying devices. Threats of magic power are sometimes used to reduce scorn, mistrust, and hostility. Much of this is no doubt true, but it applies less to the priest as such than to the priest who has taken over the role of medicine man, of diviner, or of magician. The same applies to what follows in this section.

Wonder-working remains, however, the great means of maintaining and promoting prominence. Deities rarely have to intervene, since the natives' great credulity and the priests' exceptional skill combine to produce marvels. As reported by P. Talbot, one such marvel consisted in cutting off a man's head, removing it, and ten putting it back in place.[7] Attestations of miracles in magical occurrences by worthy eye-witnesses have been explained by Sir Flinders Petrie as group "hypnotism." The main point for the performer is to have a ready exit in case of failure. Medicine men and rain-makers are especially exposed to popular vengeance when they fail to produce the expected results. Prophecy and divination are expressed in vague and ambiguous terms, leaving room for proper *ex-eventu* interpretations. Reputation-saving explanations are in fact readily found for random failures in cure, in wonder-making, or in prophecy. Particularly adapted to that purpose are stories about the adverse influence of spirits, since evidence in that field escapes human verification.

In line with what has just been said, it is no surprise that "impostors are undoubtedly met with among the priests at all stages of early beliefs" (*LOP*, p. 148). Yet primitive priesthood cannot be called a class of impostors. For one thing, the priest who has undergone the frightful experience of initiation is prepared to believe that he is henceforth endowed with divine powers. But he who deceives himself is on the way to deceive others. What our standards would term fraudulent practices can be viewed in their original context as conventional and acceptable means of obtaining the desired results. This is especially true of elementary medicine, partly built on symbolic magic and on the laws of self-persuasion. For example, the sucking cure (pretending to remove the cause of infection) is often a *bona fide* operation based on the belief in the efficacy of symbolic action.[8] Examples of fraudulent practices in removing the "cause" of diseases are often quoted (see *LOP*, p. 150, note). Priests of primitive societies should not be hastily condemned if they add a certain dosage of fraud to genuine performances, since even in our civilized world excellence rarely attains the height of fame without a measure of exaggeration.

---

[7] P. Talbot, *The Peoples of Southern Nigeria*, v.2 (London 1926) 197.

[8] See Y. Hirn, *The Origins of Art* (London 1900) 285.

C. Call and Initiation

It is almost axiomatic to say that from a personal point of view the value of a priesthood can be judged from the conditions required of the candidates to it. These requirements are obviously restricted when the priesthood is hereditary, as is sometimes the case among uncivilized tribes, but the rule of inheritance can rarely be strictly followed, since admittance to the profession remains open to exceptional candidates. In fact the claims of heredity, even when recognized, concern priority rather than exclusive rights. "As the principal duty of the priests—with exclusion of the magicians—is to mediate between mankind and the higher powers, so the chief qualifications requisite for entering the priesthood is the faculty of communicating with the gods" (*LOP*, p. 91). This faculty can be "proved" in a number of ways. If the candidate can "see" the spirits, if they speak to him in dreams, he is reckoned to have been chosen by the gods, since priests are generally believed to be assisted by their own tutelary deities, spirits, or demons. It is also a common conviction among the primitives that gods communicate with their chosen ones in dreams, imparting to them the formulas and the power to cure, and occasionally revealing to them the secrets of the future. In many tribes it is considered a condition for those aspiring to shamanism to have seen the god in a dream (cf. *LOP*, p. 97).* In the initiation of the medicine man among Australian tribes, piercing the candidate's tongue with a crystal plays an important role. In other cases the operation is done with a lance thrown by the ancestral spirits.[9]

In a superstitious milieu vocation to the priesthood is seen in a variety of "signs" : "miraculous" escape from dangers (lightning, for example), meaningful coincidences,** unexplained convulsions or swoons (as in epilepsy), deformities, and even insanity. Trances, caused by illness or self-hypnotism, are occasions when the gods manifest themselves to the ecstatic and take command of his movements (cf. *LOP*, pp. 107-108). Some tribes in central Australia think that children born with their eyes open will later be seers and prophets. Among the Ojebway Indians persons have been called witches for no other reason than that they were deformed or ill-looking. In some sections of the Congo, all dwarfs and albinos are elevated to the priesthood, their appearance being the sign

---

[9] See E.O. James, *The Nature and Function of Priesthood* (London 1955) 17-21.

of secret powers (cf. *LOP*, pp. 101-102). Solitariness, day-dreaming, eccentricity, and other psychological curiosities can point to a priestly vocation in a society where the abnormal is a sign of divine presence or visitation. Observing these dispositions in their priests, the candid primitives easily conclude that they belong to the priestly vocation.

In general little distinction seems to be made between the sexes as regards their qualification for priesthood. Among some peoples men take a certain precedence in the sacerdotal profession, and in a few cases we meet with clear statements excluding women from the priesthood (*LOP*, p. 192). In some regions half of the female population is included under the denomination of priestesses (*LOP*, p. 194). Among the primitives women are considered more apt for sorcery than men.*

With the exception of certain cases of adult vocation, the priestly education is generally carried out in two phases. At an early age an experienced priest or expert practitioner imparts to the novice elementary religious instruction and initiates him to the practices of the profession. This preparation includes learning the ritual songs, the sacred formulas, and also the tricks proper to the magical art. The candidate is also trained to deal with the spirit world and perhaps to use the resources of natural medicine properly. One aim of the initiation is to render the candidate absolutely fearless, especially in regard to the spirit world (cf. *LOP*, p. 117).** In the second phase, which can be the only one, the candidate's self-training is carried out : a period of asceticism, including prolonged fasts, supposedly liberates the mind or the soul and disposes the candidate for an apparition of the god, or at least prepares him to communicate in some way with the deity and, in some cases, to be seized by the spirits. Not rarely these ascetic practices are incompatible with the circumstances of ordinary life, accentuating still more the distinctiveness of priesthood. In many tribes the priests are expected to remain single and chaste, sexual relations being considered sinful *in se*. Elsewhere, however, the primitives accept with surprising tolerance the debauchery of their priests. Among some primitive peoples a special ceremony marks consecration to the priesthood.

Among the Saoras the shaman is involved in the choice of priests. "The priest's position is hereditary, and this is natural in view of his official functions. When a new priest is to be appointed, a shaman is called and he, falling into trance, asks the gods and ancestors whether the proposed candidate is acceptable to them. If they agree, the shaman summons the ghost of the last priest to hold office in the village. If he too approves, the shaman (possessed by and representing the dead priest) puts his hands on the head of the new priest and tells him to do his work well."[10]

D. Categories and Functions of Primitive Priesthood

It has been mentioned that primitive society usually consists of three basic classes, while priesthood emerges very soon as a distinct profession and social category. It is our task to differentiate the priests from the other religious specialists. We shall deal with priests and magicians, then shamanism, and conclude with a view of the main functions of primitive priesthood.

a) *Priests and Magicians*

Both religion and magic are universally found in primitive mankind. Wilhelm Schmidt, who investigated the origin of the idea of God among the primitives, and J. Maringer both hold that magic does not play an important role in the early stages of primitive societies when the belief in an all-providing supreme God is still prominent. [11] But the notion of religion varies with the different viewpoints. E.B. Tylor describes it as "belief in spiritual beings," while others define it as "the conception man forms of his relations with the superhuman and mysterious powers on which he believes himself to depend."[12] W.S. Morgan has proposed the following comprehensive definition of religion : "The realization that we are essential and contributory participants in ultimate reality, in nature and humanity."[13] Landtman observes that "religions contain an element of thought, i.e., the religious belief, and an element of action, i.e., the religious cult" (*LOP* 24). And according to J. Wach, religious experience has a theoretical expression, "doctrine", a practical expression, "cultus", and a sociological expression, "communion."[14] If the cultic element is stressed, then religion can be defined as "a propitiation or conciliation of powers superior to man which are believed to direct

[10] V. Elwin, *Religion of an Indian Tribe* 129.

[11] W. Schmidt, *Der Ursprung der Gottesidee*, 12 vols (Münster 1926-55); J. Maringer, *L'homme préhistorique et ses dieux*, trans. P. Stephano (Vichy 1958) 145.

[12] E. Goblet d'Alviella, *Lectures on the Origin and Growth of the Conception of God* (London and Edinburgh 1892) 47. E.B. Tylor's notion is in *Primitive Culture*, v. 1 (6th edit., London 1920) 424.

[13] W. Morgan, *The Philosophy of Religion* (New York 1950) 19.

[14] J. Wach, *Sociology of Religion* 18-34.

and control the course of nature and human life."[15] It is a distinctive feature of priesthood to be concerned with religion, as contrasted with magic.* The priest's mediating power rests upon his capacity to propitiate the supernatural powers or the deity and to obtain their protection. In religion man endeavors to influence personal transcendent beings by supplications expressed in sacrifices, praise, and prayer. While magic is "a practical art consisting of acts which are only means to a definite end expected to follow later on," religion is "a body of self-contained acts being themselves the fulfillment of their purpose."[16]

The *magician*, on the other hand, officiates in his own name and by his own occult methods, relying on secret manipulations of an impersonal if transcendental force, magic energy. He attempts, then, to control directly the forces of nature by means of a technique properly applied. The power of magic is embodied in the spell, and the magician's role is to pronounce correctly the sacred formulae in a precise rite strictly observed. Magic is an endeavor to extend man's power to hitherto uncontrollable phenomena, just as rational technique and empirical knowledge strive to face the natural conditions of human life. In imitative magic, acts are performed imitating that which is desired. The magician will, for example, blow smoke high into the air to cause rain clouds to appear or gather in the sky. Sympathetic magic rests on the belief that a thing is affected by what happens to its representation or effigy.[17] Thus primitive, even paleolithic, paintings of game animals (e.g., buffaloes) being hunted were in many cases intended as a magical control of the chase.** Black magic is used with the intention of harming an enemy. Even apart from this a pernicious influence is not rarely attributed to the magician, while the priest's activity is generally considered as beneficial. Frequently a discredited priest chooses to become a magician.

b) *Shamanism*

In the Arctic and Central Asian regions a large number of priests are *shamans*,*** a type of sacred persons whose principal duties include the following : curing the sick, presiding over the communal sacrifices, and

---

[15] J.G. Frazer, *The Golden Bough*, v. 1 (London 1911) 222, with reference to Cicero, *De inventione* 2.161. On religion as worship, see J. Wach, *op. cit.* pp. 26 and 40-45.

[16] B. Malinowski, *Magic, Science and Religion...* (New York 1948) 88.

[17] See J. De Vries, "Magic and Religion," HistRel 1 (1961-62) 214; J.G. Frazer, *The Golden Bough*, v. 1, pp. 63-65.

escorting the souls of the dead to the other world. While the priest serves at the altar and in the temple or shrine as the representative of the community, the shaman is rather a charismatic individual figure who, unlike the priest, does not exercise his functions in a corporate capacity. The priest is the specialist of worship and should not be confused with the magician, the diviner, the medicine man, or the shaman, even though the categories are often mixed in practice. In shamanism the mystical experience, or *ecstasis*, often called "flight to heaven," constitutes an essential element of the initiation, a period of meaningful dreams and often of hallucinations which may have a strange resemblance to fits of madness. In fact, according to Eliade, "several authors went so far as to explain Arctic and Siberian shamanism as the ritualized expression of a psychomental disease, especially of Arctic hysteria. But the chosen one becomes a shaman only if he can interpret his pathological crisis as a religious experience and succeeds in curing himself. The serious crises which sometimes accompany the election of the future shaman are to be regarded as initiatory trials."[18] In another phase of his novitiate the shaman sees the spirits and even behaves like a spirit, leaving his body to travel in the cosmic regions. It is in fact distinctive of the shaman to be *en rapport* with tutelary or auxiliary spirits, who are more or less at his command if he is not possessed by them. Sometimes "the shaman is a professional magician, but when he shamanizes he is under the influence of supernatural forces external to himself."[19] "Every initiation involves the symbolic death and resurrection of the neophyte. In the dreams and hallucinations of the future shaman may be found the classical pattern of the initiation: he is tortured by demons, his body is cut in pieces, he descends to the nether world or ascends to heaven and is finally resuscitated. That is to say, he acquires a new mode of being, which allows him to have relations with the supernatural worlds."[20] The shaman's special endowment lies in the area of prophecy and divination. His influence can be considered as beneficial, sometimes neutralizing, in point of fact, the activity of the magician.

In ancient China the shamans were credited with the possession of *mana*,* the spiritual power, and were believed to be possessed by spirits

---

[18] M. Eliade, *From Primitives to Zen* (New York 1967) 423-424. See also *id.*, "Initiation Dreams and Visions among the Siberian Shamans," in G. von Grunebaum and R. Caillois, eds., *The Dream and Human Societies* (Berkeley and Los Angeles 1966) 331-340.

[19] E.O. James, *The Nature and Functions of Priesthood* 33.

[20] M. Eliade, *From Primitives to Zen*, p. 424.

of *yang* material, the principle of light and warmth. Theirs was the power of neutralizing the element of darkness (*yin*) so as to exercise successfully their threefold function : invocation of the spirits of the dead, prophecy, and exorcism of all evil. There were shamans of both sexes. They appeared in the earliest times of China's history and, in many cases, seem to be identical with the *wu*, the exorcists. About the time of Christ, the Han dynasty willingly employed these *wu* as healers, because disease was then popularly ascribed to demoniacal possession. The line of demarcation between *wu*-ism and Taoism is ill-defined. In the South Eastern region of the province of Fuhkien, including Amoy Island, De Groot has found "everywhere a class of so-called *sai kong*, who almost exclusively occupy themselves with sacrificial work and exorcising magic." They are considered the most important representatives of the Wu-ist priesthood. The *sai kong* apparently belong to a category of priests who have taken over the functions of other specialists as well.[21]

The mystical basis of shamanism and the functions of the shaman vary with each region and milieu. The following report on the Saoras (India) reveals several typical and original features of shamanism. "The Kuranmaran, or the shaman, has the power not only to diagnose the source of trouble or disease, but to cure it. He is doctor as well as priest, psychologist as well as magician, the repository of tradition, the source of sacred knowledge. His primary duty is that of divination; in case of sickness he seeks the cause in trance or dream. Every shaman has a tutelary-wife in the Under World, and she comes to assist him in any perplexity and often guides him in his duties. He may inherit his powers, and is generally trained by his father or some other relative, but he is chosen by the direct intervention of a tutelary, and his marriage with her effects his dedication. Once that is done he is continually in touch with the gods and ancestors of the other world, and if he is adept he may develop a wide practice, for he is not confined to his own village [like the priest], but may go wherever he is summoned."[22]

c) *Functions of Primitive Priesthood*

Although distinct in theory, priesthood and the profession of magician often meet in the same person. In primitive societies "priests and sor-

---

[21] J.J.M. De Groot, The Religious System of China, v. 6 (Leyden 1892; repr. Taipei 1964) 1187-93

[22] V. Elwin, *The Religion of an Indian Tribe* (Oxford 1955) 130.

cerers almost inextricably blend into one another" (*LOP*, p. 173). Yet their respective functions clearly indicate how much they differ.

The importance and the diversity of the functions expected of the priests and magicians are not surprising when it is remembered that the primitives spontaneously see the hand of the deity in all happenings, be they natural, abnormal, or coincidental. "Rain and wind, increase of vegetation and animal life, on which the prosperity of many peoples depends, are among the savages universally ascribed to the action of the spirits" (*LOP*, p. 24).* Weather-doctors or weather-makers, rain-doctors or rain-makers, as well as weather-prophets are expected practitioners in a milieu where such a religious interpretation of the order of nature prevails. When the Aztecs of Mexico, *c.* 14th century A.D., took over the calendar and other features of Mayan civilization, they "transformed the gods connected with the weather and the crops into a sanguinary pantheon demanding thousands of victims annually to maintain the seasonal sequence.** This aspect of the calendrical ritual [then] became the chief preoccupation of the priesthood."[23] Both the professional interceding of the priests and the magician's expert manipulating of secret power are invoked in favor of the regular flow of nature's benefits and in time of calamities. The special art exercised in weather-prophecy extends to other fields, even to individual future-reading and the conduct of war and peace. Diviners, fortune tellers, and astrologers apply their particular techniques to the uneasy task of reducing the uncertainties of tomorrow. Divination is closely associated with witchcraft, a term which from medieval times has implied some connection with the devil. In several societies priestesses and sorceresses specialize in divination and medicine. Skill in interpreting signs and omens and an ability to understand the language of the spirits have always been considered as prerogatives of priesthood in the primitive societies (*LOP*, pp. 38-39).+ Apart from the "rain priesthood," there existed among the American Indians "the priesthood of the bow," a sort of war society, whose ceremonies were held to give thanks for abundant crops and to make ritual offerings of scalps to the anthropic gods, the controlers of the rain.[24]

Illness and death, above all else, the primitives think, are subject to

---

[23] E. James, *The Nature and Function of Priesthood* 211

[24] See F.W. Hodge, ed., *Handbook of American Indians, North of Mexico*, part 2 (Washington 1910) 524. See also on "rain-making," J.T. Brown, *Among the Bantu Nomads* (London 1926) 128-132, and "on priestcraft," 126-140.

the influence of supernatural agencies. Some think that gods or spirits, for various motives and in different ways, cause these evils among men. Others ascribe them to the magical machinations of evil-doers. In the Australian religions, writes M. Eliade, "death is not natural; it is provoked by someone. All dead are victims of sorcery. The magic accounts even for such emphatically 'natural' causes as being speared in combat; for, it is argued, the blow was fatal only because a sorcerer made it so."[25] Especially important, then, in time of illness is the conciliation of the spirits and the neutralizing of malicious spells, effects obtainable by the performance of proper ceremonies. The gods are known to be sharp disciplinarians, and in many cases their anger abates only through the intercession of a qualified mediator. Some diseases, at least partly mental, are directly attributed to demoniacal possession and are cured by exorcism. Among the Ojebways the benevolent priest alone is supposed to have the power to expel the demon possessing a patient. The New Zealanders are told by their priests that the spirit is sure to remain in the body of a sick person until the priests exorcise him (*LOP*, pp. 33-34). A great number of primitive peoples consider the priests as "the masters of the spiritual and magical causes of illness" (*LOP*, p. 34). and as capable of removing them. The priests are very often the only medicinemen available, the only ones who know the traditional prescriptions, which are usually based on the healing powers of the "medicinal herbs."

M. Eliade describes one method of curing in the shamanistic tradition "The most important function of the shaman is healing. Since sickness is thought of as a loss of the soul, the shaman has to find out first whether the soul of the sick man has strayed far from the village or has been stolen by demons and is imprisoned in the other world. In the former case the healing is not too difficult : the shaman captures the soul and reintegrates it in the body of the sick person. In the latter case he has to descend to the nether world, and this is a complicated and dangerous enterprise."[26]

Much of what Eliade writes on the role of medicine men among Australia's aborigines applies no doubt to other categories of those religious specialists, also called "men of high degree." [27] "They cure the sick,

---

[25] M. Eliade, "Australian Religions, Part 5 : Death, Eschatology, and Some Conclusions," HistRel 7 (1968) 245. The real problem for primitives is what H. Lévy-Bruhl calls "the bad death" (see *La mentalité primitive* 310-317).

[26] M. Eliade, *From Primitives to Zen*... 424.

[27] The expression is used by A.P. Elkin, *Aboriginal Men of High Degree* (Sydney 1945), the most important monograph on Australian medicine men, according to Eliade.

defend the community against black magic, discover those responsible for premature deaths, and perform important functions in the initiation ceremonies. But the most specific characteristic of the medicineman is his relation with the Supernatural Beings and the other heroes of the tribe's sacred history. He is the only one who is *really* able to recover the glorious conditions of the mythical Ancestors, the only one who can do what the Ancestors did, for instance, fly through the air, ascend to heaven, travel underground, disappear and reappear. Moreover, only the medicine man can encounter the Supernatural Beings and converse with them, and only he can see the spirits and the ghosts of the dead. In sum, only the medicine man succeeds in surpass ing his human condition, and consequently he is able to behave like the spiritual beings, or, in other words, to partake of the modality of a Spiritual Being.[28]

---

28 M. Eliade, "Australian Religions, Part 4 : The Medicine Men and Their Supernatural Models," HistRel 7 (1967) 159-160.

CHAPTER TWO

DISTINCTIVE FEATURES OF ANCIENT PRIESTHOODS

Having delineated common and meaningful features of priesthood in primitive societies (ch. 1) we now pass to the priesthoods of ancient literate societies, which are recorded in written sources and monuments. We have chosen to start with these priesthoods more remote from the Biblical world, leaving to a subsequent chapter what concerns the Near East. Indo-Iranian civilization and religion played a decisive role for countless generations in the cultures of India and the Far East. Within our scope we cannot do more than single out some of the more distinctive features that characterize the priesthood of this complex world, with indications of the best sources for further study. The same is true for what regards Buddhism and the Graeco-Roman world which come up conveniently for study in this same chapter.

A. Indo-Iranian Priesthoods

The most important branch of the Indo-European (also called "Indo-Germanic") family of languages in Asia is Aryan or Indo-Iranian, with two main divisions : Iranian and Indo-Aryan. * The oldest documents of Indo-Aryan are composed in Sanskrit. ** These are the Vedic Texts, *** which were probably composed before the Aryans had learned the use of writing. "A substantial body of linguistic, religious, and social evidence warrants the assumption that, at one time, the bearers of the two cultures, which find their expression in the Indian *Rigveda*+ on the one hand in parts of the Iranian *Avesta* on the other, formed a unity."[1]

a) *Priesthood in the Vedic Religion*

The earliest available information is in the *Rigveda*,+ a collection of sacred poetry, mainly liturgical hymns, covering, in all probability, the period from 1200 to 1000 B.C. To these original Vedic writings additions were made between 900 and 500 B.C. : first the *Brāhmaṇas*, a sort of prose commentary explaining the symbolic significanec of the rites ; then

---

[1] M. J. Dresden, "Mythology of Ancient Iran," in S. N. Kramer, ed., *Mythologies of the Ancient World* (New York, 1961), p. 333.

the *Aranyakas*, written by forest-dwelling ascetics; and finally the *Upanishads*, in which a mystical commentary on the rites was developed into a profound and original philosophical speculation.

1. Myth and Castes

The term "caste", a Portuguese rendering of sanscrit *varṇa*, "color", or *jāti*, "birth", designates a social category which can be defined thus : an endogamous group of persons, having a common name and a common ancestor, human or divine, traditionally of the same profession or occupation, enjoying the same rights and bound to the same duties, belonging, in a word, to a social class clearly distinct from others.[2]

The castes do not go back to the earliest vedic period. They are alluded to, in the *Rigveda*, only in the more recent Book X, which mentions the mythic origin of the four social classes : the *brāhmaṇa* (priests), the *kṣatriya* (warrior-rulers), the *vaiśya* (farmers and merchants), and the *śudra* (servants or slaves). The famous hymn 90, *Puruṣa-sukta* (vv. 1-12), reveals that the four classes originally emerged respectively from the mouth, the arms, the thighs, and the feet of the *Puruṣa*, the Primeval Man (the One with 1000 heads, eyes, and feet). The later liturgical texts, the *Brāhmaṇas*, distinguish the four classes more clearly still, while the epic and cosmogonic poem *Mahābhārata* (4th cent. B.C. to 4th cent. A.D.) identifies the mother Being as the divinity *Viṣṇu Narayaṇa* (3 B 189, 13-14). It seems that some *Rigveda* books, the 10th included, were (re) edited by the priestly authors of the *Brāhmaṇas*.[3] In fact only the members of the first three groups are *arya* (caste-men), while the menial *śudra*, the "hors-castes", are considered impure, have no rights and cannot be touched by caste-men. Their only duty is to serve obediently and gratis the *arya*. They are strictly excluded from learning the Vedas and from offering sacrifices. The term *paria* designates in southern India the humbler categories of the *vaiśya*, for example peasants and miners. But the Portuguese called *paria* all the lower social classes of India.

The *brāhmaṇa* (Eng. : "brahmans," "brahmins"), on the other hand, enjoy the greatest privileges, of which not the least is that of studying

---

[2] Cf. H. von Glasenapp, *Die Philosophie der Inder. Eine Einführung in ihre Geschichte und ihre Lehren* (Stuttgart, 1949).

[3] Cf. P. Masson-Oursel, "Les religions de l'Inde," in M. Gorce-R. Mortier, *Histoire générale des religions*, v. 3 (Paris, 1945), p. 6. On castes, cf. L. Dumont, *Homo hierarchicus, essai sur le système des castes* (Paris, 1966); J. H. Hutton, *Castes in India* (Cambridge, 1946).

and of teaching the Veda. Considered as the recipients and the custodians of all that came to man through revelation (*śruṭi*) and tradition (*smrṭi*), they are granted in the sacred books a sort of monopoly on all spiritual and moral power, even a claim to the possession of everything that exists in this world. In the later writings the *brāhmaṇa* even described themselves as gods on earth. They are those who serve the male personal god Brahmā or the impersonal absolute god *Brahman* (neutral).* The privileged status of the *brāhmaṇa* is especially accentuated in the *Brāhmaṇas.*[4] There is no limit set to the amount of gifts they are entitled to receive. They alone, it is said, are holy enough to partake of the sacrificial offerings. To slay a brahman is the only real form of murder and a crime that can be expiated only by the expensive horse-sacrifice. The *brāhmaṇa* stand above any one else on earth and claim to be exempt from royal jurisdiction.

2. *The Power of Sacrifice*

This unique status of the *brāhmaṇa* priests rests on their assumed divine origin, and also on the mystic power of sacrifice, which they regulate and perform. The Vedic hymns see in personified sacrifice the magic power by means of which the gods produced the world and the ancestors achieved their great enterprises. To the ancient ritualists sacrifice appears as creator and creation,** as center of life and of the universe, even as a living being that is created and killed and reborn again in innumerable alternations.[5] "The sacrifice which regulates the relations of man with the deities is a mechanical performance operating through the inner energy; concealed within nature, it emerges only by the magical action of the priest. The hostile and wearied gods are bound to capitulate, conquered and subdued by the very source of their power... Sacrifice has, then, all the characteristics of a magical operation."[6] According to Masson-Oursel, the vedic gods are in fact deities that spring from and subsist in the magical power of the liturgical actions and the accompanying enunciation of the sacred formulas. This ritual power is also called *brahman.*[7]

---

[4] An English edition of the *Brāhmaṇas* can be found in v. 12, 41, 43, 44 of *The Sacred Books of the East*, M. Müller, ed., (Oxford, 1882-1900). The translation is by J. Eggeling: "The *Satapatha-Brāhmana*, according to the text of the Madhyandina School."

[5] A. F. A. Hillebrandt, "Worship (Hindu)", Hastings ERE v. 12 (1921), p. 798.

[6] S. Lévi, *La doctrine du sacrifice dans les Brahmanas* (Paris, 1898), pp. 9-10 and 129 (my translation).

[7] P. Masson-Oursel, "Les Religions de l'Inde", p.6.

Such being the importance and the power of sacrifice, it had to be performed according to all the rules of the ritual. Any change of the rubrics or of the sacred formulas (*mantras*) could invalidate sacrifices and expose the priests and offerers to the greatest danger. The chief ministers of the sacrifice were *brāhmaṇa,* and they had to be without bodily defects and well instructed. It is distinctive of the ancient Indian sacrifice that it was celebrated for individuals and had no social significance. The horse sacrifice also was formally an offering of the king alone, although it was intended to secure the prosperity of the whole kingdom. In the later *gavāmayana* offering, however, involving a year long sacrificial session, all the participants are consecrated, that is, made priests, and the sacrifice is for the benefit of all and not merely of the offerer. For it is a fundamental notion of primitive and ancient sacrifice that all those who participate in it acquire a sacred character which isolates them from the profane world. Accordingly exit-rites are provided to release them from the magical circle and allow their safe return to normal life.[8] The *soma*-sacrifice, which required 16 or 17 priests for its celebration, constitutes the ma·n subject-matter of the *Rigveda.**

3. *Features of the Vedic Priesthood*

The Vedic hymns and their later commentaries do not give a clearer picture of priesthood than, say, the Biblical Psalms in regard to the religious institutions of Israel. The main functions of ancient Indian priesthood had to do with sacrifice. The ministers of sacrifice, the *Ṛtvijaḥ* (sing. : *Ṛtvij*), varied in number according to the nature and the importance of the rite to be performed. The functions attending it gradually led to a clearer differentiation of the categories of the "priests of sacrifice." In the *soma*-sacrifice there were four main celebrants.[9] The *Hotar*, "the one who offers, invokes," recited the Vedic hymns in honor of the gods, to praise them and invite them to the sacrificial feast. He was the chief figure at the sacrifice and not rarely was both the composer and the singer of the hymns. The *Adhvaryu* was the practical performer of the sacrifice. He had three assistants, and it was his task, among other functions, to prepare the *soma* or to immolate the victims. While performing his tasks he had to mutter sacred formulas or hum

[8] Cf. H. Hubert and M. Mauss, in *Mélanges d'Histoire des Religions* (1909), p. 67.

[9] Cf. A. Ballini, "Le religioni dell'India," in P. Tacchi Venturi, ed., v. 1, *Storia delle religioni* (5th ed., Turin, 1962), pp. 679-680.

verses of the hymns. The *Udgātar*, "singer," provided the sacrificial celebration with the proper accompanying melodies. The value of the sacrifice depended on their exact performance. The fourth of the officiants is in some texts called *brāhman*, though it seems that the technical use of this term to designate a special priest, among others, in the performance of sacrifice, is a comparatively recent innovation in the ritual of a particular family.[10] Originally an attendant priest who recited sacred stanzas in honor of *Indra* during the *soma*-sacrifice, the *brāhman* subsequently was made supervisor of the whole rite. In the more recent 4th Veda, called *Atharvaveda,* * at a time when magic and theosophical speculation pervaded the myth, the *brāhman* was the chief priest of sacrifice. Later on the term *brahman* (neuter) came to mean "prayer," then it expressed the symbol of absolute unity (*Brahman*) and finally it designated the deity (*Brahmā*). The Indian pantheon included among terrestrial "gods" a sacerdotal deity called *Bṛhaspati* or *Brahmaṇaspati*, described mainly as "the lord of prayer" (*brahman*), but also as adviser to the (celestial) gods, who through his mediation triumph over the demons.

Apart from the ministers of sacrifice, whom wealthy patrons selected from the sacerdotal class to perform the ceremonies, the *Rigveda* mentions another category of priests, the *purohita*, the domestic priests of the king or of wealthy nobles. It can be assumed that the *purohita* himself performed the minor rituals and superintended the execution of major sacrifices. Unlike the other priests, the *purohita* was closely associated with his master even in worldly concerns. Not rarely he was to him a sort of *alter ego*, sharing his good as well as his bad fortunes. In general, according to Ragozin, "The priests who confront us in the Rig-Veda, though already forming a distinct class (not caste), are simpler in attitude and in organization than their successors, the Brahmans."[11]

4. Later Developments

The *Upaniṣads* (600-300 B.C.) carry further the doctrine of the unity of the universe in sacrifice. The chief interest now centers on the attempt to explain the nature of the universe and its relation to the

[10] Cf. A. B. Keith, "Priest, Priesthood (Hindu)", Hastings ERE v. 10, p. 313.

[11] Z. Ragozin, *Vedic India, as embodied principally in the Rig-Veda* (2d ed., London-New York, 1899), p. 382.

self. The *brahmaṇa* should concentrate on study and teaching. Other books of this literature try to determine what value and what importance should be attributed to the various factors of religious life : sacrifice, study of the Veda, asceticism, almsgiving. Knowledge, it is now claimed, can be found outside brahmanism, and women begin to participate in the discussions on religion and truth.

Creative brahman teaching also led to the formation of theological schools, and even sects, like *Jainism,* which developed systematically the ascetic view of religion, including the absolute prohibition from destroying life. The Jain monk is forbidden to possess any property or even to be attached to any object or person. He is a homeless wanderer compelled to beg his food. In one form of the sect he wears no clothes, as a sign of absolute detachment. Jainism admitted an order of nuns and also orders of lay male and female adherents.

The term Jainism derives from the name given to the pioneer "saints" of the sect : *Jīnas,* "conquerors," or leaders of schools of thought. "Sharing in the theoretical pessimism of the Buddhist, Sankhya and Yoga philosophies, the sect aims in practice at the goal of liberation from the transmigration of the soul."[12] According to its creed, however, women cannot attain *nirvana.* The sect draws its adherents almost exclusively from the cultivated class (mostly traders), and is at least as ancient as Buddhism, its expansion being attested already in the 4th cent. B.C. Its nucleus lies in a strictly disciplined monastic order.

b) *Priesthood in Hinduism*

The Vedic religion gradually evolved into *Hinduism** between the 6th and 2nd cent. B.C. The ancient texts, mainly the *Rigveda,* the *Brāhmaṇas,* and the *Upaniṣads* became its sacred literature.**

1. *In ancient Hinduism*

In the new, more popular, religion, the priest of the sacrificial ritual loses his prominence in favor of the *purohita,* who, more than ever, enjoys the highest privileges. His skilled assistance is greatly appreciated by the kings, in two fields especially : the administration of the kingdom and the ceremonial of the imperial horse sacrifice. The Hindu epics tell of kings obeying the priest also in his role of soothsayer, astrologer and magician. Significant for the importance of the Hindu priesthood is the

---

[12] EncBrit v. 12, p. 868.

reported fact that "in the post-Vedic period 'right' or 'wrong' simply meant the exact performance or the neglect—whether intentional or unintentional—of all the details of a prescribed ritual, the center of which is sacrifice."[13]

During this same early period, as it appears in the Buddhist texts, the *brāhmaṇa* begin to adopt other professions, like trade and farming. Those who still perform their priestly duties turn their special attention to two divinities, *Viṣṇu* and *Ṣiva*, while the pantheistic outlook more and more colors popular devotion.

Some aspects of priesthood in later Hinduism are known from the *purānaṣ* and the classical Sanskrit literature (c. 200 B.C. to 1000 A.D.). An ever increasing number of *brāhmaṇa* adopt secular professions. Those engaged actively in priesthood now divide into families or classes which tend to become exclusive castes. As functions become more clearly diversified, so also the categories of priests. The village priest conducts the occasional ceremonies of the Hindu's religious life. In many cases he is also astrologer, fortune-teller and medicine-man. Other *brāhmaṇa* are in charge of the temple worship, which consists mainly in ceremonies involving the idol of a god. A third category of priests forms the personnel of the religious schools. The Hindu disciples have always shown the greatest respect for their *brāhmaṇa* teachers, who in some sects are treated as living embodiments of their god.

2. *In present-day Hinduism*

In contrast with the ancient custom the great majority of *brāhmaṇa* today adopt non-priestly vocations,* including agriculture and trade, or any calling which does not involve contact with realities ritually impure. The brahmans still claim to be by right the custodians of spiritual knowledge and the mediators between the gods and men. Although this privileged position of theirs is challenged by some sects, "it is fully and freely acknowledged by the vast majority of Hindus, who consider that they would not be good Hindus unless they employed brahmans for the ceremonies connected with births, deaths and marriages. Not all are qualified to employ them. There are many castes contact with whom would pollute the brahman. He therefore holds aloof from them, and their ceremonies have to be performed by men of their own family or

---

[13] EncBrit v. 18, p. 480.

caste."[14] Personal unworthiness, the people believe, does not impair the value of the brahman's ministrations.

Beside the *purohita*, or domestic priests, of whom we have spoken, present-day Hindu priesthood is made up mainly of temple priests and of funeral priests. Temple worship being a relatively recent institution, the temple priests hold secondary rank in the order of dignity. The lowest sacerdotal rank is that of the funeral priest who is regarded with contempt and even aversion because of his necessary involvement with corpses, considered impure and polluting.

"Brahmans of another inferior grade get a living as astrologers. Astrology plays a large part in Indian life; omens and the supposed influence of the stars constantly affect the conduct of affairs... The astronomer is an important functionary. He has to prepare a horoscope when a child is born. When marriages are proposed by parents, the horoscopes of the boy and girl have to be compared to see whether there are planetary influences which would be a bar and impediment to marriage, and whether the marriage would be a lucky one, e.g. whether the bridegroom would die before or after the bride. Auspicious days and hours have to be found for important undertakings, such as marriages, railway journeys and the operations af agriculture like ploughing, sowing and reaping."[15]

Also associated with Hindu priesthood are the "holy men," among whom the most prominent are the *guru*. The name applies to varying kinds of venerable persons, religious teachers or spiritual preceptors of any caste, who are believed to be in peculiarly close communion with God and to hold the secret of divine mysteries. "Intense feeling of reverence can easily pass into adoration, so that the Guru may actually be worshipped, either in his lifetime or after his death... Some of these Gurus are undoubtedly men of pure ascetic life, but others are not, and there have been persons among them who were probably mentally deranged."[16]

c) *Priesthoods of Ancient Iran*

It is believed that the Indo-Iranian cultural unity probably broke up around 1500 B.C.* Little is known of the primitive migration of some

---

[14] L. S. O'Malley, *Popular Hinduism. The Religion of the Masses*, pp. 188-189. In addition, the Brahman's knowledge of Sanskrit often requires his presence.

[15] O'Malley, *Popular Hinduism*, pp. 194-195.

[16] O'Malley, *Popular Hinduism*, pp. 197, 199.

Aryan groups to the Iranian plateau, although the presence there of various populations is attested several centuries later : the Scythians, Sarmatians, and Alans in the North, the Sogdians, Sakas and Parthians in the East, and the Medes and Persians in the West.[17] By the 9th cent. B.C. the two main peoples on the soil of Iran were the Medes, South of the Caspian Sea, and the Persians, North of the Persian Gulf. The Medes dominated politically until the accession of the Achaemenian Cyrus (558 B.C.).

1. Features of Zoroastrianism

Ancient Iran's national religion is usually called Zoroastrianism, from the Greek form (Zoroaster) of its founder's name, the prophet Zarathustra, whom the ancients represented as a sort of philosopher-priest.* The Zoroastrian creed is also called Mazdeism, from the name of the supreme divinity *Ahura Mazdā*, "the Wise Master". Zoroaster's advent, however, took place long centuries after the Aryan invasion of Iran, and until he came, the ancient religious traditions connected with the new settlers' Indian origin survived in a particular form unknown to us. Zarathustra's coming is traditionally set at 258 years "before Alexander," or towards the end of the 6th cent. B.C. This dating, however, is based on a very hypothetical identification of the two names : *Vistāspa*, mentioned in the *Gathas* and *Hystaspes*, father of Darius I. "A little over 1000 B.C." M. N. Dhalla thinks, "is the time most probably correct for the advent of this divine herald of Ahura Mazda."[18] The transmission of the data on this subject was not helped by the fact that "the Magi who furnished to the Greeks all the information that the latter possessed about Zoroaster, were keenly interested in pushing backwards into the past by several centuries the era of their prophet."[19] Even though the majority of present-day scholars consider Zarathustra as a firm historical figure, references to him from the canonical Avestan writings are limited to obscure allusions in the *Gathas*. The greater part of the legends around the figure of Zarathustra are not earlier than the Middle Ages.

The sacred Scripture of the Zoroastrians, and our main source of information on Iranian mythology and religion is the Avesta, which in

---

[17] M. N. Dhalla, *Zoroastrian Civilization* (New York, 1922), p. 334. His explicit distribution of the population is partly hypothetical.

[18] M. N. Dhalla, *Zoroastrian Civilization*, p. 24.

[19] C. De Harlez, *Introduction to the Avesta* (Bombay, 1921), p. 16.

its actual form constitutes only a relatively small part of the original corpus.* The canonical collection comprises among other texts : *Yasna*, "worship, adoration," texts of a liturgical character; *Yašt*, "sacrifice," hymns of sacrifical character devoted to individual deities; *Vidēvdāt*,** "law against the demons," in great part a book of religious and ritual law containing also mythological and legendary materials. Nineteen chapters of the *Yasna* form the *Gathas* ("chants"). Written in verse form and in an archaic dialect, these inserted hymns claim to transmit Zarathustra's own meditations and preachings. From the Gathas's silence on the main gods of the *Yasna* and the *Yašt*, modern scholars conclude that Zarathustra was a reformer who repudiated the traditional Indo-Iranian gods and condemned the *Haoma* cult.+ According to P. Masson-Oursel, Zoroastrianism was a very restricted religious movement until it became, under the Sassanians, coextensive with Mazdaeism. Zarathustra's religious reform in Eastern Iran was strongly monotheistic, it is believed, until the original doctrines were gradually watered down, from 500 B.C. onwards.

In the earlier sections of Avesta, *Ahura Mazdā* (later called Ohrmazd) appears as being the origin of the twin-spirits : the Holy One (*Spenta Mainyu*) and the Destructive One (*Anra Mainyu*, hence *Ahriman*). In subsequent writings, however, *Ahura Mazdā* is identified with "the Holy One" and appears as Ahriman's antagonist. In late Iranian *pehlevi* (in English, usually *pahlavi*) sources, it is *Zurvan*, god of time and fate, who is presented as the (hermaphroditic) begetter of Ohrmazd and Ahriman.[20] In fact, as noted by M. J. Dresden, "not one but two forms of religion are represented in the Avestan writings. The first is reflected in Zarathustra's own words as expressed in the *Gathas*... It posits an ethical dualism between Truth and Falsehood, which is regulated and topped off by a monotheism expressed by *Ahura Mazdā*... In the second form of religion represented in the *Avesta*... several components are present. In the *Gathas*, Ahura Mazdā is the father of Spenta Mainyu (*Yasna* 47.3) and through him he is creator of all things (*Yasna* 47.7)".[21]

The fact is, that in its later phases the Zoroastrian creed developed dualist speculations. To every material reality (*gētīk*) corresponds a

---

[20] See R. C. Zaehner, *Zurvan, a Zoroastrian Dilemma* (Oxford, 1955), pp. 419-428.

[21] M. J. Dresden, "Mythology of Ancient Iran," in S. N. Kramer, *Mythologies of the Ancient World* (New York, 1961), pp. 334-335. On the Gathas see J. Duschesne-Guillemin, *The Hymns of Zoroaster* (London 1952).

transcendent, invisible prototype (*Urbild*), called *mēnōk*. The *mēnōk* of good is in heaven, that of evil is in the world of darkness and of Evil. The demons, even though divine in a sense, are described as *gētīk* beings. *Ahura Mazdā* is pure *mēnōk*, as also the Prince of Evil and of darkness, *Anra Mainyu*. The universe was created in a state of perfection as *mēnōk* and remained thus 3000 years, until the Creator transferred it to the *gētīk* condition. Good-Evil dualism, writes H. S. Nyberg,[22] was metaphysically interpreted in the more recent phases of Mazdaeism.* It is now clearly stated that two eternally distinct principles underlie the life of the universe, the god of light and the god of darkness. They have their abode at opposite poles, one high up in heaven, the other down in the underworld.

2. *The Magi*

According to Herodotus (I, 96, 101), the Aryan Medes who settled in Iran were divided into six tribes, one of which was that of the Magi. It was a sort of sacred caste, which ministered to the spiritual needs of the Medes. The *Avesta* states that the Iranian nation as a whole was divided into three classes : the priests, the warriors, and the farmers. Unlike in the Indian society, however, these were not closed castes, nor were they endogamous. The status of the *magi* was perhaps analogous in a way to that of the Levitical tribe in Israel. It is common belief today that the *magi* were aboriginal Medians who spoke Iranian.[23] "To the classical writers in ancient times the name *magi* was synonymous with the wisdom of the East, and the words 'magic' and 'magician' are reminiscent of their fame".[24] Although the priestly character of the pre-Zoroastrian Magi remains indistinct, their original and lasting ascendancy was of a religious nature. They failed in their attempt to seize political power towards the end of the 6th cent. B.C.,** but their influence never ceased to grow during the next century, when the religion of the Achaemenians gradually became identified with that of Zoroaster. The Magi accepted and even appropriated the Zoroastrian reformation+ and won for themselves a sort of monopoly in religious leadership. According to Herodotus (1, 132), no sacrifice was lawful except that which the Magi consecrated and offered.

---

[22] G. S. Nyberg, *Die Religionen des Alten Iran* (Leipzig, 1938), p. 21.

[23] On the *magi* see G. Widengren, *Die Religionen Irans* (Stuttgart, 1965), pp. 111-113.

[24] M. Dhalla, *Zoroastrian Civilization*, p. 201.

A distinctive and original religious custom of the Magi concerned the funeral rites. Herodotus (1, 140) had noticed that instead of burying their dead encased in wax, like their Persian contemporaries, they exposed them to be devoured by carrion dogs ands birds of prey. In the orthodox communities of the Parsees (the followers of Zoroaster who migrated to India at the Moslem conquest of Iran), the custom is still maintained : the dead are placed in dakhmas ("towers of silence") to be devoured by vultures, lest they defile the earth or the fire. The Magi practiced oneiromancy, that is, divining by dreams, and were reputed astrologers.* Court astrologers were generally drawn from the *magi.* "Wise men from the East" (Mt 2 :1, RSV), the *magoi* of the Gospel also were stargazers and had ominous dreams (Mt 2 :2, 12). The Persian Magi are credited with assigning the planets to the creation of Ahriman because of their alleged irregular motion. In fact the fondness of the Magi for dualistic conceptions is reflected in a trend of the Persian sacred writings. They divided the world into creations of Ohrmazd and creations of Ahriman, to whom they did not hesitate to offer sacrifices.

3. Priesthood of the Avestan and Sassanian Periods

The oldest sections of the *Avesta* mention various categories of priests, corresponding to similar categories in ancient India, an indication of their antiquity. The Iranian *zotar* corresponds to the Indian *hótar*, the *kavi* (Avestan and Vedic) were priests or princely rulers and the name connotes "inspired knowledge." The term *usig* may have designated in ancient Iran "fire-priests", while in the *Vedas uśij* denotes a legendary family of priests. As for the term *vifra* (Vedic : *vipra*) it applies to the inspired priestly singer.

Athravan is, however, the most common term for "priest" in the *Avesta.* Linguistically it corresponds of course to the Indian (altindisch) *atharvan,* and both terms derive from the Indo-European class of fire-priests. S. Wikander, [25] in particular, claims that Vedic *atharvan* refers to a mythical being, and that *athravan* of the Avesta means priest in general, like *āsrōn,* in the *pehlevi* literature. These two Iranian terms are mostly used in fact to designate the priestly "caste", as distinct from the other social classes.

In present-day Zoroastrianism the *mobad* is the "fire-priest," while the *herbad* is a subordinate priest. More is known of the first category.

[25] S. Wikander, *Feuerpriester in Kleinasien und Iran* (Lund, 1946). On this book see *Orientalia* 20 (1951), pp. 212-215 (G. Patti).

Distant descendants of the Magi, like them a "caste" with sacerdotal functions, rather than priests in the strict sense, the *mobad* were the originators of the orthodox tendency of Zoroastrianism. Wikander distinguishes two periods in the history of the Zoroastrian tradition : one oral, and more ancient, reflecting the *herbad* tendencies; a later one, discernible in our written text of the Avesta and dependent on the *mobad* doctrinal trends. *Mobad* is the Modern Persian form of the older espression *magopat*, or *magpat* (related to "Magus" or "Magi"), which came to be used, both as a designation of the priestly caste and as the personal title of a priest to distinguish him from a layman.[26]

A large *pehlevi* work, the *Denkart* (often written Dinkard), composed after the Arabian conquest, draws its inspiration from the Zoroastrian tradition and literature. A recent author, M. N. Dhalla,[27] has collected from this work and from extant Avestan texts what amounts to a description of the Iranian priesthood, first in the Kianian period (2000 to about 700 B.C.), then in the Sassanian period (226 A.D. to 651 A.D.). Some features of his conspectus can be appositely presented at this point.

The high estimation in which the priestly class was held in the early period of ancient Iran can be seen from the fact that *athravan* is one of the titles assumed by Ahura Mazda himself. The High Priest ranked second to the king in the empire and the head of Iran's Zoroastrian clergy was called *Zarathustratema*, "the most supreme Zarathustra."

In the *Vidēvdāt* (18,5.6) Ahura Mazda informs Zarathustra that he is a real priest who remains awake through the night, seeking knowledge, and adds that he who sleeps through the night, without studying, and yet calls himself a priest, is a liar, falsely assuming the priestly office. Goddess *Anāhitā* calls a true *athravan* one who has studied the sacred law, who is wise and clever and "whose very body is filled with religious spells" (*Yašt*, 5,91). The priest never took monastic vows, in accordance with the prophet's teaching on the high merits of marriage. Women were admitted as priestesses and even allowed to perform a certain number of liturgical functions.

"All ceremonies, whether for the living or the dead, were performed by the priests. It was the athravan who invested a child with the sacred shirt and girdle, celebrated marriages, and recited the final prayers over the dead. He was a sacrificer in the fire-temple, a cleanser of the defiled,

---

26 M. N. Dhalla, *Zoroastrian Civilization*, p. 332.

27 M. N. Dhalla, *Zoroastrian Civilization*, pp. 122-126, and 332-335.

a healer of the sick, an exorciser of evil powers, an interpreter of dreams, a reader of stars, an educator of the youth, an administrator of justice, a scribe at the royal court, and a councillor of the king. Thus we find that the Iranian priest of this period monopolized all power and privilege. The priest was naturally the guardian of morals, and it is declared to be the duty of the High Priest to reclaim wrong-doers by admonitions, or to urge them to penitence for their misconduct. It was he who brought succour to the needy, by raising subscriptions among the wealthy. He travelled to distant lands to preach. The only important work in which he was not engaged was warfare."[28]

Iranian priesthood continued as an hereditary class throughout the Sassanian period. Artakhshir, the founder of the Sassanian empire and the rejuvenator of Zoroastrianism, belonged himself to the priestly caste. "He raised the priesthood to a more dignified position than it enjoyed during the Achaemenian period. He was a staunch believer in the doctrine of the unity of the Church and the State. The two, according to him, were like brother and sister, neither of whom could flourish alone. They were interwoven together like two pieces of brocade. The sacerdotal caste, under these circumstances, naturally rose to great power, and remained in the ascendancy until the last days of the empire. The most important of the Pahlavi works of this period, the Denkart, states that priests are to the other classes of society, what the head is to the human body."[29]

Beside moral qualifications, which the *Denkart* enumerates, physical qualities are required of the priests : bodily defects, such as deafness, blindness and dumbness, disqualified a priest from officiating.[30] According to Dhalla, "the primary duty of priests was to maintain religion in its purity, to perform rituals, to teach people, to lead them to goodness, and to inspire zeal for religion. The priests, it is said, should strive zealously to establish institutions for religious instruction. They were expected to exercise their great influence over the king, and to nurture his religious inclinations. A priest is declared to be a shepherd, with people for his flock, and as such he was to guide them safely on the path of duty. A good priest could not fail to inspire with righteousness those with whom he came in contact."[31] Dhalla has also collected from

[28] M. N. Dhalla, *Zoroastrian Civilization*, p. 124.

[29] M. N. Dhalla, *Zoroastrian Civilization*, p. 333

[30] Cf. *Nirangistan* [*pehlevi* written gloss of the Avestan rituals], bk. 2, 13.17.

[31] M. N. Dhalla, *Zoroastrian Civilization*, p. 334.

the written sources what can be known of the priests' means of livelihood in both periods (pp. 125-126 and 335). Besides the fees received for performing the sacrifical rituals, they would keep the land's first fruits offered to the gods and receive occasional alms. The kings willingly bestowed rich gifts on the shrines, especially from enemy booty after great victories. According to *Vendidad* (7, 41; 9, 37), the physicians were specially enjoined to charge no fees for services to the priests, but to heal them solely to receive their blessings. In the Sassanian period the high offices of the state were generally occupied by the learned members of the priestly class and the revenues of the large estates attached to the great temples provided a regular income to their priestly personnel. Still a good number of the clergy adopted secular professions to earn their living.

B. Priesthood in Buddhism

It is common knowledge that in Buddhism, which has no ritual of sacrifice, priesthood in the strict sense is not found, although the monks do guide the faithful in the ways of Buddhist perfection. Such being the case, no extensive treatment of the subject seems required. After recalling a few essential notions on Buddhism we shall briefly indicate distinctive features regarding the character and role of its professional leaders.

Under the name of Buddhism is understood the complex of religious beliefs and philosophical ideas which has developed out of the teachings of the Buddha. * "Beginning as a discipline for human deliverance from pain, it came to embrace various cults and sects. Two main branches flourished side by side for many centuries : the *Hīnayāna* (Little Vehicle) and the *Mahāyāna* (Great Vehicle). Buddhism is not a strictly logical dogmatic system of beliefs and practices in the Western sense. Its adherents require of religion not that it be true rather than false, but that it be good rather than bad. The characteristic symbol of Buddhism is the 'Wheel of the Law' (Dharma-Çakra). The most extant collection of early Buddhist teachings, the 'Buddhist Scriptures,' is the Pali Canon, which was given written form in Ceylon in the 1st century A.D. In modern times, in part under the impact of Western thought, the rise of theosophic neo-Buddhism is to be noted."[32]

[32] A. S. Rosso, "Buddhism," NCE 2 :847.

Even though Buddha taught salvation* through personal effort without dependence on any god, he is not known to have denied the existence of Hindu gods or forbidden their worship. Buddha is then by no means a theoretical atheist. His gods, however, subject to mutability, do not fit in the notion of divinity professed by Christian orthodoxy (on the problems involved see H. von Glasenapp, *Der Buddhismus — eine atheistische Religion*, Munich 1966). For Buddha, gods, men, and all living beings depend on and result from *Karma*, the sum total of the deeds done in previous existences. Original Buddhism is founded upon the permanent impermanency of all things, an exaggerated estimate of suffering, and the extinction of self as the only way of escape from the weary round of birth and rebirth. Soothill writes : "Neo-Buddhism, or Mahayanism, recognizes a Being who transcends the impermanent, and its objective is salvation to a permanent heaven through faith in, and invocation of, saviours."[33] In the Mahāyāna system the Absolute is believed to have manifested himself in several ways, especially through the Buddhas, one of whom is the Guatama. Under the influence of Hinduism the Mahāyāna sect developed in fact a pantheon of Buddhas and Bodhisattvas as well as a metaphysics of a pantheistic world soul complicated by Yoga and Tantra practices."[34] *Nirvana*, the Buddhist beatitude, is the extinction of the craving for life, the subjugation of the ego, whose desires cause suffering. In *nirvana*, a state of passionless peace and rest, lies the highest good attainable in life. Buddhism withdraws from the world, Christianity would redeem it. But Buddhism can be called the first universalist religion, admitting neither caste nor color barrier in the community.** Salvation is for all men and women, for all creatures.

Before his death Buddha formulated his doctrine and the rules for orders of monks and nuns. The initiation ceremony of the new monk included the pledge to observe ten abstentions, i.e., from killing, stealing, lying, sexual intercourse, intoxicants, eating after midday, wordly amusements, using cosmetics and adornments, luxurious mats and beds, and from accepting gold or silver.*** The pledge was binding for the duration of the monk's stay in the order. His daily exercises comprised morning prayers, recitation of scriptures, outdoor begging, a midday meal fol-

[33] W. E. Soothill, *Three Religions*, p. 108.

[34] NCE 2:849. See also C. Regamey, "Der Buddhismus Indiens" in F. König, ed., *Christus und die Religionen der Erde*, v. 3 (Wien, 1951), pp. 229-306; H. von Glasenapp, *Der Buddhismus in Indien und im Fernen Osten* (Berlin, 1936).

lowed by rest and meditation, and evening service. There were also prescribed days of fast and abstinence and regular public confession of sins. Buddha also founded a third order for lay people who were obliged only to abstain from killing, stealing, lying, intoxicants, and fornication. According to W. E. Soothill, sacrifice, prayer, and adoration are absent from original Buddhism, their place being taken by meditation.[35] *Zen*, the Chinese Ch'an system of meditation, has neither god, hereafter, soul, nor ritual. "It assumes the inner purity and goodness of man; its aims are to discipline the mind by an insight into its proper nature and to acquire a new viewpoint for perceiving the essence of things."[36] This form of prayer developed especially in Japan, where it was introduced in the 7th century.

In the later periods, and until the present day in various regions, the Buddhist monks or bonzes offer instructions in the elements of secular learning and the simpler doctrines of the faith, illustrated by references to the life of Buddha. On all important occasions of private life, birth, marriages, and sickness, especially, the monk is summoned to perform ceremonies and prophylactic rites, pronounce incantations, and expel evil influences by the recitation of sacred texts. Within the temples themselves the service consist for the most part of invocations and recitations, in which all the resident members of the community share, but at which the laity is not present, unless as accidental spectators. At the principal service of the day, however, one of the monks will deliver a sermon or an instruction which usually consists in exposing Buddhist doctrine or ethics. He does so not by virtue of his priesthood but on account of the superior knowledge with which he is credited.

Original Buddhism, with its agnostic tendencies, does not profess belief in a future life beyond this world and denies that man may or must approach God through a human intermediary. The Buddhist monks are not mediators but professionals of Buddha's way of life for the edification and the conversion of the faithful. In the mixed forms of Buddhism, however, ritual is admitted, sometimes under the influence of Christianity. In the Lāmaism of Tibet, which is of Buddhist inspiration, the higher clergy perform priestly functions and stand in greater esteem than the Buddhist monks of other lands. Christian influence is particularly noticeable in the Lamaistic service which borrows some features from the commemorative observance of the Last Supper.

---

[35] W. E. Soothill, *Three Religions*, p. 103.

[36] NCE 2:855.

Chinese Taoism professes to be founded on the ethical teaching of Lao-Tzu or Lao-Tse (6th cent. B.C.), although it tends to merge into the popular animism of the country. Influenced by Buddhism it also developed a certain type of priesthood and ritual soon after the beginning of the Christian era. At present there are two orders of Taoist priests, one celibate and one married. They reside in their own dwellings and wear the ordinary dress of the people. They do not shave the head like the Buddhist monks, but bind the hair on the top of the head. "Many lead an itinerant life, and derive a livelihood from the sale of charms. They are for the most part as ignorant of the teaching of Lao-Tzu as are the Buddhists of the teaching of Sākyamuni. They study instead the pseudo-science of astrology and alchemy."[37]

C. Priesthood in Ancient Greece

Several terms, most of them compounds of *hieros*, "sacred", occur in the Greek texts to express a variety of functions in the cult. The main expressions involved will be mentioned in the course of the present study, but it is important to examine first of all what notions of priesthood these texts and their commentators suggest.

a) The Hiereus : Preliminary Nnotions

When Homer wrote, no clear distinction had yet emerged, it would seem, between *hiereus*, "priest," and *mantis*, "diviner, seer". He mentions both categories of sacred persons together and presents the "diviner" as "instructed by sacrifices" (Iliad. 1.62 and 24.221). L. Campbell notes that "there is hardly any trace of temple-worship amongst the Greeks of the Homeric times." It was when the race of kings had departed and cities became conscious of a corporate existence that they erected temples and installed priests to serve in them.[38] Probably relying on Homer and other texts, Hesychius, the 6th cent. A.D. Greek lexicographer, defined the *hiereus* as "one divining by means of sacrifices". It appears then that the ancient Greeks believed that both the priests and the prophets were endowed with a special indwelling power qualifying them to mediate between men and the deity. "Alongside this hieratic conception, however, is the idea of general priesthood, that

[37] H. J. T. Johnson, "Priest, Priesthood (Chinese)", ERE 10:293.

[38] L. Campbell, *Religion in Greek Literature* (London, 1898), p. 126.

each may draw near to God in sacrifice and prayer. The head of the family sacrifices for the family, the leader for the race, the demarch* for the community and the magistrates for the city. Without any special priestly training the layman can see to purifications and expiatory offerings".[39] Isocrates (436-338) very likely had this general priesthood in view when he mentions the priestly office in criticizing inconsistent opinions of the people on the monarchy : "The cause of this inconsistency and confusion of feeling is that they consider the office of a king, like that of a priest, *can be discharged by any man*, whereas of all human responsibilities it is the greatest, and requires the greatest forethought."[40] Another Greek author of the same period, Aeschines, considers as a central feature of the priestly office "to offer prayers to the gods on behalf of the people."[41] A priesthood of this type could apply to broader categories of prayer professionals and other devotees, including self proclaimed apostles of new divinities.

It is difficult to decide who were and who were not "priests" among those various officials designated by terms like *epimēnioi*, "monthly cult officers," or *hieropoioi*, a word which can equally apply to "sacrificers" and to "overseers of temples or of rites". Even before the classical period there existed a distinctive notion of priesthood : the priest is the *de facto* or the appointed ministrant of a sanctuary, whatever it is, be it simply an altar or any place of cult. He is the official intermediary between the god or the gods of this sanctuary and the people who come there to pray and offer sacrifices. The priest is ministrant of his own sanctuary and only he can minister there. Only exceptionally would the same priest take charge of more than one sanctuary, even of different deities, or would more than one priest or priestess be in service at the same sanctuary.[42]

b) *Functions of the Priest*

In the ideal society he was contemplating, Plato thought, there will have to be priests, and priestesses, for the sanctuaries, to act as sacris tans (*neôkoroi*) for the gods (*The Laws* 6.759).** To serve the god was in fact in Greece, as in Egypt and generally in the Near East, outside Israel, the foremost of the original functions of the priest. This meant

---

39 G. Schrenk, Kittel ThW (Eng) 3:258.

40 *To Nicocles*, 6, tr. J. H. Freese, *The Orations of Isocrates*, v. 1 (London, 1894), p. 20.

41 *Tas euchas huper tou dēmou pros theous euchesthai* (Orations, 3.18).

42 See Ph.-E. Legrand, "Sacerdoce (*hiereus*)" DictAntGrRom 4, 2, p. 943.

of course taking good care of the statue which represented the god and in which he was thought to reside. It had to be washed, clothed, and protected. As "sacristans for the gods," the priests in the beginning also administered temple property. In later legislation the administration of the larger sactuaries was entrusted to state functionaries and even the preparation of the public religious ceremonies was in the hands of civil magistrates or of special commissions. The priest's role was often limited to the choice of the victims.

In the liturgical functions the *hiereus* played the essential role, distinct from that of other cult officials. No daily service took place in the Greek temples, but at regular intervals the priest offered sacrifices on behalf of the community. Apart from these official ministrations his cultic function consisted in assisting those who privately or in an official capacity came to offer sacrifices in the sanctuary. The priest's assistance was considered as a requisite for the validity of the sacrifice.

Sometimes he himself killed the victim, an action usually reserved to professional immolators called *thuteis* or *hierothuteis*. The priest's necessary intervention consisted in the vowing of the victim to sacrifice and in reciting the prayer which accompanied the oblation. But the priest's presence was also required to assure the exact observance of the ritual which conditioned the validity of the sacrifice. Plato includes the priest in the category of the *monophulaces*, "curators of the law," a title which applies especially to the sacrificial rites (see, e.g., *The Laws*, 800 and 877). The Greek priest neither taught nor preached; he was mainly the servant of the god and a professional of sacrifice.

c) *Admission and Appointment*

In his theory of the ideal state Aristotle expresses the wish that only "citizens" (*politai*) be admitted to the priesthood, and he explicitly excluded farmers and artisans. He would give the preference besides to "men who are already weary with years" (*Politics* 7.9.9). Other qualifications mentioned eslsewhere were probably more closely observed in practice: the candidates had to be healthy, unmaimed, and of good reputation. Priestesses were generally expected to remain chaste, and even to be virgins, or at least to have been married to one man only.*

As a rule the Greek goddess was served by priestesses and in her worship were sacrificed only female victims. In the ritual of Athena, however, and of Aphrodite, this rule was not always followed. In the case of Athena, one author suggests, the reason for the exception was her masculine character and her frequent connection with Zeus in the cult.[43] There were also cases in which priests and priestesses served in the same sanctuary. The institution of "boy priests" is a peculiar feature of the Greek cult. The priest of Athena (at Tegea in Arcadia) was a boy. "I do not know", writes Pausanias, "how long his priesthood lasts, but it must be before, and not after, puberty" (*Description* 8.47.3). In another case, mentioned by Pausanias, an explanation is given. "There are at Aegium (in Achaia) other images made of bronze, *Zeus as a boy and Heracles as a beardless youth*, the work of Ageladas of Argos. Priests are elected for them every year, and each of the two images remains at the house of the priest. In a more remote age there was chosen to be priest for Zeus from the boys he who won the prize for beauty" (*Descriptions* 7.24.4). It was thought convenient to have boy priests look after the images of gods represented as boys. The main reason seems to have been, however, the desire to be assured of the chastity of the ministrants.

No special training was required of the future priests. Each sanctuary had a fixed ritual and the celebrant simply followed its detailed rubrics. This was the more necessary since the ministrants changed often, being generally appointed for a limited period of time, from two to ten years.

In the priesthoods that are not hereditary, wrote Plato, the appointments should be made parly by election and partly by lot. "As far as priesthoods are concerned," he adds, "we must allow God to effect his own good pleasure by just leaving appointments to the inspired decision of the lot, but every man on whom the lot may fall must be subjected to a scrutiny (*dokimasia*), first as to his freedom from blemishes and legitimate birth, next as to his provenance from houses pure of all pollution, and the cleanness of his own life, and likewise of those of his father and mother from blood-guiltiness and all such offenses against religion" (*The Laws* 6.759). Plato would also prefer to have priests and priestesses appointed for one year only, at an age not below sixty (*ibid.*). The divine choice of candidates could also manifest itself through an oracle. In monarchical states appointment to the priestly office was often a prerogative of the prince or king. From the time of Alexander

[43] L. R. Farnell, *The Cults of the Greek States* (Oxford, 1896), p. 320. Herodotus cites as contrary to Greek custom the fact that in Egypt all the priests belong to the male sex (2, 35).

the Great it became the custom in Asia Minor and elsewhere to buy the priesthoods, and even the *diasustasis*, the right of succession.*

There existed in Greece a variety of hereditary priesthoods (*patriai hierosunai*) provided for *kata genous*, according to birth. In some states, dominated by an aristocracy, priesthood was the privilege of leading families. In other cases these patrimonial priesthoods became national priesthoods, without losing their hereditary character. It also happened that a family received the exclusive right to provide a sanctuary with priests for exceptional services rendered to it. Succession did not follow a fixed pattern. More generally, perhaps, the line of succession went from the elder brother to the youngest and then to the sons of the eldest member of the family. In one Poseidon priesthood of Athens the lot decided which member of the family would become the priest.

d) The Archiereus and other Titles

What has been said till now applies mainly to the *hiereus*, the "priest" in the stricter sense. Other names, which refer to a particular function only, very probably designate priests as well : *hierothutēs*, "sacrificer," *hieromnēnōn*, "cult magistrate," *kleidouchos*, "holder of the keys". The *hieropoioi* were originally "sacrificers," *hoi ta hiera poiountes*,** who also served as temple administrators. Later this became their main function, and the *hieropoioi* of Delos were magistrates rather than priests. They provided victims for the sacrifices of various cults. But they functioned as sacrificers and priests to Apollo, for whose cult no other ministrants are mentioned.

In Homer the term *amphipoloi* generally designates maids of important ladies. In other texts the term is used for priestesses serving gods or goddesses. But *amphipolos* occurs also in the masculine or in references to "priests," especially in connection with the cult of Zeus Olympus in Sicily. Some authors see in *amphipolos* an ancient cultic term, meaning "priest" and etymologically referring to the rite of circumambulation about sacred persons, objects or sites. The secular use of the the term would be secondary. A similar change of meaning has been noticed in the Latin equivalents *anculus* and *ancula* (derived from *ámbhiquolos*), persons who ministered (*ancillare*) in sacred areas. The feminine term, when secularized, became *ancilla*, "maid."

In the temple personnel of Plato's ideal society the title *archiereus* is granted to the head priest of the officiants for that year, "and the year shall be officially registered under his name, as a means of dating, so long as our society survives" (*The Laws* 12.947a).* When these chief priests die they will be granted a state burial, Plato adds, and in the funeral procession the priests and priestesses will march last. Even though these sacred persons, he explains, "are debarred from accompanying other funerals, they may follow this, as one that imparts no defilement, if the Pythian prophetess will add her sanction to our proposal" (*Ibid.*). In the Hellenistic period under the Seleucids the official *archiereus* is for each satrapy the chief priest appointed by the crown. At the same period in Asia Minor *archiereus* could designate the priest who headed the personnel of several shrines, or even of a single shrine of peculiar importance. In the Roman empire the regional temples of Asia Minor, in Pergamos, Smyrna, Ephesus, Sardis had each an *archiereus* elected annually as provincial chief priest.

Apart from continence prescribed for certain categories of priests and priestesses and the observance of other purity rules, few special obligations were imposed on the Greek priests, who, it seems, did not constitute a particularly transcendent class of professionals. In the Stoic philosophical speculation, however, only the sage is truly equipped for what a priest is called to be, and the human attainment of virtue is made the basis of priesthood. We shall see (ch. V) that in Philo the *hiereus* will become the symbol of what is highest in the domain of reason.

D. Priesthood in ancient Rome

In the Latin language of ancient Rome the term *sacerdos*, "priest," meant a professional of the cult, one who knew exactly how to perform the rites according to the prescribed rubrics. Rome's official priests had the right and the duty to regulate the cult both public and private. The Romans never called *sacerdos* the *paterfamilias* who worshipped the ancestral gods (as domestic priest) nor the magistrate who conducted the religious ceremonies prescribed by the state.**

In his *De Legibus* (II, 8, 20) Cicero distinguishes two categories of *sacerdotes*. There are those, he writes, who superintend the various forms of worship, and those whose special task is to interpret signs and portents, or explain the visions and oracles of seers and prophets. The *augures* and *haruspices* constitute, of course, the second category. Another classification distinguishes between the priests in general and the *flamines*, who were connected with the worship of particular deities Thirdly some Roman priesthoods existed on an individual basis, while others formed *collegia* and *sodalitates*. The *sodalitates* were confraternities of priests devoted to a particular cult, while the *collegia*, created by the State, were closer to being academies of theologians who made rulings regarding public cult.

The manner of recruiting and appointing priests has varied with the course of Rome's history. In the beginning the *sacerdotes publici* were named, it seems, by the king.[44] With the establishment of the republic, more democratic ways of nominating were introduced : the colleges chose new members by cooptation, while in the selection of candidates for the individual priesthoods, for the *flamines* and the Vestal Virgins in particular, the final word belonged to the *Summus Pontifex*.

Once appointed, the priests were generally installed in their office by the pontiffs and the augurs, or by the augurs only. All priests were originally patricians, but the Lex Ogulnia published in 300 B.C. gave the plebeians access to the *collegia pontificum et augurium*. One clause of this law stipulated that four of the *Pontifices* and five of the augurs be taken from among the plebeians. Other priestly offices, *rex sacrorum, flamines majores, salii,** remained closed to plebeians, but they were priesthoods with no major political significance. Persons with bodily defects were excluded from the priesthood, a ruling quite universal in ancient cults.[45] More distinctive of Roman priesthoods is the fact that their members, once admitted, kept their priestly character for life, at least according to Pliny (*Epist.* 4, 8) who specifically names the *augures* and the *fratres arvales* as possessing an imperishable priesthood.** The *leges annales*, which fixed the age of eligibility for different magistracies, have no provision as regards priestly offices. It seems that *pubertas* was the accepted *terminus a quo* age requirement for candidates to the priesthood.*** Although the priests of ancient Rome did not have to preach or to instruct the people in the beliefs of religion, they were expected to have a thorough knowledge of their particular liturgy. "Religion with the ancients was handed down by tradition from father to son, and consisted in the proper performance of certain rites and ceremonies. It was respecting these external forms of worship alone

---

44 See Dionysius of Halicarnassus (1st cent. B.C.), *Roman Antiquities*, II, 73, and Livy (c. 60 B.C.-17 A.D.), *History of Rome* I, 20.

45 See, e.g. Dionysius 2, 21 and Plutarch (1st-2nd cent. A.D.), *Moralia, Roman Questions*, 73. The latter says that an "ulcer" is also a sort of bodily mutilation or pollution because of which the augurs can be forbidden to practice their art.

that the pontiffs were obliged to give instructions to those who consulted them."[46]

If we now turn to examine more specifically the various categories of priests, we meet first the *collegium pontificum*. It was headed by the *Pontifex Maximus* who was assisted by other *pontifices*, primarily theologians and professors of sacred law, whose duty it was to preserve the religious traditions of Rome, especially by determining the forms of sacrifice and worship. They also officiated at the most important ceremonies of public worship and occasionally performed other important duties in the religious and in the secular fields. There is little doubt that the term "*pontifex*" derives from *pons* and *facere*, to make a bridge. It is quite possible that the *Pontifices* were thus named because they used to offer sacrifices from the Sublician bridge,* every year on the Ides of May, by throwing into the Tiber *argei*, human figures made of bulrushes.

When the republican regime succeeded the monarchy (c. 500 B.C.) the king's religious power became vested in the special office of the *rex sacrorum*, "the king of sacred things."[47] By its origin, this office could be considered above that of the *Summus Pontifex* but in real power and influence it remained below it. That of *rex sacrorum* was a convenient post for unwanted officials honorably discharged. The *rex sacrorum* was elected for life by the pontiffs and inaugurated by the augurs. He was the special priest of Janus, performed the *sacra publica* which were formerly the king's prerogative, had the sacred duty of appeasing the gods when exceptional portents announced threatening dangers, and regularly proclaimed on the *nundines* the dates of the monthly festivals. There were fifteen *flamines*, but only three of them, called *majores*, were members of the collegium pontificum. The term *flamen* probably derives from *flare*, "to blow," as on the fire of sacrifice. The *flamen*'s principal, indeed his only, function was to sacrifice to his god. But the *flamines* had to observe a large number of restrictions. The first in rank was the *flamen dialis*, devoted to Jupiter.** Also closely associated with this college were the six Vestal virgins, whose main duty was to look after the sacred flame in the temple of Vesta, goddess of the hearthfire. The Vestals were the only State priestesses at Rome; they were chosen for life but could renounce their office after thirty years of service. The

---

[46] L. Schmitz, in W. Smith, ed., *Dictionary of Greek and Roman Antiquities* (2d ed., London, 1869), pp. 997-998.

[47] On this office, see Livy, *History of Rome* 2,2 and Dionysius, *Roman Antiquities*, 4, 74.

Vestal guilty of violating her vow of chastity was buried alive, while her paramour would be publicly scourged to death.

The *augures* or diviners were authorities in the ancient *disciplina auguralis*, whose object was to study the signs (*auspices*) by which the gods manifested their favor or disfavor. The *augures* should not be confused with the *haruspices*, who did not form a college, are never called priests, and were of Etruscan origin. The *haruspices* are sometimes called *extispices* because their art consisted mainly in interpreting the will of the gods from the appearance of the entrails (*exta*) of animals. Some specialized in hepatoscopy, the augural examination of the liver.

The third great college of priests, also connected with the *disciplina auguralis*, especially that of the *haruspices*, was called *Quindecimviri sacris faciundis*. For the greater part of its history it was in fact composed of fifteen members, whose function was to examine the Sibylline books* at the request of the Senate, mainly when *prodigia* occurred. They would interpret these and recommend means of appeasing the gods. They also had the right and duty of supervision over the Greek cultic institutions in Rome.

Among the lesser priestly colleges figured also the *septemviri epulones* instituted in 196 B.C., mainly to administer the sacred *banquets* in honor of Jupiter, the *Luperci*, whose activity was confined to the single celebration, on February 15, of the *Lupercalia*, originally a pastoral festival, and the *Sodales Augustales*,+ a priesthood instituted for the worship of Augustus deified by senatorial decree in A.D. 14. There were also outside Rome municipal priesthoods. At their head stood the *sacerdos provinciae*, the chief priest of the imperial cult in the province or group of provinces to which he belonged.

CHAPTER THREE

PRIESTHOODS OF THE ANCIENT NEAR EAST

The Ancient Near East was populated by a large number of ethnic groups more or less related, if not always by language, at least by geography, culture, and religion. Their special connection with Israel is an additional reason for treating their priesthoods under one heading. A further grouping being desired, we have adopted that which practical reasons recommend rather than theoretical considerations.

A. Priesthoods of Mesopotamia

The peoples of Mesopotamia, mainly the Sumerians, the Babylonians, and the Assyrians, have many important features in common affecting their culture, their government, and their religion. They also differ in several respects and their history extends over a long period. The following exposition, it is hoped, will remain aware of this complex picture.

a) *Mesopotamia in its ancient Setting*

According to its Greek etymology "Mesopotamia" is the land "between the rivers," the Euphrates, namely, and the Tigris, in western Asia. The name is used in the Bible to translate *Aram-naharaim*, "Syria of the Two Rivers" (cf. Gen 24 :10; Jg 3 :8, 10).[1] The site of the tower of Babel, "a plain in the land of Shinar" (Gen 11 :2) is also located in Mesopotamia.* Of Nimrod it is said : "The beginning of his kingdom was Babel, Erech and Akkad, all of them in the land of Shinar" (Gen 10:10; cf. Dn 1:2). The name "Akkad" is reflected in the use of the term "Akkadian" to denote the *Semitic* language and population of southern Mesopotamia, as distinct from that of Sumer.

In the time of Abraham (c. 2000-1700 B.C.) Mesopotamia and Egypt were the two great political and cultural centers of Western Asia. With the coastal strip of Syria-Palestine joining them they formed "the Fertile Crescent", which during the period following 2000 B.C. was invaded

---

[1] See R. T. O'Callaghan, *Aram Naharaim. A Contribution to the History of Upper Mesopotamia in the second Millenium B.C.* Anal Or 26 (Rome, 1948).

by nomads or semi-nomads from Arabia. These Semites formed the bulk of the peoples later called Amorites, Babylonians, Chaldeans, Assyrians, Canaanites, and Israelites. The term "Semites" has been coined of course from the name *Shem*, one of Noah's sons (cf. 5:32, 10:1). In the "Table of Peoples" (Gen 10) the Canaanites, although Semitic, are listed as descendants of Ham (Africa), presumably because Canaan was long under Egypt's influence. The "Sons of Japhet" (Gen 10 :2-5) can be referred broadly to the Aryans or Indo-Europeans living mostly in Asia Minor. The Semitic language groups include *Northeast Semitic* (Babylonia and Assyria) : Akkadian, with Babylonian and Assyrian dialects; *Northwest Semitic* (Upper Mesopotamia, Syria, Palestine) : Aramaic, Ugaritic, Canaanite, Phoenician, Hebrew; *Southern Semitic* (Arabia, Ethiopia) : Arabic, Ethiopic.

The economy and culture of Mesopotamia deeply influenced the life and beliefs of the Palestinian population, Israel included. "Out of Mesopotamia came the arts of irrigation, of cuneiform writing, of architecture and sculpture, of city-state organization, of efficient business transactions. It produced magnificent textiles, finely carved gems, and seals. It codified law, and evolved modes of worship which left a deep imprint on the Hebrews. They lived in Mesopotamia during the Exile; and there much of the Old Testament as we know it took form. Out of Mesopotamia swept the conquerors most dreaded for centuries by Palestine the Assyrians, the Babylonians, and the Chaldeans."[2]

From Gen 11:31 we learn that Abraham's family emigrated from "Ur of the Chaldeans* to go into the land of Canaan; but when they came to Haran, they settled there." In Haran, or Paddan-aram ("field of Aram") lived Rebekah's brother, Laban, "the son of Bethuel the Aramean" (Gen 28:5). For several centuries the people of Northwestern Mesopotamia are referred to in cuneiform texts as Amurru, i.e. "Westerners." "This became, apparently, a general term applying to speakers of various Northwest-Semitic dialects found in the area including, in all probability, those strains from which later sprang both Hebrews and Arameans."[3] The Amorites** appeared in South Western Asia in the latter half of the 3rd millennium B.C. In Abraham's time, Amorite kings ruled in almost every state of Mesopotamia, including Mari of the later period. The Amorites were a distinctive people although they wrote in

---

[2] *Black's Bible Dictionary* (London, 1954), p. 439.

[3] J. Bright, *A History of Israel* (Philadelphia, 1959), p. 43.

Akkadian and adopted in great part the culture as well as the religion of Sumer and Akkad.

It is significant that the Hebrew traditions about Creation and the Flood, as contained in Gen 1-11, reveal contacts with similar accounts from Mesopotamia, although "the refinement produced by the purity of the Israelite faith sets a great gulf between the Old Testament accounts and the crassly pagan traditions of Babylon."[4] As regards creation and the Garden of Eden the resemblances are rather superficial, but in some features the Flood accounts of Genesis and of the Babylonian documents[5] are surprisingly similar*. Why was it distant Upper Mesopotamia and not Egypt or Canaan which influenced the Hebrew tradition on man's origins? Perhaps the only possible explanation is still "that the essential outlines of the accounts of the Creation, the Garden of Eden, the Flood, Nimrod (Gen 10:8ff) and the Tower of Babel (Gen, ch. 11) were brought from the homeland in Haran by the Patriarchs themselves."[6]

b) Sacral Kingship in Mesopotamia

For most peoples of the Ancient Near East kingship was a sacral institution, the nature and function of which scholars have been investigating in the last decades.[7] In the present study only a few more acceptable notions can be recalled among those having some connection with ancient priesthood. They can conveniently be related to three themes, the second of which will require a longer historical, treatment.

---

[4] G. E. Wright and F. V. Filson, *The Westminster Historical Atlas to the Bible* (2nd ed., Philadelphia, 1956), p. 25. See also J. Koenig, "Tradition iahviste et influence babylonienne à l'aurore du judaïsme," RevHistRel 173 (1968), pp. 1-42.

[5] On the comparative material related to Gen 2-3, see A. Heidel, *The Babylonian Genesis* (2d rev. ed., Chicago, 1951) and J. L. McKenzie, *Myths and Realities* (Milwaukee, 1963), pp. 152-156. Especially important: W. G. Lambert, "A New Look at the Babylonian Background of Genesis," JThSt 16 (1965), pp. 287-300.

[6] G. E. Wright and F. V. Filson, *Historical Atlas*, p. 25.

[7] How extensive this research has been appeais in the bibliography of I. Engnell, *Studies in Divine Kingship in the Ancient Near East* (2nd ed., Oxford 1967) 223-254. In his study of "Sumero-Akkadian kingship" (p. 16-51), this author seems to have overrated the evidence for what he calls the divinization of the Mesopotamian kings. See also C. J. Gadd, *Ideas of Divine Rule in the Ancient East* (London 1948); K.-H. Bernhardt, *Das Problem der altorientalischen Königsideologie im Alten Testament...* VetTestSuppl 8 (Leiden 1961) 67-90. Cf. n. 13.

1. The Divine Character of Earthly Kingship

It does not seem necessary to deal here with the kingship of the gods themselves, * although the Mesopotamians asserted that in the earliest times, and again after the Flood, "kingship has descended from heaven." For them, then, kingship had not always existed even if it represented the only known form of government in historical times. The statement also meant that the office and not the office-holder, was of superhuman origin.** In Egypt Pharaoh was a god; in Mesopotamia the king was a mortal entrusted with a divine mission and endowed with divine power. For the Mesopotamians kingship played an essential role in society but it was not, as in Egypt, an essential part of creation and of the cosmic order.[8] Rather than an autocratic ruler the king in Mesopotamia was a religious and sacred person, whose every action had a religious meaning and sprung from a religious intention. It is very important to remark of the Mesopotamian dynast, that while his subjects revered him, and even, at times, worshipped him as a god, the priests deliberately treated him as the humblest of penitents. For if the king was, in the popular mind, the god's delegate, he also represented, in a way, humanity before the gods and, as such, was expected to be a model for all in reverence and piety. Conscious of his special religious responsibility, the king carefully performed the prescribed rites and willingly accepted the dictates of tradition and the directives of the priests concerning fasts, abstinence, and purifications.

The Mesopotamians easily admitted the divine origin of royal power and yet firmly rejected the idea that a mortal could rank with the gods. In other words, belief in the religious character of kingship was universal in Sumer, Babylonia, and Assyria, while the deification of kings is only locally and occasionally attested, and never in Assyria. Yet, for his subjects, the king was a sacred being. Endowed with divine power on the day of his enthronement, he ceased to be a mere individual and became the vice-gerent of the deity. His earthly investiture being thus sanctioned in heaven, an aura of divinity seemed to surround him, but he remained, it was thought, a mortal being. Alleged attestations of royal deification in Mesopotamia should be read with appropriate caution. No firm conclusion can be drawn from the divine titles granted the kings by court style and protocol. "It is certain that royal statues were set up in temples and received offerings, but this does not imply that the kings thus honoured were divinities. For the manner in which their

[8] See H. Frankfort, *Kingship and the Gods* (Chicago, 1948), pp. 231, 237, 295.

sacrifices were listed differed significantly from the formula used for offerings to the gods... In this manner the royal statues acquired a certain degree of divinity, but this quality was quite independent from the kings whom they represented. It was the statue which received offerings, not the king; and neither the existence of statues nor the fact that sacrifices were made to them proves that the kings were worshipped as gods."[9] More will be said on the "divine" character of the Mesopotamian dynast in the historical outline that follows.

2. Kingship and Priesthood in Mesopotamia

The situation is very different in Sumer and in Assyro-Babylonia. Whereas the Assyrian kings clearly claimed to be priests of god Aššur, the case of the Sumerian dynasts is complex and several problems remain unsolved. A. L. Oppenheim, for example, omits to write about the priesthood of the king in Sumer "because the relationship evolving between the *l u g a l* ('king') and the *e n* ('high priest') is too complex and as yet too ill-defined to be mentioned but in passing."[10] The royal title at Sumer, *l u g a l k a l a m a*, "king of the land," meant originally merely "king of the Nippur region."

In ancient Sumer the god owned the land and all its produce, the cattle and everything else. During the 3rd Dynasty of Ur (2112-2005) the temples were still the major landowners and had to supply in turn the larger shrines of the national religious center, Nippur, the heart of the Sumerian "amphictyony".* In the historical period the head of the Sumerian city states is called *e n s i*, "vice-gerent" (of the god), a term that others define "the lord who lays the foundation of a temple."** A more ancient title, recalled in the Sumerian epics, is that of *e n*, "lord," with a probable priestly connotation.*** It is very likely then that the Sumerian city state dynast functioned also as supreme priest of the main deity, who was the real master of the city state. Thus could the king also claim authority over the priests of the other shrines. In the monuments of the proto-historical period the king is often represented as exercising the functions of a priest.[11] More likely the Sumerian king did not officiate himself but patronized the cult institutions.**** A clea-

---

[9] H. Frankfort *Kingship*, pp. 303 and 306. Cf. I. Engnells' excursus, "Comparison between the epithets of the king and the god," *Studies in Divine Kingship*, pp. 178-195.

[10] A. L. Oppenheim, *Ancient Mesopotamia* (Chicago, 1964), p. 99.

[11] A. Falkenstein, "La cité-temple sumérienne," *Cahiers d'histoire mondiale* 1 (1954), p. 796.

rer distinction between the royal and priestly prerogatives will develop in the subsequent religious history of Mesopotamia.

Semitic nomads had been infiltrating the Sumerian world and one of them, Sargon of Akkad, (2334-2279) seized power from Lugalzaggisi and founded a dynasty through which for two centuries the Semites would dominate Mesopotamia. Under their rule the Sumerian religious traditions were maintained, but the notion of a universal empire came to be understood politically. Sargon applied to himself what was said of divine universal lordship* when he claimed to be "the One who traverses the four regions of the world," while Naram-Sin, one of his immediate successors, liked to be called "king of the four regions." The king was no longer a local ruler but the effective head of a vast realm. The temples no longer claimed revenues by divine right but lived from royal donations and state subsidies. Royalty and clergy were now more clearly distinguished, although the king remained the sacred intermediary uniting humanity and the gods. His unique position, above the people, did not, however, result, as in Sumer, from a divine disposition, but from his strength and power, these two qualities marking, among the Semites, the presence of the divine. This helps to explain also why the first known deified kings in Mesopotamia belonged to the dynasty of Akkad. In Babylonia, from Sargon to Hammurabi, the determinative *d i n g i r*, "god," often accompanied the name of the king. Statues of deceased kings, considered as netherworld gods (not cosmic deities) received shares of the offerings in the temples. Besides, "the horned miter with which Naram-Sin is represented [see Pritchard ANEP n. 309] and the *kusītu* garments of the Neo-Assyrian kings are similar to those worn by images of the gods."[12] By transferring the center of the "amphictyony" from Nippur to Akkad, by replacing Enlil by Ištar, Naram-Sin was led to proclaim himself god and to separate what in Sumerian religion was united, the gods and society.** Akkadian rule ceased with the advent of the new Sumerian empire, which came to its golden age under the third dynasty of Ur and ended when the Elamites*** defeated and captured king Ibi-Sin (2212-2187). The dynasts of Ur remained devoted to the sanctuary of Nippur, but adopted the title of "king of Sumer and Akkad."

In the meantime, farther North, a new city and a new power had risen. Babylon, a bastion of the West-Semitic Amorites, triumphed over the Sumerian cities of the south, Isin and Larsa, and its great king

[12] Oppenheim, *Ancient Mesopotamia*, p. 98.

Hammurabi* secured again the Semitic domination of Mesopotamia. Kingship ideology now combines Sumerian and Semitic conceptions. The king is not god, although he remains, by the will of gods, in the divine sphere and is the object of popular veneration. The king's statue, in the temple, perpetuates his prayer, and is involved, when he dies, in the rites of the dead and of ancestor worship. Babylon became the capital of the Semitic world and Marduk, the god of the city, outrivalled the ancient Sumerian gods in the new pantheon. During this second millennium, when the peoples of Babylonia, Assyria, Mitanni, and Hatti met on the battlefield, a new name appeared among the royal titles of Mesopotamia : *šar kiššati*, "king of the totality," a style reflecting especially the domination of Upper Mesopotamia.** The Babylonian priests were generally faithful servants of the Babylonian crown. One exception can be cited : their opposition to Nabonidus certainly contributed to his downfall and to the easy victory of Cyrus the Persian over Babylon in 539 B.C. Nabonidus kept strong ties with Harran's moon-god Sin, whose temple he restored and for whom the royal mother was "priestess".*** In the eyes of the Babylonian priesthood, Nabonidus was an apostate in regard to Marduk, the national god. The king's long stay at Taima in North Arabia may be linked with his difficulties with the priesthood. An anti-Nabonidus inscription reflects the situation not long before the advent of Cyrus (See Pritchard's ANET 315-316).

Already in the third millennium the *Assyrians*, in the North, existed as a people, between the Tigris river and the mountains. They received less of the Sumerian culture than the Babylonians, with whom they were closely related by race and language. Their first capital, Aššur, on the West bank of the Tigris, bore the same name as their national deity, represented in art by the sun disk, topped by an archer shooting a shaft.**** In Assyrian polity the city played a major role ; political power was shared by the prince and the citizens. Duing the first Assyrian empire the wealthy corporations of merchants also had their say in the goverment of the state. The ancient Assyrian dynast, whose power was mostly religious, called himself *iššaku* of *Aššur*, "prince-regent of the god Aššur", and described as a "priesthood" (šangutu) his delegated power. The Assyrian ruler also claimed the title *waklu* "judge," but the incriptions designate him usually as *rubû*, "prince" or perhaps "great pontiff" (in Semitic etymology "*rubu*" means "great").++ The only ruler of Assyria who fully claimed the *royal* title is Assuruballit (end of 14th cent.), whose seal bears the words : "to... king of Aššur." When he defeated Mitanni and conquered Babylonia he also called himself "king of the totality" and "vicegerent of Enlil." During the reign of Tukulti-Ninurta I (1260-1232) the god Aššur was completely identified with Enlil, the great Sumerian sky-god. Then the religious center of world hegemony was no longer the ancient sanctuary of Nippur, but the temple of Aššur in the Assyrian capital. Assyrian royalty was never in conflict with the priesthood. The king always remained the priest of his gods, to whom he would himself offer sacrifices in the temple. His religious authority was never questioned.

3. Some Functions of Royal Priesthood

Leaving aside what concerns Sumer there shall be indicated here, not historically as in the previous section, but thematically, additional functions which the kings performed as priests in Assyro-Babylonia.[13]

The Mesopotamian dynast was of course the supreme administrator of the gods' estates, of the temples, and was thus entrusted with the privilege and the duty of distributing the revenues of the territory. As priest of the local god he looked to his worship, offered daily sacrifices, poured libations and recited prayers. This was done especially by the Assyrian rulers, who, speaking of their royal power, would say: "The gods have blessed my priesthood" or "Anu and Adad love my priesthood." A hymn attributed to Ashurbanipal, praising the Sun-god (*Schamash*), was no doubt associated with the temple-cult, as the following extracts seem to suggest.[14]

O light of the great gods, light of the earth,
  illuminator of world-regions ...
Thou didst look into all the lands with thy light ...
The attention of all the gods is turned to thy bright rising.
They inhale incense; they receive pure bread-offerings.
The incantation priests [bow down] under thee
  in order to cause signs of evil to pass away,
The oracle priests [stand before] thee
  in order to make the hands worthy to bring oracles.
[I am] thy [servant], Ashurbanipal, the exercising of whose kingship
  thou didst command in a vision,

---

13 See R. Labat, *Le caractère religieux de la royauté assyro-babylonienne* (Paris, 1939), pp. 131-147 (on the "king-priests"). Priestly functions of the kings are often alluded to in their titles. See also J. Gray, "Sacral Kingship in Ugarit," in *Ugaritica* VI (Paris 1969) 289-302. Much of what he writes there applies to the whole of Mesopotamia.

14 Pritchard, ANET, p. 387.

[The worshiper of] thy bright divinity,
who makes glorious the appurtenances of thy divinity,
[The proclaimer of] thy greatness,
who glorifies thy praise to widespread peoples.

Performing rites of purification was one of the important functions of Mesopotamian priesthood, as we shall see. The kings would act as *išippu* mostly in the collective and public ceremonials. Among these was the purification or dedication of divine statues. The essential rite was called "mouth washing" (*mis pi*),[15] through which the statue was made fit to smell, eat, and drink. Assyrian king Esarhaddon (680-669) was proud to be called "the *išippu* who purifies the statue of the great gods." The Mesopotamian dynasts would also act as purification priests when new temples were erected or dedicated.

"Mesopotamia was not the land of individual revelation and personal salvation but that of portents and prodigies. The deity manifested its will by means of meaningful deviations from the normal which had to be interpreted by highly trained experts. These manifestations concern the king mainly and the country as a whole."[16] In fact the Mesopotamian kings were deeply involved in divination, through which they hoped to increase the wisdom of their rule and the success of warfare. Few of them, however, were full-fledged diviners, since the art required a long and arduous training. "Outside the realm of folklore, the Mesopotamian diviner is not a priest, but an expert technician and, first of all, a scholar... The diviner derives information on ominous happenings or features from large compendia, the centennial accumulations of divinatory experiences, which he studies, interprets, and comments upon with the help of such philological textbooks as are at his disposal."[17]

The Mesopotamian kings exercised their priesthood more especially on certain feast days, when, for example, the statue of the god was ex-

---

[15] On the "mouth washing" and "mouth opening" ceremony see H. Zimmern, *Beiträge zur Kenntnis der babylonischen Religion* (Leipzig, 1901), pp. 138-139 and note. See also A. M. Blackman in JEgyptArch 10 (1924), pp. 47-59 and S. Smith, "The Babylonian Ritual for the Consecration and Induction of a Divine Statue," JRoyAsSoc (1925), pp. 37-60. On the "mouth-opening" funerary ritual in Egypt, see E. Otto, *Das Ägyptische Mundöffnungsritual* (Wiesbaden, 1960).

[16] A. L. Oppenheim, in V. Ferm, ed., *Forgotten Religions* (New York, 1950), p. 78. On Mesopotamian divination see *La divination en Mésopotamie ancienne et dans les régions voisines*. XIVe Rencontre Assyriologique Internationale (Paris, 1966).

[17] A. L. Oppenheim in *La divination...* p. 40. On oil-divination, which together with hepatoscopy (see above) and smoke-divination, was the barû-priest's special field, see G. Pettinato in *La divination...* 95-107.

posed to the veneration of the faithful, carried in soleum procession through the streets of the city or even taken on the sacred boat to neighbouring towns or sanctuaries. The New Year festival was the most important feast of the year in Mesopotamia. It is best known through the attestations coming from Babylon of the Neo-Babylonian period.[18] It may be incorrect to say that it reflects a myth and ritual pattern common to the whole ancient Near East; there is little doubt, however, that a part of its ceremonial results from a broadly common conception of deity and nature, as known in Mesopotamia. "The ritual reenactment of the myths was based upon the conception that the cycles of nature were the earthly counterpart of heavenly events. These heavenly events were the death of the god who represented life, his restoration through his female consort who brought him from the underworld, his combat over the monster of chaos and his victory, the creation of the universe, and the determination of the destinies. The seasonal and cosmic cycle of life and death was itself a reenactment of the myth, and the continuance of the cycle could be assured only by man's incorporation of himself through ritual into the heavenly cycle. Each new year was a new creation and a new victory over chaos, a new birth of the god from whom life came."[19] Royalty's role in these nature renewal rites can also be related to the popular assumption that the king stood before his god as the high priest of humanity.*

c) *Priesthood in Sumer*

In Sumer, as elsewhere in Mesopotamia, priesthood was eminently, but not exclusively, represented in its divinely constituted rulers. The Sumerian clergy played its role in a social and religious setting which has to be determined further.

1. Sumer: Ethnic Background and Culture

Sumer occupied the southern section of the rich alluvial plain lying between the Tigris and the Euphrates.** It can claim to have been the seat of the oldest civilisation of the Fertile Crescent. "Politically it consisted of a group of city states, several of which were continuously vying

---

[18] See "Temple Program for the New Year's Festivals at Babylon," an extract of Akkadian rituals: Pritchard ANET, pp. 331-334. On the Mesopotamian New Year festival see F. Thureau-Dangin, *Rituels Accadiens* (Paris, 1921), pp. 127-154; R. Largement in DBSuppl v. 6, c. 556-597.

[19] J. L. McKenzie, *Dictionary of the Bible* (Milwaukee, 1965), pp. 613-14.

for control of the land as a whole, and at times for that of its surrounding neighbours. Economically, it rested on an agricultural base which as a result of the application of successful irrigation techniques, provided a surplus sufficient to support large and varied groups of artisans and craftsmen, merchants and carriers, clerks and scribes, priests and temple officials, soldiers and court officials. Socially, it was characterized by the breakdown of the more primitive clan and tribal loyalties and the gradual emergence of local and national patriotisms. In the field of religion it witnessed the growth of highly complex temple cults together with the development of a polytheistic theology and mythology* which to some extent became paradigmatic for the faith and creed of the entire ancient Near East".[20]

It is likely that the first people to settle in Lower Mesopotamia, in the beginning of the 4th millenium B.C., were immigrants from Southwestern Iran. Soon afterwards Semitic elements joined them from the West and together they founded the first civilized urban state of the region. The non-Semite Sumerian invaders, who came to Mesopotamia from beyond the Caucasus, only gradually overran and conquered the Irano-Semitic state. In the beginning of the 3rd millennium political stability again returned to the region and this was the time when architecture reached its high level and the initial steps were taken towards the invention of the first Sumerian system of writing. The civilisation of Lower Mesopotamia is better known from the archaeological remains of its later stages, namely of the second half of the 3rd millenium. It is called "Sumerian" because of the language of the inscriptions, but "Sumerian" civilization "is actually a product of the cultural and biological fusion of at least three ethnic groups, the earliest Iranians whose ethnic and linguistic affiliations are at present altogether unknown, the Semites, and the Sumerians. Similarly it is obvious, the so-called Sumerian religion of the 3rd millenium is not a homogeneous Sumerian development but contains elements taken over from the preceding Iranian and Semitic peoples."[21]

According to Gen 10 :10 Nimrod founded Erech,+ a city where temple building began as early as the late 4th millennium. Erech was regarded as the home of Gilgamesh, hero of the great Babylonian epic. The city of Ur reached its greatest splendor in the 3rd dynasty (21st cent. B.C.) under Ur-Nammu, who founded the ziggurat which was completed by

[20] S. N. Kramer, "Sumerian Religion," in V. Ferm, ed., *Forgotten Religions*, p. 47.

[21] S. N. Kramer, "Sumerian Religion," p. 50 (A partly hypothetical reconstruction).

Nabonidus (6th cent.).* At the time of Abraham, Ur was an imposing city with important temples, especially that of the Moon-god Nanna and the E-Nun-makh temple (a common shrine of Nanna and his consort Nin-Gal). Another Sumerian city, Lagash, was a cultural center perhaps as early as the 4th millennium. Its *e n s i*, "priest-governor," Gudea restored the city; less than four centuries later the mounds of Lagash were deserted and remained so until the 2nd cent. B.C. There is some reason to believe, S. N. Kramer writes, that "the very idea of a paradise, a garden of the gods, is of Sumerian origin."[22] It is besides meaningful for the Genesis account (2 :21-24), that in Sumerian literature the goddess Nin-ti's name means "the lady who makes live," as well as "the lady of the rib". It is a Sumerian myth also that recounts how the shepherd-god of Erech, Dumuzi (the Biblical Tammuz)+ was carried off to die in the Nether World as a substitute for his angered and embittered wife, Inanna.

2. The Gods and the Priests

The Sumerian theologians assumed as axiomatic the existence of a pantheon composed of invisible, anthropomorphic, but at the same time superhuman and immortal beings, whom they called *d i n g i r*, a term which we translate by the word "god." But for the Sumerians the term *d i n g i r* designated any numinous power known to them. More specifically it meant the protective genius of the individual, a sort of "guardian angel." But beside this "personal god" there were the other numinous powers reflecting nature phenomena and economic functions.[23] "Be it the great realms of heaven and earth, sea and air, be it the major astral bodies, sun, moon, and planet, be it such atmospheric forces as wind, storm, and tempest, or finally, to take the earth, be it such natural phenomena as river, mountain, and plain, or such cultural phenomena as city and state, dyke and ditch, field and farm, or even such implements as the pick-axe, brickmold, and plow, each was deemed to be under the charge of one or another anthropomorphic but superhuman being who guided its activities in accordance with established rules and

---

22 S. N. Kramer, ed., *Mythologies of the Ancient World* (New York, 1961), p. 102. See also W. G. Lambert, "A New Look at the Babylonian Background of Genesis," JThSt 16 (1965), p. 298 (with references).

23 See T. Jacobsen, »Formative Tendencies in Sumerian Religion," in *The Bible and the Near East*, ed. G. E. Wright (Garden City, 1961), pp. 267-78.

regulations."[24] The most important groups of the pantheon, or assembly of the gods, consisted of seven gods who "decree the fates" and of fifty deities known as "the great gods." Among the deities can be singled out the goddess Nammu who controlled the primeval sea and gave birth to *An*, the male heaven-god, and *Ki*, the earth-goddess. The union of *An* and *Ki* produced the sky-god *E n l i l*. Enlil was the most important deity of the Sumerian pantheon, "the father of the gods," "the king of heaven and earth," "the king of all the lands." In the Myth "Enlil and the creation of the pickax," he is the god who separates heaven from earth, brings up "the seed of the land" from the earth, and produces "whatever is needed." Yet his powers are limited and he himself is banished to the Nether World for his immorality.[25]

In the Sumerian epic called Enki and Ninmah* it is stated that man was created to serve the gods by providing them with food and drink. On this last point "all the Mesopotamian accounts agree : man existed solely to serve the gods, and this was expressed practically in that all major deities at least had two meals set up before their statues each day. Accordingly, man's creation resulted in the gods' resting, and the myths reach a climax at this point. Even in *Enūma Eliš* this is clear, despite much conflation."[26] The role of the temple in Sumer reflects these conceptions. The gods came to be part of society, the ruling class exercising all basic economic and political functions of the country. The temple was the ruling god's dwelling, the center of his vast estate. "At its head, as owner and administrator, is the great god himself, and with him his divine consort and children, who may themselves own similar estates. The house is run by the god's wife, who directs a staff of divine servants. These in turn guide and lend their divine efficacy to a corps of human servants, the priests. There are chamberlains, who make the divine bed, see to the bathing and anointing of the god, keep his rooms clean and swept. There are cooks who prepare his daily meals, carvers and cupbearers, who serve at table, singers and musicians, who entertain

---

[24] S. N. Kramer in *Forgotten Religions*, p. 54.

[25] S. N. Kramer, in *Mythologies*, p. 96. On the Sumerian pantheon see J. van Dijk in H. Haag, ed., *Bibel-Lexikon* (Einsiedeln 1968) 1658-62

[26] W. G. Lambert, "A New Look ...," JThSt 16. (1965), p. 297. See also W. Harrelson, "The Significance of Cosmology in the Ancient Near East," in H.T. Frank and W.L. Reed, eds, *Translating and Understanding the Old Testament. Essays in Honor of Herbert Gordon May* (Nashville, Tenn. 1970), who writes : "The gods should not have to labor so hard to maintain order in the cosmos; let creatures be formed who can take over the hard service of the gods."

the god and his guests, and also singers of elegies who soothe his darker moods...".[27]

Introducing his recent study of priesthood in the old-Babylonian period, J. Renger gives a list of the Sumerian terms for priest, with the Akkadian equivalents. He distinguishes three main categories : cult-priests, diviners, and exorcists.[28] In his learned monograph Renger attempts to determine what names were given to the various cult functionaries in the different periods and in different places of Babylonian history. The author correctly notes that neither in Sumerian nor in Akkadian is there a term which would correspond to the English word priest, applicable to various categories of the cult personnel.

Apparently the most common Sumerian term related to priesthood is *s a n g a*, which has a variety of meanings especially in compound words. The *s a n g a* did not perform, it seems, ritual functions themselves, although they were certainly, as texts show, concerned also with providing sacrificial victims. Perhaps they can be described as priests serving also as temple officials and administrators. For practical purpose many of them were also scribes who can be credited with inventing new ideograms and perfecting the art of writing. Supposedly for that reason *s a n g a* are often mentioned in school texts.*

The Sumerian word *e n* (cf. Assyr *ēnu*), meaning "lord"** in early texts, is also used as a formative element in the names of officials, both secular and sacred. The sign itself expressed by *e n* represents an important symbol : a single gate-post with streamer, the emblem associated with the goddess *I n a n n a*.[29] More particularly *e n* means also "high priest" and has a feminine counterpart *n i n* or *n i n - d i n g i r*, "priestess". This Sumerogram means "lady (who is) a deity." The priestesses were supposed to live in chastity, their function being to represent a deity in cultic ceremonies. There was also a category of "priestesses", the *nadiātum*, to which the daughters of high state officials were often consecrated, even from their childhood. In Sippar these "religious persons" or "sisters", called *nadītum*, lived in a *gagûm* or "locked house", which was part of the Shamash temple. The *qadištum* ("holy ones") belonged to a lower class than the *nadītum* and in some texts such religious

[27] T. Jacobsen, "Formative Tendencies...," p. 274

[28] J. Renger, "Untersuchungen zum Priestertum in der altbabylonischen Zeit," Pt. 1 : ZAssyr NF 24 (1967), p. 113 ; see p. 110-188. We shall refer also to Pt. 2 :ZAssyrNF 25 (1969) 104-230.

[29] See Pritchard ANEP, n. 502 : alabaster vase from Warka and E. D. van Buren, *Symbols of the Gods in Mesopotamian Art.*AnalOr 23 (Rome, 1945), pp. 43-44.

persons are definitely associated with sacred prostitution. In Uruk, *I n a n n a* was served by a male *e n* -priest, who was often the city ruler. Moon-god *N a n n a*, on the other hand, was served by *e n*-priestesses, all of royal blood and chosen by means of extispicy.

Another category of the temple personnel in Sumer is more precisely known. It is the *i š i b*, "purification priest", "libation priest" or "exorcist." The term is borrowed from Akk. *āšipu* and became *išippu* in Assyrian. * The role of the exorcist will be examined below. It is worth noting that from Lagash, Nippur, and Ur come representations of Sumerian priests, shaven and nude, pouring libations.[30] Other sacred ministers are half-dressed when laying foundation stones of temples or when performing funerary rites.[31] No certain origin or explanation can be found for partial or complete ritual nudity. Possibly at Sumer it suggested primeval innocence. A Sumerian religious text says that in the beginning "garments for wearing did not exist... garments for wearing they knew not."[32] Perhaps the peculiar habit was a way of simplifying "exit rites" by avoiding "contamination" of beard and clothes from the contact with the sacred,[33] or else the custom was intended to show conformity to the requirements of the ritual as concerned physical beauty and integrity on the part of the sacred ministers. There is some evidence that in the protoliterate period some Mesopotamian peasants wore no clothes to work in the fields. Religious conservatism, it is suggested, could have kept this no-garment fashion for the officiants![34]

d) *Assyro-Babylonian Priesthoods*

It is customary and understandable to speak of Assyro-Babylonian culture and religion, since it is difficult to make clear-cut distinctions

---

[30] See Pritchard ANEP nn. 597, 600, 603, 605; W. Otto, *Handbuch der Archäologie.* Erster Tafelband (Munich 1939) T. 125 and 139.1.

[31] Cf. C. J. Jean, *La Religion sumérienne, d'après les documents antérieurs à la dynastie d'Isin (-2186)* (Paris, 1931), p. 205. R. Labat writes of the Assyrian *išippu* that primitively he officiated in the nude; later he put on a sort of red cloak to frighten the devils away (*Le caractère religieux...* 144)

[32] Cf. Gen 2:25 and E. Chiera, *Sumerian Religious Texts*, t. 25, lines 15 and 21 (Upland, Pa., 1924), pp. 28-29.

[33] On entrance and exit rites in sacrifice, see H. Hubert-M. Mauss in *Mélanges d' Histoire des Religions* (Paris, 1909), pp. 22-28 and 66-71 = *Sacrifice : Its Nature and Function* (Chicago, 1964), pp. 19-28 and 45-49.

[34] See H. W. F. Saggs, *The Greatness That Was Babylon* (New York, 1962), p. 182. R. Rutten mentions two other explanations: a display of reverential humility before the divinity, or the fear of offending deities allergic to certain cloth textures (in M. Brillant-M. Aigrain, Histoire des religions, vol. 4, Paris n.d., 72).

in this Semitic and Mesopotamian world of two nations interrelated in so many ways. Even their particular languages are but dialects of what is known as Akkadian.

1. Assyria and Babylonia

A very sketchy outline of the origin and political history of these two peoples has been given above. The following complementary notions deal mostly with their relation to the Biblical world and with particularities of their religious beliefs and worship.*

Israel and Juda saw Assyria as a mighty and always threatening power, while the Hebrew prophets interpreted its aggressions as divine punishment of apostasy: "Ah, Assyria, the rod of my anger, the staff of my fury!" (Is 10:5). The Assyrian domination of North Palestine began in 859 and led to the fall of Samaria (722) and the further deportation of Israelites to Assyria under Sargon II (722-705; cf 2 Kg 17). These were replaced by a mixed population from Babylonia, Elam, and Syria, who mingled with the remaining Israelites and became Samaritans. Sennacherib, son of Sargon II, took Lachish and other cities but failed to seize Jerusalem because of a plague in his army (cf. 2 Kg 18-19; Is 36-37). A Sennacherib annal, inscribed in cuneiform on a clay prism, tells of "Hezekiah, the Jew": "Himself I made a prisoner in Jerusalem, his royal residence, like a bird in a cage."[35] The Assyrian records mention the names of ten Hebrew kings of the divided kingdom.

We know from the Book of Kings how Sennacherib died: "As he was worshipping in the house of Nisroch+ his god, Adrammelech and Sharezer, his sons, slew him with the sword, and escaped into the land of Ararat. And Esarhaddon his son reigned in his stead" (2 Kg 19:37). Ashurbanipal who succeeded Esarhaddon glorified during his long reign (669-631?) Assyria's last capital Nineveh and stored there 22,000 inscribed tablets.++ Following the fall of Aššur in 614, Nineveh itself was taken and destroyed in 612 at the end of a siege supported by a military alliance of Medes, Babylonians, and Scythians. The Hebrew prophets exultantly celebrated the event (Nah 3:7; Zeph 2:13-15). The repentance of the Ninevites is an important element of the Book of Jonah and is used by Jesus to rebuke indifference to the Gospel message (Mt 12:41).

The Chaldean-Babylonian empire (612-539) succeeded the Assyrian, but the history of Babylonia remained intertwined with that of Assyria. The name Babylon, meaning "Gate of God" (Akk. *Bab-ilu*), applied to

[35] Cf. Pritchard ANET, p. 288.

both the city and the country (Babylonia), of which it was the capital. "Babylon influenced Hebrew life and religion more than any other city except Jerusalem; and ancient Babylonia molded Jewish thought more than any other land outside of Palestine. They are mentioned in Scripture more than 200 times."[36] There are two main reasons for this : Babylonia was the region of Abraham's origin and Babylon was the scene of the captivity of Judah.

The political history of Babylonia can only be confusing since the country was ruled by kings from several lands : Sumerians (cf. the 3rd dynasty of Ur), Akkadians (cf. Sargon I), Amorites (cf. Hammurabi), Assyrians (cf. Ashurbanipal), Chaldeans (cf. Nebuchadnezzar II), and Persians (cf. Cyrus). Something similar happened to Mari, one of the most brilliant cities in the Mesopotamia of the 3rd millenium B.C. Ruled in the beginning by the 10th postdiluvian Sumerian dynasty, it was then successively conquered by king En-Anna-tum of Lagash (c. 2500), king Sargon of Akkad, about 500 years later, and finally Hammurabi (c.1760). Excavations conducted at Mari since 1933 reveal that a series of Ishtar temples have been built, destroyed and rebuilt on the same site from the early 3d millennium or even earlier. The site, known as Tell Hariri, is about 7 m. NW of Abu-Kemal, a townlet on the Syrian side of the Syro-Iraq frontier. In ancient times, it was an important cross-roads for trade. The identity of the site was confirmed by an inscription found on a royal statue, thus dedicated to Ishtar : "Lamgi-Mari,* king of Mari, high-priest of Enlil, dedicated his statue to Ishtar."[37] The last temple was apparently destroyed with the city itself by the soldiers of Hammurabi. There were also uncovered ziggurats or temple-towers and a large palace with its royal archives.+ The thousands of Akkadian written clay tablets they contained provide extremely valuable information on the history, languages, and customs of the 2nd millennium B.C. They also naturally shed light on the world of the Hebrew patriarchs as they record correspondence and events which concern in great part the land and the period of their origin. The interest of Biblical scholars centers in this respect on three points : the repeated mention of a city called *Nahur* (cf. *Nāḥôr* of Gen 24:10), royal allusions to raids of Banu-Yamina, "Sons of the Right",and the expression "to kill an ass" for indicating the sacrifice which accompanied an oath of alliance.++

---

[36] *Black's Bible Dictionary* 55

[37] Cf. A. Parrot, *Mission archéologique de Mari*, v. 1 : *Le Temple d'Isthtar* (Paris, 1956), p. 70.

"An important element in the daily life of the people of Mari was *divination.* This technique or rather series of techniques for predicting future events was reduced to an empirical system by collecting and preserving in various ways the omens which preceded great events of the past, so that future diviners might know what to expect if they found similar omens. One of the favorite techniques of divination consisted of hepatoscopy, the inspection of the livers of sacrificial animals. Since the liver itself with its peculiar configuration could not be preserved, accurate clay models were made and an inscription added which gave the information concerning the event which followed. At Mari there were found 32 of these clay models dating to the beginning of the second millennium B.C.; they bear references to events which took place during the dynasties of Accad, Ur, and Isin".[38] The Mari texts mention also the use of omens to secure the most favorable conditions in warfare.

2. The Great Gods

The various types of religious literature represented in the tablets found in Mesopotamia can be classified as Myths, Liturgies, Ritual, Texts, Incantations and Spells, Omen Texts, and Astrological texts. In all of these types, a great number of gods are mentioned. For example, the descriptive list of Akkadian gods in K. Tallguist's standard book, *Akkadische Götterepitheta* (Leipzig, 1938), extends over 240 pages. Although most of them have a Sumerian origin they are better known from their status in the Babylonian pantheon which reflects a more advanced stage in the development of religion in Mesopotamia. Since Mesopotamian deities are often referred to in this chapter and elsewhere it seems convenient as well as instructive to sketch a synopsis of the appellations and attributions of six great gods pertaining to the Babylonian pantheon : Anu-Enlil-Ea-Sin-Shamash-Adad.*

[*see p. 62*]

The most widely worshipped goddess in Assyro-Babylonia was Ishtar. As Sumerian *I n a n n a* ("Queen of Heaven") her main temple was Eanna at Uruk. She gradually took over the attributes of most of the other female deities, but she is best known under three aspects : as goddess of love and sexuality, as goddess of war and conquest, and in astrology as personifying Venus.

---

[38] G. A. Mendenhall, in BiblArchaeol 11, 1948, p. 18.

Babylonian	*ANU*	*ENLIL*	*EA*	*SIN*	*SHAMASH*	*ADAD* or *Haddad*
Sumerian	*An*	*Ellil*	*Enki*	Two sun-gods *Su'en* and *Nanna*	*Utu*	*Iškur*
Other		Ass. *Illilu* Sem. *Bēl*			Hittite sungoddess of Arinna	*Baal* (Canaan.) (Hurr.) *Teshub*
Known as	sky-god king of the gods	air-god king of all lands chief of the Sum. pantheon	water-god Lord of wisdom personifying the fertilizing underground waters	moon-god	sun-god	storm-god fertility-god =OT Rimmon
Chief concern	god of kings and princes	guardian of the tables of destiny	instructor of mankind god of magic	lord of the calendar fertility of cattle	upholder of truth and justice	later linked to *Shamash* as oracle-giver
Father of	*Enlil*, of the creation gods and of the vegetation goddess.	*Nanna-Su'en*	*Asalluḫi* (*Marduk*)	*Utu* and *Inanna* (*Ištar*)		*Iškur* was son of *Nanna*.
Consort	*Antu*, then *Ištar*	*Ninlil* (air-goddess)	*Damkina*	*Ningal*		
Symbol	shrine with horned cap		ram's head or goat-fish	crescent, bull horns or cowherd	Solar disk with fourpointed star;	lightning and axe (also bull)
Chief sanctuaries	Uruk	Nippur	Eridu	Ur	Sippar and Larsa (Elabbar temple)	IMki

3. The Priests and their Functions

The main *raison d'être* of the temple in Mesopotamia was to shelter the image of the god. There it was protected from the impurities of the outside world, clothed in sumptuous garments, and made to "live," kept, that is, potent, efficient, and present. "Large amounts of food and drink, necessary for this purpose, had to be provided, stored, prepared and —after having been offered to the image— to be distributed among the personnel acoording to rank and status."[39]

Apart from serving the image of the god and performing their other sacred duties, in the cult, the temple personnel fulfilled several functions in their *milieu.*

> "Some were concerned with the treatment of the sick, therapeutically as well as prophylactically, using medical and magic procedures; others with the mediation of litigations utilizing, e.g., the awe of the Holy to establish the truth by means of oaths and ordeals. The interest of the temple in the maintenance of the cultural tradition is reflected in its endeavors to preserve social justice by regulating the system of measurements, reducing the rate of interest, and influencing the money-market by granting loans without interest in special cases. It induced the priests to evolve and develop methods of surveying, to establish and regulate the calendar, to observe, record and interpret astronomical phenomena. As theologians and scholars—both functions are difficult to keep apart—the priestly scribes collected, copied and commented upon the treasures of the religious literature as well as the text and reference books necessary to teach and study the Sumerian which was kept alive as a sacred and scholarly language. The training of priests specializing in divination-techniques of all kinds was considered of vital importance for the well-being and the security of the country."[40]

Particulars have been given above on the terminology and the functions of Sumerian priesthood. Much of this applies also to Assyro-Babylonia, * where the Sumerian religious institutions served as pattern and were in great part assimilated. In the earlier historical periods of Mesopotamia the *e n s i* (Akk. *iššaku*), as we have seen, exercised both functions of priest and ruler in the city-states of Sumer and Akkad. The

---

[39] L. Oppenheim, "Assyro-Babylonian Religion," in V. Ferm, ed., *Forgotten Religions* New York, 1950), p. 75. See also *id.*, "The Care and Feeding of the Gods," in *Ancient Mesopotamia*, pp. 183-198; D. N. Freedman-G. E. Wright, ed., "The Significance of the Temple in the Ancient Near East," in *The Biblical Archaeologist Reader* v. 1 (New York, 1961), pp. 145-200. J. J. van Dijk observes that the tower-temple or ziggurat had its prototype in the primitive hill of creation and destiny (in H. Haag, ed., Bibel-Lexikon, edit. 1968, c. 1660).

[40] L. Oppenheim, *Forgotten Religions*, p. 76.

supreme sacerdotal office was later delegated to other sacred persons, who were called *šangu maḫ* or *šešgallu* in Akkadian.

The Assyro-Babylonian priestly categories included, as in Sumer, the purification priests. Called *ašuppu* in Akkadian, their principal role in the Babylonian religion consisted in providing protection against the evil spirits and the demons by performing rituals and reciting incantations.* This specialized function was necessitated by the development in Assyro-Babylonia "of an elaborate system of demonology** entailing jinns, ghouls, vampires, malignant disembodied ghosts (*edimmu*), and vast hordes of hostile spirits... which lurked in graves and solitary places, on mountains and in dens of the earth, and in marshes. They roamed about the streets, sliding through the doors and walls of houses, and were borne on the wings of the mighty winds that swept the land. Wherever they occurred they brought misfortune, sickness and death in their train."[41] A sick man could often be cured, it was thought, by expelling the evil spirit dwelling in him. This the exorcist-priest could do by means of magic. A pig, for example, cut in pieces and lain on the sick man, would serve as *puḫu*, "substitute," into which the proper spell could drive the evil spirit : "Give the pig in his stead, and give the flesh as his flesh, the blood as his blood, and let him take it; its heart... give as his heart, and let him take it."[42]

It was the function of the *kalû*-priest "to appease the heart of the great gods" by chanting hymns and liturgies to the accompaniment of musical instruments. The *bâru*-priests or "seers",*** on the other hand, interpreted signs and omens, observed the new moon and the planets, indicated the lucky and unlucky days, explained the intricacies of the calendar. Their activities are frequently mentioned in the state correspondence of the Assyrian kings. Sennacherib always consulted his seers before beginning his various campaigns against Syria and Palestine.

In Babylonia priesthood gradually became hereditary; the special, often sacred knowledge of the rituals was transmitted from father to son. The priestly candidate underwent a specific training which could be long and exacting if he learned Sumerian and cuneiform writing. For the temple singers and instrumentalists the course lasted three years.

---

[41] E. O. James, *Nature and Function*, pp. 49-50.

[42] See R. Campbell Thompson, *The Devils and Evil Spirits of Babylonia*, v. 2 (London, 1904), p. xxxiii. This author sees in this expelling rite a parallel to the story of the Gadarene swine (Mk 5:1-20). More often, *goats* were used as "substitutes", like the *mašḫuldubbu*-goat (see R. Caplice in *Orientalia* 36, 1967, 292-294).

We have seen that the influence of the Mesopotamian priesthood on the ruling power varied according to the states and the periods. The kings of Babylonia and Assyria never surrendered, however, the prerogative they had to appoint higher clergy officials, a right which they often exercised in favor of their own relatives.

We can conclude this exposition of Mesopotamian priesthood by quoting some generalizing reflections of a present-day scholar. "The only individual who could approach the deity in prayers, and expect an answer, was the king, according to the Assyrian concept of kingship which differs in essential points from the Babylonian. Endowed by birth and status with an extraordinary amount of that 'divine' spark which endued his person with the supernatural awe-inspiring radiance of all beings and things divine, he had to live a life strictly regulated by ritual and moral obligations... In contradistinction to the Religion of the Common Man without cult, priests or temples, we have here the Royal Religion with one adherent, the king, subjected to complicated obligations and duties, and enjoying unique privileges in his relation to the deity. It was up to the religious genius of a small nation in the western-most section of the rain-agriculture area, called Palestine, to claim for every human being the responsibilities, obligations and privileges which in Assyria were restricted to the king and high priest. The ultimate success of this revolutionary movement relegated the Religion of the Common Man to the substratum of superstition and folklore which survives all revelations and reforms."[43]

B. Canaanite Priesthood

It is true that our certain knowledge of Canaanite ritual and priesthood remains, at the present time, limited and on many points conjectural. Yet Canaanite culture and religion undoubtedly played an important role in the Ancient Near East and their relevance to the study of Israelite traditions is increasingly being confirmed. There is an additional reason for devoting to the Canaanites more than could be expected in view of the state of present-day knowledge : the area of their meaningful presence included also Southeastern Syria and Palestine.

[43] L. Oppenheim in V. Ferm, ed., *Forgotten Religions*, pp. 78-9.

a) Ugarit, Phoenicia, and Canaan

Ras Shamra or "Fennel Promontory" is the mound on the North Syrian coast which concealed the ancient city of Ugarit, where C. F. A. Schaeffer of Strasbourg has been excavating since 1929. The discoveries, writes Mitchell Dahood, "include enormous quantities of pottery, weights, bronzes, jewelry, statuary, stelae, tombs, constructions such as temples, palaces, private homes, sanitation systems, and above all, texts."[44] Most of the tablets are written in a previously unknown cuneiform alfphabet of 29 or 30 signs.* "The widely held view that Ugaritic is a Canaanite dialect whose closest affinity is to biblical Hebrew, especially in the poetic books, has been winning the day," Dahood notes.[45] The oldest tablets start in the first half of the 14th century B.C., but texts continued to be written down, until c. 1190 B.C. C. H. Gordon explains the special importance of Ugaritic in cultural studies mainly from the fact that "Ugaritic was produced at the crossroads of the Cuneiform and East Mediterranean worlds, and of Canaan and Anatolia, during the pivotal era of ancient Near East history : the Amarna age."[46] Our knowledge of the "Canaanite" language has greatly increased with the discoveries of Ras Shamra. It was partly known from the *Amarna letters* sent by vassal Canaanite kings to the Egyptian court in the early 14th cent. B.C. "Composed by Canaanite scribes little conversant with the Babylonian language they are employing, besides containing numerous Canaanite glosses to Babylonian words, they constantly betray in form and idiom the native Canaanite speech of their writers."[47]

In many respects Ugaritic has much in common with Phoenician and Canaanite : language, literature, culture. The Canaanites are known to most people only as the unhappy precursors of Israel in Palestine. W. F. Albright clarifies the subject when he observes that the word "Canaanite" is "historically, geographically, and culturally synonymous with 'Phoenician'." Consequently in his study he employs "for convenience" the term "Canaanite" to "designate the Northwest Semitic people and culture of western Syria and Palestine before the 12th century B.C." and the term "Phoenician" to "indicate the same people and culture after this date." The name "Canaan," he explains, is a west Semitic expression meaning "belonging to [the land of] Purple,"

---

44 M. Dahood, *Psalms I* (The Anchor Bible, New York, 1966), p. xviii.

45 *Idem.*, p. xix.

46 C. H. Gordon, *Ugaritic Textbook* (Rome, 1965), p. 2.

47 W. L. Moran, "The Hebrew Language in its Northwest Semitic Background," in *The Bible and the Ancient Near East* (New York, 1965), p. 60.

and the Greek name "Phoenicia" probably refers to the "purple" industry.[48]

Introducing his study of "Canaanite Religion in the Bronze Age" Albright states that "the ethnic identity of the people later known as 'Canaanites' was already established no later than the end of the 4th millennium B.C.". In the third millennium the civilization of Phoenicia, southern Syria, and Palestine was quite homogeneously Canaanite. This distinctive presence in these areas was maintained in spite of extraneous army and population movements, even when the Mesopotamian influence on Syro-Palestine was the strongest (2300-1900 B.C.). After extending his inquiry to include also later periods (up to 1200 B.C.), Albright concludes : "There is not the slightest reason to doubt the existence of a uniform higher culture throughout western and southern Syria as well as Palestine, during this whole period."[49]

b) *Canaanite Deities*

The Old Testament is avowedly inimical to the belief and practices of Canaan. Israel's austere faith, matured in the wilderness, faced a serious challenge when confronted with Canaanite fertility cults and all the permissive morality connected with them. This is also illustrated in the dramatic contest staged on Mt. Carmel between Elijah and the "prophets" of Phoenician Baal (Melkarth), whose worship Achab's Tyrian wife Jezebel endeavored to promote (1 Kg 18.17-38). The 8th century Hebrew prophets, and later ones also, crusaded against the syncretist cults (cf. Is 1:29-30; 4:13), while the Deuteronomists emphasized that the removal of the Canaanite inspired "high places" had to accompany the renewal of the covenant. Official Israelite zeal in that direction reached its peak with Josiah who "smashed the sacred pillars, cut down the sacred poles," destroyed and desecrated the other "abominations," the cultic sites contaminated with Canaanite worship (2 Kg 23; cf. 2 Kg 17:11). The Canaanites, on the other hand, "contributed to their Hebrew successors not only the basis of the language in which the Hebrews wrote their Scripture,[50] but also ceramic arts, music and musi-

[48] W. F. Albright, "The Role of the Canaanites in the History of Civilisation" in *The Bible and the Ancient Near East*, p. 438.

[49] W. F. Albright, *Yahweh and the Gods of Canaan* (New York, 1968), pp. 96 and 100. (Hereafter *Yahweh*).

[50] See e.g., J. Gray, *The Legacy of Canaan. The Ras Shamra Texts and Their Relevance to the Old Testament*. 2d rev. ed. (Leiden, 1965), pp. 258-331 and W. F. Albright, *Yahweh*, pp. 4-25.

cal instruments, and architecture. Solomon's temple at Jerusalem was built from a Canaanite (Phoenician) model; Phoenician craftsmen, loaned by King Hiram of Tyre, executed much of the work (1 Kg 7:13-14)".[51]

Of the Ugaritic texts discovered at Ras Shamra the longest and most important composition is the Baal cycle, a collection of episodes about the Canaanite gods (*c.* 2000 lines). Next in importance are the *Legend of King Keret,* a semi-historical poem (*c.* 500 lines) and the *Epic of Aqhat* (c. 400 lines). One of two other mythological poems is named after its invocation, *The Beautiful and Gracious Gods*, and describes the birth of the twin deities Dawn and Dusk. The other tablets treat of a variety of subjects.[52]

In the myths *El* designates a particular deity, the senior god of the pantheon, where he was always the final authority, even though as a "remote high god," as a *deus otiosus*, he interfered little in the day-today affairs of the world. *El*'s royal status, unlike that of Baal, was never menaced nor eclipsed, although his kingship was static while that of Baal was dynamic.[53] But *El* is also the most common and most ancient Semitic appellation for "god."* Typical OT uses of the name *El* in connection with the God of Israel can be cited : "I am the God of Bethel" (*ha'ēl bêt-ēl*, Gen 31:13); "I the Lord God (*yhwh 'elōheka*) am a jealous God" (*'ēl qanā'*, Ex 20 :5=Dt 5:9). But as a proper name of God *'ēl* is usually followed by a determinative, as in *'ēl-roī*, "God of seeing" (Gen 16:13), *'ēl-šaddai*, "Mountain-God" (Gen 17:1), *'ēl-'ôlam* "everlasting God" (Gen 21:33), *'ēl-'elyôn*, "God Most High" (Gen 14.18).

Having in mind the first generations settled in Canaan the author of the Book of Judges states that "the people of Israel did what was evil in the sight of the Lord and served the Baals... and the Ashtaroth" (2 :11,13). The nature god *Ba'al* typified in fact distinctive features of Canaanite religious belief and practice. He "was the epitome of all the *baalim*, just as was El of all the *elim*".[54] Albright describes his titles and

---

51 *Black's Bible Dictionary* 89. On "Phoenician and Israelite religion in Contact," see W. F. Albright, *Yahweh*, pp. 197-212.

52 Translated sections of the Ugaritic texts can be read in ANET, pp. 129-155.

53 J. Gray, *The Legacy of Canaan*, p. 155. Cf. W. Schmidt, *Königtum Gottes in Ugarit und Israel. BZAW* 80 2d ed. (Berlin, 1966), pp. 58-64.

54 T. H. Gaster, "The Religion of the Canaanites," in V. Ferm, ed., *Forgotten Religions*, p. 122. Baal is never presented in the Poems as son of El but he is the brother of Anath, and the latter is clearly a daughter of El (M.C. Astour, "Some New Divine Names from Ugarit," in JAmOrSoc 86, 1966, p. 279).

his essential role in Ugaritic myth : "There is a good reason to believe that *Ba'al* was coming into use as a personal name of the god during the Hyksos period (17th and 16th cent. B.C.), when Hadad was identified with the Egyptian storm-god Seth. Baal is not only storm-god, but is also king of heaven and earth. He is thus the Canaanite equivalent of Greek Zeus and also of Babylonian Marduk, in so far as the latter was considered to be the active head of the pantheon. His terrestrial home was on Mount Casius or *Ṣaphôn* (Zaphon or Zephon) and, because of this association, he was called Baal-zephon (*Ba'al ṣaphôn*).[55] Among Baal's favorite titles in the epic are 'Triumphant (*Al'iyan*) Baal'. 'Cloud-rider' (*rākibu 'arapāti*),* and 'Majesty, Lord of the Earth'."[56]

The Canaanite pantheon included also *Dagan* ("Corn") described in the texts as father of Baal and the genius of the crops. An early 2nd millennium B.C. temple is dedicated to him at Ugarit and he appears as Dagon in the OT (cf. Jg 16:23; 1 Sm 5:2-7). Another god was *Kôshar*, the divine smith, whom a Phoenician tradition preserved in Greek sources presents as the inventor of magical incantations and the first to "trick out words" in verse. There were also three main goddesses, or three personifications in which different aspects of femal distinctiveness appeared to predominate : motherhood (Aṯrt), sexuality and fertility ('Aṯtart), beauty and virginity (*'Anat*). Jezebel is known from the OT to have been patroness to hundreds of "prophets" of Ba'al and *Ashērâh* (1 Kg 18:19), and an *Ashērâh* statue was removed from the Jerusalem temple at the time of Josiah (2 Kg 23:6). The other two goddesses were also, like Mesopotamian Ishtar, associated with warfare. The Deuteronomic expression "*'ašterôt* of the flocks", to mean the choicest ewes (7:13; 28:4) reflects 'Ashtarth's or (Greek) Astarte's fertility trait. Astarte appears in 1 Kg 11:5 as "the goddess of the Sidonians" and in Jeremiah as "the Queen of Heaven" (7:18; 44:17-19, 25).

c) *Ritual and Priesthood*

Since any reconstruction of the Canaanite cult and priesthood from the published Ugaritic texts is largely conjectural, restraint in that field is recommended and will be observed, although a more extensive treatment could be expected to serve our purpose.**

---

[55] Lit. "Ba'al of the North" (cf. Ps 48:3; 76:5; 87:1; Ezek 28:14-16). The title "the great King" in Ps 48:3 can allude to the supreme Phoenician deity, but an Assyrian or Persian monarch would also be referred to as "the great king" (cf. Ps 47:3).

[56] W. F. Albright, *Yahweh*, p. 109. The divine name *Bel* is the Assyro-Babylonian form of Baal, and was used for Enlil, later for Marduk (Heb. "Merodach"; cf. Jer 50 :2).

Which gods were worshipped at Ugarit and what sacrifices were appropriate for each of them we know from a list of offerings found at Ras Shamra. The general terminology includes such Semitic terms as *dbḥ* "sacrifice" (Heb *zebaḥ*), *ndr*, "vow" (H. *neder*), *mtn*, "gift" (H. *mattān*), *mnḥ*, possibly an "offering" (H. *minḥâh*), *nsk*, "pour" (as a libation; H. *nāsak*). A more precise relationship with the OT can be drawn from specific sacrificial terms like *šlm(m)*, "peace offerings(s)," corresponding to the Heb. *šᵉlamîm*, "communion-sacrifice",[57] or *šrp* "burnt-offering" (H. *śārap*), similar in meaning to the Heb. *'ôlâh*, "holocaust." *Molk* and *šᵉlamîm* sacrifices appear as deified personifications in the "canonical list of the Pantheon", and it has been recently suggested that Iṯm in *Šgr w* Iṯm, a newly published "double divine name," corresponds to the Heb. *'āšām*, "guilt-offering" (cf. Lev 5 :14-26; Is 53 :10).[58]

The autumnal New Year festival was an important occasion also at Ugarit. The drama of Baal was then enacted.

> "The texts about Baal were the liturgy of the festival. Baal's conflicts with Prince Sea [*Yam*] and with *Môt* ["death"], his descent under the earth and his triumphant return,* the building of the temple, the festival of its dedication, and the sacred marriage, all took place in the cult in a realistic and vivid presentation which lasted throughout the days when the autumnal New Year festival was celebrated. The worshippers were active participants in the cult, weeping and lamenting when Baal descended under the earth and joining wholeheartedly in the joyful celebration when he returned triumphantly after defeating his enemies ...
>
> But the purpose of the celebration was not simply to give the worshippers a good time. The point was that the year which lay ahead was in this way lived through and experienced in sacramental anticipation. It was not simply a dramatic presentation but a creative means by which the course of the year was determined, the aim being to ensure Baal's victory and with it fertility and crops in fields and pastures. In accordance with a conception which seems to us to be magical in character, this was what was done in the cult. What took place was a kind of 'imitative magic.' In the cult Baal triumphed over his enemies and by his enthronement and the erection of his temple ensured rain and fertility for the coming year. Thereby creative forces were set in motion and what we today call nature was stimulated to action."[59]

---

[57] Cf. R. Schmidt, *Das Bundesopfer in Israel: Wesen, Ursprung und Bedeutung der Alttestamentlichen Schelamim* (Munich, 1964).

[58] Cf. M. C. Astour, "Some New Divine Names from Ugarit," JAMOrSoc 86, 1966, pp. 281-2.

[59] A. S. Kapelrud, *The Ras Shamra Discoveries and the Old Testament* (Oxford 1965), p. 65. There are echoes of these joyous festivals in the OT (cf. Dt 12:2; Is 57:5; Jer 3 : 6-13). It is, however, mainly an exercise in conjectures to present Israelite festivals as

There existed in Mesopotamia a distinctive kingship-priesthood ideology. What has been said above on this subject applies in the main also to the religious conception of Ugarit, where the king-priest, as epitome of the corporate life of his people, was reckoned to be particularly qualified to approach the deity on behalf of the community. In the *Krt* and *Aqht* texts only kings *Krt* and *Dn'el* performed priestly functions and it is they who received divine revelation regarding their progeny, a matter of concern for the whole community and even for the cosmic order. Apart from these texts from the heroic past there is no evidence that the king continued to be the mediator of divine revelation or that the prophetic office existed at Ugarit, as in Israel and to a certain degree as in Mesopotamia.[60] What the king did in the ritual reenacted "sacramentally" on earth the mythic situations involving the deities.

The administrative texts, which describe the *real* situation, show that at Ugarit, as in Mesopotamia, the kings delegated their priestly power. In one text,[61] a high priest, *Atnprln*, is named alongside king *Nqmd* (Niqmad), and the lists of state grants mention no less than twelve different families of priests. Combining a number of testimonies T. H. Gaster draws the following picture of the temple personnel. "The temple staff consisted of priests (*kohanim*), superintended by a 'high priest', sacristans (*qedoshim*),* choristers (*sharim*), doorkeepers, watchmen, barbers or branders, and such artisans as smiths, masons, builders, etc., charged with the maintenance of the sacred edifice. A 'man of the gods' —perhaps a generic term for a sacerdotal official-- is also mentioned, as well as female votaries known as 'sacred women.' The temple personnel subsisted on regular portions of the offerings allotted to them in accordance with a fixed scale."[62] Mention is also made in the texts of *yṣḥm*, "makers of (?sacred) vestments" and of *psl*(*m*), "sculptor(s)";

---

adaptations or "historicization" of Canaanite institutions. See Kapelrud 66-68; J. Gray, *The Legacy...* 199-201.

60 J. Gray, *Legacy of Canaan*, p. 216. Cf. Id., "Canaanite Kingship in Theory and Practice," Vet Test 2 (1952), pp. 193-220; E. De Langhe, "Myth, Ritual and Kingship in the Ras Shamra Tablets," in S.H. Hooke, ed., *Myth, Ritual and Kingship* (Oxford, 1958), pp. 122-148.

61 A colophon to C. H. Gordon, UT, n. 62, LL 54-56 (p. 177), transl. in *id.*, *Ugaritic Literature* (Rome, 1949), p. 49. In *UT*, gl. n. 412, Gordon describes *atnprln* as "name of high priest and narrator of sacred myths." The term *nqd*(*m*), "shepherd," is also used as a title of *Atnprln* with a sacral significance, possibly attested also when Mesha, king of Moab, is called *nōqēd* (2 Kg 3:4). See also Gordon, *UT*, gl. n. 2297 : *rb klmm*, "high priest."

62 T. H. Gaster, in *Forgotten Religions*, p. 134.

possibly of sacred images. Fifty families are listed as *ytnm*, a category of temple attendants; the expression is echoed in the Heb. *netînîm* (Ezra 2:58; 8:20), "those given" (to the temple), seemingly non-Jewish temple servants (cf. Jos 9:27 1 Chr 9:2).

C. Hittite Priesthood

A century ago our knowledge of the Hittites* was practically limited to the sparse notions contained in the Old Testament. These can be recalled, although they have in fact little to do with the historical Hittites concerned in this section.[63] The "Hittites" of the OT are numbered among tribes of Palestine, with the Amorites, the Canaanites, the Jebusites and others (Gen 15:19-21; cf. Num 13:29; Jos 3:10). Literary critics explain that in the Genesis narratives various traditions designate differently the pre-Israelite populations of Palestine : for the Yahwist they are Canaanites, Amorites for the Elohist, and Hittites (sons of Heth) for the priestly writers. These attributions, writes R. de Vaux, are not always justified but they correspond well to the temporal succession of the names.[64] Since Suppiluliuma I (first part of the 14th cent.) the Hittites also dominated the region of Ugarit.

Israelites dealing with "Hittites" are reported in various connections : a burial ground for Sarah (Gen 23:4-20), the wives of Esau (Gen 26:34; cf. 36:2), king Solomon's horse trade (2 Chr 1:17). We are also told that upon hearing "the sound of chariots, and of horses...", the Syrians said : "Behold, the king of Israel has hired against us the kings of the Hittites and the kings of Egypt to come upon us" (2 Kg 7:6). In Joshua's program, Israelite God-given territory would include "all the land of the Hittites to the Great Sea" (Jos 1:4). In these and in other references to the "Hittites", scholars point out, the Bible reflects the Assyrian usage of the name Ḫattu, which, since Shalmaneser III (858-824 B.C.) until Esarhaddon (680-669), was understood to include the whole of Palestine. [65]

For what concerns the historical Hittites it will be seen that our know-

---

[63] See R. de Vaux, "Les Hurrites de l'histoire et les Horites de la Bible," RevBibl 74 (1968), p. 502. The *Oxford Annotated Bible*, however, relates "*Heth* (the Hittites)" of Gen 10:15 with the people "who once established a powerful empire in Asia Minor, and disappeared as a world power in the twelfth century B.C." (p. 12).

[64] *Art. cit.*, p. 503, n. 103.

[65] R. de Vaux, "Hurrites..." RevBibl 74 (1968), pp. 502-03.

ledge of their priesthood is comparatively limited, mainly perhaps because only a small portion of the available source-texts has been transcribed and translated. Since Hittology is a relatively new science, it seems apposite to introduce the subject with longer than usual preliminary remarks.

a) *The Hittites*

A vast documentation on the Hittites became available in the beginning of this century with the discovery at Boghazköy* of thousands of clay tablets on which court scribes had written down annals and religious texts for the royal archives. Scholars soon realized that the language of this documentation was not Semitic even though Sumero-Akkadian cuneiform characters were used. The fact is that the Hittites, Indo-European in language, were Oriental in their culture. They came from beyond the Caucasus to settle in Armenia and central Anatolia. It is a peculiar feature of their distinctiveness to combine, in a way, the Indo-European and the Mesopotamian cultures.

Three periods are discernible in the history of the Hittites. Little is known of the earliest, proto-Hittite period, which concerns the aboriginal population who spoke a non-Aryan language, identified simply as *Hatti* by the local documents. The second period, the Hittite period proper, covers the second millennium B.C., during which the Indo-European groups came to power and imposed their language, at least in the administration. The great Hittite empire followed, with its double phase : the old kingdom (18th-15th cent.) and the empire (15th-13th cent.).** The third period starts with the collapse of the empire (about 1200 B.C.). But the neo-Hittites of north Syria perpetuated for five centuries the traditional Hittite culture and preserved the Hittite Hieroglyphic writing.***

Modern scholars apply the term "Hittite" to the official language of the Hittite empire, although the Hittites themselves called this language *Nesili*, "Nesite," from the ancient capital Nesa, or also perhaps "Kaneshite," if Kanesh (modern Kültepe) is the same place as Nesa. Two other Indo-European languages are represented in the texts, "Palaic" spoken in the North (probably in the region of later Paphlagonia), and "Luwian," spoken in the South (mainly in the Cilician plain). Some of the texts are in Hurrian,**** while others are in Sumerian and Akkadian, the languages of diplomacy and higher learning at the time.

The Indo-European origin of the Hittites is reflected also in the political and legal institutions of their Anatolian kingdom. But in religion and worship they preferably assimilated the local traditions and borrowed from Mesopotamia, refashioning their own cults in a new syncretistic combination. The Hittites held to the tradition that every deity was to be worshiped in the native idiom of its origin. Thus were specimens of so many languages preserved at Bogazköy. In fact the texts found there are chiefly concerned "with prayers, cult instructions, festive and magical rituals, records of divination practices, and mythological lore of religious significance."[66]

It is noteworthy that in the Hittite texts Evil is never imagined in the form of devils as it is in Babylonia. The cause of all trouble is rather *paprātar*, "uncleanness," or *alwanzātar*, "sorcery," the result of black magic. These are impersonal forces, not demons. Disease results from divine wrath; it is punishment of sin, confession of which can bring divine forgiveness. Typically, king Mursilis II discovered through a series of oracles that a plague had come to the country because his father had violated the oath of a treaty.* He recalls in his confessing supplication : "For twenty years now men have been dying in my father's days, in my brother's days, and in mine own since I have become the priest of the gods." Then having described the plague at length and all that he had done to discover the reason of divine anger he says : "And because I have confessed my father's sin, let the soul of the Hattian Storm-god, my Lord, and (those) of the gods, my lords, be again pacified! Suffer not to die the few who are still left to offer sacrificial loaves and libations!"[67]

b) *Hittite Deities*

As reflected by the written documents Hittite religion shows a highly developed polytheistic system, which contains also traces of previous stages when natural phenomena, including fetishes, were the object of animistic worship.+ The Hittite gods are numerous, multinational, and anthropomorphic in character. Some are divinized personifications, as of Justice, Truth, and even Sin.[68] Sumero-Akkadian deities came to the Hittites through the mediation of the Hurrians. "Only the myths of foreign origin were written as real literary compositions —we may call

[66] J. Puhvel in EncBrit, v. 11 (1964), p. 558.

[67] Text from ANET, p. 395. (compare 2 Sam 24:17).

[68] Cf. G. Furlani, "La religione degli Hittiti," in P. Tacchi Venturi, ed., *Storia delle Religioni*, v. 1 (ed. 5, Torino, 1962), p. 424.

them epics— whereas those of local origin were committed to writing in connection with rituals."[69]

The main god of the Hittites is "the storm-god (or 'weather-god') of Hatti", also called "the storm-god of heavens." His Hittite name is, however, always written with the ideograms of the Mesopotamian *Hadad.** The Storm-god, as provider of rain, was the supreme god all over West Asia outside Babylonia proper, and is the central figure in the Anatolian, Hurrian, and ancient Syrian myths.[70] The Hittite storm-god is the real king and owner of the land of Hatti, and he has only entrusted it to the mortal king. "The Weather God's sacred animal is the bull, and according to an older conception he is a bull himself. The connection of a god of thunderstorm and rain with this animal, characterized through its force, its loud voice and its fertility, is easily understood."[71]

More distinctively Hittite is the sun-goddess of Arinna, "the mistress of the Hatti lands, the queen of heaven and earth... queen of all countries."[72] Her Hattic name was *Wurusemu,* but she is called *špš'arn* in a Ras Shamra (Ugarit) text. We do not know what her name was when the Great King of the Hittite empire was her high priest. Her high rank in the pantheon follows a trend of the ancient cults of Asia Minor. Her personality, unlike that of the Sun-God, has little to do with the sun, since her symbolic attributes are the lion and the dove.[73] The great Babylonian goddess *Ishtar* was also known in Anatolia.+ The Hittite queen or the queen mother would offer sacrifices to the sun-goddesses revered by the previous queens.

c) *Hittite Priests*

As the Hittite gods were numerous, so also must have been the priests who attended to their needs and conducted their worship. Each day the

---

69 H. G. Güterbock, "Hittite Mythology," in S. N. Kramer, ed., *Mythologies*, p. 143.

70 Cf. H. G. Güterbock, *Mythologies*, p. 173.

71 H. G. Güterbock, *Forgotten Religions*, pp. 88-9.

72 H. G. Güterbock, *Forgotten Religions*, p. 90.

73 Cf. R. Dussaud, "Les Religions des Hittites et des Hourrites, des Phéniciens et des Syriens," in *Mana : Introduction à l'histoire des religions*, I. Les anciennes religions orientales, 2 (Paris, 1949), pp. 335-386. H.G. Güterbock writes that the Indo-European god *Agni* (see ch. 2 above) is mentioned twice in Boghaszköy, but that "the contexts are too fragmentary to prove his identity with the Indian Fire-God" (*Forgotten Religions* 94) See, however, H. Otten and M. Mayrhofer, "Der Gott Akni in den hethitischen Texten und seine indoarische Herkunft," Orlitz 60 (1965) 545-552.

gods had to be washed, clothed, and given their food and drink. As masters of the land they also received regularly their tribute in the form of first fruits and animal sacrifice. "The cult took place in temples, though open-air sanctuaries also existed. To judge from the temples at Hattusa, the cella containing the cult-statue was so located that it was accessible only to the priests and usually was invisible to the general body of worshippers."[74] There were, however, processions of statues of gods, which then would appear in public view. The texts tell of various categories of priests but their functions are not always clearly identified and their names are only known by their corresponding Sumerian ideograms. Apart from the priests properly so called the texts speak of temple officials generally called "the men (or the women) of the house of the god", who were more or less directly involved in the cult itself. Only the highest officials lived within the temple precincts. The lowest category of attendants also included workers, farmers, and cattle breeders, employed in the temporal management of the temple properties. In fact the main temples were not only places of worship but also great economic and financial centers.

The highest ranking sacerdotal category was expressed by the ideogram *sanga*. Every temple had its *sanga* and the other priests were subordinates in regard to him. The king himself is sometimes called the god's *sanga*. The man in charge of the sacred vessels is identified in the Sumerian ideogram as "the one who holds the copper." Among the Hittites, as elsewhere, a host of cantors participated in the religious functions. They sang or recited ritual texts in Hittite or in any of the major languages of the empire. Their functions correspond to that of the Mesopotamian *kalû*, who sang hymns with drum accompaniment. Among the priests of sacrifice figured the *harsiyalâs*, whose task it was to offer the bread to the gods, and the *ispantuzziyalâs*, in charge of the libations.

To the Mesopotamian *bârû*, diviner and interpreter of the will of the gods, corresponded the Hittite diviners, technicians of the numerous foretelling media used in Hatti. For divining played an important role in the private and the public life of the Hittites. The omen literature, well represented in the Hittite texts, touched various areas : astrology, hepatoscopy, extispicy, oneirology, and ornithomancy. It lacked originality, however, since most of it was borrowed from Babylonia. The priests performed the function of divining by examining the entrails of

---

[74] W. L. Moran, "Hittite and Hurrian Religions," NCE v. 7, p. 36

the sacrificial victims. Other diviners watched the flight of birds or fowl for possible omens. The Hitties also practiced liver haruspicy, already known in Assyro-Babylonia and later fully developed by the Etruscans. The models of the liver found at Boghazköy came from Mesopotamia. They were used for the training of the haruspices and bore, for that purpose, inscriptions stating the meaning of the various shapes of different parts of the liver. In Hatti, as elsewhere, signs in heaven were also important and it was the function of the astrologers, priests very often, to discover their meaning and to suggest, if necessary, the proper ways of appeasing the gods.*

The Hittite king was apparently considered by his subjects as the religious head of the nation as well as its supreme judge and military commander. Through the rites of consecration he embodied all the life forces of the nations, became identified in a way with the national divinity and could be called "son of the god." Normally, however, the Hittite king was divinized only after his death. As elsewhere in the Near East, the royal consecration included the anointing and the imposition of a new name. The king usually delegated his sacerdotal functions, but at certain feasts he officiated personally as chief priest. The historical texts mention more than once that the king had to postpone a military campaign in order to perform his religious duties. "If one reads the descriptions of the elaborate ritual feast celebrated by the king, covering several days and sometimes including travels all around the shrines of the country, the special prescriptions which aim at keeping the king from contagion with anything ritually unclean, the oracles which were consulted to investigate possible neglects of the cult and the prescriptions for the compensation of such neglects, one can hardly imagine how the Hittite kings found the time to do anything else."[75]

The priestly duties of the king were many. Not rarely the king is represented as offering the sacrificial blood by pouring it at the foot of the god. Before entering the sphere of the holy, he put on the great sacerdotal cloak and covered his head with the skull cap. The king, like the priests, had to be protected against defilement, from which only prolonged purification rites could deliver him. Distinctive of the Hittite king's sacerdotal prerogatives was the power of evocation, through which he could summon the deities of enemy nations to come over to Hatti carrying along enemy possession. Thus, after obtaining a victory

[75] H. G. Güterbock, *Forgotten Religions*, p. 95. On "The Priestly Dress of the Hittite King," see A. Goetze in JCuneiformS 1 (1947) 176-185.

the king could freely lay an interdict on enemy territory and make of it pasture land for the weather-god's bulls.

From the "Instructions for temple officials"[76] we learn that the priests and their attendants had to "be very reverent" in regard to the word and the will of the gods, and act only according to their pleasure. In this document the priests are reminded of their other duties : observe cleanliness in the preparation of the sacrificial loaves; avoid appropriating any of them for their own use; celebrate the festivals at their proper time. They must have great respect for the temple and its precincts. Non-Hittites were forbidden under penalty of death from "approaching the gods," and priestly offenders of the temple precinct were also liable to capital punishment. As regards the temple property they are the caretakers of the god and have no right to take for themselves what belongs to him. It was required of the priests to have no physical defects, and to be holy, at least ritually. The king as well as the priests had to observe a number of ritual taboos. Should they have contracted any impurity, as that resulting from conjugal relations, they had to purify themselves before officiating in the cult. Transgressors of this regulation could incur capital punishment. Finally, the Hittite priests were expected to respect the traditional forms of the cult, and the conditions were set for the introduction of new elements in the ritual.

D. Priesthood in Ancient Egypt

Ancient Egypt* was in close contact with the Semitic world chiefly from the New Kingdom onwards. The Egyptians themselves had a mixed origin,** although their religious culture was distinctively national and original. Egypt's monuments and the texts associated with them are in great part products of the nation's religious sentiment, which priesthood served to promote and preserve. Even a cursory study of Egyptian priesthood involves questions which concern central aspects of the brilliant civilization proper to the Nile valley.

a) *Pharaoh and the Gods*

The founders of Egypt's theocratic monarchy and their successors were believed to be the incarnation of the gods they happened to serve.[77]

---

[76] See ANET, pp. 206-210.
[77] See H. Frankfort, *Kingship*, pp. 39-40.

The king was then the divinely constituted mediator between heaven and earth. He was the supreme pontiff in worship as well as the sovereign "shepherd" of the two-lands, concentrating in his divine person the temporal and the spiritual powers "When Pharaoh assumed dualistic titles or called himself 'Lord of the Two Lands,' he emphasized not the divided origin but the universality of his power... The universe as a whole was referred to as 'heaven and earth'. Within this concept 'earth' was again conceived dualistically, as 'north and south', the 'portions of Horus and the portions of Seth', 'the two lands,' or 'the two (Nile) banks'. The last of these synonyms demonstrates their non political character most clearly... They belong to cosmology, not to history or politics, for the whole of mankind and all the lands of the earth were subject to Pharaoh".[78] In theory it was the king who officially worshiped the gods and performed the other external acts of religion. This explains the complete absence of the priests from the rites and the offering scenes depicted on the walls of the temples. In practice, however, the priests performed the rites and managed the temples in the name of the king.

The political and religious status of the Pharaohs is best reflected in their titulary. Two examples can be given, then briefly explained. The following is the full titulary of Sesostris I (12th Dyn.) as interpreted by Sir Alan Gardiner : *Horus 'Life-of-Births', Two Ladies 'Life-of-Births,' Horus of gold 'Life-of-Births,' King of Upper and Lower Egypt 'Kheperkerēʿ'* ['the *ka* of *Rēʿ* comes into being'], *Son of Rēʿ 'Sesostris'* ['man of (the goddess) Wosret'], (may he be) *granted life, stability and wealth like Rēʿ eternally.* The second example is the titulary of Tuthmosis III (18th Dyn.) : *Horus 'Strong-bull-arising-in-Thebes', Two Ladies 'Enduring-of-kingship-like-Rēʿ-in-heaven,' Horus of gold 'Powerful-of-strength, holy-of-diadems,' King of Upper and Lower Egypt 'Menkheperrēʿ'* [the form of Rēʿremains(?)'], *Son of Rēʿ, 'Tuthmosis* ['Thoth is born'] *beautiful-of-forms', beloved of Hathor, lady of the turquoise.* Gardiner first explains the basic notion of the titulary and its composition in five elements :

> "The underlying idea is that the king, while being the temporary re-incarnation of Horus, of the goddesses described as the Two Ladies, or of the golden Horus, reveals his individuality by exhibiting the divine nature under some aspect peculiar to himself; thus Sesostris I is the Horus who infuses life into all who are born, Thuthmosis III is the golden Horus who is powerful of strength and whose diadems are holy. Similarly, the names in the two 'cartouches' or 'royal

---

[78] H. Frankfort, *Kingship,* p. 19.

rings' described the nature of the king in his capacity of 'King of Upper and Lower Egypt' and of 'Son of Rē'', respectively. Whereas an Englishman distinguishes two different kinds of name, Christian and family name, the Egyptian kings distinguished five, which we term the Horus name, the *nebty* name, the golden Horus name, the *prenomen* and the *nomen*."[79]

The *Horus name* represents the king as the earthly embodiment of the old falcon-god Horus, the dynastic god of Egypt, like the sun-god *Rē*ʿ. The *nebty* name, featuring "the two ladies," presents the king as identified with the two principal goddesses of the period immediately preceding the 1st Dyn., when Egypt was still divided into two kingdoms :vulture-goddess *Nekhbet* and cobra-goddess *Edjō*, representing respectively Upper and Lower Egypt. *Horus of gold* is the probable meaning of the monogram which constitutes the third element of the titularies, but it is not known to what god exactly it refers. The *prenomen* and *nomen* are invariably written within 'cartouches'* or "royal rings." The *prenomen* is the principal name and is almost always compounded with the name of the god *Rē*ʿ. The *nomen* or name in the *cartouche* was, as a rule, that borne by the king before his accession to the throne; it is, Gardiner writes, almost the equivalent of our family name (e.g. Sesostris and Tuthmosis). The term "Pharaoh," which in theE gyptian original means "Great House," first referred to the palace itself or to the court, but later (from Akhenaten) became a respectful designation for the king.

Most of the gods in the Egyptian pantheon are *local gods*. Several of them will be mentioned with their place of origin, their emblems, their family ties and main concern.** We first meet the triad of Thebes [the ancient capital of (Southern or Upper) Egypt] : *Amon*, *Mut*, and their son Khonsou. Amon, the "Mysterious One," supplanted *Montou* as the king's god in the 11th Dyn., and became *Amon-Rē*ʿ, in accordance with the theology of Heliopolis. His headdress usually consists of a cylindrical cap surmounted by two feathers. Mut is often identified with other goddesses, including Hathor and Edjo. She wears a vulture headdress with double crown, while Khonsou, the moon-god, appears as a young man with the lunar crescent above his head. *Seth*, god of Ombos, probably worshipped in the prehistoric period in the whole of Upper Egypt, later became an opponent of Osiris and Horus, locally identified as his brothers. He figures among the malevolent gods and is represented as a fabulous animal or as a man with such an animal's head. Ramheaded

---

[79] A. Gardiner, *Egyptian Grammar* (2d ed. rev., Oxford, 1950), pp. 71-72. What follows draws from *id.*, pp. 72-76.

Knoum is especially known as the god of Elephantine, where he supplied the waters of the Nile. His legend makes him the Creator who fashioned the world and the body of every man [see ANEP, n. 569]. *Hathor*, goddess of Aphroditopolis and Denderah, where she was the wife of Edfu's Horus, was the goddess of love and of joy. She is represented as a cow or as a woman with the head or the horns of a cow. *Anubis*, god of Cynopolis in Middle Egypt, was a god of the dead who figures on the monuments as a man with the head of a dog.

Other local gods belong to Lower Egypt. Sky-god *Horus*, from Behdet in the Delta, is the protector of the Pharaonic monarchy. He appears on the monuments as a hawk wearing a crown or as a man with the head of a hawk [see ANEP, p. 189 and n. 566]. In the mythology of Memphis, his place of origin, *Ptah* was creator of the world and the sovereign of the gods. Patron of sculptors and smiths, he was known to the Greeks as Hephaistos. The sacred animal of his incarnation was the bull Apis. As a human figure he is clothed in a tight-fitting garment and often holds the composite scepter. God of Busiris in the Delta, *Osiris* was later known in the whole of Egypt as a god of the dead. He is usually represented with a mummiform body and wearing a tiara. God of Hermopolis in the Delta, *Thot* was a moon-god who patronized writing and time computing. He has the head of an ibis, sometimes topped by a lunar disc. Another tradition makes him a monkey. From the Delta also came *Isis*, whose name means "the seat." Originally a sky-goddess she was known in the cult as the wife of Osiris and the mother of Horus. The horned moon-disc is usually included in her headdress. Finally, mention must be made of *Atum*, god of Heliopolis (near Cairo) who was later identified as the setting sun while Khepri (cf. *ḫprr, scarab*) was the rising sun.

Besides the gods with whom mythology was provided by the local cults, there were those whom speculation elaborated, to represent the cosmic elements. These *cosmic gods* were not strictly speaking worshipped in the cult. First among these was *Rēʿ*, the Sun. He travelled in the sky, with his equipage, on two boats, one for the day and one for the night. He entered at night in the body of the sky-goddess, *Nūt*, and emerged from her in the morning as a new-born sun. Beside him he had a daughter, *Maat*, who personified justice. Other cosmic gods personified the earth, the air, and the abyss: respectively *Gheb*, *Shu*, and *Nun*. No particular mention can be made here of the lesser gods, the genii, the deified heroes, and the sacred animals.

The theologians of Egypt attempted very soon to coordinate the data of tradition regarding the gods, mainly their hierarchy and their functions. According to the system of Heliopolis, for example, there existed in the beginning only primordial water. The sun-god Atum, having created himself, it explains, produced the first divine couple, after which the other cosmic gods were generated. While Heliopolis had two Enneads, or groups of nine gods, Hermopolis had its Ogdoad, the eight gods, whom Thot had created by utterance (*Shabaka* text). From the egg which they created came forth the Sun, who in turn produced and organized the universe. Other sanctuaries had their own cosmogonies. A further speculation, always active, followed the line of syncretism and tended to merge the divinities. Thus the theologians of Memphis identified all the gods with *Ptah*, while later the assimilation centered on sun-god *Rēʿ*. In the Ptolemaic inscriptions the various local gods are declared to be the manifestations of "Him whose Name is hidden."

b) The Personnel of the Temples

The Egyptian priests in their official function were at the exclusive service of the god dwelling in the temple to which they were assigned. The personnel of the great temples was considerable. To keep up the large properties, to prepare the sacred food, to weave the prescribed fabric, and to provide for the god's processions on ground and water, numerous groups of artisans and workers added the service of their respective competence to the devoted attendance of the priests. A papyrus informs us that under Ramses III (12th cent. B.C.) the temples of Amon in Thebes employed 81,322 people. The temple property included 433 gardens, 924 sq. m. of fields, 83 boats, 46 workyards, 64 market towns, and 421,362 beasts.[80] At Heliopolis and Memphis, in the North, the personnel equalled respectively only 1/7th and 1/27th of that of Thebes, the capital of the united kingdom (New Empire).

In Egypt, as elsewhere, the ministers of the cult and their attendants came only gradually to form an organized clergy. From the earlier periods documentation on the subject is scanty. Given, however, the remarkable stability of the Egyptian institutions in general, it can be assumed that the organizational pattern of the clergy known from later sources also reflects what existed since the foundation of the main temples. There was a chief priest in each of them although Egyptian has no

[80] See H. D. Schaedel, *Die Listen des grossen Papyrus Harris* (Leipziger Ägyptologische Studien 6; Glückstadt-Hamburg, 1936), pp. 45-48.

fixed term to designate this function. He is called "the greatest of those who see *Rēʿ*" at Heliopolis, "the chief of the artisans" in Memphis, and in Hermopolis (*Schmun*) he was known as "the great(est) of the five of Thoth's house." More often the chief priest is called the "first prophet of the god". He represented the king in the temple(s) entrusted to him, was by right responsible minister of the cult, and the chief administrator of the temple property. The high ranking clergy included all those who were privileged with "contemplating all the transformations of the god," those, that is, who would come near to the Holy of holies. They are called "servants of the god" (*ḥm-nṯr*), or "prophets," by the Greeks, who knew them mostly as oracular interpreters. The "second prophet of the god" seems to have been the general manager of the temple property and revenues. It is impossible to determine the particular functions of the other "prophets." Only the priests of high rank were permanently on duty. In the later periods, at least, the great majority of the priests belonged to the "temporary personnel" divided in four groups (*phylae* in Greek). Each of the groups carried out the religious service for one month, three times a year. A complete inventory of the sacred objects and temple accessories was made every time a new *phyla* took over.[81]

There were two main categories of priests among the standard clergy.* The ones are called *Wab*, "pure," "clear," perhaps because, originally at least, they would test the blood of the animal victims and declare: "It is pure!" They were bound to a special "purity" as called to touch daily the divine statue or carry it in procession on the sacred ship. From their ranks came the *stolists*, well known from the Greek documents. These specialized officiants or cult technicians were entrusted with the personal care of the god, a function to be explained below. Applied in the beginning to a privileged class of priests, the term *Wab* became later the common designation for "priest".** The "lector priests", called *ḫry-ḥb(t)*, "holder of the ritual book," formed the other category of priests. As "scribes" they wrote the sacred books, as "readers" they recited the liturgical hymns and conducted the sacred ceremonies. Their knowledge of the sacred writings recommended them for sorcery and the magical

---

[81] Some egyptologists think that the *horologues* (priest-timekeepers; *Stundenpriester*) were volunteers (perhaps laymen) who did an hour service at the temple. S. Sauneron, however, believes they were astronomers who established the "hours" in which each act of the cult should start (*The Priests of Ancient Egypt*, tr. Ann Morrissett, New York 1960, p. 66).

art. They were renowned for their wisdom and those who were horoscope-priests would suggest appropriate names for the royal progeny.

It is difficult to draw a clear distinction between the lower clergy and the lay personnel of the temples.The priestly dignity can likely be attributed to the *overseers* who directed the various activities permitting the material functioning of the temples. The feminine personnel, more or less related to the temple cult, belonged to two very distinct categories. Their were first the so-called "concubines of the god" or "recluses," and the singers of the royal harem. They were not, however, sacred prostitutes but ladies-in-waiting in the retinue of the queen, who was considered as the spouse of the god and the head of the feminine personnel employed in the temples. Generally speaking Pharaoh's human mother does not seem to have played any part in the theology of kingship. She was no more than the vehicle of the incarnation. In the second category can be numbered all those voluntary women auxiliaries who contributed their talents to the temple as singers, musicians and dancers.

c) *Installation and Obligations*

The priestly service of a god was often transmitted from father to son and their existed priestly dynasties. Royal favor or disfavor could always change the course of succession. The king usually appointed the highest dignitaries but left subordinates to provide for the lower offices. The council of the priests within the various temples assigned the particular tasks and suggested names for filling the vacancies even of the higher offices. No evidence of an elaborate installation ceremonial has been found. When Nabounnef was appointed "first prophet of Amon," king Ramses II used the following formula : "Thou art henceforth high priest of Amon : his treasuries and his granaries are under thy seal. Thou art the head of his temple, all his servants are under thy authority..." Then the monarch gave the high priest of Amon his two rings of gold and his scepter of election.[82] At Thebes, after the ritual bath in the sacred lake, the new priest was again sprinkled with water in the temple itself, and following this symbolic baptism his hands were anointed, which simply means that he was officially appointed to his office.[83]

---

[82] Quoted by S. Sauneron, *Priests*, pp. 46-47, from the inscription of the Theban tomb of Nebunnef. See J. H. Breasted, *Ancient Records of Egypt*, v. 3 (Chicago, 1906), pp. 104-105.

[83] See S. Sauneron, *Priests*, p. 48 and H. Bonnet, *Reallexikon der Ägyptischen Religionsgeschichte* (Berlin, 1952), art. "Salben," 638-649.

The secrets of the profession were eventually communicated to the newly initiated, including, no doubt those magic formulas permitting "the enchantment of heaven, earth, hell, and the seas—to see the sun climb to heaven with its cycle of gods, the moon rise, the stars in their place."[84] For the temple was not simply a building, but a miniature image of the world, a kind of model representing symbolically the regions of the universe where the god moved, and this, writes Sauneron, "seems the evident explanation of the various symbols turned over to the young priest at the moment of his installation."[85]

More is known of the *obligations* imposed on the priests. Being by office guardians of the divine Presence, the Egyptian priests had to safeguard the ritual purity required of those who approach the deity and touch the sacred effigy. Twice a day and twice during the night, reports Herodotus, the temple officials bathe in cold water. They also wash the mouth with a little natron diluted in water and shave the entire body every other day "so that no impure flea or vermin shall impede them in the practice of their religion" [*Hist.* 2.37]. To further contribute to bodily cleanliness they received circumcision and had no sexual relations, at least during the periods of their actual service in the temple.

The Egyptian priest had, in addition, to abstain from whatever the god was allergic to as regards food and clothing. One candidate to the priesthood thus expressed his credentials : "I present myself before the god, being an excellent young man, brought to the edge of heaven... I came from *Nun* (primordial waters) and I have rid myself of all that was evil in myself; I have set aside my clothing and ointments such as those used by Horus and Seth. I come before the gods in the holy of of holies, full of fear in his presence."[86] If the Greek and Latin authors writing on Egyptian customs are to be believed there was little that the priests could eat without offending the gods. It is likely that their lists of forbidden food are collections referring to different places and periods artificially assembled and thus misleading as to actual practice. It is certain, however, that the Egyptian priests could wear no wool clothing within the temple precinct because the gods would not tolerate

---

[84] S. Sauneron, *Priests*, p. 49. The text is quoted from "The Tale of Setnau" or, more precisely, „The Story of Prince Khamwise," supposedly a son of Ramses II and a *sĕtom*-priest of Ptah (hence "Setnau"). The tale, written in Demotic, is translated in B. Lewis, ed., *Land of Enchanters*. Trans. B. Gunn (London, 1948), pp. 67-83.

[85] S. Sauneron, *Priests, ibid.*

[86] S. Sauneron, *Priests*, p. 48. The text is from a statue in the Cairo museum.

fabric obtained from living creatures. In Egypt, as in Israel, the priestly vestments were made of fine linen. In contrast to the custom in other religions they were generally of a simple standard cut and pattern, neither eccentric by defect nor extravagant by excess. Only the sash, worn across the chest, could be indicative of a particular function, with the exception of the chief priest and of a few specialized officials who could wear a distinctive dress. Wearing white sandals seems to have been one of the privileges of the priestly class.

d) *Functions and Concerns*

Apart from his essential function, which was to serve the god of his temple, the Egyptian priest was especially devoted to the task of fixing and preserving the divine words and sacred rituals in the traditional hieroglyphic language.* In Egypt the priests were often the men of culture, whose knowledge and wisdom bore upon a variety of domains.

1. Guardians of the Presence

The Egyptian priests were neither mediators, like the king, nor ministers of sacrifice, nor exponents of beliefs and morals. They had almost nothing to do with the personal religion of the people and if they happened to be saintly or learned this resulted rather from their individual tendencies, even though, of course, their call favored such ideals. They are not known, as a group, to have lived on the edge of society, like other holy orders of men. They were bound to a number of purity regulations mainly or only during the periods of their service at the temple. By virtue of their profession the Egyptian priests had a very precise role to play : "maintain the integrity on earth of the divine presence, in the sanctuary of the temples, where this presence has consented to dwell—and this is all. Their action contributes to the essential theological role of the Pharaonic monarchy : to maintain the universe in the form in which the gods have created it. It is a work of specialists, a task of technicians... They are delegated by the king to perform in his place certain material rites necessary to the general welfare."[87]

It is clear that the Egyptian temple is intended to be *ḥwt-nṯr*, the "palace of the god", not a place of worship. The peristyle courts lead to gloomy recesses, including the dark chapel, the holy of holies. There the god consents each morning to let the statue which represents him

---

[87] S. Sauneron, *Priests*, pp. 34-35.

embody something of his immaterial being. The essential duty of the priests is to obtain the proper conditions for this sort of incarnation. When dawn breaks, the watchman of heaven gives a signal and the world of the temples stirs to a new day. Having performed their ablutions the priests join ranks toward the sanctuary for the sacred functions. The priest named to appear before the god breaks the clay seal and opens the door of the chapel. The morning hymns resound, alternately sung by the soloist and the chorus : "Thou art risen, thou art in peace : rise thou beautifully in peace, wake thou god of this city, to life! The gods have arisen to honor thy soul, O holy winged disc who rises from his mother Nūt! It is thou who breaks thy prison of clay to spread on the earth the powdered gold, thou who rise in the east, then sink in the west and sleep in thy temple each day... Thine eyes illuminate the night! Thy brows wake in beauty, O radiant visage which knows not anger!"[88]

Meanwhile the chief stolist removes what is left of the spent candle, lights another, and moving along the sacred ship he opens the naos and contemplates face to face the venerated idol, where the divine power comes to reside. The instant of cosmic import arrives when the officiant, placing his hands on the statue, restores its soul after the lethargy of the night. Then in respectful posture he repeats four times the formula of prayer : "I worship thy Majesty, with the chosen words, with the prayers which increase thy prestige, in thy great names and in the holy manifestations under which thou revealed thyself the first day of the world."[89] In the meantime the sacred food has been brought to the temple. It is symbolically offered to the god and to the secondary divinities of the sacred area before being distributed for the subsistence of the temple personnel. There is a ruling "that one lives on the provisions of the gods; but this is always food which leaves the altar after the god is satified."[90]

The toilet of the god comes next. He is washed, dressed in new material, or at least four strips of fine linen or byssus are offered to him : white, blue, green, and red. On solemn occasions the stolist also presented to the god one by one his precious ornaments kept in the treasury. To end the divine toilet, the priest smears the brow of the statue with the

---

88 S. Sauneron, *Priests*, p. 83. See also a text of "The daily ritual in the temple," from The Berlin Papyrus 3055, in Pritchard ANET, pp. 325-26.

89 S. Sauneron, *Priests*, p. 84.

90 S. Sauneron, *Priests*, p. 85. Instruction from the temple of Edfu.

cosmetic oil *medjet.* This also contributes to fortify the divine presence, protects the god from injury and immunizes it against the insidious attacks of evil powers. The final rite consists in presenting five grains of natron, salt and resin to the god, before veiling his face. The stolist then closes the doors of the naos and seals the fastening with clay. Before retiring he sprinkles with holy water and fumigates with incense the chapel and its *sancta*, to purify the air of all hostile presences. The other two services, at midday and in the evening, took place outside the central shrine and concerned mainly the secondary divinities : sprinkling of holy water, burning of incense, libations, food offerings and purifications. In all these ceremonies, of course, the personnel involved and the details varied with the different sanctuaries.

At regular intervals each month the god was led out in procession. His statue, enclosed in a little chapel of wood, was placed on the sacred ship, which was carried on the shoulders of the priests throughout the village. "Before the ship walked the chaplain, incense burner in hand, spreading the fumes from the turpentine grains to chase away the evil spirits which could prowl alongside the ship. Behind followed the priests, impressive in their immaculate linen clothing, perhaps chanting some sacred hymn. And around them moved the crowd of the faithful and the idle, noisy and excited, giving out shouts of joy or joining their voices with those of the sacred singers."[91] At regular stations there was a halt before the little street altars, which received the ship. While the carriers rested, other priests performed rites and gave out oracles in written form.

2. *Devoted to the Written Word*

Apart from the essential task of guarding the Presence, perhaps the main concern of the Egyptian priests was the written word. Living in the land of the papyrus, convinced that no real change could take place in the stable world of their cosmology, they would seek in the ageless formulas of their sacred writings the religious solutions of perplexing problems and events. What appears as a breach in the customary order of things is but an exception, they thought, eternally foreseen by the divine Architect and its explanation can be found in some hitherto unnoticed text which certainly situates the anomaly in the pattern eternally set for the future of the world.

---

[91] S. Sauneron, *Priests*, p. 93.

Obsessed with the written word the priests took every care to increase its volume and preserve it throughout the generations.* To the priestly scribes the pictorial hieroglyphs were more than a means of expression. These symbols, they thought, constitute an epitome of the universe, of its laws, of its history, which originated in the initial utterance of the divine words contained in the sacred writings. The sacred text, when pronounced, retains something of the primeval power which the words of creation had. Such belief naturally led the scribes to speculate on the occult forces enclosed in the hieroglyphs and to develop new combinations of the awesome signs. They perfected their techniques in the "houses of life", real institutes of sacred wisdom, where were prepared the rough drafts of the texts which the sculptors would engrave or the artists paint on the walls of the temples and in the interiors of holy places. In the "houses of life" were also written and transcribed the scrolls for the daily rituals and in their archives were stored the originals of the most important theological texts. Niches hewn out of the thickness of the temple walls received the liturgical texts of current usage and in some cases an inventory of these temple "libraries" was engraved on the wall.

3. *Manifold Wisdom*

The professionals of ancient Egypt's religious life constituted as well the literate and erudite class of the country along the Nile. By duty and inclination they were expert scribes and from necessity many of them became knowledgeable in practical astronomy, geometry, and architecture, while others applied their talents to history, geography, oneirology, medicine and magic. These disciplines can be viewed as secondary applications of wisdom, for which ancient Egypt was rightly famous (see 1 Kg 5:10; Is 19:11; Gen 41:8). St. Stephen told the Jews: "Moses was instructed in all the wisdom of the Egyptians" (Acts 7:22). It can be assumed that learned priests were his main instructors. It is common knowledge that the "sayings of the wise" in Pr 22:17-24:22 are, indirectly at least, dependent on the Egyptian "Instruction of Amen-em-ope."[92] In the 4th cent. B.C. there lived in Hermopolis (near Mel-

[92] See ANET, pp. 421-424. The "Instruction for King Meri-ka-Re" (ANET, pp. 414-418) also has biblical relevance. See J. M. Glinchey, *The Teaching of Amen-em-ope and the Book of Proverbs* (Washington, 1938); *Wisdom in Israel and in the Ancient Near East* (presented to H. H. Rowley = VT Suppl. 3 Leiden, 1955), esp. a study of G. von Rad on Job 38 and Egyptian wisdom (pp. 293-301). Add T.N.D. Mettinger, *Solomonic State Offi-*

laoui) Petosiris, the high priest of Thoth. His tomb was rediscovered in 1919 and samples of his maxims can be read on the walls of his resting place :

> He who walks in thy path, he will not falter : since I have been on earth and and until this day, when I have come to the perfect regions, there has been found no fault in me ...
>
> Oh you living ... if you listen to my words, if you heed them, you will find their worth. It is good, the path of the one who is faithful to the Lord; he is blessed whose heart turns toward this path. I will tell you what befell me, I will teach you the will of the Lord, I will make you enter into the knowledge of his spirit.
>
> If I have come here to the city of eternity, it is because I have done good on earth, and that my heart has rejoiced in the path of the Lord, from my infancy to this day. Every night the spirit of God was in my soul, and at dawn I did as he willed. I practised justice, I detested evil. I had no dealings with those who ignored the spirit of the Lord ... I did all this, thinking that I would come to God after my death, and because I knew that the day would come when the Lords of Justice would make the final division, on the day of Judgment ...
>
> Oh you living, I will have you know the will of the Lord. I will guide you to the path of life, the good path of those who obey God : happy is he whose heart leads him toward it. He whose heart is firm in the path of the Lord, secure in his existence on earth. He who has in his soul a great fear of the Lord, great is his happiness on earth.
>
> It is useful to walk in the path of the Lord, great are the advantages reserved for him who follows it. He will raise a monument to himself on earth, he who follows in the path of the Lord. He who holds to the path of the Lord, he will pass all his life in joy, richer than all his peers. He grows old in his own city, he is a man respected in name, all his members are young as an infant's. His children are numerous and looked upon as first in the city; his sons succeed him from generation to generation ... He comes finally to the city of the dead, joyfully, finely embalmed by Anubis, and the children of his children live on in his place ... You have walked in the path of your master Thoth; thus, after having received the favors he grants you on earth, he will please you with like favors after your death.[93]

Ancient Greek writers seem to have considered Egypt as the cradle of all wisdom and knowledge. It is hard to believe all the Greek biographers who state that their famous compatriots received in Egypt part of their advanced training. Yet some did seek to learn from the the priests, who often found their visitors "more inclined to credit faith

---

cials. Conjectanea Biblica. OT ser. 5 (Lund 1971) 140-157 on "The Scribal School and Egyptian Influence."

[93] The Maxims of Petosiris, published by M. G. Lefebvre, *Le Tombeau de Petosiris* (Cairo, 1924); trans. in S. Sauneron, *Priests*, pp. 12-13.

to the reasoning of the spirit than to the fantastic stories of a thousand-year tradition."[94] In any case, the broad range of the priestly concerns is well illustrated by Clement of Alexandria describing the procession of god Osiris, as it was organized in the great Hellenistic city :

> At the head comes a singer, carrying a musical instrument; they say he has to know two books of Hermes, one containing the hymns to the gods, the other the royal biography. Behind him comes the soothsayer, holding in his hand his insignia, the clock and the astronomical palm. He has to know by heart the four astrological books of Hermes ... Then comes the hierogrammate coiffed with feathers, with a book in hand and the small palette in which he keeps the black ink and the calam which he used for writing. This personage has to know the writings which are called hieroglyphics, concerning cosmography and geography, the path of the sun, of the moon and the five planets, the topography of Egypt and the description of the Nile, the prescriptions relating to sacred objects, to the places which are dedicated to them, the measures and the utensils used in the ritual. Behind, comes the stolist who carries the arm of justice and the vase of libation; he knows everything relating to the instruction of what is called "moschosphragistical", knowledge of the marks of animals, and the ten precepts which relate to the veneration of the gods in the country, which includes : Egyptian piety, treaties on fumigations, offerings, hymns, prayers, processions, feasts etc. Last comes the prophet, holding the hydria conspicuously against his chest, followed by those who carry up the offerings as they are invoked. In his capacity of chief of the temple, he knows the ten books which are called hieratic thoroughly, and comprehends the totality of the priestly wisdom on the subject of the laws and the gods.[95]

The knowledge which the priests had of astronomy, geometry, and architecture was a practical one, serving definite purposes : to determine correctly the holy seasons, time precisely the liturgical moments, assure in the building or restoring of temples the proper cosmic orientation and the right sense of proportions. The priests had little interest in history, since their theology professed that all the happenings of this world are aligned to a fixed pattern dependent on a primordial divine ordination. * On the other hand, they had a special fondness for a discipline which has been called "religious geography." It produced the sacred repertories which could supply accurate information on holy sites, their temples, priests and sacred vessels, on the divinities worshipped and the legends concerning them, on feasts and relics as well as on the various soil resources.** In the later period it was customary

[94] S. Sauneron, *Priests*, p. 114. Pythagoras (6th cent. B.C.) is credited with spending 22 years in the temples of Egypt. Other famous Greek travellers in Egypt would include Homer, Thales of Miletus, Solon, Democritus and Plato.

[95] *Stromata* 6.4. Trans. in S. Sauneron, *Priests*, pp. 139-40.

of the faithful to sleep in the temple in the hope of having significant dreams. Often these were obscure and had to be interpreted, the task of the *oneirocrites*, as the Greeks called such specialists among the priests. We know how Joseph interpreted Pharaoh's dream (Gen 41) and a papyrus of the New Kingdom period gives the significance of certain type-dreams.[96] In the Coptic translation of Gen 41:8, 24 the "magicians" (Heb. *ḥartummîm*) are called "Scribes of the House of Life." Some of the priests had a certain knowledge of medicine, a science which received special attention in the "House of Life." In illness, it was believed, evil forces are at work. Incantations and magic formulas constitute the surest cure. At the propitious moment the priest-reader would spell out potent names and numbers, or place on the sick person statues and amulets charged with the curing power of the animating spirit. On the other hand, a relief from the temple of Kom Ombo shows a collection of surgical instruments and several medical texts have been found in the vast lot of papyri from the temple of Tebtunis. Specialized texts, such as the Edwin Smith Surgical Papyrus, testify to very rational knowledge and practices.[97] These interventions remained, however, secondary and exceptional activities, in no way characteristic of the Egyptian priesthood.

e) Evaluation and Summary

The conduct of the Egyptian priests, as individuals and as forming the temple communities, was not always of course above reproach. There was, for example, in the middle 12th century B.C., at Elephantine, the scandal which involved the priests of the god Knoum, the great ram of the cataract. Following the exploits of their leader, Petanonqi, they did not refrain from violent methods to appropriate for themselves the temple treasures and the contents of its stores. Another unedifying story concerns the rivalries between the family of Peteisis and the priests of a provincial cult of god Amon. The strife arose from the disputed attribution of priestly benefits and lasted 150 years, with sporadic incidents of violence including blows and even murder.[98] These

[96] See an example in S. Sauneron, *Priests*, p. 161.

[97] Cf. S. Sauneron, *Priests*, p. 161. See also G. Lefebvre, *Essai sur la médicine égyptienne de l'époque Pharaonique* (Paris, 1956).

[98] See S. Sauneron, *Priests*, pp. 16-23. There exists a French adaptation of the story : J. Capart, *Un roman vécu il y a XXV siècles* (Paris 1914), from F.L. Griffiths, *Catalogue of the Demotic Papyri in the John Rylands Library*, Manchester, v. 3 (Manchester 1909) 60-112; 218-253 : "The petition of Peteêsi."

are fortunately exceptional episodes of a very long history in which the priests seem to have lived up to the ideal of their profession as they understood it.

The Egyptian priests were well aware of the dangers that threatened their moral life. At Edfu the officiants of the sacrificial processions could read every day, inscribed on the temple doorposts, reminders of their obligations, especially in regard to ritual purity and the proper use of sacred offerings :

> Oh you prophets, great and pure priests, guardians of the secret, priests pure in the Lord, all you who enter in the presence of the gods, masters of the temple ceremonies ! Oh all you judges, administrators of the land, stewards in your month of service ... Turn your gaze toward this dwelling in which His Divine Majesty has placed you ! When he sails to heaven, he looks here below : and he is satisfied as long as you observe the law ! Present yourself not in a state of sin ! Enter not in a state of impurity ! Speak no lies in his dwelling place ! Hold back no supplies, collect no taxes injuring the small in favor of the mighty ![99]

As a result of the rotation system adopted in their employment the Egyptian priests spent long periods in the secular life. Too permissive relaxation while they were off duty is ruled out by another Edfu inscription : "You who are men of importance, never let a long time pass without an invocation to Him; when you are away from Him present offerings to Him and praise Him in His temple... Frequent not the abode of women, do nothing that is not done here."[100] The same inscriptions extol the beatitude of the faithful priest in terms that allow for broad applications :

> How happy is he who celebrates Thy Majesty, oh great God, and who never ceases to serve Thy temple ! He who extols Thy power, who exalts Thy grandeur, who fills his heart with Thee ... He who follows Thy path, comes to Thy wateringplace, he who is concerned for Thy Majesty's designs ! He who worships Thy spirit with the reverence due the gods, and who says Thy office ... He who conducts the service regularly and the service of the holy days without error ... You who tread the path of *Re* in his temple; who watch over his dwelling place [occupied] to conduct His holy days, to present His offerings, without cease: enter in peace, leave in peace, go in happiness ! For life is in His hand, peace is in His grasp, all good things are with Him : there is food for the one who remains at His table; there is nourishment for the one who eats of His offerings ! There is no misfortune nor evil for the one who lives on His benefits; there is no damnation for the one who serves Him; for His care reaches to heaven and His security to the earth : His protection is greater than that of all the gods.[101]

---

99 Sauneron, p. 25, quoting *Edfu* 3, pp. 360-362.

100 *Ibid.*

101 *Id.*, p. 26; Edfu 5, pp. 343-44.

From the 3rd century A.D. we have this picture of the Egyptian priests, which, although idealized, certainly reflects authentic qualities and genuine aspirations :

> Through contemplation, they arrive at respect, at security of the soul and at compassion; through reflection, at knowledge; and through the two, at the practice of the esoteric and dignified customs of former times. For to be always in contact with divine knowledge and inspiration excludes greed, represses the passions and stimulates the vitality of the intellect. They practice simplicity in living and in dress, temperance, austerity, justice and non-attachment ... Their gait is measured, their gaze modest and steady, without wandering to every side; their laughter is rare and does not go beyond a smile, their hands are always hidden under their habit ... As to wine, some never take any, others take very little, for they say wine harms the veins, and in confusing the head prevents speculation.[102]

To express their filial devotion to the gods they worshipped, the Pharaohs built temples and endowed them with great prodigality. The land of Egypt, it was claimed, belongs to the sovereign. "In giving the god a part of this land, the king assured the material life of his clergy, guaranteed the regularity of his offerings, and thereby interested the god in the political fate of his dynasty."[103] Not rarely the clergy was richer than the king, and wealth usually engenders power. Being well aware of this, the kings sometimes kept the power of the clergy in check by appointing as their head a non-Theban high priest, foreign to the locally well organized machinations and intrigues. A notorious conflict opposing clergy and monarchy reached its peak at the end of the 14th century when Amenophis IV (Akhenaten) transferred the seat of goverment from Thebes to Amarna (Akhetaton), in order to better promote the monotheistic worship of Aton, the radiant sun-disc. The conflict came to an end with the death of the controversial reformer. His successor, young Tut-ankh-amon, returned the capital to Thebes and abolished all the measures taken by Akhenaten against the gods of tradition.

About the year 1000, in the beginning of the 21st dynasty, a military man, Herihor, who took the title of first prophet of Amon, gained political power with the support of the army and the Theban clergy. He finally succeeded in supplanting the king and in having his own name appear in a cartouche where the Ramesside monarchy was for-

---

[102] Porphyry, *On Abstinence* 4.6-8 quoted in S. Sauneron, *Priests*, p. 10. Porphyry, philosopher and disciple of Plotinus, lived in Alexandria in the 3rd cent. A.D.

[103] S. Sauneron, *Priests*, p. 172.

merly represented. But the rule of the king-priests was short-lived, owing to their lack of personal and political prestige. Having no real authority, writes Sauneron, "the clergy reigned by the voice of its god : Amon gave out his decrees regarding everything; the political weakness of the priestly sovereigns hid itself behind the scarecrow of the divine oracle."[104] In their proper religious fields the Egyptian clergies preserved a relative autonomy and most of their privileges during the Greek and Roman periods, until Theodosius, in 384 A.D., ordered the closing of all the temples and brought to an official end what had been a prestigious era in the history of Egypt and of mankind.

E. Priesthood among the Ancient Arabs

This long chapter on the Near East will close with a brief investigation of priesthood among the Arabs of "the time of ignorance," Muhammad's designation of the heathen period which preceded his coming. Our knowledge of the pre-Islamic Arabs derives mainly from early Muhammedan writers, a source singularly unreliable as regards the previous centuries and to be used cautiously.*

Two categories of religious personnel deserve special mention : the *kāhin* and the *sādin*. The *kāhin*, in Muhammad's time (c. 570-632), was a diviner, not a priest. He had no direct connection with the cult and felt inspired, in his soothsayings, by a supernatural power, as ecstatics of a more advanced stage, through whom the inspiring daemon is believed to speak. The *sadins*, on the other hand, were, among the ancient Arabs, sanctuary attendants and custodians, or, as we would say today, sacristans and sextons. They would guard the shrines and what was in them : sacred idols, holy vessels, and treasures. They had no function as regards sacrifices, which, among the ancient Arabs, were offered by the chiefs of families or clans and by ordinary persons, at least in normal circumstances. But it was a distinctive function of the sadins to give oracles, in the name of the god in whose sanctuary they served. Their oracular technique will be discussed below.

Persistent debates among scholars center on the following question : what connection is there between Arabic *kāhin* and Hebrew *kōhēn*, "priest"? The terms are obviously related, but it is not known for certain in what manner. Some would derive *kāhin* from the Aramaic

---

104 S. Sauneron, *Priests*, p. 186.

kāhen, while others believe that *kāhin* is not an arabicised form but a genuine Arabic word in its origin.* Apart from the term, the *kāhin*, as described above, had little in common with the Israelite priest, although he can be compared to the Israelite prophet.[105] But perhaps the *kāhin*, as he appears in our late sources, is quite different from the cultic person that may have been originally designated by the term.** In that matter, then, no firm conclusion can be drawn from the comparative study of this religion's personnel.

Even though he may never have been "priest" at all,+ the Arabic *sādin* can be compared in his distinctive functions to the Israelite priest of the early period. Both were firmly connected with a specific sanctuary and both gave oracles in the name of the divinity. Unlike the diviners (*kāhin*), whose soothsaying sprung from a personal gift, the sadins exercised an hereditary function and their oracular performance was based on the traditional method, called *istiqsām* : they obtained divine sentences at the sanctuary by drawing lots with headless arrows(*azlām*).++ This was later prohibited by the prophet (Coran : V, 4), but the heathen Arabs regularly resorted to that type of oracular consultation. The expression *qōsēm qesamim* in Dt 18:11 means to obtain an oracle from a god by some method of drawing lots, as in the case just mentioned.[106] In Biblical Hebrew, *qsm* is commonly used to convey the notion of divination. Its connection with the Arabic *istiqsām* is particularly close in Ezek 21:26-27 (=21:21-22), where Nebuchadnezzar is represented as resorting to belomancy ("casting of arrows") to find out which to attack first, Rabbah or Jerusalem. He holds in his right hand the result of his inquiry : "The oracle (*haqqesem*) Jerusalem," that is, the arrow marked "Jerusalem" (see also Num 22:7 ; Jos 13:22 ; 1 Sam 6:2 ; 28:8 ; 2 Kg 17:17 ; Is 3:2 ; Jer 27:9).

In the next chapter questions related to the origins of Israelite priesthood will recur and more comparative material will be adduced. Various

---

[105] See A. Guillaume, *Prophecy and Divination among the Hebrews and other Semites* (London, 1938), pp. 61-106; J. Pedersen, "The Role played by Inspired Persons among the Israelites and the Arabs," in *Studies in Old Testament Prophecy*, H. H Rowley, ed. (Edinburgh, 1950), pp. 127-142. On kahins and sadins see also A. Haldar, *Associations of Cult Prophets among the ancient Semites* (Uppsala 1945) 161-198. He finds in these notions a confirmation of his thesis that "no clear distinction can be made between 'sacerdotal' and 'prophetic' oracles" (p. 199). According to F. Buhl, *kāhin* is a sort of generic term under which can be designated the *ḥāzī*, "seers" (cf. 1 Sam 9:9) and the sign interpreters : the *'ā'if*, for the flight of birds, and the *qā'if*, for footprints (*Das Leben Muhammeds*, tr. from Danish by H.H. Schnaeder, Leipzig 1930, p. 82).

[106] See S. R. Driver, *Deuteronomy* (3d ed., ICC, Edinburgh 1902), pp. 223-224.

conjectures and conclusions are proposed in comparative studies of the ancient Arab-early Israelite organized forms of worship. The following can be quoted as deserving special attention: "We have not been able to detect any traits in Moses himself which remind us of the oracle-consulting sanctuary attendant, or of the Arabian *sādin* whose status in nomadic society was equivalent to that of the Hebrew *kōhēn*, but in all the Old Testament texts, late though they are (mostly P, some Deuteronomistic), which will speak of the Levites ministering around the sanctuary and caring for the Ark, we detect the essence of the *sādin*, and there is no particular reason to deny that those texts made use of a traditional concept in saying what they had to say."[107]

[107] A. Cody, *A History of Old Testament Priesthood* (AnalBibl 35, Rome, 1969), p.52.

CHAPTER FOUR

ISRAELITE PRIESTHOOD

Israelite priesthood has been the object of numerous studies. Some present the OT texts systematically while others dwell on special problems that arise from textual obscurities or contrasting evidence. The biggest and most discussed problem concerns the origin and the status of the Levites and their relation to priesthood. Among the recent comprehensive studies one should be singled out, that of Père Roland de Vaux in his well known *Ancient Israel*[1] (henceforth quoted as VAI). Particular aspects of Israelite priesthood are treated in the Biblical lexica under a number of proper names.[2] Few new solutions to thorny problems will be offered here, the purpose being rather to inform on the common data, indicate the consensus, if it exists, and suggest, in the notes especially, which solutions, in debatable questions, should be preferred.

A. Preliminary Notions

After explaining the Heb. terms for "priest," what is specifically sacerdotal will have to be distinguished from older or occasional forms of cultic ministration. The origin of Israelite priesthood will also be briefly discussed, especially as related to the greater Near Eastern context.

a) Terminology

Kōhēn is the only noun used to designate the priests of Yahweh, although it is also used for priests of foreign gods, whether Egyptian

---

[1] R. de Vaux, *Ancient Israel. Its Life and Institutions*, tr. by J. McHugh (2d ed., London, 1965), pp. 345-405. See also A. Cody, *A History of Old Testament Priesthood* (AnalBibl 35; Rome, 1969).

[2] The *Encyclopedic Dictionary of the Bible*, tr. and adapted by L. Hartman from A. Van den Born's Bijbels Woordenboek (New York 1963 = EncDictBibl) will be cited occasionally. See also G. A. Buttrick, ed., *The Interpreter's Dictionary of the Bible*, 4 v. (Nashville, 1962); J. L McKenzie, *Dictionary of the Bible* (Milwaukee, 1965). In our text English quotations from the Bible are generally taken from the Revised Standard Version (RSV).

(Gen 41:45), Phoenician (2 Kg 10:19), Philistine (1 Sam 5:5), Moabite (Jer 48:7), or Ammonite (Jer 49:3). Melchizedek was priest of (lit. "to") God Most High (*l*ᵉ' *ēl 'elyôn*; Gen 14:18); Abiathar was expelled from being priest to the Lord (*l*ᵉ*yhwh* : 1 Kg 2:27); Jonathan and his sons were priests to the tribe of the Danites (Jg 18:30). Other texts use the simple genitive : priests of Yahweh (1 Sam 14:3), "of Dagon" (1 Sam 5:5), of (the Egyptian city of) *'On* (Gen 41:45), of (the people of) *Midyān* (Ex 3:1), or priests of the high places (*bāmôt* : 1 Kg 12:32).

The Hebrew verb *kihēn* derives from the noun and means "to act as a priest" (Ex 31:10), "to serve as priests of the Lord" (Lev 7:35; 2 Chr 11:14).* There is also a noun *kehunnah* meaning "priesthood" (Ex 29:9) but *kōhēn* has no feminine since there were no "priestesses" among Israel's sacred personnel. The etymology of *kōhēn* is not known, although a similar term occurs in the Ugaritic texts and in Nabatean.** Another noun for "priest" derives from the root *kmr*, "which was used from about 2000 B.C. in the Assyrian colonies of Cappadocia, then in ancient Aramaic, and later on in the dialect of Palmyra and in Syriac" (VAI, p. 345). The corresponding Hebrew word *k*ᵉ*marîm* is used only three times in the Bible, always in the plural and as designating pagan (Zeph 1:4) or idolatrous priests (Hos 10:5; 2 Kg 23:5).***

b) Priesthood and Priestly Actions

The specific functions of Israelite priesthood will be explained in a later section. Before proceeding further, however, it seems that we should state here what is essential in the notion of this priesthood and to whom it applies in the strict sense. "The priesthood properly so called did not appear until the social organization of the community had developed considerably; then certain members of the community were entrusted with the special tasks of looking after the sanctuaries and of performing rites which were becoming ever more and more complicated" (VAI, p. 345). The Israelite priests of the earliest periods were, it seems, sanctuary attendants, and oracular consultation was their principal activity.[3] The questions to which the sacred losts would answer "yes" or "no" grew into elaborate formulations which formed a prelude to the broader instructions on the *tôrâ*. With the establishment of the temple cult the Israelite priests became mainly the ministers of the altar. Their teaching role declined, until after

---

[3] See A. Cody, *Old Testament Priesthood*, p. 13.

the Exile it was gradually taken over by the scribes and the doctors of the Law.

In Israel, as elsewhere, worship preceded the establishment of priesthood. From Genesis we learn that Cain, Abel, and Noah offered sacrifices (4:3-4; 8:20), that Abraham (12:7, 13:18, 22:2), Isaac (26:25) and Jacob (33:20, 35:7) built altars, on which they also burned holocausts to the Lord. Jacob, besides, consecrated pillars by pouring oil over them (28:18; 35:14). We know from Judges that Gideon was requested to pull down the altar of Baal, to build one to the Lord his God and to offer a bull as holocaust, which was manifestly accepted (14:16, 23). At Shiloh, Samuel's father, Elkanah, who was not a priest, also sacrificed to the Lord of Hosts (1 Sam 1:4, 21; 2:19).

Priests were not the only sacred persons who were leaders in worship. In the Ancient Near East and in Israel also, although with a difference. kings promoted worship and even personally officiated in the cult. There is an echo of ancient priest-king ideology in the features of Melchizedek (Gen 14:18) and in the oracle to the king of Ps 110 : "You are a priest forever, according to the order of Melchizedek" (v. 4). In Israel Solomon, Jeroboam, Joas, Josiah and others built temples or founded sanctuaries, recruited and appointed their personnel, published ordinances to organize or reform worship, even supervised their enforcement in person. What is more, the historical texts show the kings personally performing priestly acts (cf. VAI, pp. 113-114). Saul, David, Solomon offered sacrifices or had sacrifices offered. The factitive interpretation is, however, excluded in other cases, where, for example, it is said that Jeroboam "went up to the altar to burn incense" (1 Kg 12: 33) or that king Ahaz "drew near to the altar and went up on it, and burned his burnt offering and his cereal offering, and poured his drink offering, and threw the blood of his peace offerings upon the altar" (2 Kg 16:12-13). David and Solomon performed a rite reserved to the priests (Num 6:22-27) when they blessed the people in the sanctuary (2 Sam 6:18; 1 Kg 8:14), and David wore the linen ephod, the vestment of officiating priests (2 Sam 5:14). After the Exile, some of these actions appeared as unlawful intrusions of the kings into liturgical worship. According to Chronicles, Uzziah became a leper (cf. 2 Kg 15:5) because he himself burned incense on the altar in the temple of the Lord (2 Chr 26:16-21).

When the ancestors and the patriarchs offered sacrifices no organized priesthood existed, to which this sacred duty could be entrusted. It will be noted besides that even the later laws reserve to the priests only those rites of sacrifice in which the altar is proximately involved (cf. Ezek 44:16; Num 16:5). Anointing made the Israelite kings sacred persons, but not priests, especially since at the time of the monarchy priests were not anointed. Considering their highly representative office the kings naturally found occasion to act also as religious leaders, mainly in ceremonies involving the nation or the state. The rites remained, however, normally the concern of the priests (cf. 2 Kg 16:15). The unique statement of Ps 110.4, seen in its proper context, does not validly contradict what has been said.[4]

In his different functions the Israelite priest was a mediator : as oracular consultant and as teacher of the *tôrâ* he represented God before men; as minister before the altar he represented men before God. What is true of the high priest can be applied to every priest : "Every high priest chosen from among men is appointed to act on behalf of men in relation to God, to offer gifts and sacrifices for sins" (Heb 5:1). The concluding remarks of Père de Vaux can be appositely quoted here : "The priest was a mediator, like the king and the prophet. But kings and prophets were mediators by reason of a personal charisma, because they were individually chosen by God; the priest was *ipso facto* a mediator, for the priesthood is an institution of mediation. This essential feature will reappear in the priesthood of the New Law, as a sharing in the priesthood of Christ the Mediator, Man and God, perfect victim and unique Priest" (VAI, p. 357).

c) *The Origin of Israelite Priesthood*

Monarchy and priesthood are institutions which had been long established in the Near East when Israel became a nation. It can be assumed that Israelite priesthood received its basic character from the milieu of its origin, although the influence of the new religion changed its form and functions. In the JE story of the golden calf at Sinai, the Levites, as a result of their loyalty and zeal, are entrusted with the priestly office; having killed 3000 offenders they are told by Moses : "Today you have ordained yourselves* for the service of the Lord, each one at the cost of his son and of his brother, that he may bestow a blessing upon you this day" (Ex 32:29). In a passage which might be redactional the presence of priests among the people is mentioned before the Sinai revelation (Ex 19 :22, 24).

---

[4] On the priest-king of Ps 110, see VAI, p. 114, and the references given in H. J. Kraus, *Psalmen* v. 2 (Neukirchen, 1960), p. 752.

The existence of a pre-Decalog Hebrew priesthood has been related to the close connection (attested in the tradition) between Moses and the Midianite priest Jethro. "It would therefore seem highly probable that there were links between the Israelite cultic organization and the ancient traditional institutions of the friendly Midianite tribes. This is confirmed by the references to the priestly oracle of the sacred lot, Urim and Thummim (cf. Dt 33:8; 1 Sam 14:41; 28:6), which in method is reminiscent of the Arabian arrow-oracle.[5] Finally, though often queried, there is the obtrusive fact of the relationship between the Hebrew 'Levi' and the homonymous Minaean term for priest.[6] We must conclude that there is a strong probability that Midianite tradition played a part in determining the form of the Israelite priesthood."[7] More will be said on this subject, especially in connection with the Levi/Levite problem.

B. Priests and Levites; Traditions and Conflicts

No serious investigation of OT institutions can be conducted unless due attention is also paid to the streams of tradition which led to the texts as we have them. This applies particularly to the present study, since the redaction and edition of the texts that are likely to be informative depend largely on these priestly circles being investigated. It is clear, for example, that the varying biblical interpretations of the Levitical status reflect historical ambitions and rivalries. Some texts set forth a program of action, others sanction, justify or explain what has already taken place. Attention will be called especially to the writings of the Deuteronomists (D), of Ezekiel, of the Priestly traditions (P), and of the Chronicler (Chr, Ezra, Neh). Not wishing to lead unprepared readers into a labyrinth of riddles we shall first present an overall picture of the most disquieting problem, that of the priest-Levite relations. We shall do so taking into account also some results of a recent scholarly study* in which A. H. J. Gunneweg[8] investigates the history of the

[5] See N. A. Faris, *The Book of Idols* (Princeton Or. Stud. Princeton, 1952).

[6] See F. Hommel, *The Ancient Hebrew Tradition as illustrated by the Monuments*, tr. E. McClure and L. Crosslé (London, 1897), pp. 278-288.

[7] W. Eichrodt, *Theology of the Old Testament*, tr. J. A. Baker, v. 1 (London, 1961), p. 393. See also L. E. Binns, "Midian Elements in Hebrew Religion," JThSt 31 (1930), pp. 337-354.

[8] A. H. J. Gunneweg, *Leviten und Priester. Hauptlinien der Traditionsbildung und Geschichte des israelitisch-jüdischen Kultpersonal.* (FRLANT 89; Göttingen, 1965).

traditions that lie behind the varying Biblical statements on the subject of our present concern.

a) The Levites in the Early Traditions

Ancient sources, not apparently colored by distinctive tendencies, and interests, represent the Levites as enjoying a particular juridical status in the Israelite amphictyony.[9] On account of this and because no territory was assigned to them, they were considered as strangers everywhere and were reckoned among the *personae miserae*. Their amphictyonic membership found expression in the fact that their eponym Levi was consistently listed among the sons of Jacob. There are indications that the Levites from the beginning based their claim to be the only group called to the priesthood of Yahweh on a special status in the amphictyony.[10]

The grim story of the Levite of Ephraim and his concubine (Jg 19-20) "emphasizes the moral demands God makes on his people" (JB) and reflects at the same time the peculiar conditions of isolation experienced by the Levites in the confederation. More significant is the very ancient narrative related to the Danite migration, which probably took place at the beginning of the period of the Judges. Micah at first installs one of his sons to act as priest in his household shrine. When a young Levite from Bethlehem* presents himself he willingly takes him as priest and says: "Now I know that the Lord will prosper me, because I have a Levite as priest" (Jg 17:13). At this early period, then, a certain prestige was attributed to the priestly dignity of the Levites. It should be noted also that the two Levites are described as "sojourning" (*gar*) in their respective regions, Ephraim (19:1) and Judah (17:7), much like the resident aliens (see Ex 12.48, and JB), to whom the Levites are compared elsewhere, together with the other *personae miserae*: "the Levite, the sojourner (*gēr*), the fatherless, and the widow" (Dt 26:12). A frequent expression of Deuteronomy, "The Levite that is within your towns" (12:12, 18;14:27), belongs to the same context: "And the Levite, because he has no portion or inheritance with you, and the sojourner, the fatherless, and the widow, who are within your towns" (lit. "your gates": Dt 14:29; cf. 16:11;14). The list of Levitical towns (Jos 21) possibly expresses "the dispersal of the Levite population after

[9] On amphictyonies, see VAI, p. 93.

[10] See A. Gunneweg, *Leviten und Priester*, pp. 78-81.

the foundation of the Temple and after the organization of the official cult at Bethel" (VAI, p. 367). Although it belongs to the latest edition of the Book of Joshua it clearly distinguishes priests and levites— the document probably reflects a pre-exilic tradition.

Other ancient texts can be more likely linked with early controversy involving the Levites. In the oldest of these, Jacob, about to die, describes the character and foretells the destiny of his twelve sons and of the tribes they represent (Gen 49). In these oracles, perhaps dating in their present form from David's time, Levi and Simeon are severely blamed for their violence and the punishment is announced : "I will divide them in Jacob and scatter them in Israel" (vv. 5-7). This appraisal is quite evidently related to the tradition condemning the treacherous attack on the inhabitants of Shechem in the Dinah episode (Gen 34:30). Jacob's oracle explains as a punishment the dispersal of two tribes, whose eponyms, Simeon and Levi, belong to the group of the four oldest sons of Leah : Reuben, Simeon, Levi, Judah. It is probable that the "Levi" concerned here is, like Simeon, a secular tribe historically dispersed, perhaps by vengeful Canaanites. "The consequences of their act, the vengeance of the Canaanites, the two tribes had to bear alone; Israel, according to the indication given in Gen 49:6 and 34:30, did not feel any call to interfere on their behalf or make common cause with them."[11] Whereas Wellhausen sees no relation between the dispersed Levi secular tribe and the later priestly caste of Levi, Gunneweg is quite convinced that Gen 49 on the one hand, and Dt 33, on the other, are not to be considered as traditions concerned with two different realities, namely a lay tribe of Levi and "the Levitical priests," but as opposing traditions about the same object, "Levi"-Levites.[12]

Another early tradition, preserved in the "blessing of Moses" (Dt 33),* presents an entirely different picture of "Levi," when it says of the tribe of that name :

> And of Levi he said,
> "Give to Levi thy Thummim,
> And thy Urim to thy godly one,
> whom thou didst test at Massah,
> with whom thou didst strive at
> the waters of Meribah;
> who said of his father and mother,
> "I regard them not";

---

[11] J. Wellhausen, *Prolegomena*, p. 144.

[12] A. Gunneweg, *Leviten und Priester*, p. 220.

he disowned his brothers,
and ignored his children.
For they observed thy word,
and kept thy covenant (vv. 8-9).

This text and the narrative on the Micah Shrine (Jg 17-18) suggest that "in the first half of the eighth century, at the very latest, the priestly tribe of Levi was quite certainly in existence, and alone exercised the priesthood" (VAI, p. 362). As Gen 49 is related to Gen 34, so Dt 33 is connected with the tradition behind the episode of the golden calf (Ex 32). It will be seen that the varying accounts of Aaron's role during the Exodus may reflect opposition to the pretensions of the Aaronite priesthood (cf. also Num 12). The episode of Ex 32 could have been written as an anticipated condemnation of later bull worship at Bethel. What the author of Ex 32 contemptuously calls "calf" was probably the effigy of a bull, one of the symbols of godhead in the ancient East. Dt 33:8 alludes to Massah and Meribah, names which became memorials of Israel's faithlessness (Dt 6:16; 9:22; Ps 95:8). Meribah was one of the springs of Kadesh (Num 20:13, 27:14; Dt 32: 51), as were also, it seems, Marah (Dt 15:23) and Massah. Thus the origin of Levitical priesthood is connected with Kadesh. Probably the oracle by lot was already in possession of the Kadesh (pre-Israelite) priesthood and Moses allowed it to remain. Eichrodt conjectures that an alliance existed between Moses and the priestly clans of Kadesh against "opposition coming from the ancient Hebrew priesthoods."[13] In any case the ancient texts speak in favor of the special prerogatives of the priestly tribe of Levi.

b) *Deuteronomy* : *Levite-Priests*

Deuteronomy's concept of Levite-priests will be more easily understood if some features of the book, pertaining namely to its literary form, theology, purpose, provenance, and authorship are first recalled.

Rather than divine law in codified form, like Lev 12-26 (Holiness Code), Deuteronomy is a collection of material for an exhortatory proclamation of the Law. While "the Priestly Document" appears mainly as direct speech of God, in great part concerned with ordinances for priests, Deuteronomy is divine instructions delivered to the lay community through the medium of priestly interpretation. The prophetic element in the book is mostly a form of expression making more

[13] W. Eichrodt, *Theology* v. 1, p. 394.

plausible its claims to be authentically Mosaic.[14] Whereas in P a *kābôd-mô'ēd* ("appearance" in the Meeting-Tent) theology is in the foreground, Deuteronomy favors the sublimated theology of the Name, which does without a visible presence of the Lord. "Deuteronomy stands in the tradition of the old Yahweh amphictyony of Shechem. Or rather, it proposes to re-introduce this old cultic tradition in its own advanced period and to set it forth as the form obligatory upon Israel for its life before Yahweh."[15]

The origin of Deuteronomy is possibly related in fact to some great cultic celebration, namely the old festival of the renewal of the Covenant at Shechem. This is in many ways suggested in Deuteronomy : insistence on the obligations of the Covenant (4:13, 23, 31, 29:1-25); the blessing-cursing formulae (cf. ch. 27-28 and Jos 8:32-35); the distinctive notion that Moses put the stone tablets in the ark (10:1-5). It is known that the cult of the ark was central in the old Israelite amphictyony. The author of Deuteronomy intends to persuade his hearers that the Mosaic revelation and law are relevant to his own generation (cf. the frequent use of "this day"). Deuteronomy is often a theological re-statement of old traditions with the purpose of establishing the pure Yahwist faith in the agricultural environment of Canaan.

The provenance then of Deuteronomy is to be sought in the North rather than in the South. The frequent allusions in the book to the "Holy War" concept (cf. 7:16-26; 9:1-6; 31:3-8) and to warfare (20:1-20; 21:10-14) has led G. von Rad to suppose more precisely that Dt is the product of a revival movement having as one of its aims the re-building of the old Israelite militia to replace the dispersed mercenary army.[16] Beside this martial ideology the book contains a great deal of old cultic material worked over in homiletic form. It can be argued that the country Levites, living "within your towns" (Dt 12:12) were the actual spokesmen of the movement to revive the militia, as well as the re-interpreters of the ancient cultic traditions. "Just as old painters and sculptors sometimes put a selfportrait hidden away in the corner of a big composition, so we could perhaps see in the priestly preacher of the Holy War, as he is shown us in Deut 20, one of the Levites who are certainly to be credited with the working out of Deuteronomy. The Levites had a close connection with the Holy War, for the Levites and

---

[14] See G. von Rad, *Studies in Deuteronomy* (Stud. in Bibl. Theol. 9; London, 1953), p. 69.

[15] G. von Rad, *Studies*, p. 41.

[16] On the "Holy War" concept, see G. von Rad, *Studies*, pp. 45-69.

the Ark belong together (2 Sam 15:24), and the Ark was plainly the Palladium of the Holy War.* Only we must always bear in mind in this whole connection that we are dealing with traditions that have been revived."[17]

It will be easily objected that the Levites can hardly have composed a book supporting a cause which would tend to suppress the country shrines where they earned their living (cf. Dt 12:5-6). This stringent law, providing for only one place for sacrificial worship, was the basis of the great reform carried out by King Josiah (2 Kg 22-23). Dt never mentions, however, the city of Jerusalem, but only "the place" (*māqôm*), at which the name will dwell (12:5). An obvious reason is that Jerusalem could hardly be mentioned in discourses supposedly spoken by Moses.+ "It is being increasingly recognised," answers von Rad, "that the demand for centralisation in Deuteronomy rests upon a very narrow basis only, and is, from the point of view of literary criticism, comparatively easy to remove as a late and final adaptation of many layers of material."[18] He also suggests that Deuteronomy comes from a period when there existed perhaps a body of Levites "turned proletarian which had evidently long outgrown the cultic sphere proper and was buying itself with the scholarly preservation and transmission of the old traditions."[19]

Deuteronomy equates priests and Levites, who appear to have the same functions. In Dt 31:9 "the priests the sons of Levi" carry the ark, and the same is done in 31:25 by the Levites. Both in fact belong to one category, "Levite-priests," even in Dt 18:1, where one should read : "The Levite priests, all the tribe of Levi" (VAI, pp. 362-364). Elsewhere the members of the tribe are called "the priests, the Levites", or "the Levitical priests" (RSV CCD; cf. Dt. 17:9, 18, 18:1, 21:5, 24:8, 31:9). In a passage which may be an editorial insertion the origin of their office is set during the wilderness wanderings : "At that time the Lord set apart the tribe of Levi to carry the ark of the covenant of the Lord, to stand before the Lord to minister to him, and to bless in his

---

[17] G. von Rad, *Studies*, p. 67 See *Idem*, *Deuteronomy*, tr. by D. Barton (London, 1966), p. 25. "We must assume that the Levites in particular were responsible for this warlike movement of renewal," that they were, in other words, the main promoters of the noted militant piety. The amphictyonic militia ideology is also connected with the expressions *'am yhwh* (cf. Jg 5 :11; 20:2; 2 Sam 1:12; Dt 14:21; 27:9), "people of the Lord" and *'am ha'āreṣ*, "people of the land" (see *id.*, *Studies*.. 62-66).

[18] G. von Rad, *Studies*, p. 67.

[19] G. von Rad, *Studies*, p. 68

name, to this day" (10:8). Among the priestly functions assigned to Levi in "the blessings of Moses", teaching the law is given a more prominent place than offering sacrifices (Dt 33:8-10). In the rest of Deuteonomy also the Levitical priests* appear mainly as proclaimers of the law (27:14-26), as guardians (17:8-13) and interpreters of the *tôrâ* (31:9-13) : "Deuteronomy confirms that the sacrificial cult plays a surprisingly small part in the ministry of the Levites. They are in the first place priests of the divine law."[20] This agrees well enough with what will be proposed on the origin of the tribe.

The peculiar connection of the Levites with the amphictyony or the tribal confederacy is again set forth. They are ministers of the ark (Dt 10:8, 18:7), as at Gilgal (Jos 3:3-6), and they officiate at the great central sanctuaries, like Shechem (Dt 27:14; Jos 8:33). H. J. Kraus gives the following picture of the Levites' activity as compared with that of the *kōhanîm* ("priests") :

> In the official cult of northern Israel at the sanctuary of Bethel newly founded Jeroboam the king deliberately excluded the Levites (1 Kg 12 :31). *Kōhanîm* were appointed who were familiar with the ritual of a Canaanite sanctuary and whose duty it was to offer worship before the calf image. The official sanctuaries with their varied worship accordingly empowered officials who could adapt themselves to the new sphere and who in particular took over the dominant sacrificial cult as their main function. The Levites, however, were scattered throughout the country, living in towns and villages as *gērîm* ["resident aliens"] and had the support of the conservative, land-owning classes, the *'am hā'āreṣ*. It would be a mistake to identify these *l^ewiyyîm* ["Levites"] who lived in the country towns with the *kohanîm* of the unofficial sanctuaries and the cults of the high places who were active everywhere. The Levites, however, did not maintain their position only in the country towns, but also at the ancient Jahweh sanctuaries, particularly at Shechem and Gilgal. Through the common activity of the *l^ewiyyîm* and the *'am hā'āreṣ* the Levites again came to the fore in the time of Josiah, and Deuteronomy gives proof of this movement. Under the impetus of the great revival of ancient Israelite traditions the Levites made good their claim to the service of the Ark and in the sphere of the central sanctuary at Jerusalem."[21]

The distinctive character of Levitism has been presented in even sharper contrast. According to A. H. J. Gunneweg, behind the conflict of the traditions stood the historic struggle of Levi for the living conditions of the Yahweh amphictyony as against the new, once Canaanite, now Yahwist sanctuaries with their priesthoods, the Aaronites in parti-

---

20 H. J. Kraus, *Worship in Israel*, tr. G. Buswell (Richmond, 1966), p. 97.

21 H. J. Kraus, *Worship*, pp. 98-99.

cular. It was a period when a multitude of sanctuaries replaced the one amphictyonic center, when new state regulations gradually replaced the amphictyonic ordinances. In this situation arose the conflicts between the conservative group of amphictyonic Levi and the professional priesthoods. Levi claimed to represent the genuine Yahwist priesthood. The oppositional activity of the Levitical circles found its literary expression in Deuteronomy, with its known tendencies: amphictyonic restoration, centralization, insistence on the Levitical status. The identification of Levites and priests was not presupposed but declared as a programmatic theory. From the most ancient times Levi's concern was to teach and transmit the ancient amphictyonic traditions. This function and the particular status of a landless class characterized Levi.[22]

The prescriptions regarding one central sanctuary (Dt 12:1-14) are not a codification of the reform of Josiah (2 Kg 22-23), but, dating from before it, should be related in some way to the reform of Hezekiah (2 Kg 18:4). They belong to the last stage of a movement* which had long tended to centralize worship in the great national sanctuaries of Jerusalem and Bethel. Deuteronomy proposes a solution to one existing problem: the Levitical priests of the local sanctuaries in the provinces are deprived of their revenues. Their right to officiate in the central sanctuary, like the other priests, and to receive an equal stipend, is now expressly declared (Dt 18:6-8). Obviously, however, not all could find employment at the central sanctuary of Jerusalem, and the writer of Deuteronomy consequently commends to the charity of the Israelites "the Levite that is within your towns," along with other categories of persons having no assured means of livelihood (12:12, 18, 19, 14:27, 29, 16:11, 14, 26:11-13). Commending the Levites and the *personae miserae* to the charity of the Israelites was an application of the principle that all the members of the community must have their share of Israel's God-given patrimony of salvation. This is a distinctive Deuteronomic doctrine. The tribe of Levi as landless could appear as a prototype of the ideal people of God. It is elsewhere explicitly mentioned that the proposed arrangement failed on the main issue during the reform of Josiah: "However, the priests of the high places did not come up the altar of the Lord in Jerusalem, but they ate unleavened bread among their brethren" (2 Kg 23:9). Apparently the clergy of Jerusalem,

---

[22] A. Gunneweg, *Leviten und Priester*, p. 221. "In Deuteronomy, the distinction between priests and Levites lies under the surface." (VAI, p. 364).

jealous of their own privileges, did not allow them to take part in the liturgy (cf. VAI, p. 363).

It is not certain, however, that 2 Kg 23:9 should be related to Dt 18:6-8. This last text contains a disposition on the privileges of the Levites domiciled in the provincial regions, * while it can be argued[23] that 2 Kg 23:9 wishes to make it clear that "the (Yahwistic) priest of the high places" (not to be identified with the Levites), who were transferred to Jerusalem by Josiah, do now live there, *but* do not minister at the altar, do not, in other words, share the same rights as the Jerusalem priests. These provincial priests are demoted from their sacerdotal rank, they are not excluded from participating in the cultic life : "They ate unleavened bread among their brethren" (2 Kg 23:9). The particle *'āk* ("but"), in 2 Kg 23:9, does not then introduce a statement contradicting the stipulation of Dt 18:6-8, as is sometimes assumed. It is in fact hardly conceivable that the Deuteronomist who wrote 2 Kg 23:9 would have, as it were, expressed regret that "priests of high places" were prevented from officiating in Jerusalem, or that he would have conferred unrestricted praise on Josiah (23:26), if the Levites had been demoted in defiance of the stipulation of Dt 18:6-8.

c) *Ezekiel : Priests* and *Levites* now

Whereas Deuteronomy, in its distinctive teaching at least, tends to identify priests and Levites, these are explicitly distinguished in the writings of Ezekiel, who was himself a priest. This is presented in Ezekiel as resulting from a new legislation now introduced. The main text is found in a section (ch. 40-48), which has been called "a blueprint for the religious and political rehabilitation of the Israelite nation" (JB, p. 1411). In this oracle "the rebellious house" of Israel is told : "No foreigner (*ben-nēkar*), uncircumcised in heart and flesh, of all the foreigners who are among the people of Israel, shall enter my sanctuary" (44:9). "This is a reference to the public slaves employed in the Temple, the descendants of these slaves employed by Solomon (cf. Ezra 2:55-58), the *n^{e}thinim* ('given') whose origin went back to David, according to Ezra 8 :20" (VAI, p. 364). These temple servants will be replaced by the Levites : "But the Levites who went far from me, going astray from me after their idols when Israel went astray, shall bear their punishment. They shall be ministers in my sanctuary, having oversight at the gates of the temple, and serving in the temple ; they shall slay the burnt

[23] See A. Gunneweg, *Leviten und Priester*, pp. 120-125.

offering and the sacrifice for the people, and they shall attend on the people, to serve them" (Ezek 44:10-11).

Ezek 44 belongs to the Zadokite layer of the prophet's writings.* It reflects the Zadokite endeavor to further broaden the separation between the priests and the minor clergy to the detriment of the latter. Some authors would identify Ezekiel's Levites with the Levites who had served the small sanctuaries where worship was not always pure, with those Levites namely, mentioned in Deuteronomy, whom, it is thought, 2 Kg 23:9 called the "priests of the high places," and whose worship was suppressed in Josiah's reform (VAI, p. 264). It is possible, here again to hold a different view and to relate the Levites of Ezek 44:10 to the "rebellious Levites" mentioned in the stories of Num 16-18, which serve to confirm the claim that the Aaronic priesthood, not the Levites, are divinely appointed to full priestly status (cf. Num 16:10.40). While Deuteronomy, we repeat, identified priests and Levites, the priestly document and Ezekiel distinguish the Levitical priests and the Levitical minor clergy. The first group are in P the Aaronite priests of the tabernacle and in Ezekiel the Zadokites who serve at the altar of the temple (cf. 40:46).**

These Levites of an inferior degree who can be called Levitical ministers of the temple or 'house' are exceptionally called "priests" in Ezek 40:45.46a and 42:13. This may reflect the situation of a period when the distinction between priests and Levites was not yet clear.+ Of the Levites it is also decreed : "They shall not come near to me, to serve me as priest (*l^{e}kahēn lî*), nor come near any of my sacred things (*'al-kol-qādāšay*); ++ but they shall bear their shame, because of the abominations which they have committed. Yet I will appoint them to keep charge of the temple (*šomrê mišmeret habbayit*), to do all its service (*l^{e}kol 'abōdātô*) and all that is to be done in it" (44:13-14). Similar expressions are used for the Levites of P : "And their charge (*mišmeret*)+++ was to the ark, the table, the lampstand, the altars, the vessels of the sanctuary (*kele haqqōdeš*) with which the priests minister, and the screen; all the service pertaining to these" (*wekol 'abōdātam* : Num 3:31), but all this is, of course, connected with the tent of meeting (*'ōhel mô'ēd*; cf. Num 4 :31), not with the temple.

Ezekiel then sets forth the functions and duties of the privileged class of priests. "But the Levitical priests, the sons of Zadok, who kept the charge of my sanctuary when the people of Israel went astray from me, shall come near to me to minister to me; and they shall attend on me to offer me the fat and the blood, says the Lord God; they shall enter my sanctuary, and they shall approach my table,* to minister to me, and they shall keep my charge" (44:15-16). Then follows the enumeration of the rules of purity which they have to observe by reason of their close contact with the holy things (44:17-31). Ezekiel is known to have scrupulously distinguished the sacred from the profane (eg. 45:1-6, 48:9-10). Special exit rites are provided for officiating priests : "And when they go out into the outer court to the people, they shall put off the garments in which they have been ministering, and lay them in the holy chambers; and they shall put on other garments, lest they communicate holiness to the people with the garments" (44:19; cf. 42:14).

The priests of the higher category are also called "sons of Zadok" in Ezek 40:46, 43:19, 48:11. The first of these texts reads : "these are the sons of Zadok, who alone among the sons of Levi may come near to the Lord to minister to him." We shall see that also the Aaronites insistently claimed to be of Levitical lineage. The distinction between the priests who serve the sanctuary and the Levites who serve the temple finds applications in other areas too : different rooms assigned to each group (40:44-46), different allotments in "the holy district" (45:4-5), different properties (48:11-14), different kitchens in which to cook the sacrifices (46:20-24). All this, of course, was more idealistic than practical. It is part, in its own way, of Ezekiel's fantastic world.

d) *The Priestly Writings : Priests and Levites* always

Ezekiel and P have much in common, as we have seen, even on the subject that concerns us now. What is perhaps distinctive of each is that Ezekiel presents the distinction between priests and Levites as an innovation, while P sees it as having existed ever since Moses. This of course agrees with P's habit of describing later or even postexilic institutions against the background of the sojourn in the desert, of seeing, in other words, the past through the eyes of the present. There is little doubt that both Ezekiel and P, each in his own way, ratify, legalize, or explain concrete situations in which one faction of the Jerusalem clergy dominated another. Concerning the legislation of the Priestly Code, de Vaux writes : "It is hard to admit that legislative arrangements like those in Numbers can have been inspired by an idealistic description like that in Ezekiel. It is more probable that both texts, Numbers and Ezekiel represent two parallel trends originating from a common source, i.e. the situation created in Jerusalem by the reform of Josiah.

Indeed, it is not impossible that the laws in Numbers are a development of rules issued towards the end of the monarchy by the priests in the Temple" (VAI, p. 365).

The Priestly writings, also called Priestly Code(P), contain materials preserved and edited by the Jerusalem priesthood. The main body of P, especially as legislation and ritual, accounts for Ex 24-31, the whole of Leviticus, and the greater part of Numbers. "It is generally agreed that this priestly material in its present form comes from a relatively late period. The compiler, however, has relied upon independent source materials, such as the so-called Holiness Code (chs. 17-26), and upon numerous traditions which reach back to ancient times" (OAB, p. 122). P editors have left their mark also in the combining of the previous traditions with their own. Although the laws of Leviticus (P) are placed in the ancient setting of Mount Sinai, Lev 18:25-27, for example, clearly presupposes a time after the conquest.*

Whereas Deuteronomy's interests center on the Levites, P's main concern is with Aaronite priesthood. According to Num 3:6-9, the Levites were placed at the service of Aaron and his sons, were "given" to Aaron, and served the Dwelling (*miškān*); according to Num 8:19, they were "given" to Aaron and his sons for the service of the tent of meeting (*'ōhel mō'ēd*); "according to Num 18:1-7, which is the principal text, they were to serve Aaron and the Tent and they were 'given', but Aaron and his sons performed the strictly priestly functions, such as the service of the altar and the sanctuary, and of 'everything which stands behind the veil.' Here there is an evident parallel with Ezekiel" (VAI, p. 365). Similarities of expression have been noted above.

The aim of the Priestly legislation is not to degrade the Levites but to mend their historical status, to provide them with proper means of livelihood.[24] Yet the statements of P on the duties and privileges of Levites admit variations that may reflect historical rivalries. Whereas, for example, in Num 3:31 the handling of the holy vessels is entrusted to the Levites, Num 18:3 explicitly excludes them, as does Ezek 44:13 from such service : "They shall attend you and attend to all duties of the tent (*ûmišmeret kol- hā'ōhel*); but shall not come near to the vessels of the sanctuary (*'el-kᵉlê haqqōdeš*) or to the altar, lest they, and you, die." The tendency to limit the authorized area of the Levites, of the sons of Kohath especially, is also felt in Num 4, which warns them

[24] See A. Gunneweg, *Leviten und Priester*, p. 223.

against touching the holy things (*qōdeš* : v. 15) before they are wrapped up by the priests, or to approach the most holy things (*qōdeš haqqadōšim* : v. 19). These texts seem posterior to Ezekiel.

More will be said on the views of P in connection with the family of Aaron. It can be recalled here that "the distinctive feature of the *tabu*-concept, the idea of the divine reality as a spatially restricted entity, remained decisive for the whole religious thinking of the priesthood ... It was the Priestly law that most vigorously developed the ideal of the holy people, that is to say one set apart from all others (cf. Lev 17-26, and Ezek 40-48)".[25] The strict separation of the sacred from the profane reflects the same ideology, which led to elaborate rules concerning the handling of the holy vessels, the ritual purity of the priests, and the ceremonial vestments.

e) The Chronicler : Levites and Priests

The Chronicler shows, like Dt, a great interest in Levites, while, unlike the Deuteronomist, he admits with Ezekiel and P, a clear distinction between priests and Levites. Also distinctive is the Chronicler's tendency to ascribe to ancient times situations and ideas of a later date or even of his own period; "to make it worse, the annotators of his work have added ideas and customs from their day, too, and backdated them as well" (VAI, p. 390). It is therefore difficult to reconstruct a coherent picture of the events, facts and institutions surveyed by the Chronicler, who, as a theologian, is more interested in their interpretation than in their historical sequence or the objective accuracy of his description.

"The Books of Chronicles ... are a work of post-exilic Judaism, in a period when the nation, despite its political dependence, enjoyed a measure of self-rule by favour of its eastern overlords. The priesthood was its guide, the Law its charter. The Temple and its ritual were the centre of national life" (JB, p. 491). Throughout his work the Chronicler gives prominence to religious and liturgical activities, and for this reason, his accounts provide rich information on the temple personnel. In these accounts David, highly idealized, becomes the real founder of the temple and its ritual. The author of Chronicles, very probably a Jerusalem Levite, possibly a singer, also wrote Ezra and Nehemiah, at about the same time, not long after 300 B.C. In the restored commu-

---

[25] W. Eichrodt, *Theology* v. 1, pp. 407-408.

nity which these two books describe, the Chronicler "sees a realization of the ideal God-governed society for which he has pleaded in the Books of Chronicles" (JB, p. 495).

The Chronicler's work is then a basic source for all the aspects of Israelite Levitism and priesthood. Our present interest centers on the views this work reflects regarding the distinction between priests and Levites. The Chronicler's views on Levites have been outlined in the following way.

> They have the principal role in looking after the Ark of the Covenant (1 Chr 15-16); their duties in the Temple are laid down even before it is built, and there too they play the principal part (1 Chr 23-26). They are the predominant figures in the religious reforms of Ezechias (2 Chr 29-31) and of Josias (2 Chr 34-35). But even apart from these long texts, they are found intervening everywher e,whether their action is relevant or not. The attention paid to genealogies, which was already showing itself in the days of Esdras, develops even further. The ancestry of all the Levites is traced to the three sons of Levi, Gershom, Qehath and Merari (1 Chr 6 :1-32; 23 :6-24), in perfect harmony with the Priestly tradition recorded in Num 3-4; even people like Samuel, who, in the pre-exilic books, had no Levitical ancestry, are given a place in these genealogies (VAI, p. 391).

The connection of the Levites with the service of the ark is a fundamental notion in the Chronicler's work. David is quoted as saying : "No one but the Levites may carry the ark of God, for the Lord chose them to carry the ark of the Lord and to minister to him for ever" (1 Chr 1:52). Later, it is also said, "he appointed certain of the Levites as ministers before the ark of the Lord, to invoke, to thank, and to praise the Lord, the God of Israel" (16 :4), and "David left Asaph and his brethren there before the ark of the covenant of the Lord to minister continually before the ark as each day required ... and he left Zadok the priest and his brethren the priests before the tabernacle of the Lord in the high place that was at Gibeon" (1 Chr 16:37, 39). It is also noted that the Levites carried the ark into the newly built temple (2 Chr 5:4-5), thus acquiring the right to serve there. In additions made to the Chronicler's work the claim of the Levites is, however, obscured by the priestly editors who say that the Levites carried the tabernacle and assisted "the sons of Aaron for the service of the house of the Lord" (1 Chr 23:26, 28). In P the functions of the Levites are connected with the tabernacle (*miškān* : Num 1:50; 3:8) and the tent of meeting (*'ōhel mo'ēd* : Num 8:19). In the amphictyony setting of Deuteronomy the first duty of "the tribe of Levi" is to carry the ark of the covenant of the Lord (Dt 10:8). Following this tradition the Chronicler felt authorized to modify his source : "And all the elders of Israel came, and the priests took up the ark" (1 Kg 8:3; cf. 2:26). He wrote : "And all the elders of Israel came, and the Levites took up the ark" (2 Chr 5:4). *

The three main categories of the cult personnel are mentioned beside the lay people ("Israel"; see Ezra 2 :70) in a verse describing the return from the Babylonian exile : "Now the first to dwell again in their cites were Israel, the priests, the Levites, and the temple servants" (*netînîm* : 1 Chr 9:2). Elsewhere also the Chronicler clearly distinguishes priests and Levites (13:2, 15:14, 23:2, 24:6, ...). According to the Masoretic text, however, the Deuteromic expression *hakkōhanîm hallᵉwiyyîm* ("priest-Levites") occurs in two passages. The first has to do with the reform which followed Athaliah's death : "And Jehoiada posted watchmen for the house of the Lord under the direction of the priests-Levites ..." (2 Chr 23:18). The second concludes the description of Hezekiah's great passover festival : "Then the priests-Levites arose and blessed the people, and their voice was heard, and their prayer came to his holy habitation in heaven" (2 Chr 30:27). The use of the formula can be added to the list of the Chronicler's literary inconsistencies. ** But the ancient versions and other witnesses read "the priests and the Levites." In any case, these passages, too, concern the Chronicler's favorite subject : the theme of the reform carried out by priests and Levites. Thus are the priests and Levites expressly mentioned as those who cleansed the temple under Hezekiah (2 Chr 29:4-25; cf. 2 Kg 18:4). Under Josiah, workmen carried out repairs in the temple (2 Kg 22:3-7). The Chronicler, adding to his source, ascribed the conduct of the operation to the Levites, especially to the singers (2 Chr 34:12-13).

As in P and in previous literary arrangements, genealogies serve the Chronicler to combine the various traditions according to their relative importance in the new contexts. He has a distinctive version of the lineage of the Levites (1 Chr 6), already known from Ex 6:14-25. The main change results from the introduction of Zadok, who was not listed in the P system. Thus the Chronicler completes the line which runs from Levi and Aaron to Zadok and Ezra (Ezra 7:1-5). He gives final expression to the assumption that appurtenance to the lineage of Levi is a basic requirement to become a member of the cult personnel.

While using the three-name genealogical schema, known from P (Num 3:21, 27, 33; 1 Chr 6:1), to catalogue the ancestry of the Levites, the Chronicler, when on his own, uses the following order : Kohath, Merari, Gershom (1 Chr 15:5-7). Kohath is mentioned first presumably because his sons were entrusted with privileged functions in connection with the tent of meeting (Num 4:4-20). Elsewhere one name of the schema is dropped (2 Chr 34 :12) or only two groups are named : "And the Levites, of the Kohathites and Korahites, stood up to praise the Lord, the God of Israel, with a very loud voice" (2 Chr 20:19). The Kohathites especially were highly ranked at the period of the Chronicler: some of them "had charge of the showbread, to prepare it every sabbath" (1 Chr 9:32), a responsibility entrusted to Aaron by Lev 24:5-8. In P the Kohathites can only spread the cloth over the table of the bread of the Presence (Num 4:7).

It can be noted in conclusion that although the Levites constitute in the Chronicler's work a distinctive group, the term "Levite" refers in practice to a broad notion covering heterogeneous categories of temple functionaries who sooner or later were "Levitized" while remaining very distinct in their functions. The main nucleus of the Jerusalem Levites, though, had been constituted by those who had "left their common lands and their holdings and came to Judah and Jerusalem, because Jeroboam and his sons cast them out from serving as priests of the Lord" (2 Chr 11:14). Of similarly faithful Levites the Chronicler wrote : "The Levites were more upright in heart than the priests in sanctifying themselves" (2 Chr 29:34).

C. Eponyms and Priestly Families

Historical and literary perspectives will still be taken into account in this section which deals with the priestly families and their natural or eponymous ancestors, although a more thematic and systematic approach is intended. The present inquiry will go further into the real organization and functioning of Israelite priesthood; hopefully, it will also incidentally clarify other aspects of worship in Israel.

a) Levi and his Tribe

The preceding study has sought to determine the respective standpoints of the main Israelite traditions on the claims and functions of the Levites in their correlation to the priestly status. Questions have now to be answered that concern the origin of the Levitical tribe and the role of its eponymous ancestor, Levi.

1. Gen 49 and Dt 33 re-examined

We have seen how differently two ancient texts present the tribe of Levi. An interpreter puts it this way : "The Levites were an ancient warlike tribe that became a priestly caste (Dt 33:8-10 ...)" (OAB, p. 501; also p. 260). Diverging interpretations of these texts have been proposed and important issues remain unsettled. About the Genesis oracle it is noted that "Simeon was a non-priestly group which very soon lost its autonomy and whose members were scattered throughout the territory of Judah. It is reasonable to conclude that there was also a non-priestly tribe called Levi which suffered the same fate" (VAI, p. 368).* For various reasons other critics assume, on the contrary, that the tribe of Levi had always been priests and that its members lived scattered among the other tribes. Against this, writes de Vaux, "we know that Levi formed part of the old system of the twelve tribes; it is improbable that at some later date, when tribal divisions corresponded to territorial divisions, a tribe which had no territory was introduced into the twelve tribes" (VAI, p. 368).[26] We will examine more closely Dt 33:8-11, then attempt to clarify a problem : What brought about the connection between the secular tribe which disappeared and the priestly tribe of Levi ?

Verse 8 of the "Blessings of Moses" (Dt 33) reads in the Hebrew : "And of Levi he said, thy Thummîm and thy Urim to thy godly one (*le'iš ḥasîdekā*), whom thou didst test at Massah, with whom thou didst strive at the waters of Meribah." The significance of these localities for the origin of Hebrew priesthood has been mentioned. It is not clear, however, why Levi should be connected with these names which recall the testing. On the other hand it is probable that by *'iš ḥasîdekā* Moses is meant,[27] and in that case the reference could be to the leader's role in events similar to those recalled in Dt 32:51 : "... because you broke faith with me in the midst of the people of Israel at the waters of Meribath-kadesh, in the wilderness of Zin; because you did not revere me as holy in the midst of the people of Israel." In fact Levi and Moses are so closely linked in the Levi blessing that it is hard to decide to whom this or that statement applies. Verse 9 expresses another distinctive feature of the Levite tribe : the Levites' disengagement from family ties (see also Ex 32:29) allows his closer attachment to God himself and exemplifies the exigencies of his covenant. Verse 11 formulates the

---

[26] On the "secular tribe" of Levi, see A. Cody, *Old Testament Priesthood*, pp. 29-38.

[27] Thus F. Zorell, *Lexicon Hebraicum*, p. 257 and A. Gunneweg, *Leviten und Priester*, pp. 38-41. Wellhausen even builds a theory on the allusion to Moses : "The history of Moses is at the same time the history of the priests... As Dt 33:8-11 informs us, all priests honoured Moses as their father not as being the head of their clan but as being the founder of their order" (*Prolegomena* 135 and 143).

conviction that Levi's claims to the priestly status will not go unopposed.

2. From a Secular to the Priestly Tribe

Levi is listed among the twelve tribal eponyms in the original expression of the amphictyonic structure of Israel (Gen 35:23-26, 49:3-27; Ex 1:2-4; Dt 27:12-13; 33:6-25; Ezek 48:31-35; 1 Chr 2:1-2). Problems arise when this arrangement is compared with the other system in which Levi is omitted and Joseph is replaced by Ephraim and Manasseh (Num 1:5-15, 20-43; 2:3-31, 7:12-83, 13:4-15, 26:5-51; Jos 13-19, 21:4-7, 9-39). In the second and more recent way of listing, the ancient eponymous system is re-used to describe the territorial and political situation of a later period when the well established ethnic group of Ephraim and Manasseh had replaced Joseph, and when landlessness characterized the Levites more than ever.

Between the system including Levi and the one without him, it has been suggested, there does not lie the disappearance of a tribe but the distinction between a purely amphictyonic membership and a classification involving new geographical, historical and genealogical conditions.[28] More probably, however, as already mentioned, there had existed a secular Levi tribe, which for reasons suggested by the Bible itself did not survive in its autonomous identity but was dispersed at an early date. The survivors probably associated, like the remainder of Simeon, with Judah, also son of Leah. "But, whereas the Simeonites integrated themselves into the surrounding population, the descendants of Levi specialized in cultic functions" (VAI, p. 370).* This would have taken place on a limited scale only, since at that early period Israelite sanctuaries could hardly provide employment for a large number. Maybe the relation between the original tribe of Levi and the later priestly tribe can be sought in connection with the origin of Moses, as Wellhausen proposed. "It is perhaps correct to say that Moses actually was descended from Levi (cf. Ex 2:1), and that the later significance of the name Levite is to be explained by reference to him. In point of fact, the name does appear to have been given in the first instance only to the descendants and relations of Moses, and not to have been transferred until a later period to those priests as a body, who were quite unconnected with him by blood, but who all desired to stand

[28] See A. Gunneweg, *op. cit.* 63

related to him as their head."[29] This is, of course, conjecture, but it agrees remarkably well with the assumed mention of Moses in Dt 33:8.

As the origin of priesthood has been connected with Midian so also is the origin of the Levites sometimes associated with Arabian tribes. The Hebrew term *lēwy* denotes one of the sons of Jacob (Gen 29:34), the tribe of that name (Num 3:6) and, with the article, the Levites : *hallᵉwiyyîm*. "Among the inscriptions discovered in the Minaean script and dialect at El-Ela, the ancient Dedan, in northern Arabia, there are several which contain the word *lw*' or, in the feminine, *lw't*. This word has sometimes been translated 'priest' or even 'Levite,' by reason of its resemblance with the Hebrew *lewy*; and some writers have concluded that the Israelites adopted the institution of Levites from those early Arabs with whom they had been in contact at Sinai" (VAI, p. 369). A more accurate investigation reveals, however, comments de Vaux (*ib*), that the words *lw*' and *lw't* do not mean "priest" or "priestess", but denote an object given to a god, a pledge. It is besides more likely, he adds, that the Minaeans had themselves borrowed the term *lewy*, perhaps from Jews who lived in the region at a certain period, modified its sense and given it a feminine which did not exist in Hebrew.

All these discussions should not let us forget the fact that according to the Bible a positive intervention of God set apart the descendants of Levi to perform sacred functions (Num 1:50). They had no portion in Israel (Dt 18:1) and no territory was allotted to them, for "the Lord God of Israel is their inheritance" (Jos 13:33). They are provided with special revenues (Num 18:21-24), and with real estate in the territories of the other tribes, i.e. the Levitical towns (Jos 21:1-42). Acoording to ancient law, found in Ex 13:2, 22:29, all the firstborn sons of the Israelites were consecrated to the Lord, or redeemed through a sacrifice (Ex 13:13, 34:20). Later legislation explains that God has taken for himself the Levites as substitutes for the first-born (Num 3:13, 8:17, 18). Their consecration to the Lord's service is represented as a sacrifice (Num 8:10-13). The Priestly tradition further specifies that the Levites are "given" to Aaron and his sons to be their assistants (Num 3 :6, 8:19, 18:6), while the Elohistic tradition linked their priestly consecration to an act of zeal performed in opposition to Aaron (Ex 32:25-29).

b) *Moses and Gershom*

In the very ancient story of the Dan migration Micah's Levite is identified as "Jonathan the son of Gershom, son of Moses" (Jg 18:30).

[29] J. Wellhausen, *Prolegomena* 145.

There is no reason to doubt the truth of this detail, nor "to deny the Levitical ancestry of Moses himself, which is asserted by Ex 2.1 (Elohistic tradition) and traced in detail both by the Priestly tradition (Ex 6:20; Num 26:59) and by the Chronicler (1 Chr 5:29, 23:13)" (VAI, p. 362). Ex 2 :1 describes the birth of Moses in the following terms: "Now a man from the house of Levi went and took to wife a daughter of Levi. The woman conceived and bore a son." This text explains Moses as a Levite, as born from a priestly family. It shows that when the tradition it represents originated, a lineage of Levi stock existed, or at least that Levitical clans were already assumed realities.[30]

Kohath, son of Levi (with Gershom and Merari : Num 3:17) was father of Amran (Num 26:58). From Num we also learn : "The name of Amran's wife was Jochebed the daughter of Levi who was born to Levi in Egypt; and she bore to Amran Aaron and Moses and Miriam their sister" (Num 26:59). In spite of inconsistencies in the spelling and in the assumed ancestry of Gershom or Gerson,* family ties of Moses with the Levi lineage is well attested. The Levites are generally divided into three classes, representing three families, the Gershonites, the Kohathites and the Merarites (Ex 6:16-19; Num 3:17-37). But Num has preserved a division of the Levites into five clans : Libnites, Hebronites, Mahlites, Mushites, Korahites. The "Mushite" clan, associated by Num 3:33 with the Merari family, is certainly connected with the name and the family of Moses (Heb : *Mōsheh*).

It is obviously difficult to classify Moses in any of the ordinary categories applicable to a leader of a nation; "he is neither a king nor a commander of an army, nor a tribal chieftain, nor a priest, nor an inspired seer and medicine man. To some extent he belongs to all these categories; but none of them adequately explains his position."[31] Old Testament writers gave him a variety of names : prophet (Dt 18:15-18; Hos 12:13), holy prophet (Wis 11:1), the greatest of the prophets (Dt 34:10), servant of God (2 Kg 21:8; Ps 105:26; Mal 4:4; Bar 2:28), God's chosen one (Ps 106:23), man of God (1 Chr 23:14), man of mercy (Sir 45:1), priest (Ps 99:6). Deuteronomy characterizes him as the mediator between God and his people (5:24-28), the messenger who proclaims God's will for social, political and cultic life. Even if priestly features** appear in his person and action,[32] Moses belongs to the cate-

---

[30] On "Moses the Levite in Ex 2.1-2," see A. Gunneweg *Leviten und Priester*, pp. 65-69 and T. J. Meek, "Moses and the Levites," AmJSemLang 56 (1939), pp. 113-120.

[31]. W. Eichrodt, *Theology*, v. 1, p. 289.

[32] See P. Volz, *Mose* (Tübingen, 1907), p. 100, who, however, later modified his view. For further discussion, see A. Cody, *Old Testament Priesthood*, pp. 41-50.

gory of charismatic leaders and not to the institution of the later religious leaders known as priests. In respect to Israel he belonged as leader to all its families and clans, he was the mediator of the covenant which bound together all the tribes in the amphictyony. He was then, in a way, *gēr* in Israel, like the Levites, who had no territory of their own. It may be significant that Moses called his Levite son Gershom (= "*ger*" by "name"), because, he said : "I have been a *sojourner* (*gēr*) in a foreign land" (Ex 2:22).

c) *Aaron and the Aaronites*

Aaron is no doubt also the eponym of a class of priests, whom, for convenience's sake, we shall call "the Aaronites". What we know of Aaron derives from texts which appear purposefully edited. A study of Aaron centers therefore on the study of the traditions concerning him. Among these the tradition of the Aaronites is of course prominent and it will be studied in distinctive texts, of which Gunneweg has offered a consistent and plausible interpretation.[33]

1. Aaron in the Older Traditions

Aaron appears in JE Pentateuch texts beside Moses in various incidents that marked the origin of Israel as a nation. It is generally admitted that several features of Aaron's figure described there derive from sources that are not primary, that do not pertain, that is, to the original relation of the facts.* The appearance of Aaron as a sort of Moses' duplicate in Ex 7-10 does suggest that purposeful redactors have tampered with previous accounts. The passages in which Aaron plays a more autonomous role are also significant in their own way.

Ex 15:20 presents Miriam simply as the sister of Aaron. The omission of Moses in this context indicates that the source which elsewhere calls the two men brothers (Ex 4:14, 6:20, 28:1) may not be primary. Num 12, seemingly an Elohistic narrative, tells how Miriam criticized the conduct of Moses and became leprous in punishment. In our present texts Aaron sides Miriam in a role which probably reflects a polemic against him. A later insertion (vv. 2-8) introduces reflections on Moses' unique relation to God, without a word on Miriam's original complaint (v. 1). A more accurate investigation of the texts shows, however, that Aaron did have a role to play in the original narrative : he was the

---

[33] See A. Gunneweg, *Leviten und Priester*, pp. 81-98.

first to discover Miriam's illness and to intercede in her favor. Miriam's punishment is in part presented in terms of ritual uncleanness and confinement (compare the use of *sgr*, "shut up", in vv. 14-15 and Lev 13:4-5). In this context Aaron's role seems related to the ritual function of the priest described in Lev 13-14.

Other passages as well suggest that even before P Aaron's role had to do with cultic functions. In the battle against the Amalekites (Ex 17:8-16) Aaron and Hur assist Moses in imparting the prolonged blessing on which victory depends. The Lord's command to appear before Pharaoh is in J given to Moses alone. Yet Aaron's presence is then mentioned, precisely when Pharaoh asks them to intercede in his favor (Ex 8:8, 9:27f., 10:16f.). "It appears as if the Jehovistic editor had held Aaron's presence to be appropriate precisely at the intercession."[34] The composite character of the text appears in the fact that Moses then makes his prayer in the singular (8 :12, 30, 9 :33, 10 :18). Besides, it does not seem accidental that Pharaoh bids both Moses and Aaron offer sacrifices and worship their God (Ex 8:25, 10:8). This can only mean that Aaron was at a very early period acknowledged as the eponym of a priesthood. Other texts confirm this assumption. When Jethro, the priest of Midian, visited Moses at the camp, he celebrated a sacred meal, to which it is said, also "Aaron came with all the elders of Israel to eat bread with Moses' father-in-law before God" (Ex 18:12). The elders here are the secular delegates of the Hebrews; if Aaron is mentioned it must be as their religious representative. He appears in the same capacity at the covenant celebration of Ex 24:1, 9-11, together with two other priestly eponyms, Nadab and Abihu (cf. Lev 10:1-3). If he is then told to function as judge with them, it is not in his distinctive role but as representing Moses during his absence. Furthermore the judiciary is not incompatible with the priestly office (Dt 17:8-15). The distinctive appearance of Aaron in the contexts mentioned can be attributed to the influence of the priesthood which has elected him as eponym.

2. *Aaron and Bethel*

In the JE narrative of the golden calf (Ex 32) the rebuke of Aaron contrasts the priestly prestige and intercessory role attributed to him by P in Ex 25-31 (see OAB). The episode can be seen to reflect a polemic against schismatic worship at Bethel, where Jeroboam asked his sub-

[34] J. Wellhausen, *Prolegomena*, p. 143, note.

jects to adore Yahweh under the cultic symbol of the "golden calves" or young bulls, one for Bethel and one for Dan (1 Kg 12:26-29). The possible connection of Aaron with this aberrant form of worship (cf. 1 Kg 12:32) can be represented in the following way: "Perhaps certain groups which claimed descent from Aaron had with them a bull which was a sign of the divine presence, to guide them in their wanderings (Ex 32 :1, 4; 1 Kg 12 :28), just as the groups which belonged to Moses had the Ark to go before them and to indicate the stages of their journey (Num 10 :33-36)" (VAI, p. 334).* The formula, "These are your gods, O Israel, who brought you up out of the land of Egypt!" may well have been a cultic exclamation used at Bethel (1 Kg 2:28) and reproduced in mockery by the editors of the Sinai episode (Ex 32:4, 8). Certain scholars assume that the Exodus account of Aaron's golden calf and the story of Jereboam's golden calves are in some way interdependent. It is particularly remarkable that the two eldest sons of Aaron, Nadab and Abihu, should bear names virtually identical with those of the two recorded sons of Jeroboam, Nadab and Abijah. Either Jeroboam deliberately imitated Aaron, they think, or "most of our account of Aaron's golden calf was tendentiously narrated by the Zadokite priesthood of Jerusalem with a view to discrediting the northern kingdom and its bull cult." That the Zadokites also accepted later Aaronite descent would explain that Aaron is partly exculpated in the Exodus narrative, by being presented as "merely submitting to popular pressure."[35]

It is noted that Jeroboam appointed for his high places "priests from among all the people, who were not of the Levites" (1 Kg 12:31). This reflects the polemical intention of the Deuteronomic editor, for whom only Levites are legitimate priests. In spite of 1 Kg 12:31 it can be assumed that Aaronites functioned at Bethel even before the Jeroboam schism and that the type of worship which the king officially sanctioned and reactivated had a prehistory in the Northern sanctuary.

In some ancient texts, then, Aaron appears beside Moses as his colleague, in others as his rival. This change may reflect the growing importance of the Aaronites and of their central sanctuary, probably located at Bethel. These Aaronites, now royal functionaries, needed to

---

[35] M. Aberbach and L. Smolar, "Aaron, Jeroboam and the Golden Calves," JBiblLit 86 (1967), p. 140. See also R. Brinker, *The Influence of Sanctuaries in Early Israel* (Manchester, 1946), pp. 262-63; I. Lewy, "The Story of the Golden Calf Reanalyzed," VetTest 9 (1959), pp. 318-322.

reconfirm the legitimacy of their priesthood when their status changed with the distintegration of the amphictyony. Other groups, however, opposed the change and continued to hold that the amphictyony founded by Moses with its particular form of worship had to be maintained. The action of the Levites against the worshippers of the golden calf (Ex 32:25-29) would represent the reaction of their circles to the abandonment of the ancient and only legitimate institution.

3. Aaron the Levite (Ex 4 : 3-16)

The passages (probably E) which describe how Aaron was appointed the mouthpiece of Moses (Ex 4:13-16, 27-31) appear in their present context as interpolations. Their origin, too, is connected with the purpose of setting Aaron beside Moses as his partner or rival. Here, however, Aaron is called "the Levite" (4:14). The appellation does not stand simply for "the priest"; its meaning has to be clarified in the light of the literary tradition concerning Levi and the Levites. "Levite" must be understood in the meaning it had in the pre-Josiah traditions : membership in a body of persons conjoined under the eponym "Levi" and characterized by a peculiar amphictyonic status and specific functions in the confederacy. Applied to Aaron the appellation reflects an attempt by the Aaronites to give to their eponym a status which essentially belonged to Moses, the mediator and originator of the covenant confederacy. As the Levites in Dt 33:10 claim to be priests, so also the Aaronites in Ex 4:14 claim Levitical prerogatives.

This was the beginning of a trend in which Levitehood was gradually absorbed into priesthood. Two other claims are distinctive high points of the process : P genealogies place Aaron in the Levi lineage (Ex 6:16-25); Aaron is denied any inheritance, like the Levites (Num 18:20). Finally Levitehood was classified as minor clergy. Gunneweg notes (p. 98) how serenely the Aaronic claims are introduced in the texture of the ancient literary traditions : Aaron is a brother, a partner, a helper to Moses, who is never blamed. In contrast stands the strongly polemical attitude of the other camp, the Levites, struggling to retain their rights (Ex 32:25-29; Dt 33:11).

4. The Eleazar-Phinehas Problem

Aaron's third son, *Eleazar*, succeeded his father as high priest (Num 20:24-28; Dt 10:6). Ithamar's elder brother and father of Phinehas (25:7), he assisted Moses in taking the census of the tribes (Num 26:2-3) and cooperated with Joshua in apportioning the land of Canaan (Num 34:17; Jos 14:1, 19:51). Eleazar was buried "at Gibeah, the town of Phinehas his son, which had been given him in the hill country of Ephraim" (Jos 24:33). In postexilic Jerusalem the house of Eleazar undoubtedly played a more important role than that of Ithamar (see 1 Chr 24 and *infra*). The genealogy of Moses and Aaron (Ex 6:14-27) traces the priestly ancestry from Levi, Jacob's son, to Aaron and through Eleazar to Phinehas, while Ithamar is not even mentioned.

The Eleazar house based its credentials also on *Phinehas*, whose promotion is most clearly set forth in Num 25:10-13 : as a result of his peculiar zeal in opposing intermarriage with the Midianites, "a covenant of perpetual priesthood" is granted to him and to his descendants. He becomes a priestly figure *sui juris*, whereas in the P conception anyone is priest who can claim to be of Aaron. The episode and the exceptional privilege founded on it most likely reflect the pretentions of a Jerusalem priestly family* to the exclusive rights of drawing from its own ranks the legitimate high priests. These Eleazarites could also point out that Phinehas had been chief priest in Israel when the Transjordan tribes planned to set up a separate sanctuary (Jos 22:13, 30, 32) and still later on at the time of the war against Benjamin (Jg 20:28). In postexilic Jerusalem certain priests, including Ezra himself, traced their lineage back to Phinehas (Ezra 7:5, 8:2), whose memory was recalled in later ages (Ps 106 : 30-31; Sir 45:23-25).

The origin and the growth of Eleazar as eponym may have been favored by the consonantal identity of his name with that of a son of Moses, *Eliezer* (Ex 18:4), ancestor through Rehabiah of a Levite clan (1 Chr 23:15-17). The Levite priest Jonathan of the Danites was Moses' grandson and the priestly circles of Jerusalem at the time of Hezekiah associated Moses with the bronze serpent worshiped as an idol (2 Kg 18:4; cf. Num 21:8-9; Wis 16:6-7). It is probable that the Eleazar-Phinehas tradition was introduced into the P complex by interested priestly circles of Jerusalem. Yet the possibility remains that the Eleazar-Eliezer figure took shape before P, although the name became only later the eponym of the most important priestly class of Jerusalem. Through the contamination of traditions and the overwhelming development of the Aaron-priest speculation, Eliezer-Eliazar, son of Moses, became an Aaronite, while the two names were later distinguished and pronounced differently.

It would seem impossible to identify Phinehas, son of Eliezer-Eliazar, with *Phinehas*, son of Eli, since the latter was severely blamed for his conduct (1 Sam 3:29-36), while the first, as we have seen, received the reward of his exceptional zeal (Num 25:10-13). But Jerusalem became the successor of Shiloh, as the Israelite central sanctuary (Jer 7:12), when the sacred ark, captured and returned by the Philistines (1 Sam 4:11, 6:21), was transferred to David's capital (2 Sam 6). There was also a transfer of priestly lineage : the prominent priestly house of Jerusalem linked its origin to Phinehas, son of (Eli)-Eliezer-Eliazar. The prediction that the house of Eli would be punished (1 Sam 2:27-36) is clearly an insertion designed to justify the exclusion of Abiathar and his descendants (1 Kg 2:27.35). The correlation Eli-Eliazar-Eliezer (son of Moses) would clarify some references of the inserted passage concerning Eli : "I revealed myself to the house of your father when they were in Egypt subject to the house of Pharaoh. And I chose him out of all the tribes of Israel to be my priest ..." (1 Sam 2:27-28). The same hypothesis can explain the quite sudden appearance of "Eli the priest" (1 Sam 1:9). The account of his origin would naturally have interfered with the devised genealogical scheme. It may be that the combination Eliezer-Eliazar-Phinehas is much older than P, older even than the Jerusalem priesthood.

The graduated character of the buildup of the priestly ancestry appears quite plainly in two passages. In the verse which introduces the ritual of the installation of the priests (Ex 28-29) "the sons of Aaron" are mentioned first without their names, then Aaron's name is repeated and followed by that of each Aaronite : Nabab and Abihu, Eleazar and Ithamar (28:1). Secondary additions are also noticeable in Num 3:1-4, where, with curious repetitions, the promotion of the Aaronites to the priesthood is linked to the mere statement of the Aaronic genealogy. Another lineage was concurrently built up to make Aaron descend from Levi (Ex 6:16-25). This provided the link with the oldest Israelite traditions, took into account the Deuteronomistic conceptions, and brought the whole Jerusalem cult personnel under Levi ancestry.

Ithamar, the fourth and youngest son of Aaron and Elisheba (Ex 6:23), was consecrated to the priestly office with his father and brothers (Ex 28:1). He assumed a role of direction in respect to the Levites (Ex 38:21), the Gershonites (Num 4:28), and the Merarites (Num 4:33, 7.8).* This may reflect actual features of the second temple organization. Ithamar occupies thus a rank above the lower Levitical cult personnel, although he comes second in regard to Eleazar, "chief over the leaders of the Levites" (Num 3:22). It is then very likely that Ithamar was the eponym of the second most important priestly class of postexilic Jerusalem (1 Chr 24:1; Ezra 8:2). "According to 1 Chr 24:3, the priesthood of Shiloh, of Nob and of Jerusalem itself, until the dismissal of Ebyathar, was descended from Ithamar" (VAI, p. 360). The later relations between the Ithamarites and the Eleazarites will be examined below.

5. *Korah versus Aaron*

Num 16 combines the accounts of two clashes which opposed subordinates and their leaders (see also Sir 45:18-19). From the JE tradition (vv. 1b-2a, 12-15, 25-34) we learn how the Reubenites Dathan and Abiram revolted against the civil authority of Moses and in punishment were swallowed up in an earthquake (cf. Dt 11:6). Verses of the P tradition (1a, 2b-11, 16-24, 27a, 35) deal with the religious claim of the Kohathites against the Aaronites. In this part of the episode Korah and his company of 250 Levites question the privilege of their rivals and apparently claim for themselves full priestly status (v. 10). On the invitation of Moses, who wishes to submit them to God's judgment, they offer incense, each in his own censer, thus performing what priests only were allowed to do. In reaction to this act of temerity "fire came forth from the Lord and consumed the two hundred and fifty men offering the incense" (v. 35; cf. Lev 10:1-3).[36]

The original version of the religious controversy in the story dealt, it seems, with the absolute separateness of priesthood, not with its relevance or its distinctiveness in respect to the laity. The way P conceived the role and function of priesthood could lead to regard this institution as a wall separating God from the people rather than as a force of mediation. Protest could especially arise against the postexillic attempt to combine in the high priest the three powers of priesthood, prophecy, and kingship. God's judgment in the story was not originally intended to decide who is priest and who is not, but who is holy, or more precisely, what is holiness.

The point of the controversy has then shifted to concern divine call to priesthood (cf. the use of *hiqrîb*, "cause to come near" in vv. 5, 17, with that of *qrb*, "come near," in Num 18:3, 4). The background of the controversy remains obscure, because what we have in Num 16 is a one-party version, that of the priestly editors. The whole Korah story looks like a new edition of a late P narrative dealing with a contro-

---

[36] On the whole episode, see A. Gunneweg, *Leviten und Priester*, pp. 171-184.

versy on the absolute separateness of priesthood in the post-exilic community, involving besides Moses and Aaron 250 leaders of the congregation and notables of the religious life. Korah's name, conspicuously absent from v. 35, may have been included only later.* The rest of ch 16, vv. 36-50, can be interpreted along the same lines. The people told Moses and Aaron: "You have killed the people of the Lord" (v. 41), by involving the 250 in a judgment of God on your concept of holiness, of which your opponents were unaware.

Korah is described in v. 1 as "the son of *Kohath,* son of Levi" (cf. Ex 6:18, 21). The family of Kohath had a particular importance as being related to the Aaronites. The Levite Amran, son of Kohath, was the ancestor of Aaron and Moses (Ex 6:20; Num 3:19). It can be assumed that historically the Kohathites were the closest rivals of the Aaronites. In Num 4 the prerogatives of the Aaronites are re-stated together with the limitations of the rights of the Kohathites. On the other hand, the Korah clan was at a certain period the most prominent group among the Kohathites and as such could stand as their representative. Thus is the episode of Num 16 partly a dramatic account of struggles suggested in Num 4, or more generally of conflicts between priests and Levites.

The house of Korah was not wiped out with the judgment of God against the rebellious company. On that occasion, we read in Num 26:11, "the sons of Korah did not die." Three of these, named Assir Elkanah, and Abiasaph, headed "the families of the Korahites" (Ex 6:24), who formed one of the five Levitical clans mentioned in Num 26:58. The Korahites were both gatekeepers (1 Chr 26:1, 19) and singers (1 Chr 6:37; 2 Chr 20:19). Pss 42, 44, 45 are called "*maśkil* of the sons of Korah," while Pss 46-49, 84-85, 87-88 have the inscription "a psalm of the sons of Korah." Perhaps the episode of Num 16 reflects a distinctive feature of the character of the Korahites. "Korahites were always the same, full of intrigue, battling their way forward, first as doorkeepers, then as singers, and finally even usurping Priestly functions!" (VAI, p. 393).

The story of Aaron's budding rod (Num 17) belongs to a tradition independent of Num 16. It was inserted in this context because it, too, deals with a divine judgment designed to prove Aaron's peculiar separateness. It says nothing of Korah and his company. The story is often interpreted as an etiology explaining how the Levites have acquired priesthood.[37] This, however, is an unlikely P theme. Others assume that

---

[37] See H. Gressmann, *Mose und seine Zeit* (FRLANT 18; Göttingen, 1913), pp. 103-104

it is not Aaron the high priest who is involved here but Aaron the leader of the tribe of Levi. But such a role is otherwise not assigned to Aaron. The story reflects rather the later introduction into the P system of the Levite component of the priestly lineage. No party struggle is involved but a popular illustration of the P solution to the old problem concerning the Aaron-Levi relation. The story may have been told first to explain the presencc in the temple of a relic preserved from Aaron's staff.

d) Zadok and the Zadokites

Later tradition regarded "the sons of Zadok" or the Zadokites as constituting the official Jerusalem priesthood (Ezek 40:46, 44:15, 48: 11), and providing the only legitimate high priests (2 Chr 31 :10).Their place in the Israelite tradition raises questions that have to do with both Zadok and his descendants.

1. Who was Zadok?

While Levi and Aaron could be conceived merely as eponyms for Levites and Aaronites,* Zadok (Heb. *Ṣādôq*) is no doubt an historical person. His name appears in the list of the officials of the early monarchy (2 Sam 8:17, 20:25) and in the "history of David's family and the disputed succession" (2 Sam 15:24-35, 19:12; 1 Kg 1:8, 32). After the capture of Jerusalem from the Jebusites Zadok appears suddenly as David's official "priest," with Abiathar (2 Sam 8:17, 19:11, 20:25; 1 Chr 18:16).[38] After David's death Zadok sided with Solomon, while Abiathar sided with Adonia in the struggle for the succession (see 1 Kg 1). As a result Solomon, at the beginning of his reign, banished Abiathar to Anathoth (1 Kg 2:26), and Zadok became the only official "priest" in Jerusalem (2:35), although both Abiathar and Zadok, the "priests," are still named among the "high officials" in 1 Kg 4:1-4. Later tradition, as we have said, gave prominence to "the sons of Zadok", a name also applied to the leaders of the Qumrân sect.

Zadok's name occurs for the first time in 2 Sam 8 :17 : "And Zadok the son of Ahitub and Ahimelech the son of Abiathar were priests".

---

[38] On Zadok and the Zadokites, see A. Gunneweg, *op. cit.*, 98-114; VAI, pp. 373-374; J. Bowman, "Ezekiel and the Zadokite Priesthood," GlasgowUnivOrSocTransaction 16 (1955-56) 1-14; E. Auerbach, "Der Aufstieg der Priesterschaft zur Macht im alten Israel," *Congress Volume* (VetTestSuppl 9, Leiden 1963) 236-249.

It has long been suspected that the verse is in disorder, since in 1 Sam 22:20 Abiathar is called "son of Ahimelech, the son of Ahitub." It may be that in 2 Sam 8:17 the name of Ahitub has changed place accidentally, or else was deliberately transferred to make him father of Zadok. The original reading would have been : "Zadok and Abiathar, son of Ahimelech, son of Ahitub, were priests." Thus Zadok would be left without a genealogy (VAI, p. 373).

Where did Zadok come from ? According to 1 Chr 16:39 David "left Zadok the priest and his brethren the priests before the tabernacle of the Lord in the high place that was at Gibeon." Some scholars give this information credit and explain : under David Abiathar was in the service of the Ark and Zadok in the service of the Tent, which, at the time, was kept at Gibeon (cf. 2 Chr 1:3). In the early texts, however, Zadok, is never mentioned except, like Abiathar, in connection with the Ark (cf. 2 Sam 15:24-29). "A second suggestion is that Zadok was one of the priests at Qiryath-Yearim (1 Sam 7:1), and that he took part in the transfer of the Ark to Jerusalem ; according to 2 Sam 6:3-4, the cart was driven by Uzzah and 'Ahyo' ; it is suggested that instead of 'Ahyo,' we should read *'ahiw*, meaning 'his brother.' This brother would in fact be Zadok, who afterwards remained at Jerusalem as one of the two men who carried the Ark : and Uzzah would have been replaced by Ebyathar (2 Sam 15:29). There is no text which formally contradicts this theory, but neither is there one which gives it positive support ; it is certainly possible, but it is not proven" (VAI, p. 374).

The similarity between the two names, Zadok and Melchizedek, is quite obvious, especially in the consonantal Hebrew. Another king of Jerusalem was called Adonizedek (Jos 10:1). Zadok cannot, however, be identified with Melchizedek, as A. Bentzen has suggested,[39] nor even be considered heir to the priestly kingship represented in Gen 14:18-20. Rather than as an historical person, Melchizedek can be seen as a type or prototype of the Jerusalem priest-king. It is unlikely that David would have installed as chief priest a political adversary recently defeated. * A plausible hypothesis can be formulated : Zadok was priest of the Jebusite shrine of *'el-'elyon*, "God Most High," when David conquered the city, and the king appointed him to serve with Abiathar in the new Yahwist sanctuary (2 Sam 8:17). There exist, however, no indications that a sanctuary of *'el-'elyôn* was later used for the cult of

---

[39] A. Bentzen, *Studier over det sadokidiske praesteskabs historie* (Copenhagen, 1931), pp. 8-9.

Yahweh. The Ark was kept in a Tent until the end of David's reign, and when Zadok is mentioned in the Bible it is always in connection with the Ark or the Tent (cf. 2 Sam 15:25; 1 Kg 1:39; see VAI, pp. 374 and 311). No firm conclusion then can be drawn on the origin of Zadok, but this last hypothesis, as formulated, deserves further study.*

2. The Zadokites and the House of Eli

Perhaps Zadok was for the ancient sources, like Melchizedek, *apatôr, amêtor, agenealogêtos* (Heb 7:3), but thus he would not remain, given the importance of the ancestry in the priestly traditions. In 2 Sam 8:17, discussed above, Zadok appears as son of Ahitub. This difficult reading could derive from an intentional change designed to make of Zadok a member of the house of Eli. For in the tradition Ahitub is "son of Phinehas, son of Eli, the priest of the Lord in Shiloh, wearing an ephod" (1 Sam 14:3). Ahitub is also father of Ahijah (*ibid.*), often considered as the same person as Ahimelech, father of Abiathar (1 Sam 22:9, 11, 20, 23:6, 30:7). After the destruction of Shiloh by the Philistines (1 Sam 4) Ahimelech functioned as chief priest at Nob, near Jerusalem (Is 10:32; Neh 11:32). Nob is called "the city of the priests" (1 Sam 22:19), and there David took refuge with Ahimelech who gave him food and weapons (1 Sam 22:1-9). Because of this, Saul destroyed the whole priestly family of Nob, except Abiathar, who escaped and fled to David (22:9-23).

In two of the Chronicler's genealogies Zadok appears as Ahitub's son (1 Chr 6:8, 12, 53; Ezra 7:2). In two others he is his grandson, through Meraioth (Neh 11:10; 1 Chr 9:11). This change indicates how weak was the tradition on the matter. The Deuteronomistic oracle of 1 Sam 2:27-36 announces the substitution of the house of Eli by that of Zadok. Zadok was not then historically of the house of Eli and the tradition which tends to affirm it can be contested. If the present reading of 2 Sam 8:17 is not a simple error of transmission, it is a deliberate theological alteration designed to clarify the Zadokites' origin, which later appeared objectionable. In other words "the purpose of the scribes in making Zadok a descendant of Ahitub was to legitimatize his claim to the high-priesthood after Abiathar, grandson of Achitob, had been deposed in his favor by Solomon (3 Kg 2:35)".[40] The association of Zadok with the Elids would have appealed to David himself as showing that in its personnel also the Jerusalem cult continued that of

[40] EncDictBibl, c. 27.

Shiloh. The transfer of the ark had been of great importance : "By its installation in the city of David the Ark elevated Jerusalem to the status of an amphictyonic cultic centre and brought the ancient Israelite traditions and institutions of the tribal confederacy to the 'chosen place' ".[41]

Apart from 2 Sam 8:17 questions can be raised as to the historical reliability of other elements in the genealogical line Eli-Phinehas-Ahitob-Ahimelech-Abiathar. They concern mainly the assumed link between the Shiloh (Elid) priesthood and that of Nob. It is not said, for example, how the Elid turned up in Nob, how this place could have become in a short time such a large center of worship (1 Sam 22:18-19), if its priesthood consisted merely of a few Elid refugees. Perhaps the newcomers added their number to the indigenous, now converted, ministers of the cult. A peculiar genealogical notice reads : "... Ahijah the son of Ahitub, Ichabod's brother, son of Phinehas, son of Eli, the priest of the Lord in Shiloh, wearing the ephod" (1 Sam 14:3). Through the unexpected mention of Ichabod (cf. 1 Sam 4:19-22), the story of the Elids is linked with the history of king Saul's rise to power, to which Ahijah was associated (cf. 1 Sam 14:18). As Ahimelech is also son of Ahitub (1 Sam 22:9-12) he is made a Elid together with his son Abiathar.*

It is also significant that in the history of the succession Abiathar is not any longer named "Abiathar, son of Ahimelech" (1 Sam 22 :20, 23:6, 30:7) but simply Abiathar (2 Sam 15:24, 17:15, 19:12, 20:25). It is then possible that Abiathar was not historically but was made a member of the house of Eli. Although this assumption would require further demonstration, it can be said that there existed three autonomous traditions dealing respectively with the Elids, with the priests of Nob, with the Zadokites. They were eventually joined by a genealogical tie.** Chronology and genealogy have often served the Biblical authors in expressing the accomplishment of the divine will. Thus an oracle had said that one Elid only would be saved from the impending catastrophe (1 Sam 2:33), namely Abiathar, who alone escaped at Nob (1 Sam 22:18-23) and was later substituted by Zadok the "faithful priest" (v. 35; 1 Kg 2:35).

---

[41] H. J. Kraus, *Worship in Israel*, p. 182; Cf. M. Noth, "Jerusalem und die israelitische Tradition," *Gesammelte Studien zum Alten Testament* (2d ed., München 1960) 172-187.

e) Eleazarites and Ithamarites

In the census of the first return from Babylonia priests are mentioned who were excluded from the priesthood as unclean because they failed to find their names registered in the proper genealogies (Ezra 2:62; Neh 7:64). Ancestry also served contending priestly families as a basis for claiming or confirming prominence with respect to other groups. This has been amply illustrated in the preceding pages. A few points have to be clarified regarding the situation in the postexilic community. An annotation of the Chronicler, reflecting this situation, tells how David organized the priests "with the help of Zadok of the sons of *Eleazar*, and Ahimelech of the sons of Ithamar (1 Chr 24:3). This indicates clearly that in this tradition at least the line of Zadok claimed descent from Aaron, through Eleazar, while the priesthood of Shiloh and Nob, or the Eli line, traced their lineage back to Aaron through Ithamar. It is noteworthy that the Ithamarites in the postexilic period appear in 1 Chr 24:3 as collaborating with the Eleazarites or Zadokites. We do not know for certain how this accord was reached, but several indications can be examined usefully and a possible solution proposed. Only the broad lines of a complex question will be presented and then recalled in a simplified schema.

In Ex 6:2-7.7 the call of Moses and the appointment of Aaron are recapitulated by the P tradition (cf. Ex 3:1-6.2). In 6:14-27 the priestly lineage is traced from Levi to Aaron and through Aaron's third son Eleazar to Phinehas. In Ex 28:1 the Lord says to Moses : "Bring near to you Aaron your brother, and his sons with him, from among the people of Israel, to serve me as priests—Aaron and Aaron's sons, Nadab and Abihu, Eleazar and Ithamar." Num 3 :3. calls these four sons "the anointed priests, whom he ordained to minister in the priest's office." "But Nadab and Abihu died before the Lord when they offered unholy fire before the Lord in the wilderness of Sinai; and they had no children.* So Eleazar and Ithamar served as priests in the lifetime of Aaron their father" (v. 4). According to P the Eleazarites differ from the Ithamarites as providing the high priests from their ranks, a privilege never granted to the sons of Ithamar.**

In Ezekiel the Jerusalem priests are called "the sons of Zadok" (40:46, 43:19, 44:15, 48:11) "because it seemed useful and natural to classify them under the name of the Davidic priest in Jerusalem, the first known Israelite priest in Jerusalem. The title was perhaps Ezekiel's invention; at least there is no evidence that it is founded on carefully preserved genealogies."[42] In P, in the Chronicler's work, and in some postexilic Psalms (115:9, 118:3, 135:19), the priests are called "sons of Aaron" or those of "the house of Aaron." It is in fact clear that in postexilic Jerusalem the official priesthood in Israel was considered as Aaronite. Zadok and his successors had in some way linked themselves to the Aaronite lineage (cf. Ezra 7:1-5). The individual priests would claim their priestly rights by proving that they belonged to one of the two great branches of the Aaronite family, the Eleazarites or the Ithamarites (1 Chr 24:3; Ezra 8:2).

The fact that the priests are called "sons of Aaron" in the postexilic writings certainly reflects what was happening in the little world of the Jerusalem priesthood. We have seen above (c. 2) how the name of Aaron is connected with the Bethel priesthood. Some authors suggest that these Aaronites became the dominant priestly family in Palestine during the Exile and managed to have their eponym recognized even in Jerusalem as the common priestly ancestor. It is, however, unlikely that the sanctuary of Bethel was reactivated after the reform of Josiah. No evidence indicates, besides, that a non-Zadokite group maintained continuity of worship in Jerusalem during the Exile.

A more probable solution assumes that an agreement had been reached in Babylonia between the Zadokites and a rival group. This can be identified as the family of Abiathar, representing the house of Eli and claiming descent from Aaron, through Ithamar.* As a counter-measure the Zadokites also claimed Aaron as their ancestor, through Phinehas and Eleazar (1 Chr 6:4-15) (VAI, p. 396). After Ezra's reform the agreement previously concluded led to practical conclusions and the Ithamarites were again admitted to share the functions of the Jerusalem worship with the sons of Zadok and thus was priesthood recognized as the common privilege of all the sons of Aaron. Thus the Chronicler, tracing back the situation of his day to David's ruling, tells how the king organized the priests "with the help of Zadok of the sons of Eleazar, and Ahimelech of the sons of Ithamar" (1 Chr 24:3).

The following schema recapitulates with significant names and references the assumed lineage of the two great families, who lived as rivals before being reconciled under a single patronymic name.

---

[42] J. R. Bartlett, "Zadok and His Successors at Jerusalem," JThSt 19 (1968), p. 17.

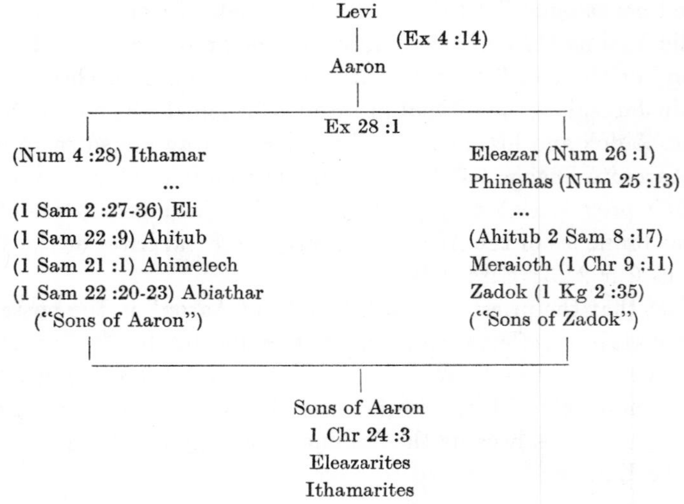

D. The Priestly Office

The various OT traditions present their distinctive viewpoints on the disputed question of the status of the priests and Levites. In the Israelite religious world priestly families contended for preeminence and their lot was often bound to that of the ruling powers. Yet the priestly office was, in Israel, a reality with definite features and duties. This reality we shall now examine, giving proper attention to the determining factors connected with the literary traditions and the historical perspectives.

a) The Installation of Priests

In Israel priesthood was an office, not a vocation. A special divine calling would go to kings or prophets, but not to individual priests.* No divine intervention is noted in the priestly appointments made by Mikah (Jg 17:5, 10) and Eleazar (1 Sam 7:1), while it is well known that kings appointed and dismissed the personnel of their official sanctuaries (1 Kg 2:27, 12:31). The tribe of Levi, it is true, was set aside by God himself for the holy service (cf. Num 3:12, 41, 8:16), but there is no mention of a particular charisma for the individual members of the tribe. Priesthood was in fact hereditary in Israel, as professions generally were in the ancient Middle East. Jonathan's sons succeeded their father as priests of the tribe of the Danites (Jg 18 :30) and it is well known that Eli and his sons were priests at Shiloh (1 Sam 1-2), while Ahimelech and his family provided the priestly service at Nob (1 Sam 22:11). This system assured the maintenance of the sanctuaries and continuity in divine worship. But it could also lead to excessive institutionalism, crass conservatism, and a lack of zeal in performing the sacred duties. Any man of priestly descent could be admitted to the priesthood, unless he was excluded from it by physical impediments (see Lev 21:16-23). Just as the sacrificial offerings must be unblemished (Lev 22:17-25) so must the ministers of the altar be without bodily defects. "Because the priest is to 'come near' to God and to share God's sanctity in a special way, a physical defect in him would be an affront to God who created the physical world without blemish" (JB, p. 159).

1. "To Fill the Hand"

The Priestly Document describes more than once the ordination of the Israelite priests, of Aaron, that is, and his sons. Instructions on the building of the sanctuary and on its ministers are given in Ex 25-31. The formula ordinarily used, "God said to Moses," asserts the divine authority behind the religious institutions of Israel. Yet what is described in these chapters, as elsewhere in P, combines elements of great antiquity with others that reflect the development of worship and also the situation in the postexillic temple (see JB, p. 109). In the last chapter of Exodus the instructions are briefly recalled, but then the ritual of sacrifice (Lev 1-7) interrupts the narrative. The directives of Ex 28-29 on priestly ordination (cf. Ex 40:12-15) and investiture are finally carried out in Lev 8-9. We have in this ceremonial a model ritual full of religious teaching. It is impossible to know how close this pattern was followed in the actual practice.

The Hebrew Bible uses quite consistently the phrase *millē' yad*, "to fill the hand," to express the making of a priest. This is rendered, even by RSV, in several ways : more often "to ordain" (Ex 28:41),* but also "to consecrate" (1 Kg 13:33; 2 Chr 13:9; Lev 16:32, 21:10), and "to install" (Jg 17:5, 12). In this last text layman Micah "installs" his son and later his Levite as priests, he does not really "ordain" them. Jg 17:5, 12 is in fact the oldest Biblical texts where the expression "fill the hand" is used for the appointment of a priest. Outside P the phrase also occurs in connection with the zealous Levites "who ordained themselves" (Ex 32:29) and with those persons "from all the people" whom

Jeroboam "consecrated to be priests of the high places" (1 Kg 13:33). To sum up, "fill the hands" was "an old expression for investment with priestly prerogatives" (OAB, p. 106). Its literal meaning is quite obviously forgotten when it is applied to the "consecration" of an altar (Ezek 43:26).

The cognate noun *millu'îm*, "fillings" (of the Lord), appears in the phrase "ram of ordination" (Ex 29:22, 26:27), the victim of the installation sacrifice, which included the "wave offering" (Ex 29:24-28; cf. Lev 7:29-36).* In this same late P context an attempt is made to link the sacrificial rite with the Hebrew expression for "ordain." Having mentioned a number of sacrificial offerings (parts of the victim, bread, and oil) the ritual reveals what Moses had to do next : "You shall put all these *in the hands* of Aaron and *in the hands* of his sons, and wave them for a wave offering before the Lord. Then you shall take *from their hands*, and burn them on the altar in addition to the burnt offering..." (Ex 29:24-25). Putting these things in the hands of the priests signified that they were authorized to receive their portion of the offerings (1 Sam 2:12-17).+ The wave-offering ceremony had probably a broader significance : "By so performing, for the first time, the ritual gesture of a minister of the altar, the man was invested with priestly power" (VAI, p. 346).

2. *Consecrated*

A text (P) of the second Temple period outlines thus the instruction given to Moses for the installation of priest : "And you shall put them [the vestments] upon Aaron your brother, and upon his sons with him, and shall anoint them and ordain them ["fill their hands"] and *consecrate* them, that they may serve me as priests" (Ex 28:41). The Hebrew term translated "consecrate" is *qiddēš* ("to make, declare holy"), an intensive verbal form of the root *qdš* meaning "holy," which appears also in the causative form *hiqdiš*, "to make holy" (1 Chr 23:13). The Priestly writers have stressed in the notion of holiness the aspect of *separateness* from whatever is profane (*ḥōl*), accentuating in the Mosaic experience of God the awe-inspiring unapproachableness of Yahweh. Consecration or sanctification expresses the positive aspect of that which is or becomes holy, while purification removes the obstacles hindering the approach to God and the holy. For example, by their vow the Nazirites become temporarily "separated" (*nzr*) from normal life and consecrated to God. What belongs to Yahweh worship participates in this type of holiness; the ark, the sacred utensils (Num 4:15), the victims (Ex 28:38, 29:34), the showbread (Lev 24:9), the incense (Ex 30:35), the anointing oil (Ex 30:25), and the priestly vestments (Ex 28:2) are all holy, while the altar of sacrifice (Ex 29:37) and the altar of incense (Ex 30:10) are most holy.

The term *qiddēš* is used twice again in this divine declaration : "I will consecrate the tent of meeting and the altar; Aaron also and his sons I will consecrate, to serve me as priests" (Ex 29:44; cf. Ex 21:15; 40: 13). To approach the sphere of God's holiness, to minister in the holy forbidden precinct, the priests have to be consecrated, that is "set apart" from the sphere of the profane. This meaning is borne out also where it is said of the men of Kiriath-jearim that "they consecrated (*qiddēš*) Eleazar, son of Abinadab, to have charge of the ark of the Lord" (1 Sam 7:1). The notion of "setting apart for God's service" is often expressed by a verb in the causative, *hibdîl*, "to separate." Thus the Lord himself "set apart the tribe of Levi to carry the ark of the covenant of the Lord ..." (Dt 10:8). The Levites were prepared for their office by a special purification ceremony (Num 8:5-13) on many points similar to the "ordination" of the Aaronic priests (Lev 8). Thus, says the Lord to Moses, "you shall separate (*hibdil*) the Levites from among the people of Israel, and the Levites shall be mine" (Num 8:14). Later, Moses would remind the rebellious Korah party : "Is it too small a thing for you that the God of Israel *has separated* you from the congregation of Israel, to bring you near to himself, to do service in the tabernacle of the Lord, and to stand before the congregation to minister to them" (Num 16:9). Of Israel as a whole it is besides written : "I am the Lord your God, who *have separated* you from the peoples" (Lev 20:24). Lev 19:2 expresses the keynote of the so-called "Holiness Code" (Lev 17-26). Israel's holiness is derived from the nation's relation to the holy God, not from any intrinsic quality of the people (OAB, p. 146).

Singularly set apart, consecrated, sanctified for the service of God in his holy domain the priests are bound to observe distinctive rules of ritual purity (Lev 21:1-15). They can attend only the funerals of close blood-relatives and even then will refrain from certain mourning rites. They are not allowed to marry a woman who has been a prostitute or one whom her husband has divorced. They are to avoid the risk of contaminating the holy with the profane. Besides wearing special vestments those about to perform sacred duties must prepare themselves by proper purifying rites (Ex 30:17-21); they wash their hands and feet (Ex 40:31-32), and abstain from wine and alcoholic drinks (Lev 10:

8-11). They may not partake of their portion of sacrifice while in a state of ritual uncleanness (Lev 22:1-9).* Even stricter prescriptions rule the life of the chief priest, whose office brings him in contact with the most holy things (Lev 21:10-15).

After their purification the Levites were presented "before the Lord," that is, before the tent of meeting, and there, it is said, "the people of Israel shall lay (*samak*) their hands upon the Levites, and Aaron shall offer the Levites before the Lord as a wave offering from the people of Israel, that it may be theirs to do the service of the Lord" (Num 8:9-11). Thus the fact is recalled that the Levites are, in a way, sacrificed instead of the first-born of the people (v. 16), and that they belong to Aaron and his sons, just as the waved sacrifice belongs to the priests (see Ex 29:24). Neither of these rites applied to the priests** who were not, as such, equated to sacrificial victims. The late P ritual does, however, include in the consecration of Aaron and his sons a rite similar to that used for the altar :+ Moses took some blood of the sacrificed ram of ordination "and put it on the tip of Aaron's right ear and on the thumb of his right hand and on the great toe of his right foot," doing afterwards the same for Aaron's sons (Lev 8:23-24; cf. Ex 29:19-20). Thus their whole person was consecrated for office.

According to the postexilic ritual, the high priest was anointed (Ex 29:7; Lev 8:12). In the last redaction of the Pentateuch the anointing is extended to all the priests,++ but apart from the P texts there is no certain evidence for the anointing of priests before the Hellenistic period (VAI, p. 105). Neither Ex 29:5-8 nor Lev 8:13 mention the anointing of priests also, as could be expected. But according to Ex 29:21 and Lev 8 :30 both Aaron and his sons were sprinkled with anointing oil. They then partake in the communion meal from the sacrifice of ordination and observe the following prescription : "You shall not go out from the door of the tent of the meeting for seven days, until the days of your ordination are completed, for it will take seven days to ordain you" (Lev 8:33; cf. Ex 29:35-37).

3. *The Priestly Vestments*

We shall treat of the vestments of the priests and of the high priest, leaving, however, for a subsequent development (c; 1) the garments related to the oracular function : the ephod and the breastpiece concontaining the Urim and Thummim.

In preparation of the investiture of Aaron and his sons Moses is instructed to have special garments made for them. Some are for Aaron only (the high priests) while others will be worn by his sons (all the priests). Their description reflects the custom of the second temple, which, however, had no doubt, a long history, knowing as we do how little subject to change is the priestly tradition, particularly in what concerns sacred vestments. Moses then is told :

> You shall speak to all who have ability whom I have endowed with an able mind, that they make Aaron's garments to consecrate him for my priesthood. These are the garments which they shall make : a breastpiece, an ephod, a robe, a coat of checker work, a turban, and a girdle; they shall make holy garments for Aaron your brother and his sons to serve me as priests (Ex 28 :3-4).

The "robe" (*me'il*) or "cloak" was in ordinary life a loose-fitting garment with short sleeves or sleeveless. It was worn by Samuel (1 Sam 2:19), by Saul (1 Sam 24:5), by David (1 Chr 15:27) and by other princes (Ezek 26:16). Aaron's robe, the blue robe of the ephod, was ornamented with little bells (Ex 28:31-35) which were thought to protect the priest from demonic attack, lest he die when he entered the holy place. The next garment mentioned is the *kuttōnet,** ("coat"), better rendered "tunic" (CCD, JB), which was an inner garment worn next to the skin, by ordinary people as well, since the time of Adam and Eve (Gen 3:21)! Among the gifts offered for the second temple after the Exile, figure a number of priestly "tunics" (Neh 7:70, 72). Aaron's *kuttōnet* was "of checker work" (RSV) "brocaded" (CCD), or "embroidered" (JB), varying translations of the Heb *tašbēṣ*.

On the *miṣnephet*, the high priest's "turban," there was a "plate" (*ṣîṣ*) of pure gold, seemingly a sort of golden "flower" (*ṣîṣ* : 1 Kg 6:18), symbol of life and salvation, inscribed : "Holy to the Lord" (Ex 28:36). Lev 8 :9, describing the actual investiture of Aaron by Moses, should probably be understood as follows : "And he set the turban upon his head, and on the turban, in front, he set the golden flower, the sign of consecration (*nezer*),** as the Lord commanded Moses." The anointing of the postexilic high priest had a royal significance. This can be said also of his headdress : the *nezer* is mentioned among the royal insignia (2 Sam 1:10; 2 Kg 11:12; Ps 89:39). In these texts the meaning suggested is obviously that of "crown" or "diadem." In Ps 132:18 it is said that the *nezer* of the Davidic king "will blossom."*** The headdress called *saniph*, which Joshua receives, is a "royal" apparel in Is 62 :3 and elsewhere;+ the *miṣnephet* itself (Ex 28:4) is worn by the prince in Ezek 21:31 (RSV 21:26). According to Zech 3:5, 9 a clean turban (*ṣaniph*) is placed on the head of the High Priest Joshua. Perhaps influenced by

Christian usage, CCD translates *miṣnephet* by "miter," while the *Bible Pirot-Clamer* prefers "tiare." "Last of all, the breastplate covered in precious stones (Ex 28:15-16) recalls the rich breastplate worn by the Pharaohs, and by the kings of Syria in imitation of them, as the finds at Byblos show; it is quite likely that the kings of Israel also wore a similar breastplate" (VAI, p. 400).*

The "girdle" or "sash" (*'abnēṭ*) to be worn by Aaron is embroidered with needlework (Ex 28:4, 38). As for Aaron's sons, the priests, they have to be provided with tunics, girdles and caps (*migba'ôt*); to them it is also prescribed to wear "linen breeches" (*mikn^{e}sê bād*), "to cover their naked flesh." They "shall be upon Aaron, and upon his sons, when they go into the tent of meeting, or when they come near the altar to minister in the holy place" (Ex 28:42 f.).** All the priests' vestments, it seems, were made of linen; wool is forbidden in Ezekiel's temple ordinances (44 :17). Linen is, in fact, the ritually clean fabric, worn by priests (Lev 6:10), by angels (Dan 10:5), and by the Lord's scribe (Ezek 9:2 :OAB).

In the ceremony of ordination sacrificial blood and anointing oil are sprinkled on Aaron and his sons, as well as on their garments; "and he and his garments shall be holy, and his sons and his sons' garments with him" (Ex 29:21; Lev 9:30). The ceremonial change of garments, finally, figures among the entrance and exit rites which condition the contact with the holy (Lev 16:4) and the return to normal life : "When the priests enter the holy place, they shall not go out of it into the outer court without laying there garments in which they minister, for these are holy; they shall put on other garments before they go near to that which is for the people" (Ezek 42:14).***

b) The Various Offices

Leaving for a subsequent section the study of the functions and duties of Israelite priesthood we shall here examine first the hierarchical organization of the priests and then discuss briefly the role played by the lower ranking Levitical personnel.

1. Chief Priests and Senior Officials

Although few statistics can be produced, it is certain that the Israelite sanctuaries and especially the temple were staffed with a large number of priests, apart from the lower functionaries (see VAI, pp. 377-378). There were eighty-five persons "wearing the linen ephod," with Ahimelech, at the sanctuary of Nob (1 Sam 22:18). In the first caravan returned to Jerusalem after the Exile a total of 4,289 priests are mentioned (Ezra 2:36-39; Neh 7:39-42).

There were obviously dignitaries among those priests. We usually think of the "high priests," but the term *hakkōhēn haggādôl* "high priest," occurs only four times in pre-exilic texts: once it designates Jehoiada in Jehoash's reign (2 Kg 12:11), three times it refers to Hilkiah under Josiah (2 Kg 22:4, 8, 23:4). Both of them are more often called "the priests." They were in fact "chief priests," and the postexilic term "high priest" used in these contexts must have been introduced by later editors. Although the king was in Israel the patron of priesthood, there exists no real reason to suppose that he performed the functions of high priest, explaining thus the late appearance of the term. It is true, however, that Joshua, the postexilic high priest, is made recipient of the royal crown in Zech 6:11, although Zorobabel, the civil governor, was, it seems, originally meant in the text. In fact the "royal" character of the high priest was asserted only little by little (VAI, p. 378).

The head of the clergy is then usually identified simply as "the priests." Jehoiada (2 Chr 23:9; Jer 29:26), Hilkiah and Uriah (2 Kg 16:10-11) were "the priests" in different periods of the monarchy, Zadok had been appointed "the priest" by Solomon (1 Kg 2:35), and even sooner Heli (1 Sam 2:11), Ahimelech (1 Sam 21:1-2), and Abiathar (1 Sam 23:9) functioned as "the priests." The Priestly Document naturally speaks of Aaron, "the priest,"* while in 2 Chr 31:10 the formula is expanded to "the priest, the head of the house of Zadok." Another title *kōhēn hārō'š*, "chief priest," occurs in connection with those taken to Nebuchadnezzar at the fall of Jerusalem: "And the captain of the guard took Seraiah the chief priest (lit. "head priest"), and Zephaniah the second priest, and the three keepers of the threshold" (2 Kg 25:18= Jer 52:24). In 2 Chr 19:11 Amariah, who served under Jehoshaphat, is given the title of chief priest, as also Azariah, who, with eighty priests of the Lord, withstood king Uzziah for burning incense to the Lord (2 Chr 26:20).

Both "the priest" and the "chief priest" stood at the head of the priestly personnel in their respective centers of worship. Yet "one should not imagine that this head of the priesthood had the importance or the rank which the high priests had after the Exile. Before 587, the principal priest had control over the clergy of Jerusalem only, and he was himself responsible to the king (cf. 2 Kg 12:8, 16:10), whereas the high priest after the Exile was the religious and civil head of the community" (VAI, p. 378).

In the text quoted above (2 Kg 25:18), Zephaniah is mentioned as the "second priest" (*kōhēn mišnè*), an office which is also referred to in connection with Josiah's reform : "And the king commanded Hilkiah, the high priest, and the priests of the second order (*kōhanê hammišnè*), and the keepers of the threshold, to bring out of the temple of the Lord all the vessels made for Baal, for Asherah, and for all the host of heaven" (2 Kg 23:4).* The "keepers of the threshold," three in number according to 2 Kg 25:18, were, as it seems, the senior officials of the temple, and not mere doorkeepers. They were in charge, under Josiah, of the collections of money destined to repair the temple (2 Kg 12:9, 22:4).

The *ziqnê hakkōhanîm*, "the elders of the priest" (JB), or "the senior priests" (RSV) held also an important position among the Israelite clergy. During the Sennacherib siege, a distressed Hezekiah sent a group of these to prophet Isaiah, along with Eliakim and Shebna (2 Kg 19:2= Is 37:2). They are mentioned again, together with "the elders of the people," as accompanying Jeremiah in the symbolic action of the broken flask (Jer 19:2). As the "elders of the people" (cf. 1 Sam 30:26-31) were very likely the heads of families, so also it can be assumed that the "elders of the priests" were the heads of the priestly families : "thus they would be forerunners of those men who headed the various divisions of the clergy after the Exile, the origins of which are attributed to the time of David by 1 Chr 24:1-18" (VAI, p. 379).

2. *The High Priest*

The title *hakkōhēn haggādôl*, "the high priest," is mentioned in Ezekiel and occurs only rarely even in the postexilic texts of the Hebrew Bible : three times in the Pentateuch (Num 35:25,28,32),** four times in the Chronicler, as applied to Hilkiah (2 Chr 34:9) and to Eliashib (Neh 3:1, 20, 13:28), once in Sir 50:1 (Heb) eulogizing Simon "the high priest," while all other uses refer to Joshua, the contemporary of Zerubbabel. "The title, therefore, certainly existed from the moment of the return from exile. A papyrus from Elephantine,+ dated 408 B.C., refers to the high priest of Jerusalem ,Yehohanan, as *kahna rabba*, which is the Aramaic equivalent of *kōhēn gādôl*. On the other hand, the term was rarely used, and people usually said simply 'the priest,' as they had done before the Exile, and as the Priestly texts of the Pentateuch have it. It is only in the Mishnah and in the Talmudic treatises that the title is commonly used, either in Hebrew (*kohēn gādôl*) or in Aramaic (*kahna rabba*)" (VAI, p. 398).

Azariah, "the chief priest" (2 Chr 31:10), is called *n^e^gîd bet ha'elōhîm*, "chief officer of the house of God" (RSV), a few verses further (v. 13). The same Hebrew formula (see also 1 Chr 9:11) elsewhere concerns the high priest Seraiah and is translated by another interpreter "prefect of the Temple of God" (Neh 11 :11, JB). The term *nāgîd* had been used in connection with the anointing of Saul "to be prince (*nāgîd*) over my people Israel" (1 Sam 9:16, 10:1) and to describe David "prince over Israel" (2 Sam 5:2, 7:8) as well as Hezekiah, "the prince of my people" (2 Kg 20:5). In the Chronicler's period and language *nāgîd* normally applies to officials and men of high rank, but the three texts relating to Azariah and Seraiah may preserve the nobler religious meaning of anointed prince or God appointed leader. According to J. Morgenstern, the king in the pre-exilic period functioned as "the supreme ecclesiastical authority and officiant of the nation," with a chief priest over every local sanctuary. In the early post-exilic period "the anointed priest," also called "the priest who was the greatest of his brethren," superseded the king as the chief priest and the recognized head of the theocratic community. Only after 411 B.C. did the office of *kōhen gādôl*, "high priest," in the true sense of the term, come into being.[43] The high priest is in fact called *hakkōhēn hammašîaḥ*, "the anointed priest," in Lev 4:3, 5, 16, a title which refers to a rite of his consecration. And in Dan 9:25 and 11:22, the phrases "an anointed one, a prince" (or "Anointed Prince") and "the prince of the covenant" refer to the high priest.

Recapitulating the instruction given to Moses concerning the Tabernacle and its ministers, Ex 40 describes the ritual of the priestly consecration :

> Then you shall bring Aaron and his sons to the door of the tent of meeting, and shall wash them with water, and put upon Aaron the holy garments, and you shall anoint him and consecrate him, that he may serve me as priest. You shall bring his sons also and put coats (=tunics) on them, and anoint them, as you anointed their father, that they may serve me as priests : and their anointing shall admit them to a perpetual priesthood throughout their generations (vv. 12-15).

In Ex 29:4 and Lev 8:6 also, a full bath is required in view of the pre-consecration ritual purity, whereas washing the hands and the feet suffices before entering the tent of meeting (cf. Ex 40:29). But the high priest will take a full bath before entering the holy place (Lev 16:4). In

43 J. Morgenstern, "A Chapter in the History of High-Priesthood," AmJSemLang 55 (1938), p. 377.

other instances, regarding both the priests and the laymen, washing of persons of clothes is prescribed to remove uncleanness contracted by the contact with the carcass of unclean animals (Lev 11:25), with a person having an itching disease (13:34), with the ashes of a red heifer (Num 19:7-10), with the scapegoat (Lev 16:26), or in various other cases (Lev 15:16-20, 16:28, 19:19). These washings and purifications, as well as many others, very often archaic customs of primitive belief, served in their new context "to separate Israel from the pagan world around it, and to inculcate the idea of Yahweh's transcendent holiness and of the holiness which his chosen people ought to preserve" (VAI, p. 460).

The passage quoted above (Ex 40:12-15) belongs, like most of the P writings, to the latest redaction of the Pentateuch, and is, therefore, postexilic. What concerns the anointing of the sacred ministers reflects besides a practice that did not exist before the Exile. In the P tradition itself one series of texts reserves the anointing to the high priest alone (Ex 29:4-9; Lev 4:3, 5 16, 6; 13), while another asserts it of all the priests.[44] Taking into account all these facts and others mentioned above, it can be reasonably assumed that "after the disappearance of the monarchy, the royal anointing was transfered to the high priest as head of the people, and later extended to all the priests" (VAI, p. 105). For in ancient Israel anointing is a religious rite reserved to the king, whom it constitutes *per antonamasian* the "Anointed One" (1 Sam 24:6),* the *mashiaḥ* (*messiah*), main protagonist of the Messianic hope (Ps 2:2).[45] In the next chapter the high priests and their anointing in the light of sources belonging to the later Jewish period will be studied. For the present, the issue is the mode of succession of the Zadokite high priests.**

Twelve successors of Zadok are listed in 1 Chr 6:9-15 (= MT 5:34-41), from Ahimaaz, Zadok's son (2 Sam 15:36), to Jehozadak, the father of Joshua who was the first high priest after the restoration (Hag 1:1). Since Zadok's ancestors (1 Chr 6:3-8) are also twelve in number, from

---

[44] Ex 28:41, 30:30, 40:12-15; Lev 7:35-36, 10:7; Num 3:3. On anointing see VAI, pp. 105 and 399-400. The existence of two traditions left its trace in Lev 6:13(=20), where the verse starts with a plural and continues with a singular; unless this is a collective singular including the whole line of high priests (see M. Noth, *Leviticus* 55-56).

[45] On "royal messianism" see J. Coppens, *Le messianisme Royal* (Paris, 1969) (with extensive bibliography) [=NouvRevTh 90 (1968), pp. 30-49, 225-251, 479-512, 622-650, 834-863, 937-975]. On royal anointing see R. de Vaux, "Le roi d'Israel, vassal de Yahvé," *Bible et Orient*, pp. 287-301 [=Mélanges Tisserant, v. 1 (Rome, 1964), pp. 119-133].

the making of the Tent in the desert to the building of the Temple, a period of 480 years (1 Kg 6:1), or twelve generations of 40 years, it can be assumed that the genealogical symmetry is deliberately designed to set the foundation of Solomon's Temple as marking the middle year in the history of Israel's sanctuary (cf. VAI, p. 375). Other indications point to an artificial arrangement of successors. Besides being incomplete the list includes names of persons not related to each other as father to son. Thus Azariah (v. 9) was one of Zadok's sons (1 Kg 4:2), not his grandson. Furthermore, the series Amariah-Ahitub-Zadok appears twice (in vv. 7-8 and 11-12). The list appears in fact to have been composed from several groups of names. Historical evidence can line up ten distinctly identified persons, whose names would account for all the leading priests at Jerusalem from Zadok to the Exile : Zadok (1 Kg 2:35), Azariah (1 Kg 4:2), Amariah (2 Chr 19:11), Jehoiada (2 Chr 24:2, 15), Zechariah (2 Chr 24:20), Azariah (2 Chr 26:17), Urijah (2 Kg 16:10), Azariah (2 Chr 31:10), Hilkiah (2 Kg 22-23), Seraiah (2 Kg 25:18).

Having re-examined the whole question, J. R. Bartlett concludes : "We notice that there is not much evidence that the succession from priest to priest was hereditary. Apart from Zadok and his son Azariah, whose case we shall discuss below, no priest is clearly said to have his son as his successor".[46] It is certainly clear, he adds, that Zadok's was not the only priesthood in Jerusalem under David and Solomon. David's sons were priests (2 Sam 8:18), so was Ira the Jairite (20:26), and under Solomon Zabud the son of Nathan was also priest (1 Kg 4:5). It is unlikely in fact that exclusive prerogatives were granted to one priestly family; it would have prepared the way for the eventual growth of a dangerous rival power, threatening that of the king.*

Another plausible source can throw light on the mode of succession of the leading priests. It is the distinctive meaning of the words *nāgîd*, "prince," *rōʾš*, "head," and *gādôl*, "great," used in their titles. Account being taken of what these terms suggest in other Biblical contexts there is reason for believing that "the leading priests in Jerusalem between Zadok and the exile were not yet primarily the chief cultic officers of the nation, taking their office from their lineage, but were rather men chosen and appointed by the king for their outstanding ability to take office as 'the chief priest,' and as one of the 'rulers of the

[46] J. R. Bartlett, "Zadok..." JThSt 19 (1968), pp. 7-8.

house of God,' with administrative oversight of the temple."[47] Perhaps the truth is that hereditary succession was the general rule,* while the king not rarely exercised his right to appoint unprivileged "outsiders."

3. The Minor Clergy

In the course of our study of the differing traditions on the priest-Levite problem the status of the lower-ranking personnel has been also discussed. It is not our intention to give a complete picture of their duties and activities, but we shall single out the more prominent and distinctive features of their function in and around the Israelite sanctuary and temple.

The Levites were originally ministers of the ark, and this, as stated, was connected with their special role in the amphictyony, a concept of Deuteronomy, which also states clearly the initial vocation of the Levites : "At that time the Lord set apart the tribe of Levi to carry the ark of the covenant of the Lord, to stand before the Lord to minister to him and to bless in his name to this day" (10:8). The Chronicler naturally sees this vocation actualized by an ordinance of David : Then David said, "No one but the Levites may carry the ark of the Lord and to minister to him for ever" (1 Chr 15:2). Elsewhere texts are obscured by the contamination of traditions, but the fact remains that the Levites were primarily meant for the service of the ark. The ark was, however, soon set to rest permanently in the sanctuary and the Levites are represented in Ezekiel and the Priestly tradition as minor clergy at the service of the Zadokite and Aaronic priests.

According to the Chronicler David himself distributed the priests into twenty-four classes (1 Chr 24), classified the Levites as Gershonites, Kohathites, and Merarites (1 Chr 23), and instituted from among them twenty-four classes of singers (1 Chr 25), as well as several classes of gate-keepers (1 Chr 26:1-19). "In these chapters he is describing a later situation in which door-keepers and singers had been incorporated into the Levites; but he is not inventing everything. Though the pre-exilic texts never mention the singers or the door-keepers, every large sanctuary in ancient times had them, and the liturgical services of the Temple always needed such men" (VAI, p. 382). The Psalm titles, which probably echo an authentic tradition, suggest the same conclusion,

---

[47] J. R. Bartlett, "Zadok..." JThSt 19 (1968), p. 15. See the discussion, pp. 11-15. These leading priests were chosen from priestly families, not from one only.

as regards singers, from whom small Psalm collections got their names. The attribution of psalms to Asaph, Heman, Ethan and the sons of Korah, S. Mowinckel believes, reflects "a dependable tradition concerning the circles in which these psalms came into being... They are the names of such persons—historical or legendary— as were supposed to be the ancestors of the guilds of the temple singers."[48] There are indications that the first choir of singers for the temple at Jerusalem was recruited from among non-Israelites (VAI, p. 382). In any case, since singers and gate-keepers returned from the exile (Ezra 2:41-42; Neh 7:44-45), it must be assumed that their office existed during the first temple period, although presumably they would not then have been Levites, but free laymen employed in the temple. These free men are to be distinguished from the *n^etinim*, "those given" (to the temple), mentioned expressly in Ezra 2:43, 58, 70; 7:7, 24; 8:17, 20; Neh 3:26, 31; 7:46, 60, 73; 10:29; 11:3, 21 and 1 Chr 9:2. These were mostly foreigners who, like the Gibeonites (Jos 9:27) had come into the hands of the Hebrews usually as captives of war, and had been dedicated as temple servants (Ezra 8:20 : OAB, p. 274).

In the Chronicler' system the three head singers under David trace their ancestry to the three sons of Levi : Heman descends from Kohath, Asaph from Jahath, Ethan (= Jeduthun : 1 Chr 25:3) from Merari (1 Chr 6:33-47 = MT 6:18-32). Under these three great names are distributed twenty-four divisions of musicians, whose names are listed in a highly artificial arrangement.* The varying order of names in the ancestors' lists seems to result from rivalry among the groups of singers. The sons of Asaph, who had been in exile, were given seniority, but the sons of Heman claimed the same privilege on other grounds (see 1 Chr 6:33, 15:17, 19).

Six families of gate keepers returned from exile, according to Ezra 2:42 : a total of 139 persons (cf. Neh 7:45, 11:19), who appear levitized as descendants of Korah in 1 Chr 9:17-19 (cf. 1 Chr 6:7). It is said there of Shallum, Akkub, Talmon, Ahiman and their kinsmen : "they were the gatekeepers of the camp of the Levites," in the desert days (cf. 2:17). But the Obed-edom guild of gate-keepers were later promoted to be singer-musicians (1 Chr 16:41-42), presumably because Jeduthun, Obed-edom's father (1 Chr 16:38), had been a singer. The Korahites, known as gatekeepers (Ex 6:24; 1 Chr 26:1), are given as singers in 2 Chr 20:19 and a number of Psalms are attributed to their guild

[48] S. Mowinckel, *The Psalms in Israel's Worship*, v. 2 (Oxford, 1962), p. 96.

(Pss 42-49, except 43, and 84, 85, 87, 88), The frontiers separating the two offices apparently had become less clearly defined.

The minor clergy was active in other offices too. According to 1 Chr 32:2-5, the 38,000 Levites numbered in the census were assigned their duties by David himself, in the following way : "Twenty-four thousand of these shall have charge of the work in the house of the Lord, six thousand shall be officers and judges, four thousand gatekeepers, and four thousand shall offer praises to the Lord with the instruments which I have made for praise." These figures are indeed fantastic, but they show the relative importance of the duties involved. The large figures of 1 Chr 23:4-5 are to be interpreted within their literary context, as modes of expressing how great was David's vision of the temple and its worship as an ideal religious institution. The same is true of the amount of gold and silver David invested to prepare the building of the temple (1 Chr 22:14), some five billion dollars ! (see OAB, p. 521). As regards the musicians and the gatekeepers more sober figures are supplied further on by the Chronicler himself, 288 and 96 persons respectively (1 Chr 25:9-31 ; 26:7-11).

The first and largest category of Levites are devoted to the service of the temple in various capacities,* known also from chs 3, 4 and 8 of Numbers, where the Levites assist the Aaronic priests. As for the "officers" (*šōṭ^e^rim*) or "clerks", mentioned in 1 Chr 23:4, they could have been secretaries, and the LXX translates the term by *grammateis*, "scribes" (JB). More precisely they should be described as "clerks of the courts, assistant officials," also appointed for duties unconnected with the temple (1 Chr 26:29).**

c) *The Priestly Duties*

The main duties of the Israelite priests, which are manifold, can be related to one or another of the three capital functions stated in Moses' final blessing, when he associates the name of Levi with the prerogatives of priesthood : "Give to Levi thy Thummim, and thy Urim to thy godly one... they shall teach Jacob thy ordinances, and Israel thy law ; they shall put incense before thee, and whole burnt offering upon thy altar" (Dt 33:8a, 10). The general meaning of the text is clear : the Israelite priest is dispenser of oracles, instructor in the Law, minister of the altar. The nature and order of these duties corresponds well enough to the pattern which, as far as we know, characterizes the development of priestly function, from an originally mantic mold to the later prominence given to sacred knowledge and sacrificial rites. Priesthood itself, as comparative study shows, even when initiated as a religious venture founded on individual charisma and revelation, gradually emerges as an institution established on tradition and devoted to its preservation. The priest, at this stage, becomes mostly the official who safeguards and applies the prescribed set of regulations.[49] Sacrificial worship in Israel came to be predominantly an institution regulated by statute, effecting atonement independently of any spontaneous feeling on the part of the individual. Yet the prophetic element associated with priesthood tempered somewhat the natural consequences of its distinctive development.

1. Dispensing of Oracles

To Jethro, who advises him to cease judging all the people alone like a bedouin chief, Moses explains : the people come to me "to inquire (*daraš*) of God" (to seek a verdict by oracle) and "I make them know the statutes of God and his decisions" (*tôrōtāw* : Ex 18:15-16). It was ruled, however, that henceforth ordinary cases would be handled by lay leaders (18 :21-22; cf. Num 11 :24-25), while cases without legal precedent would be submitted to Moses himself (Ex 18:26). In the later situation "every one who sought the Lord (*kol mebaqqēš Yhwh*) would go out to the tent of meeting," where "the Lord used to speak to Moses face to face, as a man who speaks to his friend" (Ex 33:7, 11). This personal privilege of Moses (Num 12 :6) the priests did not share but had to consult the Lord by means of the ephod and of the Urim and Thummim.

In the more ancient texts, prior to the P tradition, the *ephod* is first mentioned in the book of Judges. We learn that Mikah the Ephraimite, who had a shrine, "made an ephod and teraphim,* and installed one of his sons, who became his priest" (17:5). The Danite spies looking for a favorable place to re-settle their tribe ask Mikah's Levite, now his priest, to inquire (*šā'al*) of God about the success of their mission, as if to consult an oracle was his main function. It is not said how he did it, but later the Danite warriors take him to be the priest of the tribe and carry along "the graven image, the ephod, the teraphim and the molten

[49] On the religious structure of priesthood, see W. Eichrodt, *Theology*, v. 1, pp. 402-406. Specifically on Dt 33:8-11 see A. Deissler, *Der Priesterliche Dienst*, v. 1 (Freiburg i. Br. 1970) 24-32.

image" (Jg 18 :5, 18-20). Nothing indicates in these texts that the ephod was worn as a garment.

Leaving aside Gideon's ephod (Jg 8 :7), a singular case, * we find that the ephod is mentioned several times in the first book of Samuel as an object which is carried (*nāśa'*)[50] as a receptacle for the oracular lots.** These lots, Urim and Thummim, had a conventional meaning, probably "yes" or "no", and when drawn gave the divine answer (1 Sam 14 :41).+ The use of alternatives with successive eliminations could work out even an elaborate answer (cf. Jos 7 :14-18). "The care of the sacred lots was reserved to the Levitical priests (Num 27 :21 ; Dt 33 :8). After the reign of David the practice was discontinued and never resumed (cf. Ezra 2 :63). But the name was still used for part of the high priest's vestment" (JB, p. 361).

In other texts the linen ephod (*'ephôd bād*) is a light ceremonial garment, a loincloth, with which young Samuel (1 Sam 2:18) and king David (2 Sam 6:14) are girded (*ḥāgûr*) at the waist. Mention of the ephod recurs next only in the postexilic texts of the Priestly tradition, describing the vestments of the high priest (see e.g. Ex 25:7 ; Lev 8:8). Here the ephod is "a sort of apron hung on the front of the priest's body and fastened around the waist by means of an attached belt; it was made of fine linen cloth (*šēs*) which was embroidered with gold thread and purple and scarlet woolen yarn ; each of its two shoulder straps bore a large precious stone set in gold filigree work. This ephod served primarily as a support for the breastpiece, which was an oracular instrument" (EncDictBibl, c. 673). The breastpiece (*ḥošen*)[51] of judgment, i.e. of oracular decision (Ex 28:15, 29, 30) was a pouch containing the sacred lots (cf. Pr 16:33), Urim and Tummim (Lev 8:8). But the garment piece was now merely ornamental, serving perhaps to connect artificially the high priest's ephod with the ancient oracular ephod. According to a later development, stones engraved with the names of the Israelite tribes were fixed on the ephod and on the breastpiece, for the obvious purpose of reminding Yahweh of his people (Ex 28 :12, 29).[52]

---

[50] See 1 Sam 2:28; 14:3; 22:18; 23:6; 30:7. RSV has in 1 Sam 14:3 "wearing an ephod," but the translation "carrying an ephod" is proposed in the note. According to J. Morgenstern the "ephod," related as term to the Arabic *kubbe*, was originally a tent-shrine, which housed the tribal deities (*teraphim*). After the Settlement it became a miniature cult-object (HebUCAnn, 18, 1944, 1-52).

[51] On the ephod and the breastpiece see I. Friedrich, *Ephod und Choschen im Lichte des Alten Orient*. Wiener Beiträge zur Theologie 20 (Freiburg i. Br., 1968).

[52] See J. S. Harris, "The Stones of the High Priest's Breastplate," AnnLeedsUnivOrSoc 5 (1963-65), pp. 40-62.; cf. J. Massingberd Ford, "The Jewel of Discernment (A Study of Stone Symbolism)," BZ 11 (1967) 109-116.

To sum up, it can be said that "ephod" in the Biblical evidence is a cultic term concerned with oracular consultation as a function of priesthood. Outside Israel the word *'epod* occurs in Ugaritic, apparently to designate a kind of garment.* The same meaning can be read behind the feminine plural *epādātum* of the Old Assyrian texts from Cappadocia. Perhaps the garment gradually became a distinctive priestly garb and the name was received as such in the Israelite cult terminology. The most ancient representatives of Israelite priesthood, it can be assumed, dispensed oracles by drawing from a pouch of their "ephod" the sacred lots. This was a singular form of oracular consultation comparable to the *istiqsām* of the *sadin* among the ancient Arabs.

The use of the Urim and Thummim** as oracular devices disappeared early, as we have seen, probably even before the building of the first temple. "Achab and Joram of Israel and the kings of Judah contemporary with them (1 Kg 20:13-14, 22:6; 2 Kg 3:11) consult Yahweh through prophets, in circumstances where Saul and David used to consult him by the ephod" (VAI, p. 353). From 2 Kg 22 :14-20 we learn that on Josiah's command (v. 13) Hilkiah the priest and his assistants sought and obtained oracular advice from Huldah the prophetess in connection with the words of the scroll found in the temple. In post-exilic Jerusalem there was no priest to handle the Urim and Thummim (Neh 7:65), which, says the Jewish tradition, were absent from the second temple.+ It is, however, probable that in individual cases the priests continued to give answers in God's name, although no recourse was made to the traditional means of consultation. Biblical evidence can be adduced in support of this (e.g. Os 4:6; 7:26; Mic 3:11; Jer 18:18; Mal 2:7), even without raising the question of the so-called "cultic prophets."

2. *Instruction in the Torah*

Besides handling the Urim and Thummim the Levitical priests have the duty, Moses said (Dt 33:10) to "teach" Israel the Lord's ordinances (*mišpāṭîm*) and his law (*tôrâ*).++ In Dt the Levites are primarily priests of the divine law and the sacrificial cult plays a surprisingly small part in their ministry.[53] The Hebrew word for "to teach," used in this context, is *yārâh*, conjugated as a causative, and as such it also serves to form the word *tôrâ*,+++ as well as *môreh*, "teacher" (Pr 5:13), a term

[53] See H. J. Kraus, *Worship in Israel*, p. 97.

applied also to God (Job 36:22). To correct the situation among the new settler in occupied Samaria the king of Assyria commanded : "Send there one of the priests whom you carried away thence; and let him go and dwell there, and teach them the law of the god of the land. So one of the priests... came and dwelt in Bethel, and taught them (*w*ᵉ*yōrēm*) how they should fear the Lord" (2 Kg 17:27-28). Centuries later, the Chronicler recalled that "for a long time Israel was without a teaching priest (*kōhēn môreh* : 2 Chr 15:3). Jeremiah's enemies argued that the disappearance of their censurer would not affect the work of three classes of spiritual leaders, "for the law shall not perish from the priest, nor counsel from the wise, nor the word from the prophet" (Jer 18:18; cf. Ez 7:26). The priest being one who teaches (cf. Mic 3:11), it is not surprising that the Lord himself proclaims through his prophet : "Because you have rejected knowledge, I reject you from being a priest to me" (Hos 4:6). The knowledge *of God* is of course involved here, as in other texts of Hosea (5:4, 6:3, 6) and this conforms to the programmatic statement of Dt 33:10. Malachi showed a particular respect for the priestly "instruction" : "For the lips of a priest should guard knowledge (*daʿat*) and men should seek instruction (*tôrâ*) from his mouth, for he is the messenger of the Lord of hosts" (2:7; cf. 2:6, 8, 9). The priest performed his teaching duty in the sanctuary to which he belonged,* mainly in the temple, where, it was expected, "the God of Jacob would teach" the nations "his ways," "for out of Zion shall go forth the law, and the word of the Lord from Jerusalem" (Is 2:3).

Ezekiel prophesied thus on the land of Judah : "Her priests have done violence to my law (*tôrātî*) and have profaned my holy things; they have made no distinction between the holy and the common, neither have they taught the difference between the unclean and the clean, and they have disregarded my sabbaths, so that I am profaned among them" (22:26; cf. 44:23). Aaron is instructed "to teach the people of Israel all the statutes (*ḥuqqîm*) which the Lord has spoken to them by Moses" (Lev 10:11). Among these figure especially the precept of distinguishing the clean from the unclean, the holy from the profane (v. 11). After the Exile Haggai requests from the priests a decision, a *tôrâ*, about the effects of touching clean and unclean things (2 :11-13). The priest was a specialist of these cultic precepts, but his teaching role gradually extended, when these simple instructions or *tôrôt*, were collected and included in a vaster *corpus*⁺ called "the Law of Elohim" (Jos 24:26), "the Law of Yahweh" (Ps 1:2), "the Law of God which was given by Moses" (Neh 10 :29). "And Moses wrote this law (*tôrâ*), and gave it to the priests the sons of Levi, who carried the ark of the covenant of the Lord, and to all the elders of Israel" (Dt 31:9). When Jeremiah complains, "the priests did not say, 'where is the Lord?', those who handle the law did not know me" (2:8), he in fact considers the priest as being normally the interpreter of the Torah, understood as regulating the moral conduct, as defining the conditions of access to proper worship, as governing generally the relations of man with God. After the Exile the priests increasingly shared with others the task of teaching the Torah. "The Levites, who by then had been taken away from strictly priestly functions, became preachers and catechists. In the end, teaching was given quite apart from worship, in the synagogues, and a new class arose, of scribes and teachers of the Law. This class was open to all, priests and Levites and layfolk alike, and eventually displaced the priestly cast in the work of teaching" (VAI, p. 355).*

3. *Offering of Sacrifices at the Altar*

In the beginning of this chapter we have seen that the patriarchs, private Israelites, and leaders of the nation offered sacrifices in the earlier period of its history. Yet the priests were the normal ministers of sacrifice and as early as the 9th or 8th century the Blessings of Moses consider this function as their privilege,+ particularly if it involves ministering at the altar: "They shall put incense before thee, and whole burnt offerings upon thy altar" (Dt 33:10). The compilers of the Holiness Code based the special rules of purity for priests on their function at the altar: "They shall be holy to their God, and not profane the name of their God; for they offer the offerings by fire to the Lord, the bread of their God; therefore they shall be holy" (Lev 21:6).

The commonest word for "a sacrifice" is *zebaḥ* (1 Sam 15:22), while the corresponding verb *zābaḥ* denotes both the slaughtering of animals for food (1 Sam 28:24; Dt 12:15) and the sacrificial immolation (2 Sam 6:13; Dt 15:21). The altar is consequently called *mizbēaḥ*. The immolation of the victims was not, however, the essence of sacrifice, but its preparation. "The Priest's role, properly speaking, did not begin until the victim was brought into contact with the altar, and it consisted in pouring the blood around the altar" (VAI, p. 416). This conforms to the importance of the blood in OT sacrifice: "For the life of the flesh is in the blood; and I have given it to you so that you may on the altar perform the rite of expiation for your lives; for it is the blood which expiates by the life which is in it" (Lev 17:11). The blood was the holiest part of the victim and its ritual manipulation was reserved to the priest,[54] whose privilege it was also to place upon the altar that part of the sacrifice which belonged to God.[55] To "go up to the altar" is in fact the distinctive feature of the priestly function (1 Sam 2:28; 2 Kg 23:9) and only the descendants of Aaron could offer incense because it had to be burnt on the altar.[56]

According to Chronicles, "Aaron was set apart to consecrate the most holy things,* that he and his sons for ever should burn incense before the Lord, and minister to him and *pronounce blessings* in his name for ever" (1 Chr 23 :13). Deuteronomy formulates somewhat differently the duties of the Levitical priests, but it includes blessing : "At that time the Lord set apart the tribe of Levi to carry the ark of the covenant of the Lord, to stand before the Lord to minister to him and *to bless*, in his name, to this day" (Dt 10 :8; cf. 21 :5). "Ministers of the altar" (Jl 1:13), the Israelite priests were also "the ministers of the Lord" (Jl 1:13, 2:17) and as such pronounced blessings in his name (Num 6: 22-27).[57] This was done in the temple, mainly in connection with the sacrifice (Lev 9:22, Sir 50:20-21). Later, blessings would be pronounced in the synagogue and only by a priest.

The concentration of worship in the Jerusalem temple brought to an increasing prominence the whole apparatus of the cult, especially that of sacrificial worship. This "resulted partly from the interest taken by the king in the cultus and its outward display, but also from the natural tendency to elaboration characteristic of great cultic centers. The earlier proportion between sacrificial worship and the imparting of the *tōrā* was consequently invented; compared with the lucrative traffic of the Temple the ministry of God's word declined in importance and interest, and as a result the priestly profession lost any really profound influence."[58] The prophet Hosea, using the formula, "like people, like priest," deplores that the priests of his day do not dispense to the faithful the knowledge of God, that "they feed on the [sacrifices for] sin of

---

[54] Cf. Lev 3:8, 13; 4:5-7; 17:6.

[55] Cf. Lev 1:7-9; 4:10, 19, 31, 35; 5:12; 6:14-15; 9:7-20; Ezek 43:19, 27.

[56] Num 16:40; 1 Chr 23:13; 2 Chr 26:16-18.

[57] On the OT priestly blessing, see C. Westermann, *Der Segen in der Bibel und im Handeln der Kirche* (Munich, 1968), pp. 45-47.

[58] W. Eichrodt, *Theology*, v. 1, p. 400. We do not treat here of the revenues of the clergy. See VAI 379-382, 403-405 and O. Eissfeldt, *Erstlinge und Zehnten im Alten Testament* (Leipzig 1971); for the later period see E. Schürer, *Geschichte des jüdischen Volkes im Zeitalter Jesu Christi*, v. 2 (4th ed., Leipzig 1907) 297-317.

my people; they are greedy for their iniquity" (Hos 4:6-9). Those priests who failed to instruct the people on the correct use of sacrifice fell implicitly under the censure of the prophets who condemmed the excessive estimation of ritual worship not conducive to a truly moral life (Hos 6:6; 1 Sam 15:22), who repeatedly reminded their generation that the offering of victims alone cannot lead to the Lord (Hos 5:6; Jer 29 :13), cannot replace the duty of being just, charitable, humble, and of avoiding evil (Mic 6 :6-8; Is 1 :11-17).

How distinctive Israelite priesthood was in respect to the contemporary priesthoods of the pagan world, how superior to them in its functions and requirements, this is a theme which rightly held the attention of older authors, and to which we shall return in the general conclusion. In Israel, as elsewhere, the priests were the specialists of worship, and worship in the OT is often described as *'abōdâ*, "service,"[59] to which the Levites are dedicated : "And Aaron shall offer the Levites before the Lord as a wave offering from the people of Israel, that it may be theirs to do the service of the Lord" (Num 8:11). The cult was "for Yahweh," not for Israel, and the presence of Yahweh is a theme usually connected with the cult (cf. Zeph 1:7; Zech 2:13). By the cult Israel expected to be brought to the remembrance of Yahweh.[60] The Israelite priest, as the leader in worship, performed the mediatorial role which was recalled at the beginning of this chapter. The Epistle to the Hebrews will explain of course that the OT cult institution was earthly and deficient (8-10). Yet the Levitical priests played a providential, and beneficial role in sustaining a temporary form of valid worship until "the time of reformation" (Heb 9:10), until the new covenant would be inaugurated by the sacrifice of Christ, Priest and Victim.

---

[59] "To serve God," Ex 3 :12; 9 :1,13. The cult as "service" of the Lord is mentioned, e.g., in Num 4:4; Jos 22:27; 1 Chr 24:3; 2 Chr 35:16.

[60] See Ex 30:16; Lev 2:2; Num 5:15.

CHAPTER FIVE

JEWISH PRIESTHOOD AT THE TIME OF JESUS

When the Jewish people solemnly renewed their adherence to the covenant and the law at the time of Ezra, the priest-scribe, and Nehemiah the governor (Neh 8-9), it was a turning-point of Israel's history. The law had become, in a new manner, the constitution of the community. This law community would survive without political nationality. In the following centuries this complex of beliefs and practices which is called "Judaism" or "later Judaism" gradually gave a new religious physiognomy to the community reborn after the national disaster.* During this period the priests increasingly tended to be only cult functionaries while the doctors of the law gained in prominence. The temple of Jerusalem remained the only lawful place to offer sacrifices. Synagogal worship, being non-sacrificial, had need of priestly ministers, while it provided the scribes and rabbis with ample opportunities to promote the study of the law, especially on Sabbaths. Yet priesthood maintained its determining influence on Jewish religion at least until the destruction of the second temple in 70 A.D. We shall examine anew some of its essential features in the light of the literary sources more or less contemporary with the life of Jesus : mainly the New Testament, the works of Philo, of Flavius Josephus, and the rabbinical writings. The community of Qumran, whose distinctive existence falls within the period under study, will receive some attention, especially as regards priestly messianism, a concept not unconnected with the high priesthood of Christ himself.

A. A Class and its Divisions

Being an hereditary institution Jewish priesthood tended to become a caste, firmly established in its traditions and privileges. We shall see how it was organized, after examining the statements of the New Testament on the Jewish priests and Levites.

It is remarkable that the Greek word for priest, *hiereus*, is used in the NT only in regard to the Jewish priests (cf. Mt 8:4), to Christ (Heb 10: 21), and to all Christians in general : "And he made us a kingdom, priests to His God and Father," which is often smoothed out to "a kingdom of priests" (Rev 1:6).[1] In this last sense the term appears to be taken figuratively, like *hierateuma*, "priesthood," in 1 Pet 2:5, 9 (designating the prerogatives of the baptized), dependent of Ex 19:6, where all Israel is said to be consecrated to God in a special way.[2] Apart from the Epistle to the Hebrews no NT writing passes judgment on Jewish priesthood as a whole although in the parable of the good Samaritan the priests and Levites are understood not to have acted as might have been expected of them (Lk 10:31-32). As Jesus recommended that his followers practice and observe what the scribes and the Pharisees sitting on Moses' seat said should be done (Mt 23:3), so also he would likely acknowledge the validity of the Jewish priests' ministry at least for the time being. Having cured a leper he told him : "Go, show yourself to the priest, and offer the gift that Moses commanded, for a proof to the people (Mt 8:4; cf. Lk 17:14; Lev 13:2-17). Thus the priest himself will be brought to testify in favor of the authority of Jesus. But by expelling the merchants and money changers from the temple area (Mt 21:12-17; Jn 2:13-25) he indirectly rebuked those who apparently tolerated their presence there.

The priests of Jesus' time are not otherwise mentioned in the Gospels. As for the chief priests and high priests (*archiereis*), they are often mentioned as responsible for Jesus' death together with the scribes : "The chief priests and the scribes were seeking how to arrest him by stealth, and kill him" (Mk 14:1). Jesus himself had prophesied : "The Son of Man must... be rejected by the elders (*presbyteroi*) and the chief priests and the scribes" (8:31). Having rejected Jesus the chief priests also opposed the church he had founded (Acts 4:6).* Luke notes, however, that with the progress of the word of God "the number of the disciples multiplied greatly in Jerusalem, and a great many of the priests were obedient to the faith" (Acts 6:7).

---

1 On the spiritual worship of Christians, see S. Lyonnet, "La Nature du culte dans le Nouveau Testament," in *La Liturgie après Vatican II*. Unam Sanctam 66 (Paris, 1967), pp. 357-384.

2 On Ex 19:6, see W. L. Moran, „A Kingdom of Priests," in *The Bible in current Catholic Thought* (New York, 1962), pp. 7-20. On the much debated 1 Pet 2:4-10, see J. H. Elliott, *The Elect and the Holy. An exegetical Examination of 1 Peter 2:4-10 and the phrase basileion hierateuma*. SupplNT, 12 (Leiden 1966), with bibliog., pp. 230-242 : "The significance of *hierateuma* lies not in its cultic connotations, but together with *basileion*, in its designation of the electedness and holiness of the Divine Regent's Community" (p. 223).

At the time of Jesus the total number of Jewish priests entitled to exercise cultic functions exceeded 7000, while the Levites were not fewer than 9000, according to one interpretation of available figures.[3] Obviously not all of them could officiate at the same time. They were grouped into twenty-four divisions or "courses"* which took weekly turns in performing the daily duties in the temple at Jerusalem. We learn from the Chronicler that in his day such divisions already existed and their origin is attributed by him to the initiative of king David himself, who organized the Sons of Aaron "according to the appointed duties in their service" (1 Chr 24:3). The number of "courses" may have varied somewhat during the Biblical period,[4] but it was constantly twenty-four later on,** as we know from the Jewish sources.[5]

In theory none of these "courses" had precedence over the others. In practice, however, the "course" to which the high priest or the main officials belonged must have been more influential than the others. Thus Josephus states that great advantages came from being of the first course, that of Jehoiarib (1 Chr 24:7), which had given the Hasmonean high priests and other national leaders.+ The apportioning of rights, of privileges, and especially of revenues among the "courses" was a natural hotbed of rivalries and struggles. Josephus reports that not long before the end of the second temple chief priests deprived other priests of their tithes, even by violent means. These conflicts had repercussions in politics. In the outbreaks of revolt that led to the events of 70 A.D., notes Josephus, the chief priests tried in vain to prevent the priests from abandoning the customary sacrificial offering for the Roman rulers.[6]

These divisions (*maḥleqôt* : 1 Chr 28:13) or "courses" are subdivided into family categories each called *bet 'ābôt,* "house of the fathers," and in service categories, or *mišmarôt,* "watches."++ In the later rabbinical terminology *mišmār* is the "course," while *bet 'abôt* is the subcategory. At the head of the "courses" stood the "leading priests" (*śārîm*; cf. Ezra 8:24) or "officers of the sanctuary" (*śārê qōdeš*; 1 Chr 24:5). They could have been the same officials as the *rā'še 'ābôt,* "the

[3] See J. Jeremias, *Jerusalem in the Time of Jesus,* trans. F. H. and C. H. Cave from 3d German ed. (Philadelphia, 1969), pp. 203-04. He relies mainly on 2 texts : *The Letter of Aristeas* (§ 95) and a remark by Josephus in *Against Apion* 2.8, §108.

[4] While 1 Chr 24:7-19 speaks of 24 priestly "courses," Neh 10:3-9 and 12:1-7 mention 22, and Neh 12:12-21 has 20.

[5] See Josephus *Ant.* 7.14.7 § 365-367.

[6] Josephus *Jewish War* 2.17.2, § 410.

heads of the fathers" (of the Levites), mentioned in 1 Chr 15:12. In the rabbinical writings occur other expressions, like "the elders of the priesthood" and "the eldest of the father's house," to denote the leaders of various categories in Jewish priesthood. *

The division of the Levites into twenty-four classes apparently took place at the time of the Chronicler (cf. 1 Chr 23:6-24).** About 1 Chr 23:1-23 commentators note: "Twenty-two heads of fathers' houses are usually found here, and various attempts have been made to increase this number to twenty-four, since there were twenty-four courses of priests (24:7-18), of singers (25:9-31), and of gate-keepers (26:2-11a), but all have been more or less arbitrary. The statement of Josephus (Ant 7.14.7) that David divided the Levites into twenty-four classes may have been derived from 1 Chr 24:31."[7] Like the priestly courses, so also the Levitical classes were headed by *śarîm* and *rā'šîm* (cf. 1 Chr 15:4-12; Neh 12:22,23). The Greek terminology corresponding to these and other Hebrew titles will be examined in connection with the particular offices of the Jewish priesthood.

B. Hierarchy and Functions

Though the teaching of the Law and its interpretation had become the prerogative of the scribes in the later Jewish period, the priests remained the professionals of religion through their control of the cult, without which the faithful felt unable to fulfill their religious duties. No sacrifice, it was thought, could be validly offered except through the mediation of the priests. The Law stipulated in fact that only the "sons of Aaron" were the legitimate ministers of the altar. This ministerial priesthood had a hierarchy whose offices received further determination in the Jewish postbiblical writings, as will now be seen. ***

a) *The High Priest*

At the head of the whole priesthood was the high priest (*hakkōhēn haggādôl*), known in Greek as *archiereus* and called *kahna rabba* in the Aramaic language spoken in Palestine. What the high priesthood meant to the devout Jews of the end of the 2nd century B.C. is reflected in the eulogy of Simon the High Priest found in the 50th chapter of Eccle-

[7] E. L. Curtis-A. A. Madsen, *The Books of Chronicles* (ICC, Edinburgh, 1910), p. 263.

siasticus. As a cultic person the high priest performed the most meaningful rites on the great Day of Expiation (Lev 16). A new distinctive trait was added to his office in the later periods : the high priest was also the political head of the nation during the periods of independence under the Hasmoneans, some of whom, were both high priests and kings. Even when the nation was ruled by foreigners the high priests played an important political role as heads of the sanhedrin and also as representing the Jewish nation in its dealings with the Roman authorities. The manifold social involvement of the high priest explains why he officiated in the cult only rarely. He had to present personally the sin-offering of the people on the Day of Expiation and later practice expected him to make also the daily offerings during the week preceding the feast. Apart from this he officiated whenever he wanted. Josephus states that as a rule he would officiate on Sabbath days and on the New Moon and New Year feasts.[8] Both the priest-kings John Hyrcanus and Alexander Jannaeus are known to have occasionally performed the sacred functions.[9]

Joshua ben Sira wrote of the high priest : "When he put on his glorious robe and clothed himself with superb perfection and went up to the holy altar, he made the court of the sanctuary glorious" (Sir 50:11). Philo, the Jewish philosopher, and Josephus,[10] after him, have insisted on the symbolical significance of the high priest's vestments. Philo who wrote that "the highest, and in the truest sense the holy, temple, of God is, as we must believe, the whole universe," also states that the high priest's dress "would seem to be a likeness and copy of the universe (*apeikonisma kai mimēma tou kosmou*)".[11] The high priest's vestments were, in a way, a symbol of the Jewish religion. Herod the Great, then Archelaus, and the Romans after them, considered it to be a protection against uprisings to control these vestments and store them in the fortress Antonia. If Emperor Claudius in a decree signed in his own hand on June 28 of 45 A.D. disposed of this matter, it is because he saw in the struggle for the vestments a struggle for religion itself. Josephus writes : "After Archelaus, when the Romans took over the government, they retained control of the high priest's vestments and kept them in

---

[8] See *Jewish War* 5.5.7, § 230.

[9] See *Ant.* 13.10.3 and 13.5, §§282, 372.

[10] *Ant.* 3.7 (§§ 151-187) and 3. 8-9 (§ 214-218).

[11] Philo, *The Special Laws,* 1.12. §66 and 1.16, § 84. On the symbolism of the high priest's dress see *ibid.* 1.16-17. § 84-97.

a stone building, where they were under the seal both of the priests and of the custodians of the treasury and where the warden of the guard lighted the lamp day by day. Seven days before each festival the vestments were delivered to the priests by the warden. After they had been purified, the high priest wore them; then after the first day of the festival he put them back again in the building where they were laid away before. This was the procedure at the three festivals each year and on the fast day."[12]

According to Lev 21:13-14 the high priest could marry only a Jewish virgin. When Philo, commenting on these two verses states that she had to be also a priest's daughter he verry likely expresses what the custom suggested.[13] These and other regulations, intended to perpetuate a pure lineage, had a lesser meaning when under Herod the Great and the Roman rule high priesthood was certainly no longer hereditary and for life. The office had become involved in politics and exposed to the intrigues of rivalry and simony. Yet Jewish sources speak of the "lifelong sanctity" of the high priest.* The deposed high priests kept their titles, as also did even their eventual substitutes of a few hours on the Day of Atonement. It seems that in the last period of the second temple even the high priest was not any more or not always anointed, since the Mishnah knows of high priests installed by investiture only.[14] Maimonides states that anointing had ceased with the Exile.[15] It is, however, unlikely that the Hasmonean priest-kings would have neglected anointing. This and the mention of the high priests as "Anointed Ones" in late texts (Sir 45:15; Dan 9:25-26; 2 Macc 1:10) suggest rather that the custom of anointing the high priests disappeared entirely only during the Herodian-Roman period.

b) *Chief Priests and High Priests*

"Seven days before the Day of Atonement the High Priest was taken

---

12 *Ant.* 18.4.3. § 93-94. These festivals are Passover, Pentecost, and Tabernacles, while the fast day refers to the Day of Atonement. On this great day, however, the high priest wore a simple white vestment (cf. Lev 16:4; *Yoma* 3.7; 7.1-4).

13 *The Special Laws*, 1.22, § 110.

14 Cf. *Horayoth* ("Decisions"), 3.4. The *Jerusalem Talmud* reads in the mention of "anointed" in *Yoma* 1.1 the implication that the high priest meant there is one who has received the unction (in the 1st temple period) as distinct from one promoted later by investiture (in M. Schwab's edition, v. 5, p. 166).

15 *The Code of Maimonides*, 8, "The Book of Temple Service," Treatise 2, ch. 1, § 8, in the M. Lewittes edition (New Haven, 1957), p. 44. He was then consecrated solely by putting on the special vestments of high priesthood.

apart from his own house unto the Counsellors' Chamber and another priest was made ready in his stead lest aught should befall him to render him ineligible. R. Judah says : also another wife was made ready for him lest his own wife should die, for it is written : 'He shall make atonement for himself and for his house'; 'his house' that is his wife. They said to him : If so there would be no end to this matter."[16] Thus reads the first of the Mishnah provisions designed to insure the availability of the high priest for the great feast day. It may be that the *raison d'être* of the *s^e^gan,** "deputy high priest," the second highest ranking official in the Jewish priesthood, was not to replace the high priest on the occasion mentioned, but it was very likely the custom to designate him for such an office, unless another substitute was found to be more appropriate. During the main ceremony of the Day of Atonement the *s^e^gan* stood at the right of the high priest, and the chief of the father's house at his left.** When the moment of reading came, the *s^e^gan* received the scroll from the chief of the synagogue and gave it to the high priest. The *s^e^gan* was in charge of the daily cult, and being a permanent official he could safeguard the liturgical continuity despite the rotation system of service. He was besides the prefect of the temple, *stratēgos tou hierou*, whose special duty it was to have its external order respected. According to late Jewish sources the *ro'š hammišmar*, head priest of the weekly course, conducted the ceremony which concluded the period of purification prescribed for leprosy and childbirth.

Another important office was held by those responsible for the temple treasure, which included both the sacred vessels and the temple fund. The fund or money reserve, large enough to tempt even political rulers (cf. *Ant* 17.7.1-2, § 105-118), was kept in the "treasure" (*gazophulakion* : Lk 21:1; Jn 8:20). The *gizbarîm* or *gazophulakes*, the "treasurers",*** ranked among the highest officials + and were also entrusted, it seems, with tasks formerly in the hands of the Levites. ++ The *amarkelim*, mentioned only once in the Mishnah,+++ may have been connected with the treasury. The Jerusalem Talmud states that the *amarkelim* and the *gizbarim* received orders from two higher officials, called *qatôlîqîn*, and explains that in the official protocol the following order of precedence was followed : the king, the high priest, the *qatôliqos*, the *amarkal*, the *gizbar*.++++

The New Testament often refers to a group of officials whom it calls

---

[16] *Yoma* 1.1 (Danby Translation).

hoi archiereis, "high priests" or "chief priests." Since there was only one high priest at any given time, the use of the term in the plural calls for an explanation. The expression "high priests" occurs in association with "the rulers" (*hoi archontes* : Lk 23:13, 24:20), with "the scribes and the elders",[17] with "the scribes" alone, [18]with "the elders" alone.[19] It is used only once alone : Saul "has authority from the chief priests to bind all who call upon thy name" (Acts 9:14).

These "high priests"* obviously formed a distinctive group and had a decisive influence in the deliberations of the Sanhedrin especially on points affecting the Jewish religion nationally. Apart from the ruling high priest the group very probably included the former high priests deposed by Herod or the Roman procurators and possibly also other leading members of the priestly families. "On the morrow their rulers and elders and scribes were gathered together in Jerusalem, with Annas the high priest and Caiaphas and John and Alexander" (Acts 4:5-6). When the zealots elected Phanni as high priest, Josephus contends, they deprived of their claims "those families from which in turn the high priests had always been drawn."[20] Josephus and the Mishnah attribute also judicial and administrative authority to "the sons of the high priests". These are the various categories that may be intended by the NT *archiereis.*

If *archiereis* is translated "chief priests" the meaning of the term can be more easily broadened to include other high officials, namely the *s^egan*, the heads of the priestly courses, the *amarkelim* or *stratēgoi*,+ and the *gizbarim*. These officials, it is claimed, formed, together with the high priest, an "established College with oversight of the cultus, control of the temple, administration of the temple treasury, and supervision of priestly discipline".[21] One thing is certain : there existed a priestly aristocracy whose standard of living contrasted sharply with the modest condition of the common priest (*kōhēn hedyôt*). The frequent use of *archiereis* in the NT reflects an interpretation of the facts. When the opposition arose against Jesus, "it was not the work of a single individual, nor of the supreme holder of priestly rank alone, but of the religious authorities in general. Along with the scribes, the main oppo-

---

17 Mt 16:21; 27:41; Mk 8:31; 11:27; 14:43, 53; 15:1; Lk 9:22.

18 Mt 2:4; 20:18; 21:15; Mk 10:33; 11:18; 14:1; 15:31; Lk 20:19; 22:2; 23:10.

19 Mt 21:23; 26:3, 47; 27:1, 3, 12, 20; Acts 4:23; 23:14; 25:15. See EncDictBibl, art. "Chief Priests," c. 357.

20 *Jewish War* 4.3.6, § 148.

21 G. Schrenk, in Kittel ThW (Eng), p. 270.

nents were the chief priests as a whole, i.e. the priestly aristocracy, the leading official representatives of the sacral life of the nation. As a body, they rejected Christ as a transgressor."[22] This verdict, which will sound harsh to many, does not necessarily mean that all the officials agreed to condemn Jesus.

c) *Priests and Levites*

At the time of Jesus there were, as it seems, several thousand priests qualified for service, who considered it an honor to officiate in the temple when their "course" was on duty. Perhaps only half of these priests had their permanent residence in Jerusalem, the others living in other parts of Judaea and even in more distant regions. While on duty no priest was allowed to drink wine. According to the Mishnah, "if a priest served [at the altar] in a state of uncleanness his brethren the priests took him outside the Temple Court and split open his brains with clubs."[23] No priest having a blemish could "approach to offer the bread of his God," although he could "eat the bread of his God, both of the most holy and of the holy things."[24]

Other prohibitions affecting more generally the ordinary life of the priests had been incorporated in the priestly law and continued to be binding in the later periods. Certain permanent bodily defects excluded admittance to active membership in the priesthood.* "From the priest," Josephus writes, "Moses exacted a double degree of purity. For not only did he debar them, in common with all others, from the aforesaid practices [cf. Lev 20], but he further forbade them to wed a harlot, he forbids them to wed a slave or a prisoner of war, aye or such women as gain their livelihood by hawking or inkeeping or who have for whatsoever reasons been separated from their former husbands."[25] Ezekiel's prescription that a priest may marry only a virgin or a priest's widow was not incorporated in later law.+ These regulations on priestly marriage have the same foundation as those regarding the purity of the priests : they are concrete expressions of belief in the holiness of the priestly state. On the age of admittance to the priesthood there is no

---

22 G. Schrenk, *Ibid.*, p. 272.

23 *Sanhedrin* 9.6 : H. Danby, *The Mishnah*, pp. 396-397.

24 Lev 21:16, 22-23; *Ant* 3.12.2, § 278. "Just as the sacrificial offering must be unblemished (Lev 22:7-25), so the priest who offers it must be without bodily defect" (*Oxford Annotated Bible*, p. 149).

25 *Ant.* 3.12.2, § 276.

clear regulation, but one Jewish source suggests a minimum age of twenty.* The candidate who had been accepted by the Sanhedrin (cf. *Middoth* V, 4) was consecrated by the rites which have been described above (see Ex 29 = Lev 8).**

There is little in the later Jewish sources that is distinctively informative on the Levites of the NT period. One author thus summarizes his findings : "On the Levites devolved the Temple-police, the guard of the gates, and the duty of keeping everything about the sanctuary clean and bright. But as at night the priests kept watch about the innermost places of the Temple, so they also opened and closed all the inner gates, while the Levites discharged this duty in reference to the outer gates, which led upon the Temple Mount (or Court of the Gentiles), and to the 'Beautiful Gate,' which formed the principal entrance into the 'Court of the Women'."[26] There were, besides, the singers, and membership in this group also was gained by birth. They were considered as lower in rank than the gatekeepers and the Talmud states that a Levite who did his colleague's work at the gate actually incurred the penalty of death.[27] From Josephus we learn that "those of the Levites who were singers of hymns urged the king [Agrippa II] to convene the Sanhedrin and get them permission to wear linen robes on equal terms with the priests," a favor which they obtained.[28] Josephus follows later Jewish tradition when he presents Korah as "one of the most eminent of the Hebrews by reason both of his birth and of his riches," who being jealous of Moses "proceeded to denounce him among the Levites" : Moses "in defiance of the laws had given the priesthood to his brother Aaron, not by the common decree of the people, but by his own vote, and in despotic fashion was bestowing the honours upon whom he would."[29] This tends to show that the vanity of honors has attracted from the earliest times even those dedicated to work for the glory of God. Perhaps Korah's main mistake was to have understood priesthood as an office of honor, rather than as a call to serve both God and one's fellowmen.

---

[26] A. Edersheim, *The Temple, its Ministry and Services, as they were at the Time of Jesus Christ* (London, 1874), p. 65.

[27] See *'Arakin* ("Vows of Valuation") 11b, quoting Num 3:38 (p. 63 in Soncino edit.).

[28] *Ant.* 20.9.6, § 216-217.

[29] *Ant.* 4.2.2, § 14-16.

C. Priesthood at Qumran

The community of Qumran and the finds that were made there certainly belong to the period presently under study. In spite of the enormous importance justly attributed to the Dead Sea scriptures this matter will be treated only briefly here because the scrolls do not contain very much that directly concerns our subject. After inquiring about the Sons of Zadok and connected problems we shall examine two conceptions that could be related to the representation of the High Priesthood of Christ.

a) "*Sons of Zadok*"

The middle section (col. V-IX) of *The Community Rule* (1QS) contains the statutes relating to the Council of the Community. It opens with the following statements :

> And this is the Rule for the men of the Community who have freely pledged themselves to be converted from all evil and to cling to all His commandments according to His will. They shall separate from the congregation of the men of falsehood and shall unite, with respect to the Law and possessions, under the authority of *the sons of Zadok*, the Priests who keep the Covenant, and of the multitude of the men of the Community who hold fast to the Covenant. Every decision concerning doctrine, property, and justice shall be determined by them (V, 1-3).[30]

The designation "the sons of Zadok" (*bny ṣdwq*)* refers here exclusively, it seems, to the priests, who are considered as occupying a position of leadership in the society. The *Damascus Document*+ (CD) quotes, however, Ezek 44.15 as follows : "The Priests, the Levites, and the sons of Zadok who kept the charge of my sanctuary when the children of Israel strayed from me, they shall offer me fat and blood." Then it adds : "The Priests are the converts of Israel who departed from the land of Judah, and (the *Levites* are) those who joined them. The *sons of Zadok* are the elect of Israel, the men called by name who shall stand at the end of days" (III, 31-IV, 2).[31] In this case "sons of Zadok" designate the community as a whole. An early editor of the Document suggested,

---

[30] Translation of G. Vermes, *The Dead Sea Scrolls in English* (Baltimore : Pelican Books, rev. reprint, 1965), p. 78. The original edition of *The Community Rule* (*serek hayyaḥad*), formerly called *The Manual of Discipline*, appeared in M. Burrows *et al.*, ed., *The Dead Sea Scrolls of St. Mark's Monastery*, v. 2 (New Haven, 1951).

[31] Tr. G. Vermes, p. 100.

correctly, it seems, the following explanation : "The Party (of the reformers), though originating apparently with the priests and Levites, came to embrace a strong lay element, just as the Pharisaic party, though in the main a lay movement, came ultimately to embrace a section of the priests."[32] Another passage of *The Community Rule* suggests what background led to the use of "sons of Zadok" to describe the members of the community : "He (the Master) shall separate and weigh *the sons of righteousness* (*bny hṣdwq*) according to their spirit" (9.14). This *bny hṣdwq* (with art.), like *bny ṣdq* (no art.) of 3.20.22, may be taken as designating the community as a whole. "Ezek 44:15 played an important part for the religious circles from which 1QS and CD originate, not because it contains the name of Zadok, but because it was possible by means of the Midrashic canon of interpretation, to read the meaning 'sons of righteousness' into it. 1QS IX, 14 emphasizes this by using the article."[33]

The formula "sons of Zadok" is also used at the very outset of *The Rule of the Congregation** (1QSa) :

> This is the Rule for all the congregation of Israel in the last days, when they shall join the Community to walk according to the law of the sons of Zadok the Priests and of the men of their Covenant who have turned aside from the way of the people, the men of His Council who keep His Covenant in the midst of iniquity, offering expiation for the Land.[34]

In this passage, as well as in 1.24 and 2.3 where "sons of Zadok" occurs again, the Zadokite origin of the leading priests is insisted upon, and this suggests to some authors that persons of high priestly Zadokite lineage headed the Qumranic movement, even though the Community's claims to have the legitimate high priests did not concern the present but the future.[35] The same work mentions another category of priestly officials : "The sons of Levi shall hold office, each in his place, under the authority of *the sons of Aaron*" (I, 15-16). These are called elsewhere "the sons of Aaron the Priests" (II, 13). According to *The Community Rule*, when a man enters the Covenant "they shall examine his spirit

---

[32] R. H. Charles, *The Apocrypha and Pseudepigrapha of the Old Testament*, v. 2 (Oxford, 1913), p. 785.

[33] P. Wernberg-Møller, *The Manual of Discipline.* Studies in the Texts of the Desert of Judah, v. 1 (Leiden, 1957), p. 91.

[34] Tr. G. Vermes, p. 118.

[35] See J. Carmignac et al., ed., *Les textes de Qumran, traduits et annotés*, v. 2 (Paris, 1963), p. 17. More generally on the meaning of "Sons of Zadok" in the Qumran community see G. R. Driver, *The Judaean Scrolls* (Oxford, 1965), pp. 226-266.

in community with respect to his understanding and practice of the Law, under the authority of the sons of Aaron ... and of the multitude of Israel" i.e. of the Sect (V, 21).

Furthermore, "the sons of Aaron alone shall command in matters of justice and property, and every rule concerning the men of the Community shall be determined according to their word" (9, 7). Perhaps no clear distinction is to be sought between "sons of Zadok" and "sons of Aaron", the first formula exalting status and authority, the second recalling more generally the ancient privileges of the priestly class. Or else it can be said that the "sons of Zadok" represent the supreme governing body of the Community, while the "sons of Aaron" are all the priests to whom traditionally the Israelites owe submission in religious matters.

Fervent devotion to the Law, a distinctive feature of later Judaism, characterizes even more clearly the religious attitude of the Qumran sectarians forming the Community of the Renewed Covenant. Whoever approaches the Council of the Community "shall undertake by a binding oath to return with all his heart and soul to every commandment of the Law of Moses in accordance with all that has been revealed of it to the sons of Zadok, the Keepers of the Covenant and Seekers of His will, and to the multitude of the men of their Covenant who together have freely pledged themselves to His truth and to walking in the way of His delight."[36] Wherever ten Covenanters live together one of them at least must be a priest capable of interpreting the Law for them at any time of day or night. The general members of the Community are to keep vigil for a third of every night of the year, to study the Law and pray together (CR 6, 2-8). In fact the Righteous Teacher who instituted the Community is neither a Messianic figure, nor a prophetic forerunner: he is a Zadokite priest who initiated the Covenanters in the true meaning of the ancient Scriptures and established a new discipline in anticipation of the Messianic era.[37]

Priests and Levites are often mentioned in the Qumran scriptures. According to *The Community Rule* they bless the God of Salvation, with those entering the Covenant; they recite the favors of God and

[36] *The Community Rule* 5.7-10 (Tr. Vermes, p. 79).

[37] Cf. F. M. Cross, *The Ancient Library of Qumran* (New York, Anchor Books, rev. ed., 1961), pp. 160 and 223. The Essenes, he also states, "are piiestly apocalyptists, not true ascetics" (p. 78). On "the Righteous Teacher and the Wicked Priest," see Cross pp. 127-160.

recall the iniquities of the children of Israel (I, 18-23). At table the Priest shall be the first to stretch out his hand to bless the firstfruits of the bread and the new wine (VI, 4-5). On this, F. M. Cross notes : "The common meal of the Essenes is hereby set forth as a liturgical anticipation of the Messianic banquet ... No doubt in the assemblies of the Essenes the lay head and the priestly head of the community (the types of the Messiahs to come) stood in the stead of the Messiahs of Aaron and Israel."[38] At the Council meeting the Priests shall sit first, and the elders second, and all the rest of the people according to their rank (VI, 8-9). The supreme Council consisted of twelve laymen and three Priests (8.1), the latter representing, it seems, the three clans of the tribe of Levi (cf. Ex 6:16). Both the Sect as a whole and the smaller groups or "camps" (ten men made a quorum) had two superiors : one was the Priest, mainly concerned with the ritual, the other was the *mebaqqēr* "guardian," whose special field was "instruction," while his authority was mainly felt in the admission of members and in all matters regarding orthodoxy and right conduct.* He also exercised the function of "Manager" or "Bursar of the Congregation" (Vermes), if this office was not entrusted to another official. It has also been suggested that the Guardian was a Levite, and that this Levite-Guardian was also known as *Maśkil*, "Master," that is, teacher of his congregation.

A passage of the *Damascus Document*, already quoted, shows how its Essene author discovers in 1 Sam 2:35 and Ex 44:15 prophecies of the origin of his Sect : God "built them a sure house in Israel ... The Priests, the Levites, and the sons of Zadok who kept the charge of my sanctuary when the children of Israel strayed from me, they shall offer me fat blood" (CD III, 18-IV, 4). It also reveals the peculiarly priestly character of the early schismatic community. "The priests of Qumran regarded the Jerusalem sanctuary as defiled, its priests false, its calendar unorthodox. In the end of days the Essene priesthood would be re-established in the New Jerusalem, the false priesthood overthrown for ever. Meanwhile, the Essene community is organized as an ideal priestly theocracy ... The whole life of the community is shaped in the interest of priestly objectives. In short the Essenes are a counter-Israel organized by a counter-priesthood, 'true' Israel led by the 'legitimate' priesthood."[39] This peculiar theorizing was bound to affect also the course

---

[38] F. M. Cross, *Library of Qumran*, p. 90.

[39] F. M. Cross, *Library of Qumran*, pp. 128-129.

of the Messianic hope. According to Cross, all this suggests that the origin of the Essene movement must be sought for in the struggle of rival priestly houses, one being the new house of the reigning Hasmonean priests, the other claiming to represent the Zadokite priesthood. Having lost hope to establish a faithful theocracy in Israel these "orthodox" priests sought to fulfill their ideal in an apocalyptic priestly community. Ancestors of the Essene sectaries can probably be found among the congregation of the *ḥasîdîm* (cf. 1 Macc 2:42), these uneasy allies of the Maccabean warrior priests. Possibly, when Simon was *elected* high priest (*c.* 140 B.C.; 1 Macc 14:35) the Hasidic party broke into two wings : the Pharisees and the Essenes.

b) A Priestly Messiah?

The Messianic expectation at Qumran is a complex question amply debated by recent studies, several of which will be mentioned. No true consensus can be expected since authors have a varying conception of "messianism." The term *mašîaḥ*, besides, can be understood simply as "anointed", a notion applicable to both the king and the high priest. It can also be taken in the strict sense as denoting the Messiah, the future ideal king expected to establish God's reign and inaugurate a new era (cf. Is 9:2-7; Pss 2 and 110). The problem of the Messianic hope in Qumran centers on a few texts.[40] Of the Covenanters *The Community Rule* states :

> They shall depart from none of the counsels of the Law to walk in the stubbornness of their hearts, but shall be ruled by the primitive precepts in which the men of the Community were first instructed until there schall come the Prophet and *the Messiahs of Aaron and Israel* (1QS IX, 10-11).[41]

That the plural "Messiahs" must be read here* is confirmed by the fact that the "Messiah of Israel" is spoken of separately in *The Rule of the Congregation* : "The Priest... shall be the first to extend his hand over the bread. Thereafter the Messiah of Israel shall extend his hand over

---

[40] All the occurences of *mašîaḥ* in the Qumran scriptures are discussed in M. De Jonge, "The Use of the word 'Anointed' in the time of Jesus" NovTest 8 (1966), pp. 132-148. J. R. Schaefer has correctly noted : "All parties agree that the intertestamental literature speaks of an eschatological priest who is messianic both in the sense that he will be an anointed one and in the sense that he will play a leading role in the messianic age. Disagreement arises when he is called priestly Messiah," with prerogatives similar to those of the royal Messiah ("The Relationship between Priestly and Servant Messianism in the Epistle to the Hebrews," CathBiblQuart 30, 1968, 359f).

[41] Tr. Vermes, p. 87.

the bread..." (1QSa II, 18-21). The Priest can mean in this text the high priest, as often in the OT (cf. Lev 4:3, 15, 16), that is "the Anointed Priest" (Lev 4:3-12), and be an equivalent of the Messiah of Aaron" of 1QS IX, 11.* The "meal" in 1QSa refers to a future meal to be eaten first when the Messiah appears. "The sect as yet thinks of only one Messiah, a lay figure, but the eschatological priest is already so important in their thinking that when the two are mentioned together the Messiah is specifically referred to as being 'of Israel' to distinguish him clearly from the sacerdotal figure".[42] The title "Messiah of Israel" is not found in the OT, where the king is called *m^e^šiaḥ yhwh* (1 Sam 24:6, 10), but it occurs three times in the Targum.[43] Another section, partly restored, of *The Rule of the Congregation*, should probably read as follows :

> This shall be the assembly of the men of renown called to the meeting of the Council of the Community when the *Priest-Messiah* shall summon them. He shall come at the head of the whole congregation of Israel with his brethren, the sons of Aaron the Priests, those called to the assembly, the men of renown; and they shall sit before him, each man in the order of his dignity.
>
> And then the *Messiah of Israel* shall come, and the chiefs of the clans of Israel shall sit before him, each in the order of his dignity, according to his place in their camps and marches.
>
> And before them shall sit all the heads of family of the congregation, each in the order of his dignity (1QSa II, 11-16).[44]

According to K. G. Kuhn "the entire passage shows us with complete certainty the concept of two Messiahs : (1) the Messiah of Aaron, the high priest and head of the entire Congregation of Israel, and (2) the Messiah of Israel, the political leader, subordinate and second in rank to the former."[45] Other interpreters are not so sure. "That the Zadokite hierocracy envisaged a High Priest as its future 'ecclesiastical' Head need not be questioned. But the claim that he was also viewed as a "Messiah" in the same sense (though with different functions) as 'the Messiah of Israel' must, I think, be viewed with reserve. The fact that the High Priest took precedence of the Messiah of Israel may mean very little; presumably he would do so in any Temple rite or priestly

---

[42] J. F. Priest, "The Messiah and the Meal in 1QSa," JBiblLit 82 (1963), p. 100.

[43] Targ. Is 16:1, 5; Targ. Micah 4:8.

[44] Tr. Vermes, p. 121. (Paragraphs and italics are mine; brackets indicating restored text are omitted.)

[45] K. G. Kuhn, "The Two Messiahs of Aaron and Israel," in *The Scrolls and the New Testament*, K. Stendahl, ed. (New York, 1957), p. 57.

function but this does not mean that we are to regard the High Priest as in the strict sense a 'Messianic' figure."[46]

In the *Testaments of the Twelve Patriarchs*, which belong to the cycle of Essene writings, the expectation of two Messiahs is also clearly expressed : "To me [Judah] God has given the kingship, to him [Levi] the priesthood; and the kingship he has subordinated to the priesthood."[47] Having "named all of the messianic passages of the *Test.XII Patr.*," with the exception of later Christian interpolations,* Kuhn concludes confidently : "All of them exhibit, with complete unanimity, the concept of the priestly Messiah of Levi and [of the] political and royal Messiah of Judah, the latter ranking after the former."[48] The *Damascus Document*, as we have it, speaks, however, of the "coming of the Messiah (sing.) of Aaron and Israel" (12.23; 14.19; 19.10) of the future appearance of the "Messiah from Aaron and from Israel" (20.1). Since the plural meaning, it is claimed, "has been definitely confirmed by the evidence from 1QSa, the singular can be understood only as a secondary correction by a medieval copyist of the CD."[49] Thus the text would have been conformed to the entire extra-Qumranic Jewish tradition which knows only of the royal Messiah from Judah. Yet this is a lame explanation, since a Qumran fragment containing CD 14.19 shows that already in the 1st cent. B.C. the phrase "the Messiah of Aaron and Israel" was clearly understood in the singular.[50] Perhaps a change occurred in the Messianic expectation. J. F. Priest "has attempted to show that in the earliest stage the sect technically thought of only one Messiah, the lay figure common in Jewish Messianism, though their priestly interest was well on the way to creating a Messiah of Aaron."[51]

---

[46] M. Black, *The Srolls and Christian Origins* (London, 1961), p. 147.

[47] *Test. Judah* 21.2-5.

[48] K. G. Kuhn, "Two Messiahs", p. 58. E. Cothenet is ready to accept a "double messianic expectation" in Qumran, provided the term Messiah is not given the precise sense it has in the NT (in J. Carmignac, ed., *Les Textes de Qumran*, v. 2, p. 145).

[49] K. G. Kuhn "Two Messiahs", p. 59. Having examined other texts, like CD 2.12 and 6.1, Kuhn concludes (p. 60) that *mashiaḥ* in the CD was originally used only in the plural, either as noun (Messiah) or as adjective ("anointed"). According to R. Deichgräber, "the singular *mšyḥ* in the oldest copy of CD from Cave 4 at Qumran does not oppose the supposition that CD expected two messianic personalities" ("Zur Messiaserwartung der Damaskusschrift," ZATWiss 78, 1966, p. 33).

[50] See J. T. Milik, *Ten Years of Discovery in the Wilderness of Judaea*. StBiblTh 26 (London, 1959). pp. 125-126.

[51] J. F. Priest, "The Messiah and the Meal" JBiblLit 82 (1963), p. 100.

c) *Melchizedek at Qumran*

In the next chapter we shall have to examine the OT background of the use which the author of the Epistle to the Hebrews makes of Melchizedek to describe the high priesthood of Christ. We must now attempt to determine what role, if any, Melchizedek played in the Jewish religious conceptions at the time of Jesus. It is quite possible that the author of the Epistle owes very little to these conceptions, since he explicitly refers to the Genesis narrative and to Ps 110.4. Yet he certainly did not deliberately exclude what his Jewish contemporaries, especially in the Essence circles, had to say on the matter.

To begin with what is easiest, the Qumran finds include an Aramaic text which is a free re-working of the biblical stories contained in several chapters of Genesis. The work is related to other texts composed or used by the Essenes, and its date of composition (probably 1st cent. B.C.) also suggests its Essene origin. The contents of the scroll, however, neither exclude nor indicate that this Genesis Apocryphon is of Essene origin. This is how it relates the Melchizedek episode (Gen 14, 17-20) :

> [The king of Sodom] came to Salem, that is Jerusalem, while Abram was camped in the valley of Shaveth—this is the Vale of the King, the Valley of Beth-haccherem. Melchizedek, the king of Salem, brought out food and drink for Abram and for all the men who were with him; he was a priest of the Most High God and he blessed Abram and said, "Blessed be Abram by the Most High God, the Lord of heaven and earth. Blessed be the Most High God who has delivered your enemies into your hand." And he gave him a tithe of all the flocks of the king of Elam and his confederates.[52]

It is noteworthy that Salem is identified with Jerusalem and that Melchizedek is clearly made king of Salem. On the other hand, there is no attempt to explain "king of Salem" as "king of peace" (Heb 7:2). The king's name is written in one word, while the MT has *malkî-ṣedeq*. To "brought out bread and wine" the author, significantly perhaps, has substituted "brought out food and drink."* He shows no trace of finding a cultic relevance in the original narrative.

In his study on "Wine in OT cult," E. Busse gives a qualified but affirmative answer to the question : "Is Gen 14.18 to be interpreted sacrificially ?" There was, he thinks, a sacral meal, in which Abram and Melchisedek entered into a new fellowhip and *'ēl 'elyôn*, the "God Most

---

52 lQApGn, col. 23, lines 13-17. Text and translation in J. A. Fitzmyer, *The Genesis Apocryphon of Qumran Cave 1* (Rome, 1966), p. 65. See his commentary, pp. 154-158.

High," was involved in the sacred rite.[53] Even granting that this precise interpretation is largely conjectural the fact remains that the solemn celebration of Abram's triumph is hardly conceivable in its ancient context without some kind of sacrifice being offered.* This being so, Gen 14.18 is more correctly read as follows : "And Melchizedek king of Salem brought out bread and wine, for he was priest of God Most High."** In Israel as well as in Babylonia, bread and wine + are common sacrificial offerings.[54] In one text at least, the vases for the wine libations are closely associated with the bread of the Presence (Ex 25: 29-30), the "bread of God." Thanksgiving offerings can take the form of a wine libation : "I will lift up the cup of salvation and call on the name of the Lord, I will pay my vows to the Lord in the presence of all his people" (Ps 116:13-14).++ Even the verb *hôṣî'*, "brought out", used in Gen 14:18, is not necessarily non-cultic. In Jg 6:18 the term occurs in parallel with *hinnîah,* "set before," used elsewhere in a sacrificial context (Dt 26:4, 10).

In any case no conclusion can be drawn from *Genesis Apocryphon* concerning the cultic character of Abram's encounter with Melchizedek. It is true also that the Epistle to the Hebrews, with all its insistence on Melchizedek, does not even allude to his "offering" of bread and wine. This could indicate that the author of Heb was unaware of the original meaning of Gen 14 :18 or that he repudiated by his silence the association with pagan rites. More to the point is the fact that of Melchizedek's priestly role he retains only what he wishes to stress : Melchizedek, a non Levitical priest, without genealogy, blessed Abraham, the ancestor of the Levites.

Melchizedek is called "high priest" in *Targ.* 1 Chr 1:24 and in one reading of Targ. Gen 14:18.[55] This conception was probably formulated before the controversy arose between the synagogue and the Christian Church concerning the king of Salem. The Epistle to the Hebrews uses Melchizedek to exalt the non Levitical priesthood of Jesus. In some Patristic writings, Melchizedek, prototype of Christ, incarnates, as it were, Christian claims against the pretensions of Jewish legalism. His

---

[53] See E. Busse, *Der Wein im Kult des Alten Testamentes. Religionsgeschichtliche Untersuchung zum Alten Testament.* Freiburger Theol. Studien 29 (Freiburg im Br., 1922), pp. 37-41.

[54] See F. Blome, *Die Opfermaterie in Babylonien und Israel,* I (Rome, 1934), p. 360.

[55] The London Polyglot text of the Palestinian (Jerusalem) Targum II (fragmentary). See R. Le Déaut, "Le titre de *Summus Sacerdos* donné à Melchisédech est-il d'origine juive ?" RechScRel 50 (1962), pp. 224 and 227.

role is extolled at the expense of other biblical figures, even of Abraham. By identifying him with Shem, Noah's son (Gen 6:10), the author of the Palestinian Targum of Gen 14:18 and other Jewish writers made of Melchizedek an ancestor, even of Abraham, who was thus justified for honoring the way he did the king of Salem.

In Qumran Cave 11 was discovered the fragmentary text of an eschatological midrash in which the name Melchizedek occurs repeatedly. Although the interpretation of the fragments remains on many points hypothetical, "they do contain a number of interesting phrases revealing new facets of the Melchizedek legend in late Palestinian Judaism."[56] In a context concerned with the jubilee year (cf. Lev 25) Melchizedek apparently plays a role in the execution of divine judgment. He is seemingly involved in a statement on "atonement" and also as such could be called "a heavenly redemption-figure." "The function of Melchizedek as heavenly deliverer who protects the faithful people of God and as chief of the heavenly hosts runs parallel with that of the archangel Michael in the Dead Sea Scrolls, and in late Jewish and early Christian literature. Michael and Melchisedek are, however, not identified explicitly in the Qumran texts at our disposal. This identification is only found in certain medieval Jewish texts."[57] In these Qumran fragments, Is 52:7 (cf. Rom 10:15) is given special emphasis : "How beautiful upon the mountains are the feet of him who brings good tidings (*m^ebaśśēr*), who publishes peace, who brings good tidings of good, who publishes salvation, who says to Zion, 'Your God reigns !' " The *m^ebaśśēr* (*euaggelizomenos*) of this text is identified with "the Messiah," while "your God" (*'elōhāyik*) seems to be explained as referring to the heavenly Melchizedek, the antagonist of Belial. Apparently Melchizedek is also numbered among the "holy ones of God"* mentioned in texts like Ps 82, also quoted. Since no allusion is made to Gen 14:18-20 or to Ps 110, 11Q Melch very likely belongs to a tradition not at all represented in the Epistle to the Hebrews.

56 J. F. Fitzmyer, "Further Light on Melchizedek from Qumran Cave 11," JBiblLit 86 (1967), p. 25.

57 M. De Jonge and A. S. Van der Woude, "11Q Melchizedek and the New Testament," NTSt 12 (1965-66), p. 305.

CHAPTER SIX

JESUS THE HIGH PRIEST

Men conscious of their ultimate destiny or desirous to be liberated from their present miseries have sought from time immemorial to obtain access to the deities they worshipped and through whose help they hoped to transcend the limits of their existence. Thus did humanity more or less consciously come nearer to the true God with the help of her priests, who found in sacrifice, broadly understood, the best adapted means of worshipping and propitiating. According to the Israelite tradition, Moses, following the instructions of Yahweh, instituted a priesthood and a sacrificial liturgy in which blood played the essential role : "The life of flesh is in its blood. This blood I have given to you, in order that you may perform the rite of expiation upon the altar, for your lives; for blood makes expiation, by reason of the life that is in it" (Lev 17:11).* To Christian believers the definitive answer to man's quest of redemption is found in Christ, Priest and Victim, of whom the Author of Heb states : "Now, once, in the conclusion of the ages, for the removal of the sin, through the sacrifice of himself, has he been made manifest" (9:26). This statement, properly understood, reflects the great themes of the Epistle and it is here quoted to indicate that the present writer will insist on the close connection existing between Christ's priesthood and his sacrifice.

A. In the Epistle to the Hebrews

The Epistle has been called "to the Hebrews" since the year 200 at least.[1] Clement of Rome, Ignatius of Antioch (+*c.* 110), and the author of the Epistle of Barnabas (before 130) seem to have used Heb. Around 200, Pantaenus mentioned the Epistle "to the Hebrews", and ascribed it to Paul, who, he explains, did not sign it because he was professedly Apostle to the Gentiles, and for other reasons (see Eusebius, *Hist.eccl.* 6. 14. 4). Clement of Alexandria, disciple of Pantaenus, wrote in his

---

[1] On the place of Hebrews in early tradition, see C. Spicq, *L'Épître aux Hébreux*, v. 1 (Paris, 1952), pp. 169-196.

Hypotyposes (before 215), that Heb was written by Paul in Hebrew and translated into Greek by Luke (according to Eusebius, *Hist.eccl.* 6. 14. 2). By the end of the 4th century the canonicity of the Epistle was everywhere admitted. There are reasons for believing that its addressees were in fact Christians of Jewish extraction who could understand the elaborate parallels drawn with the Jewish liturgy and be particularly sensitive to the Author's constant use of the Old Testament. In addition, it is obvious that Judeo-Christians, more than others, could have felt attracted by the Jewish liturgy and in need of being confirmed in their adhesion to the superior liturgy of Jesus the High Priest.

The epistle draws on many points from the early Christian kerygma and in doctrines shows strong affinities with both Pauline and Johannine Christologies.[2] It will be opportunely indicated that Heb has perhaps the closest parallels with Ephesians and the First Epistle of Peter, this last writing containing what seems to be the clearest allusion to the priesthood of Christ outside Heb. Heb is, in the author's own words, a "speech of exhortation" (13:22), or, so to speak, a written sermon.* Although traditionally assigned to the Corpus Paulinum it can hardly be Paul's for a variety of reasons, the main one being that the central theme of Heb, Christ's high priesthood, is not explicitly found in any other Epistle.** One way of asserting a certain degree of Pauline authorship of the writing would be "to hold that a writer, who was at home in the world of Pauline ideas, received the commission to compose his work from the Apostle, who allowed him complete liberty in its composition, and that Paul then approved of the finished work and provided it with his own conclusion."[3]

Who this writer was cannot be determined with certainty. He must have been an original and first class mind, well versed in Scripture, eloquent, and a master of Greek prose. Heb's Greek is the best in the NT and the Epistle is constructed on a most careful plan.[4] Because of the literary, non-theological, similarities Heb has with the works of Philo,+ it has been said, probably rightly, that the writer of Heb was "a Philonian converted to Christianity."[5] Apollos would, it seems, satisfy all these requirements, taking into account the description we have of him in Acts 18:24-28 and elsewhere. Paul writes of him as if he

---

[2] See C. Spicq, *Hébreux*, v. 1, pp. 92-166.

[3] EncDictBibl c. 962.

[4] See A. Vanhoye, *La structure littéraire de l'Épître aux Hébreux* (Bruges, 1963).

[5] E. Ménégoz, *La Théologie de l'épître aux Hébreux* (Paris, 1894), p. 198.

belonged to the same category as himself and Peter (1 Cor 1 :12, 3 :22). Hugh Montefiore has persuasively restated Père Spicq's arguments in favor of Apollos, and has gone beyond most other scholars along the following line : "A possible reconstruction of events is offered here on the grounds that the Epistle to the Hebrews was written to the Church at Corinth by Apollos at Ephesus some time between A.D. 52 and A.D. 54, while Paul was on his tour of Caesarea, Antioch and the churches of Galatia (Act 18 :20-23)."[6] There apparently exists no major internal objection to such an early dating of Heb. On the contrary it would explain the distinctive originality of the writing in respect to other NT scriptures and would be suggested by certain archaic formulations. If Apollos wrote on his own, independently of Paul, it seems difficult to explain, however, that his authorship remained unknown or, at least, was forgotten when Clement of Rome used the Epistle towards the close of the first century. In any case, the "splendid indifference" of the author to the actual circumstances of Jewish sacrifice in Jerusalem suggests that he had no accurate first hand knowledge of it and that he wrote before the destruction of the temple in 70 A.D.

a) Jesus, High Priest of a Superior, Eternal Order

To be understood by his readers and to establish his doctrine the Author of Heb compares Christ's priesthood to that of the Mosaic institution. For him, however, they do not belong to the same category : one is of a superior, extraterrestrial, eternal order, the other is an earthly, temporal institution. The author brings out most clearly this fundamental distinction by referring to the priesthood of Melchizedek (ch. 7).

1. King-Priest Melchizedek

Well knowing that the Israelite priests, according to the Law and also in practice, have to be of Levi, while Jesus is of the tribe of Judah (7:14), the author of Heb finds expressed in Gen 14:18-20 and in Ps 110:4 (LXX) the revelation of God's will concerning the advent of the Messianic Priest independently of Levi and of the Mosaic institution. These two passages raise textual and hermeneutical problems that are discussed in the commentaries and in specific monographs. * Our author

---

[6] H. Montefiore, *Hebrews,* p. 12. O. Kuss, on the other hand, finds no evidence whatsoever in support of Apollos (*Der Brief an die Hebräer,* 2d ed., Regensburg 1966, p. 21).

reads these texts in the Greek Septuagint version,[7] accepts them as divine revelation, and understands their statements in a Messianic sense. Melchizedek, for him, is a type of Christ as regards priesthood. "A type presupposes a purpose in history wrought out from age to age... This consideration tends further to explain why the writer of the Epistle takes the Biblical record of Melchizedek, that is Melchizedek so far as he enters into the divine history, and not Melchizedek himself, as a type of Christ. The history of the Bible is the record of the divine life of humanity, of humanity as it was disciplined for the Christ."[8] The interest of the Author in the Israelite priesthood and sacrifice as described in the OT, not as existing in practice, could be explained along similar lines.

Concluding the Second Part (3:1-5:10) of his Epistle, our author writes that Christ in connection with his meritorious sufferings was "*proclaimed* by God High Priest according to the order of Melchizedek" (5:10). Further on he speaks of Jesus as "*become* High Priest according to the order of Melchizedek," this time in connection with his entering behind the veil as our forerunner (6:20). Only in the first main section (ch. 7) of the third part (5:11-10:39) does he, however, elaborate a parallel between the priesthood of Melchizedek and that of Christ. Since Abraham paid tithes to Melchizedek and received his blessing, he argues, it is clear that Melchizedek's priesthood ranks above that of the sons of Levi, who had Abraham as ancestor (7:1-10). The descendants of Abraham were included in him, notes Westcott, not only physically but also because "he was the recipient of the divine promises (7:6) in which the fulness of the race in its manifold developments was included" (p. 180). This is true in a sense, but it must be observed that for Paul the true posterity of Abraham according to the promises was Christ (Gal 3:16)! In any case it is implied in the author's reasoning that if Melchizedek was greater than Levi then *a fortiori* Christ was, of whom Melchizedek was a type (see *id.*, p. 181).

Now this superior priesthood of Melchizedek resembles that of Christ and must have been therefore its prophetic type. "King of justice," "king of peace" (7:2) are epithets that apply to the name "Melchizedek" and, according to Semitic mentality, to his person as well. But

7 How he reads them is explained by F. Schröger, *Der Verfasser des Hebräerbriefes als Schriftausleger* (Regensburg, 1968), pp. 130-159. Besides RSV, we have also used in citing Heb : A. Vanhoye, *A Structural Translation of the Epistle to the Hebrews*, tr. J. Swetnam (Rome, 1964).

8 .B F. Westcott, *The Epistle to the Hebrews* (3d ed., London, 1906), p. 202.

justice and peace are attributes of the Messianic King (cf. Is 9:6-7) and refer to Christ. The Author in fact calls Christ "king" implicitly both here (7:2) and in his use of Ps 110:1, 4. Melchizedek, besides, has no known genealogy, possibly like the Servant (Is 53:8), but unlike the Levitical priests, for whom it was an essential matter. The silence of Scripture suggests in addition, that Melchizedek had "neither beginning of days nor end of life" (7:3). The mystery surrounding his origin and his later fate leads the author to conclude : "Having been likened to the Son of God, [he] remains priest in perpetuity" (7:3; cf. 7:24).

This last statement raises one of the particular problems which we shall now discuss. From the fact that no end of his life has been recorded, Melchizedek is said to remain priest in perpetuity. This is less an argumentation than an illustration. The author's real proof text is Ps 110:1, 4, interpreted messianically. Having established the legitimacy of comparing Melchizedek's priesthood to that of Christ, our author draws from the Messianic king-priest figure whatever relevant traits he can find to enrich his parallel. According to A. T. Hanson he would really believe, although he does not say so explicitly, that Melchizedek was Christ pre-incarnate, who appeared to Abraham in the person of the priest-king of Salem.[9] Some ancient writers have asserted the same, long before modern scholars, and it is common Christian teaching that the Son of God was active in regard to the world as Logos and Wisdom. Among the "Catholic" Melchizedekians, some held, according to Epiphanius, who refutes them (*Haer* 55.7), that the Son of God himself appeared to Abraham *en idea anthrōpōn*, "in human form." To the question "Who is this king of justice, priest of God?", Ambrose answers: "He to whom it was said : 'You are a priest forever according to the order of Melchizedek' (Ps 109.4), that is, the Son of God, priest of the Father, who by the sacrifice of his body atoned to the Father for our sins" (*De Abraham* 1, 3.16). It is, however, very unlikely that the author would have given such emphasis to the advent of Christ (cf. 1:2, 6; 9:26), had he believed that it was really His second coming in the flesh. Rather he believed what he teaches, namely that Melchizedek was a prophetic type of Christ as regards priesthood. Furthermore he very probably considered Melchizedek to have been an historical person, the way he appears in Gen 14:18-20, unsubjected to the discerning eye of modern criticism.

---

[9] A. T. Hanson, "Christ in the Old Testament according to Hebrews," in *Studia Evangelica*, v. 2. Texte und Untersuchungen 87 (Berlin 1964) 393-406.

There is no need to seek a prehistory to Heb's use of Melchizedek, outside Gen 14 and Ps 110. These are probably the author's only sources, beside his Christian faith. His account shows no traceable theological dependence with respect to Philo's allegory on Melchizedek,* to Judaic speculation like that evidenced by Josephus, or to Qumran. In the rabbinical tradition, for example, the oracle of Ps 110 (=109 LXX), granting royal priesthood, is applied to Abraham, to whom God bestows the priesthood of Melchizedek, demoted because he named Abraham before God (Gen 14:19).[10] The author of Heb avoids such fineries of reasoning.+ It can be said, however, with G. Schrenk: "In the light of fulfillment, the truth of Christ is read back into the OT; it lays its impress upon the sayings of Scripture by way of Ps 109:4."[11] Heb retains of the Genesis narrative only that which serves to illustrate the priesthood of Christ and that which shows the superiority of Melchizedek's priesthood over the Levitical. Thus our author omits to say that Melchizedek "offered bread and wine," to God, or to Abraham, estimating this episode to be either irrelevant for his theme or likely to weaken his argumentation (superiority of M. over Abraham).

2. *Insufficiency of the Old Priesthood*

Our author will now show that the old priesthood was insufficient and had to be replaced. He has in mind the Levitic or Aaronic priesthood (7:11) and makes no mention of pagan priesthoods. He does not speculate on Melchizedek as a "holy pagan,"++ being satisfied with the Genesis statement that he "was priest of God the Most High" (7:1).

The Aaronic priesthood, instituted by Moses, was radically insufficient because it fulfilled nothing, like the Law, with which it was closely connected (7:11, 19). It is clear from 7:19, 25, 10:1 that "fulfilling" (*teleioun*) in this context has to do with approaching God, with coming into fellowship with him.[12] And this "perfection" the Aaronic priesthood did not have and could not procure, because the rites it conducted would not purify the conscience of the worshipper (9:9), in contrast to what the faithful obtain through Christ's sacrifice (10:4, 11:40, 12:23). The priesthood of non-Jewish Melchizedek, on the other hand, not subject to the dispensation of the Law, not of the order of Aaron (7:11), is to be judged differently, like the priesthood of our Lord who is not of

[10] See *Nedarim* 326 (pp. 98-99 in the Soncino edit. of *The Babylonian Talmud*).

[11] G. Schrenk in Kittel ThW (Eng), v. 3, p. 275.

[12] See G. Schrenk, *ibid.*, p. 278.

Levi but of Judah (7:14). If the whole Law was an apparent failure (see JB : Rom 8:4), so was the priesthood which supported it (7:11) and on which it was founded. By putting an end to the Law, whose end he was (Rom 10 :4), Christ in a way also fulfilled it (Mt 5 :17), replacing it by "the law of faith" (Rom 3:27), "the law of Christ" (Gal 6:2), "the law of the Spirit" (Rom 8:1). The apparent failure of the Levitical priesthood fulfilled in fact a divine purpose, since while it was still in full activity came the promise of the new priesthood (Gen 14; Ps 110) of the era of grace (Rom 5:21).

The old priesthood was insufficient for another reason as well. The Levitical priests could perform no lasting ministry bearing permanent fruit. They disappeared through death and succeeded to one another in great numbers (7:23), a circumstance which shows how restricted was their accomplishment. They had no escape from the limitations of the flesh. It is not so in the other order of priesthood, in which another has become priest "not according to a law of fleshly precept but according to a power of indestructible life" (7:16). It was, for example, because of carnal law that there were requirements for OT priesthood regarding outward descent, outward perfection, and outward purity. In the new priesthood an inward force succeeds to the Law of outward restraint and the law of carnal generation is not binding. The permanency of this priesthood is founded on an oath : "The Lord has sworn, and he will not repent : You are a priest forever, according to the order of Melchizedek" (Ps 109:4; Heb 7:17, 21). To Phinehas and to his descendants after him was granted "the covenant of a perpetual priesthood" (Num 25 :13; cf. Ex 40 :15), but this, Westcott explains, did not imply the permanence of the personal life; it was subject to the conditions of succession, and therefore to the possibility of change, while a priesthood founded on a divine oath is absolute and immutable (p. 187).

The insufficiency of the old priesthood is linked to the inefficacy of the old cultus, which the author will describe in ch. 8. The deficiency of both is stressed to show that a change was necessary (7.11-12), to underline the superiority of Christ's priesthood, and thus admonish those who would esteem no other priesthood than that of Aaron.

3. The High Priesthood of Christ

We want here to concentrate on the notion of the High Priesthood of Christ in Heb, while in the next section the sacrificial function of Jesus as High Priest will be treated systematically. Here and there also the difficult question will be raised : how and how much does Christ function as High Priest in Heaven ?

Jesus is called "Priest" or "High Priest" only in Heb and his priestly functions are scarcely described as such in the other NT writings. To present explicitly Jesus as Priest the author of Heb had to surmount obstacles which a less talented mind would have thought insuperable. He showed clearly that despite outward appearances the death of Jesus was a sacrifice, a free oblation (cf. Heb 10:5-10), and that priesthood was divinely destined to achieve in Christ, beyond its failing Aaronic exemplar, the removal of sin and the union with God.

Purification from Sins

Before explicitly stating, and then expounding, his main theme, the sacrifice of Jesus as High Priest, the author of Heb prepares its introduction by formulating or combining in a distinctive manner conceptions of Christ and his work known to primitive Christianity. Thus it was traditional to say "Christ died for our sins in accordance with the scriptures" (1 Cor 15:3). The phrase "after having effected purification from sins (Heb 1 :3) gives a ritual expression to the notion, since the concept "to purify" is current in the ritual law (cf. Lev 11-16) and is related to the expiatory rites : "For on this day shall atonement be made for you, to purify you; from all your sins you shall be purified before the Lord" (Lev 16:30). Outside Heb "purification from sins" is used in the NT only in a late text (2 Pet 1:9).* For Heb, in fact, the high priest's role is closely related to the removal of sins (cf. 5:1, 3) and this aspect also is alluded to in the phrase of Heb 1:3. The blood of Christ is not, however, meant to procure the ritual purity of the flesh but to "purify our conscience from dead works" (9:14). Having effected purification from sins the Son "took His seat to the right of the majesty on high" (1:3). Thus is introduced a distinctive feature of Jesus the High Priest : His sacrifice achieved, He rests from his work (cf. 4:10) and reigns at the right hand of God, like the king-priest of Ps 110 (cf. Heb 10:12). The author saw a connection between this title, "the Son," and that of "High Priest" as predicated of Jesus (cf. 5:5, 8; 7:3, 28).

Above Angels, yet Brother of Men

In the first part of the Epistle (1:5-2:16) the author contemplates Christ as the enthroned Lord, as glorified in consequence of His sacrifice

(2:9). This is in conformity with the kerygma, as expressed, for example, by St. Peter in his oration to the Jews : "Let all the house of Israel therefore know assuredly that God has made Him both Lord and Christ, this Jesus whom you crucified" (Acts 2:36). While for Paul Christ Jesus has been constituted Son of God in power by His resurrection (Rom 1:4), Heb presents the Son as fulfilling the prophecies relating to the expected eschatological King-Messiah (Pss 2, 45 and 2 Sam 7:14). That v. 1 and not v. 4 of Ps 110 is quoted in Heb 1:13 shows that the author is presently concentrating on the theme of the enthroned Lord, worshipped in the Christian community, although he never forgets that this King is also Priest. By quoting Ps 102, which concerns God Himself as universal Judge, the author (Heb 1:10) indicates that he is thinking of Christ as the transcendent Messiah reigning in heaven, as the real Son of God. These various titles are distinct expressions of what "the name He has inherited" (1:4) does in fact contain.

It is stressed, besides, in Heb, that Christ has obtained the transcendent state above the angels after having been ranked below them (2:5-9), in solidarity with men, whom He still calls his brothers (2:10-16). For He suffered in His human mortal nature "that through death He might render powerless him who has the power of death, that is, the devil, and deliver those who through fear of death were subject to lifelong bondage" (2:14-15). By representing the redeeming Christ as solidary with men the author recalls a traditional truth (cf. Rom 8:3), easily linked to what is distinctive of the high priest's vocation (5:1-4). All this is explicitly stated in the concluding verses of the first part, which announce the two sections of the second part : 3:1-4:14 (Jesus, faithful) and 4:15-5:10 (Jesus, compassionate High-Priest). We read :

> Hence He had in all things to be made like His brethren so that He might become a merciful and faithful high priest for the things of God in order to make expiation for the sins of the people; for in what He suffered Himself having been tested, He is able to offer help to those being tested (2 :17-18).

Whereas in Judaism heredity and specific rules tended to separate the priests and the high priests from the people, the Epistle stresses that the High Priest Jesus belongs to the generation of man, and that precisely He became a merciful and faithful high priest through human suffering and not through an external rite. The author will, however, also insist on the innocence of Jesus and write : "It was fitting that we should have such a high priest, holy, blameless, unstained, separated from sinners, exalted above the heavens" (7:26).

Faithful over his House

In the first verses of the second part of the Epistle (3:1-5:10) the "faithfulness" of Moses and of Jesus are compared. Moses is said to be faithful *in* his entire house as servant, while Christ is faithful as Son *over* his house (3:1-16). In this Christ will appear superior to Moses : as having greater glory, which He shares with the Creator himself, as being "trustworthy" (*pistos*) over a larger (only insinuated) house, and as having authority over it as Son, not merely in it as servant (Moses). Only a few of the exegetical problems which these difficult verses raise can be here dealt with.

"In his entire house," at the end of v. 2, could refer to the house of Jesus, of Moses, or of God, "the one who made him." This last meaning seems preferable, because of 10:21, "a high-priest over the house of God," and also because of Num 12:7 : "Not so with my servant Moses; he is entrusted with all my house." But in Heb 3:1, as in 3:6, "over his house" can be understood to be the house of both God and the Son, since Christ has edified the house and is Lord over it. *Oikos Theou* generally refers in the OT to the temple or sanctuary (1 Kg 6:1). In 2 Sam 7:11, 16, 19, 25, 26, 27, 29 *oikos* is used figuratively of David's dynasty (cf. 1 Chr 17:12-13), the house of David.* In a few texts God calls (the land of) Israel "my house" (Jer 12:7; Hos 9:15; Ps 114:1). In the context of Heb the "house" in which Moses is faithful as servant stands for Israel, which Moses organized in a nation and to which he gave a law, a sanctuary and cultic institutions.

Jesus, the High Priest, is called faithful over his house (3:2, 6), Spicq explains (v. 2, p. 65), "as having exactly accomplished His mission according to the divine prescriptions." The Greek *pistos* is, however, patient of another meaning, "trustworthy," which better suits the present context : Christ, the Son of God, exalted in glory, is sovereign and thus trustworthy in His role as the High Priest through whom we accede to God (10:19-25). Moses also was *pistos* over God's house, for his authority was exceptional since God spoke to him mouth to mouth and not in dreams (Num 12:6, 8). The statement then of Heb 3:2, Jesus the High Priest, "faithful to the one who made him," should be understood to mean : He is divinely accredited as worthy of being trusted, being invested with God's own authority. Similarly, we read in 1 Sam 3:20 (LXX) that "all Israel ... knew Samuel (to be) *pistos eis prophētēn tō kuriō*, accredited by God as prophet."

Beyond the debated questions relating to Heb 3.3-4 the following can be retained as certain : the author suggests that Christ's activity and power over His house can be equated to that of God himself and extend to the whole people of God, from the beginning till the end of the world (cf. Spicq, v. 2, pp. 67-68). About to introduce an exhortation, the author, however, states : "Christ, as Son [is said to be faithful], over His house; whose house we are, if we maintain the accorded right (*parrēsia*) and the glorying in the hope" (3:6). The author's generation of believers and all believing Christians constitute the privileged (not the exclusive) portion of the house which Christ has edified by his redemptive work. To illustrate this texts can be adduced from other NT writings : "Come to Him, to that living stone, rejected by men but in God's sight chosen and precious; and like living stones be yourselves built into a spiritual house, to be a holy priesthood, to offer spiritual sacrifices acceptable to God through Jesus Christ" (1 Pet 2:4-5; cf. 2:10; 3:18). As second text the whole second chapter of Ephesians could be quoted : God, it says, "who is rich in mercy ... even when we were dead through our trespasses, made us alive together with Christ, and raised us up with Him, and made us sit up with Him in the heavenly places in Christ Jesus ... So then you are ... fellow citizens with the saints and members of the household (*oikeios*) of God ... Christ Jesus Himself being the cornerstone, in whom the whole structure is joined together and grows into a holy temple (*naon*) in the Lord."

Jesus, compassionate High Priest

The author had explained that Jesus, the High Priest exalted above the angels, was not ashamed to call men "my brothers," in His redemptive role (2:5-18). When he comes, to the end of the second part, to define more closely the function of the high priest, as he understands it, he presents Jesus as the compassionate High Priest, tested in His sufferings like the other men and Himself brought to fulfillment through His sacrifice (4:15-5 :10). This distinctive teaching of Heb is perfectly consonant with the whole revealed Christian doctrine, illuminates the notion of sacrificial redemption, and goes a long way towards formulating the mystery of Christ's unique sacrifice. Between the Jewish high priest and the worshippers a certain solidarity existed, but it could not express itself, in any deep sense, in sacrifice. For the Jewish high priest did not offer himself, like Jesus. But Jesus, the High Priest, contained, so to speak, the whole of mankind in His humanity, which through sacrifice returned to God and opened to all believers in Him the way to the heavenly sanctuary (10 :19-20) : "Having been given fulfillment, He became for all those who obey Him a cause of everlasting salvation" (5:9).

The high priest, in the words of Heb, "taken from men is constituted for men in regard to the things of God (cf. 2:17), to offer gifts and sacrifices for sins" (5:1). This is a main theme in Heb, for Christ is High Priest in the fullest sense when offering Himself in sacrifice : not like the other priests, "He, having offered for all time* a single sacrifice for sins, sat down at the right hand of God ... For by a single offering He has perfected for all time those who are sanctified" (10:12, 14 : RSV). This is a recurring theme : "By that will we have been sanctified through the offering of the body of Jesus Christ once for all" (10:10). The purpose of Christ's sacrifice was the removal of sin (9:26, 28). It was also that of the sacrifices which the Jewish high priest offered, either for himself or for the people (5:3; cf. Lev 16:11, 15, 17). Elsewhere we learn that Jesus the High Priest "has no need, like the [other] high priests, to offer sacrifices daily, first for his own sins and then for those of the people; He did *this* once for all when He offered up Himself" (7:27). "This" is usually referred to the last statement only : offer for the sins of the people, since Christ has no sin (4:15). The epithets applied to Him in this same context, "holy, innocent, immaculate" (7:26), refer, however, to the High Priest after His sacrifice, "separated from the sinners and become higher than the heavens" (*ibid.*). It is then perhaps not altogether excluded that Jesus could have offered Himself in sacrifice also for the sins which in a way he had made His, namely by assuming mortality, a human condition brought about by sin. Thus St. Paul could write that God has done what the law, weakened by the flesh, could not do : "sending His own Son in the likeness of sinful flesh and as a sin offering,+ he condemned sin in the flesh" (Rom 8:3). Perhaps also can Heb 9:28, "offered once for the taking away (*anapherein*) of the sins of many," be understood somewhat in the same way as 1 Pet 2:24 : "He himself carried up (*anapherein*) our sins to the cross," i.e. to cancel them. Christ's *teleiôsis*, "fulfilment," also involved His being liberated from "the likeness of sinful flesh," and this can explain why Jesus the High Priest is said to "have *found* an eternal redemption" (9:11) and how the heavenly things themselves have to be purified with "better" sacrifices (9:23).

There exists, then, the possibility of seeing in Heb 7:27 the contrast where it seems to lie grammatically : our High Priest has no need *daily* to do what the high priests did, for this He did *once for all* by offering

Himself. This is a mere possibility, for, in fact, the author, announcing in 2:17 forthcoming developments, states that Jesus had in all things to become like His brothers to be a merciful and a faithful High Priest "in order to expiate the sins of the people." "Also for Himself" is not mentioned, as compared to what we read in 5:3 of the high priest's sacrificial function : "He has, just as for the people so also for Himself, to offer for sins" (see also 9:7). The high priest has to offer also for himself either because he is personally a sinner or because of his solidarity with the people, whose sins are to be expiated. It has been explained how this second meaning is applicable to Christ.

The Prayer of our High Priest (5:5-10)

Applying to our Lord his definition of the high priest (5:1-4) the author of Heb first explains, quoting Ps 2:7 and Ps 110:4, that Christ, like Aaron (5:4), was called by God to the high priesthood (5:5-6); then the proposition continues :

> He, "who in the days of His flesh,
> having offered petitions and supplications
> to the one able to save Him from death,
> with strong cries and tears,
> and having been heard because of His reverence,
> although being Son, learned from the things He
> suffered the obedience,
> and having been given fulfilment (*teleiōtheis*),
> He became for all those who obey Him
> a cause of everlasting salvation,
> proclaimed by God High Priest according
> to the order of Melchizedek (5 :7-10)."

This long sequence* dramatically describes how our High Priest suffered anguish and offered intense prayers in connection with His vocation.[13] Omitting details and discussions, it can be retained that in His prayer, which was heard, our High Priest asked that His passion be reckoned as a sacrifice, not one ending in death, but one leading to the resurrection (cf. 11:19, 13:20). For only such a sacrifice would make

---

[13] On Heb 5.5-10, see the detailed study of A. Vanhoye, *Textus de sacerdotio Christi* (ad usum auditorum, Rome, 1969), pp. 91-124. The connection of the passage with the Gospel tradition should be seen less in precise references, for example, to the Agony narratives, than in a general evocation of the Passion turned to sacrifice by intensive prayer. See also T. Lescow, "Jesus in Gethsemane bei Lukas und im Hebräerbrief," ZNTWiss 58 (1967) 215-239 (quite a complete study of the literary sources of the passage).

Him the High Priest who given fulfilment would bring to salvation all those who obey Him, those, that is, made participants of His priestly sacrificial *transitus* (cf. Phil 3:10, 11, 21).

Leaving for subsequent treatment the connection implied between Christ's filiation and His High Priesthood, we still have to examine the teaching of 5:9-10 on Christ's coming to fulfilment and His being proclaimed High Priest. Whereas *teleioun*, "fulfilling," used in other contexts to express what priesthood does or does not procure, means to bring closer to God, or to render apt to approach God, *teleiousthai*, "to be given fulfillment," "to be consummated," applied to Christ, is clearly connected in 5:9 with His becoming High Priest, as also in 7:28 : "For the Law constitutes as high priests men having weakness, while the word of the oathtaking ... [constitutes High Priest] a Son come to fulfilment (*teteleiōmenon*) for the [eternal] age." The terms *teleioun*, "to fulfill," and *teleiōsis*, "fulfillment," occur in the LXX to translate the Hebrew *millē' yād*, "fill the hand," and *millu'im*, "filling (of the hand)," expressions which designate the instituting of an Aaronic priest in his office or the sacrifice offered on this occasion. * It is possible, not certain, that the author of Heb thought of these expressions in using *teleioun* and *teleiōsis*.

Through the anguish and suffering, accepted and sustained in a spirit (cf. 9:14) of obedience and prayer, not only the event (the Passion) but Jesus Himself, so to speak, was transformed in a new man : "Although being Son, [He] learned from the things He suffered the obedience" (5:8). Jesus fully submitted to the will of God, exhibiting, with God's grace, in Himself, that change of heart which, as announced by the prophets, would characterize the Messianic people (Jer 31:31-34; Ezek 36:26; Heb 8:8-12). Not that Jesus Himself turned from rebellion to submission. Heb notes carefully that "entering into the world" Christ chose the path of obedience, even unto death (10:4-10; cf. Phil 2:6-8). Yet His humanity was "in the likeness of sinful flesh" (Rom 8:3), and had to be transformed, to appear before God. Having declared that heavenly things, mainly, it seems, Christ's humanity, have to be purified by better sacrifices, namely by Christ's own sacrifice (9:23),[14] the author of Heb adds immediately : "For not in a sanctuary made by hands did Christ enter ... but into the heaven itself, to appear before the face of God for us" (9:24). It is also Paul's teaching that "flesh and blood

[14] See A. Vanhoye's analysis of Heb 9.22,23 in VerbDom 44 (1966), pp. 177-191, and my own remarks on 9.23 in VerbDom 46 (1968), pp. 248-255.

cannot inherit the kingdom of God, nor does the perishable inherit the imperishable" (1 Cor 15:50). The sacrificial transformation of Christ's body expressed in the flesh the total oblation of His inner self accepted by God for the redemption of humanity.* This was Christ's *teleiōsis*, the great achievement of His priesthood. Manifested as Priest by his sacrifice (cf. 9:26), as such He was proclaimed by God when in His own *teleiōsis* he brought others to their *teleiōsis*, to their union with God (10:14) : "Having been given fulfilment, He became for all those who obey Him a cause of everlasting salvation, proclaimed by God High Priest according to the order of Melchizedek" (5:9-10).

Psalm 110 in Hebrews

Heb treats explicitly of the superiority of Christ's priesthood in 7:20-28. Several aspects of this theme have been examined above, in contrast to the insufficiency of the old priesthood. The permanency of the new priesthood founded on a divine oath was peculiarly noted. Christ's title of "guarantor of a better covenant" (7:22) will come for study below with related contexts. We wish here to examine more closely Heb's use of Ps 110:1, (LXX 109) and Christ's priestly role as Intercessor in heaven (Heb 7:25).

Ps 110 was used by Jesus himself in putting the Pharisees to a test : How can the Christ be both the lord of David and his son ? (Mt 22:44-45, parall.), and when he told the Sanhedrin : "Hereafter you will see the Son of man seated at the right hand of the Power, and coming on the clouds of heaven" (Mt 26:64, parall.).** Ps 110 :1 is often quoted in other NT writings in support of the belief that Christ, after his Ascension, sat at the right hand of God. + Heb possibly alludes to the Ascension as well, when it speaks of "a great High Priest who has gone through the heavens" (4:14), who has "become higher than the heavens" (7:26). More precisely the Son's taking His seat to the right of the majesty on high" (1:3) and the application to Him of Ps 110:1 (Heb 1:13) show how superior to the angels He is. Christ's seating at the right hand of God comes after He has effected purification of sin (1:3), offered one sacrifice for sins (10:12), or as a reward for enduring the cross (12:2). For Heb, in fact, sitting at the right hand of God is for Christ the High Priest an enthronement as the Messianic King (1:3, 13; cf. 1 Pet 3:22), a coming into His rest with the pilgrim people (3:13-4. 11; esp. 4:10), and it marks the completi on once-for-all of His sacrificial work (1:3; 10:12).

Heb 1 :3 quotes Ps 110 :1, not directly from the OT, but as used in the Christian tradition, more precisely perhaps as in primitive confessions of faith in Christ. In the Psalm "sit at my right hand" expresses rather the entering into a new state or situation : "be seated at my right hand". In Heb 1:3 what is retained is the action of sitting that took place, terminating a previous activity. In contrast to the Aaronic priests who stand each day ministering the cult, repeatedly offering the same sacrifices, Jesus the High Priest, having offered once for all one sacrifice for sins, sat at the right hand of God (10:12). In Heb 1:13 Ps 110:1 is quoted exactly as in the Septuagint.

Ps 110 was quite obviously used for the enthronement of one or more Israelite kings. The historical situation of the Psalm is a debated question. E. Podechard's interpretation,[15] a very plausible one, rests on the assumption that Ps 110 was composed to honor David, when the sacred Ark was transferred to Sion (2 Sam 6), or soon afterwards. Melchizedek, king at Shalem, the Jebusite city, was priest of *'el-'elyon* (God-Most-High : Gen 14:18), worshipped by the Phoenicians and the Canaanites. In a way David installed Yahweh in Sion, to replace the former divinity. In return (cf. Ps 2:6) Yahweh proclaimed David king and priest according to the order of Melchizedek (Ps 110 :4) and made with his family an eternal covenant (cf. also Ps 89:4, 5, 29, 30, 37; 132:11-18). The invitation of the oracle, "Sit at my right hand" (Ps 110:1), could refer, adds Podechard, to the location of the palace in relation to the Tent of the Ark (2 Sam 6:17; 7:18). It is also possible that for the enthronement the king sat on a throne beside the Ark, seat of God's invisible presence. If the Psalm is typically, not directly, Messianic, the enthronement of the Davidic king prefigured the heavenly enthronement of the real Messianic heir to David's throne (cf. Lk 1:32-33).

The author of Heb certainly considered Ps 110 as Messianic and understood v. 4 as referring to Melchizedek as a king-priest : "The Lord has sworn, and he will not repent : You are a priest forever, according to the order of Melchizedek" (cf. Heb 5:6, 20; 6:20; 7:11, 17). The main stream of Christian exegesis is agreed that this was indeed the original meaning of the Psalm. Yet this traditional view has been challenged, not too seriously, by a few authors, including H. H. Rowley, who places the Psalm in David's time but understands it as follows : In the first three verses Zadok addresses himself to the king; in the

---

[15] E. Podechard, *Le Psautier : Ps 95-100 and Ps 110.* (Lyon, 1954). See also A. Serina, *La figura di Melchisedec nel salmo CX.4* (Trapani 1971).

fourth he is spoken to by the king, who confirms him in the priesthood.[16] If this were true, then we could not say, with J. A. Fitzmyer, quoting prevailing opinion : "Ps 110:4 thus presents the king as the heir of Melchizedek succeeding him as priest forever" (CathBiblQuart 25, 1963, p. 308). In fact the concept itself of priest-king would not be mentioned in the psalm. But the king of Ps 110 may have been called "priest" as being the Messiah himself. If not, David or a Davidic heir could be referred to as priest, as exercising some priestly functions in the way Israelite kings did, as successors of Melchizedek who in Jerusalem had been priest and king.

"Always Living to Intercede"

Even though it consistently affirms that Jesus, our High Priest, offered only one sacrifice for all (7:27, 10:10), Heb nonetheless insists on the heavenly character and the permanency of Christ's priesthood : "He, due to His remaining for ever, has the permanent priesthood" (7:24); He is "cultminister of the sanctuary" (8:2, i.e. in heaven; cf. 9:24); "If He were on the earth He would not be a priest at all" (8:4). Heb, on the other hand, closely related the priesthood of Jesus to His sacrifice, in His *transitus*, that is, from earth to heaven, from His mortal to His immortal condition. The term of His sacrifice was the entrance into heaven, once for all (6:20, 9:12, 24). And as any movement is specified by its term, so also sacrifice, and thus can both the sacrifice and the priesthood of Jesus be called celestial. Christ's sacrifice is celestial for another reason as well : an eternal spirit animated it (9:14), God was at work in it. It is through divine action that the human nature was transformed in Christ's *teleiōsis*. Christ is priest forever as being of the order of Melchizedek (Ps 110:4), but also because His sacrificial *transitus* has eternal value, for Himself and for the countless generations, past and present, saved for all eternity. *

For Heb, Cody believes, Christ carries out three priestly functions in the heavenly sanctuary : He purifies the sanctuary (9:23), He appears in the presence of God (9:24), He intercedes for us (7:25).[17] It is far

---

[16] H. H. Rowley, "Melchizedek and Zadok (Gen 14 and Ps 110)," *Fs. für A. Bertholet* (Tübingen, 1950), pp. 469-470. Some recent authors put in doubt the reference to a personal Melchizedek, reading instead *malkî ṣedeq*, "my legitimate king." What is important here is that the author of Heb read Melchizedek, as in the LXX.

[17] A. Cody, *Heavenly Sanctuary and Liturgy in the Epistle to the Hebrews* (St. Meinrad, Ind., 1960), p. 193.

from sure, however, that "to purify heavenly things" (9:23) means to purify the sanctuary. There are good resons for believing that to purify heavenly things by better sacrifices refers to Christ's own sacrificial *teleiōsis*, as we have explained above and elsewhere. As the next verse explains, thus "purified" He entered into the heavenly sanctuary to appear before the face of God for us (9:24). Having entered once for all, our High Priest remains seated in the presence of God throughout eternity (10:12), priest forever (7:17, 21, 28), once for all made manifest in the sacrificial epiphany (9:26). The saving action of Christ remains forever, being eternal in quality and in value, for it was accomplished "through an eternal spirit" (9:14), still operating in virtue of Christ's sacrifice. All this is involved, and even more, in the concept of Christ's priestly presence in heaven.

Christ's presence is already an intercession, for "you have approached", the Epistle teaches, "a mediator of a new convenant, Jesus, and a sprinkling of blood pleading more insistently than Abel" (12:24). "For the Epistle to the Hebrews, Cody writes, the intercession of Our Lord is really and simply equivalent to His expiatory activity, carried out once in earthly history and brought up against eternity in the celestial order."[18] The Epistle provides, however, no evidence showing that its author believed in a celestial sacrifice of Christ, whose oblation and offering belong to the historical past only.* Heb nowhere states that Christ's sacrifice is either renewed, re-offered, re-presented, or even prolonged in heaven. There, Christ's sacerdotal activity consists in being present and in interceding (*entugchanein*).

In contrast with the Aaronic priests who, being subject to death, come and go in considerable numbers (7:23), Jesus the High Priest "has the permanent priesthood; whence He is able to save to perfection those who approach God through Him, always living to intercede for them" (7:24-25). No one can say with certainty what exactly the author meant by Christ's intercession. Perhaps he did not think of a distinctive function, having rather in mind what Christ is as the leader and the cause of men's salvation (2:10, 5:9), as the provider of their *teleiōsis* (10:14), allowing them to approach God (4:16, 7:19, 25). The concept of priestly sacrificial redemption wrought by Christ is foremost in the author's thought. As for the idea of Christ's intercessory role it probably belonged to his less distinctive conceptions. He received it from tradition and he probably had it in mind every time he says that Jesus sits

[18] A. Cody, *Heavenly Sanctuary*, p. 199.

at the right hand of God (1:3, 8:1, 12:2).[19] Similarly, it seems, Paul depends on a primitive Christological formula when he writes: "Who is to condemn? Is it Christ Jesus, who died, yes, who was raised from the dead, who is at the right hand of God, who indeed intercedes for us?" (Rom 8:34). A few verses before, Paul, more on his own, had written that the Spirit intercedes for the saints (8:26,27).[20]

The notion of *paraklētos* may be linked with that of intercessor, as referring to a heavenly advocate at the bar of God in heaven. "In place of the many advocates which Judaism found to defend the righteous before the forum of the heavenly Judge, primitive Christianity recognises only one advocate with the Father, Jesus Christ, who as the Righteous can intercede for sinners (1 Jn 2:1). The thought is common to primitive Christianity even though the word *paraklētos* does not occur in the non-Johannine writings. The living Christ intercedes at the right hand of the Father (Rom 8:34).* In intercession He places His incorruptible life at the service of His people (Heb 7:25)."[21] The author of the Fourth Gospel probably considered Jesus Himself, in his future role, as a *paraklētos*. This is what the following translation of Jn 14:16 suggests: "And I will pray the Father, and he will give you another *paraklētos*, to be with you for ever." In any case, 1 John, having called Jesus Christ *paraklētos*, adds: "And he is the expiation (*hilasmos*) for our sins, and not for ours only but also for the sins of the whole world" (2:1-2). Thus the notion of "advocate" is linked to that of expiation, as in Heb, where our High Priest, who has offered once for all his sacrifice, is said to be always living to intercede for those who approach God through Him (7:25).

In presenting Jesus as the High Priest of a superior, eternal order, the author has masterfully retained and reinterpreted these features of priesthood he found applicable to Christ, yet showing that Christ's was a radically new priesthood accomplishing a divine plan adumbrated in Scripture. In his use of comparison and typology the author finds similarities between the old and the new order of things and a certain continuity; he emphasizes, on the other hand, that Jesus, the High Priest, and his saving work differ from what foreshadowed them, not only as being more perfect but also as being of another category, indeed as being unique and definitive. Ample illustration of the author's meth-

---

19 See N. Johansson, *Paraklētoi* (Lund, 1940), p. 235.

20 See C. K. Barrett, *A Commentary on the Epistle to the Romans* (London, 1957), p. 173.

21 J. Behm in Kittel ThW, v. 5, p. 812 (see pp. 800-814 on *paraklētos*).

od can be found also in his treatment of the new cultus, as compared to the old.

b) *Jesus, High Priest of a Superior Cultus*

We have such a High Priest, Heb teaches, "who sat at the right of the throne of the Majesty in the heavens, cult-minister (cf. 8:6) of the sanctuary and of the true tent" (8:1-2). The precise meaning of this proposition will have to be determined but it is clear that Heb considers Jesus as High Priest of a cultus, no doubt of a superior cultus, corresponding to the superiority of the High Priest himself.

1. The Old Cultus, Earthly and Figurative

The Mosaic cultus, concretely represented as that of the wilderness "tent" (9:2; Ex 25-26), was an earthly (9:1) and figurative institution (8:5), destined to procure the purity of the flesh (9:13), and unable to purify the conscience of the worshippers (9:14). The author develops these points in 8:1-6 and 9:1-10. We shall only comment now what does not more conveniently come for exposition under the next heading (comparison with the superior cultus). What concerns the covenant (8:7-13; 9:15-23) will receive below a separate treatment.

Completing his presentation of our High Priest, Jesus, the author writes : "Now if he were on earth he would not even be a priest, since there are those who offer the gifts according to the Law. They serve a model and draft of the heavenly things; for when Moses was about to erect the tent, he was instructed by God, saying, 'See that you make everything according to the pattern which was shown you on the mountain' " (8:4-5). Since "there cannot be two divinely appointed orders of earthly priests" (Westcott, p. 218), the priesthood of Christ must of necessity be of another order, of a celestial order. The Aaronic priests, who offer according to the Law (cf. 7:11-12) serve a "model" (*hypodeigma*; cf. 9:23; Ezek 42:15)* and a "draft" (*skia*; cf. 10:1) of the heavenly things (*epourania*; cf. 9:23). The idea here expressed is not entirely new, since it occurs elsewhere in another form, also in the Bible.[22] David is reported to have given Solomon plans for the temple, received from God (1 Chr 28:19), much in the same way as Moses re-

---

[22] King Gudea of Lagash is reported to have been shown in a dream the plan of the temple to be built in honor of his god. See A. L. Oppenheim, *The Interpretation of Dreams in the Ancient Near East* (Philadelphia, 1956), pp. 224, 245, 246.

ceived his for the desert tabernacle (Heb 8:5; Ex 25:40). In Wis 9:8 Solomon prays thus to God: "Thou hast given command to build a temple on thy holy mountain, and an altar in the city of thy habitation, a copy (*mimēma*) of the holy tent (*skēnē*) which thou didst prepare from the beginning."

In contrast with the use made elsewhere of similar notions, Heb brings out in 8:5 the imperfection and ungenuineness of the Mosaic institution. It rose as an *hypodeigma*, a "model," an imperfect figure, a defective indication (cf. *hypodeiknymi*) of what was forthcoming; it was only a *skia* ("shadow"), a "draft" of the definitive reality expected, which Moses saw in advance as *typos* (8:5), a God made "pattern" of the future heavenly things connected with the liturgy of Christ the High Priest. While this *typos* was perfect, its earthly expression, worked out by Moses, could only be imperfect and inadequate. Thus we are introduced to the proposition that the old cultus was earthly and figurative and was bound to be replaced, for models and drafts lose their *raison d'être* when the reality they announce is an accomplished fact: "He removes the first to establish the second" (10:9).

The first dispensation had rites of worship and its sanctuary (*to hagion*), which was of the world (9:1). The insufficiency of the old cultus is variously expressed in 9:8 10. The way of the (true) sanctuary was not yet open while the first tent was in existence: being earthly it could not lead to God, as does Christ's sacrificial liturgy (the other tent: 9:11; cf. 10:9-10). This, the author continues, is symbolic for the present age (in which the old dispensation is replaced by the new: cf. 8:13), for it shows that "gifts and sacrifices are offered which are unable to give fulfilment in conscience to the worshipper." They can only remove impurities contracted by violating the prescriptions "on food, drinks, and different baptisms," being "rites of flesh in place until the time of reformation."*

2. *The "Greater Tent" as the New Sacrificial Liturgy*

Introducing the central section of the Epistle (ch. 8-9) the author refers to it as "the chief point of the things being said," then proceeds to speak about Jesus the High Priest as cult-minister of a new liturgy (8:1, 2, 6). It is only afterwards, in 9:11-12, that his main statement occurs, perhaps the most important of the whole Epistle. Having presented the Mosaic sacrificial institution, visualized as the desert "tent," and stressed its earthly character and shortcomings, he begins to expose in contrast what is the new sacrificial liturgy of redemption; set forth as follows the text stands in clearer view:

(a) But Christ, having appeared, High Priest of the good things to come,
(+b) by means of the greater and more perfect tent,
(-b') not made with hands, that is, not of this creation,
(-c') and not by the blood of goats and calves,
(+c) but by His own blood,
(d) entered once-for-all into the sanctuary, having found an eternal redemption (9:11-12).

What does "the greater and more perfect tent" represent? This has been long a debated question. The present writer will propose a new interpretation, which he considers to be the correct one, as it fits very well the immediate and the general context of the Epistle. But first let us examine the foremost solutions offered till now.

In one type of interpretation, which can be called "cosmological," the "tent", it is believed, refers to a celestial space: after his Resurrection and through his Ascension, Jesus crossed the (lower) heavens to arrive in God's presence (cf. Heb 4:14, 7:26; Eph 4:10; see Spicq, v. 2, p.256). This solution is open to serious objections: the preposition *dia* would be used twice in the same sentence with the same case (genitive) but with different meanings ("through the tent ... by his own blood"); a cosmological meaning for "tent" does not suit the soteriological context and the parallel phrase "by His own blood"; cosmic heavens are "of this creation" (cf. 1:10-12, 12:26-27); the author does not locally distinguish "heavens" from heaven. But he does distinguish "the tent" from "the sanctuary" (in 9:11-12 and in 8:2). H. Montefiore, who does not, admits the ensuing difficulty in a remarkable understatement: "It might at first sight seem slightly clumsy, to say, in effect, that by means of the heavenly Tent Jesus entered into the heavenly Tent."[23] In *The Jerome Biblical Commentary* (New York 1968) Myles M. Bourke prefers the opinion "that sees this Tabernacle as the heavenly regions, the heavenly counterpart of the earthly outer Tabernacle, through which Jesus passed (4:14) into the highest heaven, the abode of God (9:24), the counterpart of the inner Tabernacle, the Holy of Holies" (p. 397). But the objections to this view, which have been indicated, remain unanswered.

[23] H. Montefiore, *A Commentary on the Epistle to the Hebrews*, p. 153.

Looking for some metaphorical or spiritual antitype to the local sanctuary, several Fathers, both Greek and Latin, understood "the greater tent" to be our Lord's body.[24] The meaning would be that Christ has used His body and His blood (9 :12) in a priestly activity, to open for humanity the way to God. Although this last statement is true, it is not necessarily asserted in our passage and cannot be used to prove that "the greater tent" is Christ's body. For one thing *skēnē*, "tent," is never used elsewhere in the Bible to designate the body. In Wis 9:15, as also in 2 Cor 5:1, 4, *skēnos* occurs with that meaning, and *skēnōma* in 2 Pet 1:13, but not *skēnē*. It can also be objected that the mortal body of Christ can hardly be said not to be of this creation, especially in Heb with its insistence on the reality of the Incarnation (2:17, 4:18).

Vanhoye escapes this last objection by saying that "the greater tent" of Heb 9:11 is the glorified Body of Christ.* Positively he expounds at length the NT theme of the new Temple and insists on the trial incident recorded in Mk 14:58 : "We heard him say, 'I will destroy this temple that is made with hands, and in three days I will build another, not made with hands.' " Such precise reference to Gospel narratives in Heb remains, to say the least, problematic. The session at the right hand of God mentioned in the context of the "tent" (8:1) must be referred to Ps 110:1 (cf. 1:13), not to the trial narrative. Explaining the interpretation of the Fathers, Vanhoye had pointed out that "tent"=body of Christ is well adapted to the context of Heb 9:11-12, as being in parallel with "by His own blood" : flesh and blood, body and blood, are current correlatives in the NT (cf. Heb 2:14). But in Heb 9:12 "blood" stands for the sacrifice of Christ (cf. 9:14, 25, 10:19, 13:12, 20) and is not used as a correlative of "body." In proposing his own interpretation Vanhoye fails to indicate how the glorified Body of Christ can be paralleled with His blood. Besides, it must be said that Christ entered heaven with His body, rather than by His body.

Convinced that a better interpretation is available the present writer has to disagree also with Vanhoye on the precise meaning of "the greater tent," although he feels in complete agreement with him on the overall interpretation of the Epistle and particularly on the manner of understanding the sacrificial redemption wrought by Christ and formulated in Heb.

---

[24] See, e.g. Chrysostom (PG 63, 119) and Ps.Oecumenius (PG 119, 376).

The New Sacrificial Liturgy

For Westcott "the greater and more perfect tabernacle of which Christ is minister, and (as we must add) in which the Saints worship, gathers up the various means under which God reveals Himself in the spiritual order, and through which men approach to Him" (p. 259 f.). This is largely true, but "the various means" have to be determined : they are essentially the new sacrificial liturgy of which Christ by his sacrifice is the cult-minister, and for this reason the author speaks of "the greater and more perfect tent."

The attentive reading of Heb 9 and related contexts clearly indicates that the author thought of two orders of salvation, one being of this world, the other not (being of a heavenly order, not however a heavenly liturgy like that, for example, of Rev 19:10, 22:3). The author's conception can be exposed schematically :

(1) There is the old order of salvation with its cultus, seen by the author in the desert "tent" (*skēnē* : 8:5, 9:21), provisional, earthly (*to hagion kosmikon* : 9:1). This "tent" has two parts, also called "tents'': the "holy" (the first "tent" : 9:2), where the sacrificial liturgy is celebrated (9:6; cf. 10:11, 13:10)* and which leads to the "holy of holies" (9:8); the "holy of holies" (9:3), the second "tent" (9:7), in which only the high priest enters once a year, not without (the) blood (of another : 9 :8, 25). The veil separating the "holy" from the "holy of holies" prevents the free access to the sanctuary (9:3, 8). This cultus cannot purify the conscience (9:9, 10:2), give fulfillment (*teleiōsai* : 10:1), nor take away sins (10:11), since it procures only the purity of the flesh (9:10, 13). The priests of this "tent" serve "a model and draft of the heavenly things" (8:5).

(2) There is the new order of salvation, celestial, perfect, producing permanent fruits of a moral nature. The symbol of its cultus is also a "tent" (*skēnē*), whose cult-minister is the new Priest (7:15, 16,24) of the new, superior sacrificial liturgy (8:2, 6). By this true (8:2), greater, and more perfect "tent,"+ not of this creation (9:11), Christ as High Priest entered once-for-all into the sanctuary (*ta hagia* : 8:2, 9:12), that is, into heaven, unto God's presence (9:24), inaugurating a new living way by the veil of His flesh (10:20; cf. 6:19-20) and by his own blood (9:12, 10:19).

It would seem that this context shows clearly enough what "the greater tent" of 9:11 is : *the new liturgy of redemption* by which Christ the High Priest, in His sacrifice (cf. "by his own blood" :9:12), entered into the heavenly sanctuary, having found an eternal redemption. The two dispensations of salvation, the old and the new, are represented, as already said, by two liturgies, one being the prefiguration of the other. Since the first was concretely that of the "tent," the second is also called "tent," "*the* tent," because it had been mentioned already in 8:2 as "the true tent." In respect to each, four main elements are considered : the priests, the sacrifice (the blood), the purification from sins, the passage to the sanctuary by means of the "tent" (in the new liturgy the passage takes place in the sacrifice itself). The "tent" of Christ's liturgy is called "the greater tent" because it concerns the salvation not of the Jewish people only but of the whole world (cf. 2:9; Mal 1:11). It is "the more perfect tent" on account of the dignity of its Cult-Minister (8:2) and because it procures true perfection (2:10, 10:14) rendering apt to enter the sanctuary (9:11, 24). In contrast with the desert "tent" which Moses and the Israelites erected (8:5, 9:2), the tent of our High Priest's sacrificial liturgy is "not made with hands," is not "of this creation", for it is a divine work, in which Christ offered Himself through an eternal spirit (9:14; cf. 7:16),* and God "led up from the dead our Lord Jesus, the great shepherd of the sheep, in blood of the eternal covenant" (13:20).

The interpretation proposed agrees remarkably well with the correct understanding of the sacrifice of Christ as his passage to God through death and resurrection. This sacrificial liturgy involving motion, "according to a power of indestructible life" (7:16), is to be distinguished from the static condition which followed : Christ present before God (9:24) and living to intercede (7:25). Our author, theologian of the priesthood and sacrifice of Jesus, quite remarkably saw in the *transitus* liturgy of the Mosaic tent a prefiguration of Christ's own passage as High Priest from the condition of the flesh to that of the spirit (*transitus internus*), from this world to the Father (*transitus externus*; cf. 4:14; Jn 13:1). "Now, once, in the conclusion of the ages, he has been made manifest through the sacrifice of Himself, for the removal of sin" (9:26).** Read thus the statement presents the sacrifice of Christ as the epiphany of our High Priest and this conforms to what is said elsewhere of His *teleiōsis* (5:9, 7:28) and of His entry into the heavenly sanctuary by means of the sacrificial liturgy, of "the more perfect tent" (9:11-12).[25]

---

[25] For a fuller exposition of my interpretation of Heb 9.11, 12, 23 see "Sacrificium ut

"Cult-Minister of the Sanctuary and of the True Tent"

Having investigated the meaning of the new "tent" in its clearer context (9:11-12), we must now return to a section (8:1-6) where this "tent" is mentioned as "the true tent," obviously a variant description of the same notion. While in 9:11-12 "the greater tent" was clearly distinguished from "the sanctuary" (*ta hagia*), as leading to it, the two appear in 8:2 in a less discerning light. Here is the section in literal translation, omitting v. 4-5 already examined above (b, 1) :

> Now the chief point of the things being said : we have such a high priest who sat at the right of the throne of the Majesty in the heavens, cult-minister (*leitourgos*) of the sanctuary and of the true tent, which the Lord set up, not man (8:1-2). Now it is quite a different ministry (*leitourgia*) which has fall (*tetuchen*) to Him, in proportion as He is mediator of a better dispostion (*diathēkē*), which has been made law on better promises (8:6).

Nothing in the context suggests that *kai*, joining "the sanctuary" and "of the true tent" should be understood epexegetically: "the sanctuary, that is, the true tent." They are two different notions, here as in Heb 9:11-12. The difficulty is to explain why Christ is called cult-minister of both. That He was cult-minister of the true tent we knew already, since He was both the Priest and the Victim ("He offered Himself") in the great liturgy of redemption which procured his sacrificial *teleiōsis* and led him to the sanctuary (5:9, 9:11-12).

How is Christ *leitourgos* of the sanctuary ? To this question there is an answer which we propose firmly, while realizing that this new solution runs counter to prevailing conceptions.

The Jewish high priest, for Heb, was constituted to offer gifts and sacrifices (for sins :5:1, 8:3, 9:7) and every priest "stands each day ministering the cult and offering repeatedly the same sacrifices" (10: 11).* Heb does not explain, nor even mention, what the high priest did in the Holy of Holies. The sprinkling of the blood the author attributes to Moses (9:21) or he indistinctly includes it as one instance of the efficacy of the blood for purifying the flesh (9:13). It is, however, for Heb, distinctive of the High priest's function that he *enters* into the Holy of Holies (9:25), not without blood, which he offers for himself and the sins of ignorance of the people (9:7) : a means of being purified upon

---

liturgia in Epistula ad Hebraeos," VerbDom 46 (1968), pp. 235-258. I would not write now of a liturgical function, even not sacrificial, of Christ in heaven (as I do there p. 235, n. 1 and p. 245), except in a very broad sense.

entering the holy place (see Montefiore, p. 148). Heb insists on the high priest's *entering* into the Holy of Holies because this is an aspect that can be predicated of Christ's function as High Priest.

The community of Heb is a pilgrim people on its way to *enter* the place of eternal rest (3:11, 18, 19, 4:1, 3, 5, 6), into the interior of the veil (6:19), where the Forerunner Jesus *entered,* having become high priest for ever according to the order of Melchizedek (6:20). Christ having come as High Priest *entered* once-for-all into the sanctuary (9:12). He did not *enter* into a sanctuary made by hands but into heaven itself, to appear before the face of God for us (9:24). It can be concluded that in 8:2 our High Priest is called "*leitourgos* of the sanctuary" precisely because He *entered* into the sanctuary. The verse can be paraphrased thus : We have such a high priest who sat at the right of the throne of the Majesty in the heavens, as one-having-been *leitourgos* of the sanctuary and of the true tent. This interpretation is suggested by the next verse : "For every high priest is constituted to offer gifts and sacrifices, whence the need for him to have something which he might offer." The subjunctive *aorist* used here points to the one past offering, not to be repeated (cf. 7:27).

Christ himself underwent a sacrificial purification (*teleiōsis*) to enter the sanctuary (9:23-24). This He did as "forerunner" (6:20), as "leader of salvation" (2:10), as "leader and fulfiller of the faith" (12:2), therefore as head of the redeemed humanity. And this He remains, since through faith in Him, through the sacraments of the Church, mainly the Baptism and the Eucharist, believers mystically experience their own *teleiōsis* (10:14, 12:23), even before the final resurrection (cf. 9:28). Christ is effectively High Priest for ever in that sense (7:24), and this is probably the meaning which our author read in the traditional formula he inserted in his text : "Always living to intercede for them" (7:25). Nothing indicates that he thought Christ remained as *leitourgōn* of the sanctuary and of the true tent after He sat at the right of the throne of the Majesty in the heavens. To be seated is not the position of a *leitourgos* (cf. 10:11), but of one "for the remaining time awaiting until his enemies have been placed as a footstool of His feet" (10:13; cf. 1 :13), until a second time, without (offering for) sin, He will be seen to those awaiting Him for salvation (9:28), at the end of the world. Similarly Heb 4:10 says of Christ : "For He who entered into His rest, He also rested from His works just as God from His own."

3. High Priest of the New Covenant

Of Jesus the High Priest, "Cult-Minister of the sanctuary and of the true tent," Heb writes : "Now it is quite a different ministry (*leitourgia*) which has fallen to him,* in proportion as he is mediator of a better disposition (*diathēkē*), which has been made law on better promises" (8:6). While the old Aaronic priesthood was still in place the Lord had announced the advent of another priesthood, eternal in character, the priesthood of the order of Melchizedek (7:11, 21). In the same way he spoke thus to Jeremiah : "Behold days are coming, says the Lord, and I shall conclude with the house of Israel and with the house of Juda a new covenant ..." (Jer 31:31 ; Heb 8:8). And Heb adds : "In saying 'new' he has made the first old" (8:13, 10:15-17). The connection with the High Priesthood of Jesus had been suggested earlier : as He became priest not without an oath "so had Jesus become guarantor of a better covenant" (7:22). In 8:6-13 the making of the new covenant is related to the different (better) *leitourgia* in which Jesus the High Priest has been the Ministrant (8:6), and in 9:15 we read : "And because of this, of a new disposition he is Mediator," "this" referring, as it seems, to what precedes, the entry of our High Priest in heaven by "the greater tent," by the new sacrificial liturgy (9:11-14). For Heb, obviously, to a new covenant must correspond a new liturgy, and the new covenant had been mediated by Christ, High Priest for ever. What better covenant liturgy could be thought of than one of which the Ministrant is both God and man, in which the sacrifice effects the return to God of the Mediator as Head of the new humanity, of the covenant people, a liturgy in which all the sins find their expiation. Jesus himself gave a meaning to his death and formulated it : "*This is* my blood of the (new) covenant, which is poured out for many for the forgiveness of sins" (Mt 26:28). The author of Heb was aware of this logion when, citing (LXX) Ex 24:8, "Behold the blood of the *diathēkē* which the Lord disposed for you," he read instead : "*This is* the blood of the *diathēkē* which God prescribed (*eneteilato*) for you" (Heb 9:20 ; cf. 10: 29).

This *diathēkē*, "covenant" (or "disposition"), has, for Heb, the character of a *diathēkē*-testament, for its Mediator has in fact died, and his death involves an heritage (Heb 9:15-17),+ that of salvation (1:14), immediately made available in the triumph over death of Jesus the High Priest. Our author wanted his readers to understand that the Mosaic covenant, like the Aaronic priesthood, was a provisional and figurative institution, now antiquated and being replaced (8:13) by a new covenant-testament in which sin would not prevent the called from receiving the promise of the eternal heritage (9:15). The sacrifice of Jesus, which takes away sin (9:26, 28) and purifies the conscience (9:14) is also the covenant-sacrifice (Mt 26:2 par.; 1 Cor 10:25) in which the Son makes joint heirs of His eternal heritage (9:15) His brethren, the children of God (2:11-14).

c) *Titles of our High Priest*

Apart from that of High Priest the Epistle to the Hebrews attributes to Jesus several titles, some explicitly, like "the Son," others only implicitly, like "the Servant of God." Their study can shed additional light on the High Priesthood of Jesus. We will examine first the title "the Son" which is prevailingly one of pre-existence, then that of "Servant," which refers to Jesus' sacrifice, and finally other titles variously connected with Christ's exaltation.

1. The Son of God

In view of Jesus' pre-existence, Cullmann writes, the Author of Heb is interested in connecting "High Priest" very closely with "Son of God," for he quotes the confessional formula and makes it expressly recognizable as such: "Having therefore a great High Priest who has gone through the heavens, Jesus, the Son of God, let us hold fast to the profession" (4:14).[26] This Son, by whom He created, "after having effected purification from sins, took His seat to the right of the majesty on high" (1:2-3). What is here stated of the Son applies to the sacrificial work and to the exaltation of our High Priest (cf. 8:1-2). Again, what he writes of the Son, quoting Ps 110:1, "Sit at my right until I have placed your enemies as a footstool of your feet," he states also of Jesus as High Priest (10:13). The two texts, one about the Son (Ps 2:7), the other on the High Priest (Ps 110:4) are quoted together in Heb 5:5-6: "So also Christ did not exalt Himself to be made a high priest, but was appointed by Him who said to Him, 'Thou art my Son, today I have begotten thee'; as he says also in another place, 'Thou art a priest for

[26] O. Cullmann, *The Christology of the New Testament*, tr. S. C. Guthrie and C. A. M. Hall (2d ed., Philadelphia, 1963), p. 304. On the title "Son of God" see Kittel ThW v. 8 (1967) pp. 367-395 and F. Hahn, *The Titles of Christ in Christology*. Tr. H. Knight and G. Ogg (Cleveland, 1969), pp. 279-333. On the title "Son" in Heb 1-2 see A. Vanhoye, *Situation du Christ, épître aux hébreux 1 et 2*. Lectio Divina 58 (Paris 1969) 61-227.

ever, after the order of Melchizedek' " (RSV). Elsewhere the combination of the two texts is suggested rather than expressed : "Indeed, the law appoints men in their weakness as high priests, but the word of the oath, which came later than the law, appoints a Son who has been made perfect for ever" (7:28 ; see also 4:14 quoted above). In another passage, Christ, the Son (Heb 3:6), is declared faithful over His (or God's) house, which, as we have seen, He edified as High Priest (3:1) by his redemptive work. It has been explained in what sense Heb understood that Melchizedek, a prophetic type of our High Priest, has been likened to the Son of God (7:3).

"The Christology of the High Priest is combined with that of the Son of God throughout Hebrews. The writer does not forget that the theme of *obedience* belongs with the ideal of Jesus' sonship, especially since it can be related easily to the High Priest concept."[27] Although he was Son, Heb asserts, Christ learned from the things He suffered the obedience (5:8). This is also the context in which we read that having been given fulfilment, Christ became for all those who obey Him a cause of everlasting salvation, "proclaimed by God high priest according to the order of Melchizedek" (5:9-10). This can be compared to the exaltation which according to Paul Christ was granted as a consequence of His extreme self-denial (Phil 2:5-11). They are two examples, among many, of the "New Testament dialectic between deepest humiliation and highest majesty."[28] The proclamation of Christ as High Priest in connection with his *teleiōsis* may also be related to John's notion of the Cross as an exaltation (cf. Jn 13:31, 17:1). As God-man Christ by his very being was destined to be High Priest, which he effectively became gradually during his lifetime[29] and especially in his sacrificial *transitus* to God as head and representative of redeemed mankind. He is proclaimed High Priest upon achieving his mediatorial work. Being the Son of God his Priesthood could only be unique and incomparable.

The use of the anarthrous title "Son" is characteristic of Heb (cf. 1:2, 5, 3:6, 5:8, 7:28; cf. Rom 1:4) and emphasizes, Westcott explains, "the essential nature of the relation which it expresses" (p. 427). It is defined, he adds, by the personal titles "the Son" (1:8), "the Son of God" (6:6, 7:3, 10:29), "the Firstborn" (1:6), while "the Son of God"

---

27 O. Cullmann, *Christology*, p. 305.

28 O. Cullmann, *Christology*, p. 92.

29 According to E. Grässer, Heb refers to only 3 facts in the historical life of Jesus : his origin from Judah (7.14), his agony at Gethsemane (5.7), his death outside the gate (13.12) : "Der historische Jesus im Hebräerbrief," ZNTWiss 56 (1965), pp. 63-91.

is identified with Jesus in 4:14, where placed side by side the two titles "suggest the two natures of the Lord which include the assurance of sympathy and power" (W. 107). The first verses of Heb speak of Christ as Revealer and Redeemer, of the Incarnate Son who keeps his divine prerogatives while accomplishing his mission among men. Spicq who observes this (v. 1, p. 163), also notes that this is exactly the viewpoint of the Christological texts in the epistles of the Captivity (Eph, Col, Phil). This raises only one of the problems that could be discussed in connection with the title "Son". We will only suggest, to conclude, that the author of Heb must have thought of Christ as both "Son" and "High Priest" when he defined our Lord's disposition upon entering into the world as one of obedience, "Behold I have come to do thy will...," and then comments : "By that will we have been sanctified through the offering of the body of Jesus Christ once for all" (10:9-10).

2. Our High Priest as Servant

"Applied to Jesus," Cullmann writes, "the concept High Priest is closely related to that of the Suffering Servant of God. In a certain sense one could actually understand it as a variant of the Suffering Servant concept".[30] This is hardly true if the interpretation we have proposed of our High Priest's sacrificial work is correct, but it shows that there exist grounds for comparing the title of High Priest with that of Servant. James R. Schaefer feels that Heb's concept of Jesus the High Priest is rather a sublimation of the Suffering Servant concept.[31] Perhaps he has not realized how extensive the sublimation involved is, for he sees our High Priest's saving work almost exclusively in his redemptive death which *merited* him the exaltation and the entry into heaven. Schaefer failed to see or to point out the absolute newness of our High Priest' *transitus* sacrifice,[32] the one mystery perceived and formulated in its successive stages.

In his study Schaefer has well formulated several important points of comparison between Heb's conception of the High Priesthood of

---

30 O. Cullmann, *Christology*, p. 83.

31 James R. Schaefer, "The Relationship between Priestly and Servant Messianism in the Epistle to the Hebrews," CatBiblQuart 30 (1968), p. 383.

32 On "Pascha, Passio, Transitus" in early Christian writings see Christine Mohrmann's analysis in EphLit 66 (1962), pp. 37-52 : "Le déroulement même du drame de la rédemption est pour Augustin un *transitus*" (p. 49). On the theology of the sacrificial *transitus* to God see my *Rédemption Sacrificielle*, pp. 412-425.

Jesus and the Servant of God theology. "In Heb vicarious redemption ceases to be passive submission to suffering it is for the servant (Acts 8:32-35; 1 Pet 2:21-24) and becomes a positive embracing of death precisely because it is a priestly offering" (10:9-10). Similarly, "whereas the servant's innocence serves mainly to lend tragic poignancy to his death (Is 53:9, 11), Jesus' innocence in Heb serves rather to enhance the excelling quality of His priesthood (7:26)." Furthermore, the exaltation of Jesus in Heb "is eminently priestly, whereas the exaltation of the servant is more exactly a vindication of his fidelity" (p. 384 f.).

It is probably correct to say that whatever themes of servant messianism the Author of Heb has used he drew from the servant Christology of the early Church rather than directly from the OT Servant texts. The closest textual similarity occurs in Heb 9:28 : "thus Christ, offered once for the taking away of the sins of many" (*pollôn anenegkein hamartias*) as compared to "he took away the sins of many" (*hamartias pollôn anēnegken* : Is 53:12), which 1 Pet 2:24 follows quite closely. There is no verbal contact in Greek between "always living to intercede for them" (Heb 7:25) and "he made intercession for the transgressors" (Is 53:12). Psalm 22 is possibly connected with the Servant songs of Isaiah, but its v. 22 is enlisted by Heb 2:12 "not for the servant theme which it expresses, but simply to confirm Jesus' solidarity with those whom He sanctifies."[33] In Is 42:6 Yahweh declares to the Servant: "I set you as a covenant of the people and a light for the nations" (Is 42:6). But in the 4th Song (Is 52:13-53.12), which describes the Servant's sufferings and his sin-offering (cf. Is 53:10), there is no allusion, it is generally believed, to his covenant role, while our High Priest has established the new covenant in his sacrifice. It is, however, quite possible that St. Jerome correctly translated the Hebrew text of Is 52:15, "*Iste asperget gentes multas,*" "he shall sprinkle many nations." Thus the Servant would do on a vaster scale what Moses did at the inauguration of the Sinai covenant (Ex 24:8; Heb 9:21). This would fit well the logion on the Covenant-Blood at the Last Supper (Mt 26:28), with the interest Heb has for our High Priest as Mediator of the new Covenant (8:6, 9:15), and with the mention of blood sprinkling in connection with the mystery of our salvation (Heb 12:24; 1 Pet 1:2; cf. Rom 3:25).

---

33 J. R. Schaefer, "Relationship," p. 378.

3. *Other Titles*

Jesus being called only once *apostolos*, "Envoy," in the entire NT, we do not know for sure what our author (3:1) meant by this title. Later occurrences of the title are not very illuminating. Justin writes of Christ, perhaps independently of Heb (for he also calls Him "Angel") : "He is called 'Angel' and *apostolos*, because he announces (*epaggelei*) all that should be known and he is sent (*apostelletai*) to reveal everything" (*Apol* 1:64, 4). According to Pantaenus, Paul did not sign Heb out of respect for our Lord who himself *was sent* to the Hebrews as *apostolos* of the Almighty (in Eusebius, *Hist.eccl.* 6.14.4). The author therefore invites his readers to "consider the *apostolos* and High Priest of our profession, Jesus" (3:1), how faithful he is over his house. The office of "Envoy," Montefiore suggests, refers primarily to the Incarnation, for the Son was sent into the world (p. 70), as John so often repeats (cf. 3:17, 34), the most significant text being perhaps for us 10:36, where Jesus described himself as "He whom the Father consecrated and sent (*apesteilen*) into the world" (RSV; cf. 20.21).

In Rabbinic tradition a priest was a *šaliaḥ* of God (*Yoma* 19a, quoting R. Huna), and the high priest was the *šaliaḥ* ("the one sent") of the Jewish community on the Day of Atonement (*Yoma* 1,5). "Thus Jesus might be described in Rabbinic terms as a *šaliaḥ* who represented his people before God, and this was precisely his priestly work" (Montefiore, p. 70). While admitting that *apostolos* can be interpreted along these lines, Vanhoye preferably sees the term as expressing the authority of Jesus (like "faithful" in the same context), as revealing God to us (Heb 1:2, 2:3), whereas "High Priest" designates Christ as leading us to Him (*Textus de sacerdotio*, p. 48).

Setting the passion of Jesus in the divine plan of salvation the author of Heb writes : "For it was fitting that God, for whom and by whom all things exist, in bringing many sons to glory, should make the pioneer (*archēgos*) of their salvation perfect through suffering" (2:10). In the Septuagint *archēgos* is usually a political or military "leader" of the whole people, or of a part of it (Kittel Th W Eng, v. 1, p. 487). In Philo the cognate term *archēgetēs* is often predicated of Adam, Noah, or the patriarchs, especially Abraham. The notion behind *archēgos*, independently of the term, is one which suits well leaders like Moses and Joshua (in Greek : *Iēsous*, like "Jesus"), whose vocation it was to bring the chosen people to the Promised Land. Moses is in effect called "ruler and deliverer" (*archōn kai lytrōtēs*) in Acts 7:35, but he was *archēgos* only imperfectly since he did not introduce his people into the Land, while Joshua was leader only in the last phase of the journey. It is a different, superior leadership that applies to Jesus, called in Acts "Leader and Savior" (*archēgos kai sōtēr* : 5:31), or "the Author of life" (*ho archēgos tēs zōēs* : 3:15). He it is who has opened for us by his blood, by the *teleiōsis* of His humanity the new and living way leading to God (Heb 10:19-20), and in this He was also "the pioneer (*archēgos*) and perfecter (*teleiōtēs*) of our faith" (12:2), He "who inspires our faith from the beginning to the end" (Montefiore).

Paul exhorted his readers to self-discipline by citing the example of runners who compete for earthly prizes (cf. 1 Cor 9:24; Gal 2:2). In Heb 12:1 the imagery recurs in the form of a "gigantic relay race" (Montefiore), a challenge for the last competitors to "run with endurance the race that lies before us," knowing that as Forerunner (*prodromos*) Jesus entered the sanctuary on our behalf, having become High Priest for ever according to the order of Melchizedek (6:20). In fact, these two titles, *archēgos* and *prodromos* apply to our High Priest in His essential function : by means of His sacrifice He has entered into heaven itself, to appear before God for us (9:24).

To conclude, a few words on the designation of Jesus as "Christ" or "the Christ" in Heb, and its relevance to the notion of Messianic kingship. Strictly speaking, the term "Messiah" is equivalent to "Christ," since the Hebrew word *mašiāḥ* (Grecized as *messias* in Jn 1:14, 4:25) is translated *Christos* in Greek. *Christos Kyriou,* "the anointed of the Lord," is the regular designation of the Israelite king (cf. 1 Sam 9:11, 23). And because of the promises made to David in respect to his descendants (2 Sam 7:1-16; 1 Chr 17:1-15) the expected Messiah was also called "the Son of David" (Mt 1:1; Mk 10:47), as the Messianic King (Lk 19:38). The term "Christ" also applied to the high priest called in some texts *ho hiereus ho christos,* "the anointed priest" (Lev 4:16; see ch. IV, D, b, 2). As a designation of Jesus the term "(the) Christ" retains its original meaning in several texts of different NT writings (cf. Mt 23:10; Acts 17:3; Rom 9:15), but even more often, especially in Paul, it becomes part of a personal name "Jesus Christ" (cf. Mk 1:1), or is even used alone more as a name than as a title (Rom 16:18).

In Heb, as elsewhere in the NT, "the Christ" (with the art : 3:14, 5:5, 16, 11:26) designates Jesus rather as the Messiah, while "Christ" (without the art. : 3:6, 9:11, 24) is more of a personal name, like Jesus Christ (10:10, 13:8, 21), although the meaning still affects its use. Thus where "Christ" occurs for the first time in Heb, the context has changed from the earthly life of Jesus to that of his glorious state as the Son now ruling over his house (3:6). In the other two texts (9:11, 24) "Christ" designates the exalted High Priest entering into the sanctuary (in 9:14, 28 the art. points to the same person as in 9:11, 24). The Author of Heb thought of "Christ" as being the Messianic king. This is already clear from his use of Ps 2:7 and Ps 110:1, combined with Ps 110:4 and the figure of Melchizedek, the Priest-King of Salem (Heb 7:1-3). He does not call Christ "King" but alludes to such a title by describing his exaltation in terms of royal enthronement: "But of the Son he says, 'Thy throne, O God, is for ever and ever, the righteous scepter is the scepter of thy kingdom' " (1:8). It is almost certain that in "O God" the divine appellative is understood in its full sense, although in Ps 45:6, quoted here, it does not necessarily have a transcendent meaning. The idea of rest after completing a work (cf. Heb 4:10) and the use of royal imagery appear combined in the following very distinctive text: "But when Christ had offered for all time a single sacrifice for sins, He sat down at the right hand of God, then to wait until His enemies should be made a stool for his feet" (10:12-13; cf. Ps 110:1). The Messianic expectation, both royal and priestly, was fulfilled in Jesus and this the Epistle to the Hebrews has admirably expressed by describing as an *enthronement* the exaltation of Christ our *High Priest*.

B. Jesus as High Priest in the NT outside Heb

Only in Heb is Jesus referred to explicitly as (High-) Priest and only there it is demonstrated that He is our High Priest. But the other writings of the NT dwell on notions that seem to imply the priesthood of Christ. These are found mainly in the formulas that present Christ's death as a sacrifice, and in those that describe his consecration to be the Savior of the world. Since there exists no consensus on most points of the matter to be treated, our main effort will be to present in an orderly way the themes and the texts which seem more relevant and worthy to be further discussed.

a) The Sacrifice of Jesus as Priest

Several NT authors beside Heb understood that the death of Jesus was a sacrifice and described it accordingly when they presented it as a mystery of salvation. This is commonly admitted for some later texts, like Eph 5:2 : "and walk in love, as Christ loved us and gave Himself up for us, a fragrant offering and sacrifice to God" : *paredōken heauton huper hēmōn prosphoran kai thusian tō Theō eis osmēn euōdias* (cf. Ex 29:18; Ezek 20:41). Markus Barth correctly states about Rom 3:21-26 that "the words *hilastērion* and 'in His blood' make it necessary to assert that Paul thinks in this passage of Christ's death as an expiatory, atoning sacrifice."[34] According to Barth, Paul in the passage describes the sacrifice of Jesus as "brought by God," as "an act of revelation," "a judicial act," and as "changing the situation of man" (pp. 30-33). Although this will seem partially debatable to many, it shows that the notion of sacrifice can be conceived as broad enough to include redemption motifs which are often wrongly considered as non-sacrificial.

There are two other early texts which, in my opinion, also show that Paul interpreted Christ's death as an expiatory sacrifice. One is Rom 8:3, where he explains that God has done what the law, weakened by the flesh, could not do : "sending His own Son in the likeness of sinful flesh and as a sin offering, He condemned sin in the flesh." Christ's redemptive death is also very likely represented as a "sacrifice for sin" in 2 Cor 5:21 where Paul explains how God through Christ has reconciled the world to Himself: "For our sakes He made him 'sin' [=sin offering] who knew nothing of sin, so that in Him we might become the justice of God." These statements belong to the same theological contexts as the formulas of Heb : "Where there is forgiveness of these, there is no longer any offering for sin" (*prosphora peri hamartias* : 10:18) and "When Christ had offered a single sacrifice for sins (*thusia huper hamartiōn*), he sat down at the right hand of God" (10:12). John expresses the same notion otherwise when he writes: "He is the expiation for our sins (*hilasmos peri tōn hamartiōn hēmōn*), and not for ours only but also for the sins of the whole world" (1 Jn 2:2; cf. 4:10).

When the NT writers affirm that Jesus has suffered and died "according to the Scriptures" (1 Cor 15:3; Acts 3:18, 13:29; Mk 9:12, 14:21, 49; Lk 4:26-27, 24:25-27) they obviously refer foremost to the Suffering Servant texts (cf. Acts 4:24-28, 8:26-40). They followed in this the lead given by Jesus himself : "This is my blood of the covenant, which is poured out for many" (*hyper pollōn*; Mk 14:24), "For this is my blood of the covenant, which is poured out for many" (*peri pollōn*) for the forgiveness of sins" (Mt 26:28; cf. Mk 10:45; 1 Tim 2 :6). The term

---

[34] M. Barth, "Was Christ's Death a Sacrifice ?" ScotJTh occ Papers, No. 9 (Edinburgh, 1961), p. 28.

polloi corresponds, at it seems ,to the Hebrew *rabbim*, which occurs five times in the 4th Servant Song (Is 52:14, 53:11-12). It is not often enough observed, besides, that 2 Cor 5:21 has all the appearances of a condensed application of Is 53:9-11 to Christ in His sacrifice. It is important to note, for our purpose, that Servant formulations are affirmations, not denials, of the sacrificial interpretation of Christ's death. For it is said of the Servant : "In truth he made himself an offering for sin" (Is 53:10),* or in the Greek : "And the Lord determined to purify him (*katharisai*) from this stroke (*plēgē*), when his soul shall be given up for a sin offering (*peri hamartias*) ...". In the next verse is expressed (in the LXX) the will of the Lord "to justify the Righteous one (*dikaiōsai dikaion*) who is serving many (*polloi*) well, when he shall bear away their sins" (tr. C. Thomson). The same Greek expression, "to take away their sins" (*airein hamartias*) is used of Christ in Jn 1:29 and 1 Jn 2:1-2 it is said of "Jesus Christ the Righteous (*dikaios*)" that He is the expiation for our sins. All this suggests that in the Servant theology of the Passion can and must be read a sacrificial interpretation of the death of Christ.

Other relevant texts could be cited, among which 1 Cor 5:7, "Christ, our paschal lamb, has been sacrificed." The verb *thuein*, "sacrifice, immolate," is used only here to describe Christ's redemptive death, although *thusia* also occurs with the same meaning (Eph 5:2; Heb 9:26, 10:12). The NT writers, it is true, seldom directly identify Christ's death as a sacrifice. Their reticence is understandable : it was difficult to define as a sacrifice the death of one who had been executed as a criminal by the Roman authorities. Theological reflection was needed to grasp the internal and higher meaning of the drama. Besides, there was the danger of seeming to equate the unique mystery of the Cross with the known categories of pagan or Jewish sacrifices. The biblical authors do not in fact dwell on definitions. They contemplate events and in them apprehend the manifestation of God's will. This is also typical of the author of Heb who uses sacrificial language while making it clear that Christ's sacrifice is *sui generis* : "Sacrifices and offerings Thou hast not desired, but a body has Thou prepared for me ... He abolished the first in order to establish the second. And by that will we have been sanctified through the offering of the body of Jesus Christ once for all" (10:5, 9, 10).

What has been said till now is like the major premise in our reasoning: early and numerous formulations of Christ's death describe it, implicitly at least, as a sacrifice, and this certainly reflects a generalized conviction of the first Christian generation. Our second premise will be: if Christ freely gave his life in sacrifice for the redemption of mankind it is as priest that He did it. It should be legitimately concluded that even if Christ is not explicitly called priest outside Heb it is implied that He is in the texts that present His death as a sacrifice.

In his second sermon Peter expressed a truth of the kerygma formulated in varying ways by the NT writers : "What God foretold by the mouth of all the prophets, that His Christ should suffer, He thus fulfilled" (Acts 3:18). His known destiny Jesus accepted and followed in perfect freedom; of His own life he said : "No one takes it from me, but I lay it down of my own accord" (10:18). In the words of C. K. Barrett, "to prove that Jesus accepted death voluntarily was an important point in early Christian apologetic" (in loc.). Jesus freely submits to the arrest outside Gethsemane, reaffirming that the only necessity compelling Him is the fulfilment of the Scriptures (Mt 26:52-54; cf. Jn 18:4,6).

The Author of Heb has explicitated (cf. 5:1, 8:3, 10:12) what was obviously the common persuasion at the time of Jesus, that there can be no true sacrifice without the intervention of a priest. In the First Letter of Peter the Christians are described as those called "to be a holy priesthood, to offer spiritual sacrifices acceptable to God through Jesus Christ" (2.5). "It does not take a priest to offer to God the sacrifice of a contrite heart."[35] This is true and priesthood in the metaphorical sense has little in common with priesthood in the proper sense. * Yet the passage quoted reflects, apart from Heb, the conviction that priesthood and sacrifice are correlative notions. More to the point, there is a clear allusion to Christ's priesthood in 1 Pet 2:24, properly translated : "He who carried up our sins to the Cross in His Body, that dead to (our) sins we might live to righteousness." The priests "carried up" (*anapherein*) to the altar the victims to be offered in sacrifice (see Lev 4:20; 1 Macc 4:53). Christ in his sacrifice passed from the sphere of the flesh and sin (cf. Rom 8:3; 1 Pet 4:1) to God's domain. He carried our sins to the Cross, to destroy them, in this sense that those whom faith and baptism (Rom 6:4) have conformed to our High Priest in His sacrifice (Phil 3:10) are delivered of their sins, for through it our sins are expiated and the new humanity is born (2 Cor 5:17; Eph 4:24; 1 Pet 3:18). It is

---

[35] G. B. Caird, "Review of J. Colson's *Ministre de Jésus-Christ*," JThSt 18 (1967), p. 480.

very probable that Christ is referred to as Priest in the following passage, a compendium, so to say, of notions found in Heb (e.g. 7:25, 10:1): "For Christ also died for sins once for all (*hapax*), the righteous for the unrighteous, that he might bring (*prosagein*)* us to God, being put to death in the flesh but made alive in the Spirit" (1 Pet 3:18).

It can be assumed then that even outside Heb a priestly intervention is involved in the sacrifice of Jesus. If this is true the conclusion is inescapable : the NT writers considered Jesus to be both Priest and Victim. They were, however, reluctant to state it clearly for fear of associating Christ's unique Priesthood with the Aaronic institution. In his careful presentation of Christ's sacrificial liturgy and Priesthood the author of Heb successfully expressed their absolute newness in a largely traditional language.

b) *Christ's Priestly Consecration*

The connections of Heb with the Johannine writings are important and numerous.[36] It is then expected that John would at least allude to Christ's Priesthood, and it is probable that he does. In the beginning of the 5th cent. St. Cyril of Alexandria wrote in connection with Jn 17:9-11 :

> Again, He is, as man, Mediator between God and men, our truly great and holy High Priest, who offering Himself in sacrifice has appeased the spirit of his Father by his intercessions. For He is the Victim and the Priest, the Mediator, and the immaculate Offering, the true Lamb who takes away the sin of the world (*In Jo Ev* XI, 8).

Chytraeus, a Protestant theologian of the 16th cent., for the first time apparently, described Jn 17 as the "high priestly prayer." "It is a fact, Cullmann writes, that one can explain the whole prayer only on the basis of the high priestly consciousness of the one who spoke it ... The petition for the sanctification of his own (17:17) and their separation from the world (17:11-13) is a typical high priestly prayer," here understood ethically, not ritually (cf. Heb 9:13).[37] Saying "and for thy sake I consecrate (*hagiazein*) myself, that they also may be consecrated in truth" (17:19; cf. 17:17), Jesus speaks as "a servant of God, who makes himself ready for his divinely appointed task, and the task immediately

---

[36] See C. Spicq, *Hébreux*, v. 1, pp. 109-138. On the Johannine origin of the High Priest conception of Heb see C. Spicq in *Aux Sources de la tradition chrétienne. Mélanges Goguel* (Neuchâtel-Paris, 1950), pp. 258-269.

[37] O. Cullmann, *Christology*, p. 106.

ahead of Jesus was that of dying for his friends. The language is equally appropriate to the preparation of a priest and the preparation of a sacrifice; it is therefore doubly appropriate to Christ."[38] J. Gnilka believes that *hagiazein* has in Jn 17:19 a sacrificial meaning, as in Ex 13:2 and Dt 15:19, which speak of the sacrificial consecration of the firstling males of the herd and flock to God. He would not, however, easily accept G. Friedrich's claim (ZKathTh 53, [1956], pp. 275-278) that *hagios tou Theou*, "Holy One of God" (cf. Mk 1:24; Lk 4:34) refers to Christ as High Priest. Not only priests are called "saints of God"! But Gnilka is willing to read in Jn 2:21-22 the teaching that Jesus has abolished the OT cult and that he is the living *milieu* of the cult in the new community (p. 422).[39] To the Jews who wanted to stone Him Jesus had said: "Do you say of Him whom the Father consecrated (*hagiazein*) and sent into the world, 'You are blaspheming,' because I said, 'I am the Son of God'?" (Jn 10:36). In this text also, *hagiazein* means "to set apart for a sacred duty," as Jeremiah was "consecrated" to be a prophet (1:5), as Aaron and his sons were "consecrated" to be priests: "Aaron and his sons I will consecrate (*hagiazein*), to serve me as priests" (Ez 29:44; cf. 28:41, 30:30, 40:13; Lev 8:12).

Hagiazein is also correctly translated "sanctify" or "make holy (*hagios*)," and this rendering is preferable in Heb 2:11: "For the sanctifier and the sanctified are all from one." The same concept of "sanctification," as resulting from our High Priest's sacrifice, appears in Heb 10:10: "In this [God's] will we have been made holy through the offering of the body of Jesus Christ once for all (10:14, 29, 13:12). To sanctify (*hagiazein*) others by his sacrifice Jesus Himself had to be holy (*hagios*), not merely be without sin. Our High Priest's consecration was consummated by His *teleiōsis*, his Godward transformation. In the same way, "by one offering He has given fulfilment (*teteleiōken*) in perpetuity to those being sanctified" (10:14).

In his last discourses the Johannine Christ raised other themes which are associated as well with the High Priest of Hebrews. Here and there He appears as a Pioneer, as one who opens the way (Heb 10:19-20), who is the Way (Jn 14:6), first to enter into heaven once for all (Heb 9:12), to prepare a place for His disciples (Jn 14:2-3; cf. Heb 11:16). For John, with the Passion there comes for Jesus the Hour to depart

---

[38] C. K. Barrett, *The Gospel according to St. John* (London, 1955), p. 426.

[39] J. Gnilka, "Die Erwartung des Messianischen Hohenpriesters in den Schriften von Qumran und im Neuen Testament," RevQum 2 (1960), pp. 424, 409, 422.

out of this world to the Father (13:1), while for Heb our High Priest's sacrifice takes Him into the heavenly sanctuary there to appear before the face of God for us (9:12, 24). It has been pointed out above that the role of the Johannine *Paraklētos* (Jn 14:16, 26, 15:26, 16:7; 1 Jn 2:1) may be related to that of Intercessor (cf. Heb 7:25). "The Son of Man exalted on the Cross and at the same time paradoxically raised to the glory of the Father will take the place of the Accuser to reign as Intercessor, as Paraclete."[40] Further discussion of these issues lies beyond the scope of our present subject. Let us rather examine other possible priestly features of Christ outside the Epistle to the Hebrews.

c) *Priestly Blessing and Priestly Vestment*

To pronounce blessings was one of the Aaronic priest's functions, and the author of Heb found in the Genesis account of Melchizedek's blessing of Abraham proof that his priesthood was superior to the Levitical (Heb 7:1, 8). Luke's Gospel ends with a description of Christ bidding farewell to his disciples : "Then He led them out as far as Bethany, and lifting up His hands He blessed them. While He blessed them, He parted from them" (24:50-51). Thus Luke closes his Gospel in the same way he opened it, with a *leitourgia* (1:23), which is now completed by a priestly blessing. "Lifting up His hands" is correctly interpreted as a technical expression of the priestly blessing. Having performed the sacrifice "Aaron lifted up his hands toward the people and blessed them" (Lev 9:22). Similarly it is said of Simon the high priest that coming down from the service at the altar he "lifted up his hands over the whole congregation of the sons of Israel, to pronounce the blessing of the Lord" (Sir 50:20-21).* From this and other parallels P. A. Stempvoort concludes : "We can find in Sir 50 the literary background of Luke's description of the last Christophany."[41] This may be overstated but it remains very probable that Luke did allude to Christ's priesthood at the end of his Gospel.

All three Synoptics mention that the vestments of Jesus became resplendently white at the Transfiguration (Mk 9:3; Mt 17:2; Lk 9:29). This Christophany shows Jesus invested by an extraterrestrial light proper to the resurrected figures of the apocalypses (cf. Rev 3:5, 18, 4:4, 7, 9, 13, 19:14). Christ is symbolically enthroned as the Messianic

---

[40] T. Preiss, *Life in Christ*. Studies in Biblical Theology 13 (London, 1954), p. 19.

[41] P. A. von Stempvoort, "The Interpretation of the Ascension in Luke and Acts," NTSt 5 (1958-59), p. 34.

King-Priest. The celestial white vestment is a theophanic transposition of the white tunic worn by the Jewish priests.* According to H. Riesenfeld the motifs of resplendent vestments and of glory were associated in ancient times with the priestly function.[42] The exalted Christ described in Apoc 1:13 is "clothed with a long robe (*podērēs*) and with a golden girdle (*zōnē*) round his breast" (RSV). It happens that *podērēs* in Ex 28:4, 29:5 renders *me'il*, the tunic of the high priest (cf. Wis 18:24), who also wore an ornamented *zōnē* (Ex 28:39, 29:9).+ A reference to Christ's high priestly character is often read also in Jn 19 :23. The tunic (*chitōn*) of Jesus "was without seam, woven from top to bottom," like that of the high priest, which Josephus describes,++ and there was a ruling forbidding the high priest to rend his clothes (Lev 21:10). The soldiers said to one another : "Let us not tear it, but cast lots for it to see whose it shall be" (Jn 19:24). It is probable, not certain, that Apoc 1:13 and Jn 19:23-24 contain a reference to the High Priestly character of Jesus.

There are, to conclude, valid indications that presenting the death of Jesus as a sacrifice, in the way we have explained, the NT writers, even outside Heb, thought of Him as being both Victim and Priest. To this end He had received a special consecration which can be called priestly, and this was consummated in His sacrificial *teleiōsis*. More concrete but less certain allusions to Christ's priesthood can be found in His farewell blessing before the Ascension and in the Johannine description of vestments related to His person. Other priestly features have been suggested and probably more could be found, but those we have discussed seem at the present time to be the most relevant and are not to be neglected.

C. Our High Priest in Early Christian Writings

The title High Priest is rarely used of Christ in the early Christian writings, presumably because the Epistle to the Hebrews was firmly admitted in the canon of Scriptures only at a later period. Our very limited inquiry does not go beyond Origen, who died in the middle of the 3rd century. None of the texts we shall quote requires a lengthy commentary, in view of our present concern, which is to illustrate rather than demonstrate.

---

42 H. Riesenfeld, *Jésus transfiguré* (Copenhagen, 1947), pp. 107 and 116. See also pp. 115-129 : "La robe sacrée."

We first meet *Clement of Rome*, who in his (first) letter to the Corinthians alludes about 20 times to the Epistle to the Heb. He writes : "This is the way (*hē hodos*; cf. Heb 10:20), dearly beloved, wherein we found our salvation, even Jesus Christ the High-priest of our offerings (*tōn prosphorōn hēmōn*; cf. Heb 13:15), the Guardian (*prostatēs*) and Helper (*boēthos*) of our weakness. Through Him let us look steadfastly unto the heights of the heavens ..." (*Cor* 36).* Further on he addresses God in the following terms : "O Thou, who alone art able to do these things, and things far more exceeding good than these for us, we praise Thee through the Highpriest and Guardian of our souls, Jesus Christ, through whom be the glory and the majesty unto Thee both now and for all generations and for ever and ever. Amen" (*id.* 61). On the way to his martyrdom (*c.* A.D. 110) *Ignatius of Antioch* wrote to the Philadelphians, probably in dependence of Heb : "The priests likewise were good, but better is the Highpriest to whom is committed the holy of holies; for to Him alone are committed the hidden things of God" (*Philad* 9).

Some of the other texts to be quoted relate the priesthood of Christ to the investture of Joshua (Gr. *Iēsous*) the high priest (cf. Zech 3:1-10). + Apparently the earliest of these is from *Justin Martyr* who around 150 argued that in Zechariah's vision Joshua prefigures Christ the High Priest, in the mysteries of his Passion and Resurrection : "The revelation of the Jesus who was a priest of your nation in Babylon foretold the things which were to be done by our Priest, God and Christ, the Son of the Father of all things" (*Dial.with Trypho* 115). Returning to speak "of Jesus Christ, the Righteous ... of Him who was crucified as the Christ, the High Priest," Justin explains how Jesus of Zech 3 prefigured Him and us, "who have put off our filthy garments, that is our sins ... and are the true high-priestly family of God" (*id.* 116).

In Rome, about half a century later, *Hippolytus* also mentioned Joshua the high priest as a figure of Christ. In his commentary of Daniel he explains thus *christos hēgoumenos*, "anointed ruler" (Dn 7:25 LXX) :

> What "Anointed" (*christos*) is mentioned, if not *Jesus of Jōsedek* who made the people return at that period (cf. Ezra 3 :2, 8, 5 :2 LXX), and having had the holy place built, offered the sacrifice according to the rites of the Law. All the kings and priests were called *christoi* because they were "anointed" with the holy oil, aforetime prepared by Moses. Bearing the name of the Lord they foretold of Him in figure (*typos*) and in image (*eikōn*), until appeared from heaven the perfect (*teleios*) King and Priest, who alone fulfilled the will of his Father, as it is written : "And I will raise up for myself a faithful priest ..." (1 Sam 2 :35).[43]

[43] Hippolytus, *Comm. on Daniel* 4.30; my transl. of the orig. Greek : GCS, Hipp., v. 1, p. 266; the other text quoted is on p. 270f.

Referring in the same context to the statements of Dn 9:24 LXX on "sealing up sins" (or sin offerings) and "anointing the holy of holies," Hippolytus explains : "The Holy of Holies is nothing else but the Son of God who made his appearance and declared himself to be the Anointed One of the Father, sent into this world." Then he quotes Lk 4:18-19 and adds : "All those who believed in the heavenly Priest were purified by the Priest himself, and their sins were remitted. But for those who did not believe in Him ... their sins were sealed up ..." (4:32).

Tertullian refers to Joshua the high priest even more explicitly than Hippolytus his contemporary, when against Marcion who denied such truth he declares that Christ is the Messiah and Savior whose coming was prophesied in the OT :

> Thus also in Zechariah (3 :3-5), in the person of Jesus [=Joshua], in the very prefigurating mystery (*sacramento*) of the name, the true High Priest of the Father, Christ Jesus is delineated in his two advents by the double clothing : first, clad in the filthy garments, that is in the indignity of the passible and mortal flesh ... ; then, stripped of these and vested with (new) garments and a clean turban, that is with the glory and the honor of the second advent" (*Against Marcion*, III, 7, 6).

In a writing of his later (montanist) period (*c.* 217), Tertullian strongly opposes remarriage, on the grounds that all Christians are priests : "Jesus, the great High Priest of the Father, clothing us with His own garment—'for those who are baptized in Christ have put on Christ' (Gal 3:27)—has made us priests to God His Father (Apoc 1:6), as John declares" (*Monogamy* 7).[44] This is one instance of the distinctive interest Tertullian had in a theological theme thus described by the editors of his treatise *On Baptism* : "This anointing (at Baptism) is associated by all the Fathers with that of the priests and kings of the OT and with the spiritual anointing of Christ. It confers on the baptized their quality as anointed, as Christians. By it the neophyte is made participant of the Priesthood and of the Kingship of Christ" (Sources Chrétiennes, vol. 35, p. 41).

Clement of Alexandria, who knew Heb, very likely alludes to it in the following passage : "This eternal Jesus, the one great (*megas*; cf. Heb 4:14, 10:21) High Priest of the one God, who is also His Father, prays for men, and exhorts them ...".[45] *Origen,* who quotes Heb in all his

---

[44] Tr. W. P. LeSaint in AncChrWr v. 13, p. 85.

[45] *Exhortation to the Greeks,* 12 : GCS, Cl. Alex., v. 1, p. 84. He also calls Jesus High Priest in *The Tutor,* 2.8 : *ibid.,* p. 197.

writings (see Spicq, *Hébreux* v. 1, p. 171, n. 1), calls Jesus High Priest in several texts. Having in mind his opponents, who denied that our Lord had a human body, he asserts that Joshua, Zechariah's "Jesus" in the LXX (cf. Zech 3), whose filthy clothes were exchanged for clean ones, was the type of Christ, who assumed a human body "in the likeness of sinful flesh" (Rom 8:3), and voluntarily chose the filth, in the ignominy of the cross, to redeem men. Origen's original Greek, which is lost, probably was clearer than the Latin recension of Rufinus (PG 13, 1834-35).

Origen taught that prayer can be addressed to the Father alone, a theory which finds no support in the Patristic tradition. Using a formula we have seen used by Clement of Rome he writes in his treatise on Prayer : "For the Son of God is the High Priest of our offerings and our advocate (*paraklētos*) with the Father, praying for those who pray and pleading with those who plead" (*Prayer* 10.1). More distinctively, he writes further on : "There remains, then, to pray to God alone, the Father of all, but not apart from the High Priest who was appointed with an oath by the Father, according to the words ... Heb 7:20-21" (*Prayer* 15.2). Then more explicitly : "You should not pray to Him who has been set over you as High Priest by the Father, nor to the Advocate who has this office from the Father (cf. 1 Jn 2:1); but you should pray *through* your High Priest and Advocate, who can have compassion ... Heb 4:15" (*Prayer* 15.4). The same theme recurs in *Against Celsus* :

> We ought to pray to the supreme God alone, and to pray besides to the only-begotten Logos of God, the firstborn of all creation (Col 1 :15); and we ought to beseech Him, as a high-priest, to bear our prayer, when it has reached Him, up to His God and our God and to His Father and the Father (cf. Jn 20 :17) of the people who live according to the word of God" (VIII, 26).[46]

In this text Origen seems to admit that, after all, prayers can be addressed also to Christ, and this possibility he has asserted even more clearly elsewhere.[47] Another text of Origen, to conclude. Having recalled that the Jewish priests did not offer sacrifices intended to remove serious and deliberate sins (Num 15:27-31), he adds the following comment :

---

[46] Tr. H. Chadwick, *Origen : Contra Celsum* (Cambridge, 1953), p. 471; in GCS, Orig., v. 2, p. 242; the Greek text of the quotations from *Prayer* is *ibid.*, pp. 320, 334, 335, and the tr. of J. J. O'Meara in AncChrWr v. 19, pp. 42, 58, 59.

[47] See, e.g., *Hom. on Exodus*, 13.3: GCS, Orig. v. 6, p. 273; cf. *Hom. on Lev.*, 5.5; *ibid.*, p. 243. For possible explanations of the inconsistency see J. J. O'Meara in AncChrWr, v. 19, pp. 9-10.

"In the same way the Apostles also and their successors, priests (*hiereis*) according to the great High Priest, having received the science of divine therapy, know from their instruction by the Spirit for what sins, when, and how they must offer sacrifice" (*Prayer* 28.9).[48]

As the Epistle to the Hebrews became better known and studied, the Fathers and the theologians found a growing interest in the High Priesthood of Jesus and sought to formulate its mystery in the framework of dogmatic Christology. In scholastic terms Christ's Priesthood is said to be rooted in the grace of the union in one person of his two natures, human and divine. Christ received, however, it is further stated, the faculty of exercizing his Priesthood through his elevation to the supernatural order by sanctifying grace.[49] The Author of Heb, on the other hand, has spoken of the Priesthood of Christ in the framework of the Biblical message of salvation and has insisted on the following aspect : it is as High Priest that Jesus has effected sacrificial redemption.

---

[48] In GCS, p. 381 and O'Meara, p. 112. See also Origen's *Exhortation to Martyrdom* 30: GCS Orig., v. 1, p. 27, where it is stated that the High Priest Jesus Christ offered Himself in sacrifice. For patristic references on Christ the High Priest, see G. W. H. Lampe, ed. *A Patristic Greek Lexicon* (Oxford, 1961-69), pp. 238-239.

[49] See Ch. V. Heris in *Somme Théologique*, IIIa, q. 18-23 (édit. de la Revue des Jeunes), notes, pp. 357-359.

GENERAL CONCLUSION

In our religious conception, that of the Judeo-Christian world, two essential elements enter into the definition of a "priest" : he is a man dedicated or consecrated to exercise a priesthood, and one who belongs to a clergy juridically specified and organized. It can be argued, however, that the existence of a priesthood is not necessarily bound up with the existence of a clergy, nor even with the existence of priests that are mediators by office or permanent and institutional specialists of the sacred. Priestless religions exist, and in the most elementary forms of sacrifice the priestly role seems attributed to the victim rather than to the sacrificer. The priests appear as a distinctive body mainly in the hierarchical societies, in which the work is diversified into categories. Cases are conceivable in which appurtenance to a sacerdotal caste imparts less sacrificial power than a given non-priestly status. Thus a Levite in Israel would be, in a way, less "priest" than the heads of families or the kings performing priestly actions. A distinction then has to be made between sacerdotal power and priestly status. In some societies at least it is possible that a specialized priesthood has been instituted to exempt the non-priests from sacerdotal functions and sacral interdictions pertaining to them, as well as to provide competent sacrificers and mediators. Its purpose would then be to desacralize the society as a whole, not to sacralize it (in that case a non-sacral priesthood would be useless).[1] Thus the offering of the first fruits and the dedication of the firstborn to the divinity probably had among others, the purpose of allowing the return to profane use or to secular life the greater part of all the yield and progeny believed to be the god's property by right. In Israel later legislation explained that God took the Levites for himself as substitutes for the firstborn (Num 3:13, 8:17, 18).

Priesthood in the preliterate societies offers, as we have seen, a variety of features that may be reckoned as belonging to the common notion of priesthood. While the magicians developed the technique of efficacious rites to control the supernatural agencies at work in the world, the priests insisted on worship as being the appropriate means of placating them and of obtaining their favor. The magicians generally operate on

---

[1] See P. Idiart, "The Priest, Pagan and Christian" in *The Sacrament of Orders* (Collegeville, 1962), pp. 264-268.

an individual basis, but the priests usually speak for a deity, are connected with a sanctuary, or represent a tradition. The less the invisible powers are known, the more terrifying they appear to the primitives, who estimate that the ability to communicate with the divine is a priestly prerogative. At a more advanced stage of religious development, fellowship with the deity is sought and this figures among the very first fruits which the mediatorial work of the priest is expected to bring about, in one way or another, depending on the system of worship.

In Vedic religion the *brāhmaṇa* priests controlled and released the mystic power of sacrifice, with its universal significance. The validity of their mediation depended on the exact performance of the prescribed rites. In later Hinduism a varied clergy performed other priestly functions, supervising idol worship in the temples, teaching religion, and officiating at births, marriages, and deaths. The history of priesthood in ancient Iran is closely linked with Zoroastrianism; the successive classes of priests, *magi*, *athravan*, *herbad*, *mobad* were more or less connected with fire worship and pastoral ministration. In Greece the priests were closely associated with the sanctuary where they served. They played a necessary role in the valid offering of sacrifice and ministered to the statue of the god in the temples. It is not always clear what is distinctive of a *hiereus* as compared with other temple officials and sacrificers. Unlike India and Iran, the priests in Greece did not constitute as a rule an hereditary class and their admission to the priesthood was conditioned by qualifications of a physical and moral nature. The head official of the personnel of one or of several temples was called *archiereus*, the term for high priest in postexilic Judaism and the central title of Jesus in the Christology of the Epistle to the Hebrews. It is distinctive of the priests in ancient Rome that they were grouped in *collegia* and played an important role as augures and diviners. Also distinctive is the institution there of State priestesses, virgins who looked after the sacred flame in the temple of Vesta.

In treating of priesthood in the ancient Near East we have tried to respect the objective complexity of the problems involved, regarding chronology, cultures, and religious beliefs. Kingship was a sacred institution in Mesopotamia : even though generally speaking the kings were not deified, they were the vice-gerents of the deity, sacred intermediaries uniting humanity and the gods. In Sumer the city state dynast very likely functioned as supreme priest, while the Assyrian king was unquestionably the first priest of the realm, he who called himself "the *ishippu* who purifies the statues of the great gods." We have discussed the debated questions relating to the ritual reenactment of the myths at the New Year festival in Babylonia. The primitive role of the priests in Mesopotamia, as also in Egypt, was to work for the gods, to serve them, clothe them, feed them, in the place of mankind; the god, real master of the land and temple, was represented by the statue, in which he was thought to dwell and live. In view of the particular nature of the Mesopotamian pantheon we have tried to correlate the different gods worshipped in the area and to delineate their character and attributes. Derivative priestly functions have also been studied, those mainly that concern prophesying, purifying, and exorcising. We have then carefully determined what is meant by Canaanite language and culture, before examining which gods were worshipped at Ugarit, what sacrifices were offered to them, and by what names the priests and their assistants were designated. The similarities of Ugaritic cultic terminology with that of the OT have been noticed in passing. The fact that the non-Semitic Hittites combine, in a way, the Indo-European and the Mesopotamian cultures calls for special attention, more than their pantheon, partly borrowed, and their priesthood, about which few precise notions are available. Yet divining has been found to be a particularly distinctive feature of the Hittite priests.

Due to his divine origin the Egyptian Pharaoh was the born mediator between heaven and earth, the supreme pontiff in worship, concentrating in his person the temporal and the spiritual powers. In practice, however, the priests performed the rites and managed the temples in the name of the king. As guardians of the god's presence in the temple they performed the appropriate rites relating to his statue, which had to be washed, dressed, and symbolically fed, if the proper conditions for the 'incarnation" were to be procured. They preserved and studied their sacred scriptures with an equal devotion, finding the explanation of the universe in the traditional hieroglyphic texts, which, when pronounced, were believed to revive their original power. The priests formed in Egypt the class of the learned and we have seen that their wisdom found applications in a variety of fields. Like the Jewish priests they were subject to laws of purity and had to avoid in food and clothing what was thought could offend the deities they served. Among the ancient Arabs the *sādin* had something in common with the Israelite priest: he was firmly connected with a specific sanctuary and gave oracles in the name of a divinity. The *kāhin*, on the other hand, was rather of the prophetic type, even though the name is similar to *kōhēn*, the Hebrew priest.

A pre-Mosaic Hebrew priesthood, if one existed, would likely have had a prototype in this priesthood of the desert which is attested among the ancient Arabs. The origin of the Israelite priesthood and the role of Moses in its institution raise complex problems, for which the historians of the Biblical traditions offer varying solutions. We will not reexamine this argument here nor recapitulate the great debate on the status of the priests and Levites. Instead we can focus attention again on these aspects which may clarify the notion of priesthood in itself and in its comparison with the priesthood of Christ.

In recent years the excessive prominence given to the mediating role of sacral kingship in the ancient Near East[2] has led investigators to neglect the other types of mediators, the priests and the prophets. It is true, however, that the Israelite kings without being "priests" in the sense of the Hebrew *kōhēn* did exercise in regard to the nation that "natural" priesthood which was also proper on a smaller scale to the head of the family or clan. Besides, as an "anointed of God" the Israelite king was the recipient of a special grace to be, within the Covenant, mediator between God and his people (cf. 2 Kg 11:17), and as monarch he was the supreme administrator of the cultic institution. The priestly role of the Israelite kings, which gradually diminished, was later negatively reinterpreted as an undue intrusion in the sacred sphere. Whereas generally in the ancient Near East, and specifically among the Canaanites, a priest was considered to be a priest *to* a divinity (cf. Gen 14:15), the Israelite priest, primitively at least, is said to be priest to an individual, to a tribe, or to the king (cf. Jg 17:10, 18:19; 2 Sam 20:26). The statement of 1 Sam 2.35, "And I will raise up for myself a faithful priest [i.e. Zadok] ... and he shall go in and out before my anointed [the Davidic king] for ever," "is consonant with that close association of Davidic dynasty and royal temple which lay at the heart of the Jerusalemite nationalist-religious ideal expressed most explicitly in 2 Sam 7 and underlying many of the oracles of Isaiah and Micah."[3]

It is a distinctive feature of the Israelite religion that the priestly mediatorial function is seen as part of the great economy of salvation divinely instituted and offered to the people as a pure grace together with the Covenant.[4] In regard to eschatology and priesthood in the OT

---

[2] See a good review of this debate in J. Scharbert, *Heilsmittler im alten Testament und im alten Orient* (Quaest. Disp. 23;24 Freiburg im Breisgau, 1964), pp. 11-20.

[3] A. Cody, *Old Testament Priesthood*, p. 137.

[4] See J. Scharbert, *Heilsmittler*, p. 280.

it is true that the grace promised to men is of a spiritual nature (Os 2:19-20), that the new covenant is one to be written upon the heart (Jer 31:33), that the expected renewal will be a gift of the Spirit (Ezek 36:26-27). Yet Jeremiah foresees a new cult, in which the priests will have a role to play (31:14); Ezekiel described at length the future temple and its reformed cult (40-48); Malachi expects the Levites to be purified, till they present right offerings to the Lord (3:3), and in the third part of Isaiah the exiles are promised : "You shall be called the priests of the Lord ... ministers of our Lord" (61:6). And of the Gentile worshippers the Lord says : "Some of them I will take for priests and for Levites" (66:21). From these and other texts Grelot concludes : "The existence of a priestly mediation is not regarded as something transitional, which the eschatological salvation would render useless."[5] A truly redeeming mediation or sacrificial redemption was not, however, provided by the Mosaic institution. * And the hope of remedying this essential lack expressed itself in the prophecy of the Suffering Servant, the Just one who would bear the sins of all and justify a multitude (Is 53).

What this eschatological figure announced became a reality with the sacrifice of Jesus the High Priest. But although the author of the Epistle to the Hebrews alludes, as we have seen, to the Servant theology, he more commonly links the person of Jesus the High Priest to the Old Testament through the figure of Melchizedek. He does not present the priesthood of Jesus nor His sacrificial liturgy as fulfilling what the old priesthood and the old liturgy would have been in figure, but as effecting true Redemption, that which the Mosaic institution was unable to procure. In a similar way the priesthood of Christ is not a myth, although it may provide the answer to the hope expressed through myths. In fact if analogies exist for Christ's priesthood they are more easily found in the death-resurrection mysteries of the pagan myths than in the institutionalized Aaronic priesthood (cf. Idiart, pp. 270-272). For Jesus is not priest by office, he is so by nature. And in this sense His priesthood had a certain affinity with the "natural" priesthood of king-priest Melchizedek. It would be wrong to call the priesthood of Christ described in Heb "allegorical," for the reason that it cannot be compared with the Aaronic institution. For Christ is the only totally real priest, even the only possible priest in the full sense of the

---

[5] P. Grelot, *Le ministère de la nouvelle alliance* (Paris, 1977), p. 39.

term. Christ is not a priest, He is *the* Priest, whose self-offering constitutes one Sacrifice for the redemption of the world.

In the New Testament, terms and values are easily transferred from the rito-cultual to the personal-spiritual order (cf. 1 Cor 9:13, 14, 12 : 28; Rom 12:1, 15:16; Eph 4:11, 5:2; Phil 2:17; 1 Tim 4:6). This brings as well a change in the practice of worship. At the time of Jesus the sacrificial cult took place in the temple, while the "spiritual" cult, the teaching of the Law and the prophets was held in the synagogues. But the Christian churches, which do not know this duality, have replaced both the temple and the synagogues, because, as Thomas Aquinas explains, "the sacrifice of the Church is spiritual : in Christianity faith is taught and sacrifice is offered in one and the same place" (ST 1a2ae, 102.4 ad 3).

We wish to conclude with a text in which Origen, commenting on the book of Joshua, expresses in Biblical terms the replacement of the Mosaic cultic institution by the new economy of salvation :

> We have to comment also on the death of Moses; for if we do not know how Moses dies, we will not understand how Jesus reigns. When you consider Jerusalem destroyed, the altar forsaken, when no sacrifices, no victims, no libations, no priests, no pontiffs, no Levitical ministrations are to be seen, when all this has come about, then say : "Moses, my servant, is dead" (Jos 1 :2). When they no longer appear three times a year before the Lord God (Ex 23:17), nor offer the gifts in the temple, nor slay the Passover lamb, nor eat the unleavened bread, nor bring the firstfruits, nor consecrate the firstborn, when all this ceases to be celebrated, then say : "Moses, my servant, is dead."
>
> But when you see the Gentiles (or the peoples) embrace the (Christian) faith, churches being erected, altars no more besprinkled with animal blood but consecrated by the precious blood of Christ (1 Pet 1 :19), when you see priests and Levites, no more ministrants of the blood of goats and bulls (Heb 9:14), but of the word of God by the grace of the Holy Spirit, then say that Jesus has replaced Moses, that he has obtained the sovereignty, not Jesus [=Joshua], son of Nave (Jos 1:2 LXX), but Jesus, the Son of God."[6]

---

[6] Hom 2.1 on Joshua : GCS, Orig. 7, pp. 296-297. My own translation from the Latin text of Rufinus. On the disappearance of the Jewish cult see also Hom 17.1 : *ibid.* 909-910. Instead of the Heb. "Joshua, the son of Nun," the LXX text, followed by Origen, read *Iēsous huios Navē* because, as it seems, NAYN was taken for NAYH; in the ancient characters N and H were frequently confused.

BOOKNOTES

The bold figures refer to the pages in the text.

1* See, for example, the list of works given in M. Eliade, *From Primitives to Zen. A Thematic Source Book of the History of Religions* (London 1967) 635-643. On "priests, shamans, and prophets," see V. L. Grottanelli, ed., *Ethnologia. L'uomo e la civiltà*, v. 3 (Milano 1966) 387-457. On priesthood among the primitives see the older work, still valuable, of J. Lippert, *Allgemeine Geschichte des Priesterthums*, v. 1 (Berlin 1883) 13-284.

3* On "family cults" see J. Wach, *Sociology of Religion* (London 1947) 59-71. On "ancestor-worship (in Africa)," see P. A. Talbot, *The Peoples of Southern Nigeria*, v. 2 (London 1926) 298-335.

4* "Spirits," divine beings, and lesser gods are not to be confused with the "high god in the sky." On the concept of the Universal Sky-god, see E. O. James, *Prehistoric Religion. A Study in Prehistoric Archaeology* (London 1957) 256-260.

9* On the role of dreams in primitive religions see M. Eliade, *Myths, Dreams and Mysteries. The encounter between contemporary faiths and archaic realities*, tr. by Ph. Mairet (New York 1960).

9** "By the Moxo in Brazil and certain tribes in Paraguay, it was deemed necessary that aspirants to the priestly office should have been attacked and wounded by a jaguar, which animal was the visible object of their worship" (*LOP* 98).

10* On priestesses and witches, see V. Elwin, *The Religion of an Indian Tribe* (Oxford, 1955), pp. 128-144; J. C. Baroja, *The World of the Witches*. Tr. O. N. V. Glendinning (Chicago 1965).

10** Fear of the spirits is a well-known characteristic of the primitives. Belief in roaming devils pervaded Babylonian society. In Voodoo circles, as in Haiti, the gods (*loas*) and spirits are believed to haunt mountains, rocks, caves, springs, and ponds or to live in rivers or in the sea. The *hougans* (priests) and *mambos* (priestesses) visit them there and return with fresh powers. The *loas* are also present in the sacred trees growing around the *houmforts* (temples) and houses of the country. Cf. A. Métraux, *Haiti. Black Peasants and their Religion* (London 1960), pp. 60-61.

12* For different conceptions on "magic and religion" see J. G. Frazer, *The Golden Bough*, v. 1 (London 1911) 220-243 and J. De Vries in HistRel 1 (1961) 214-221. According to J. Cazeneuve a magic mentality can be applied to realities of religion. Therefore "the priests can, like the chief, be endowed with magical capabilities" (*Les rites et la condition humaine*, Paris 1958, 201). Sometimes, as among the Kikuyu, the magician is all at once priest, medicine man, and diviner (p. 437).

12** E. O. James assigns two main meanings to the symbols found in the paleolithic "cavern sanctuaries." They reflect fertility rites intended to render the animals prolific and magic hunting rites to secure success in the chase (*Prehistoric Religion*, London 1957, pp. 174-176 and 232).

12*** According to E. O. James, "the shaman is the prevailing type of magician not only among the North Asiatic peoples but also in the Pacific islands, Malaysia,

Dravidian southern India and Africa, and in some of the American Indian tribes ..." (*The Nature and Function of Priesthood*, London 1955, p. 30). On shamanism see M. Eliade, *Shamanism: Archaic Techniques of Ecstasy* (New York and London 1964); *Id.*, "Recent Works on Shamanism: a Review Article," HistRel 1 (1961) 152-186; *Id.*, "Shamanism" in V. Ferm, ed., *Forgotten Religions* (New York 1950) 297-308; J. Campbell, *The Masks of God: Primitive Mythology* (New York 1959) 229-281; H. Hoffmann, *Symbolik der Tibetischen Religionen und des Schamanismus* (Stuttgart 1967) 100-109; J. T. Hitchcock, "A Nepalese Shamanism and the Classic Inner Asian Tradition," HistRel 7 (1967-68) 149-158. Also *Studies in Shamanism* (Abo Symposium of 1962; Stockholm 1967). See details in EphemThLov 43 (1967) 24-25.

13* *Mana*, a Polynesian word, means "occult power." In all *taboo* things there is enough *mana* to destroy violators who do not possess an equivalent *mana*. A priest entering into a *mana*-charged cemetery to perform ceremonies has nothing to fear since his *mana* protects him. On *mana* see M. Eliade, *Patterns in Comparative Religion* (London 1958), pp. 19-21; F. Herrmann, *Symbolik in den Religionen der Naturvölker* (Stuttgart 1961), pp. 30-40.

15* In the thought of ancient Semites "the life-giving power of the god was not limited to vegetative nature, but to him also was ascribed the increase of animal life, the multiplication of flocks and herds, and, not least, of the human inhabitants of the land" (W. R. Smith, *Lectures on the Religion of the Semites*, 2nd edit., London 1907, p. 107).

15** The Aztecs sacrified children to the rain god and a distinctive feature of the Aztec ceremonial was the dancing of the priests in the flayed skins of sacrificial victims, since magic powers were attributed to these particular skins (cf. V. W. von Hagen, *The Ancient Sun Kingdom of the Americas*, Cleveland 1961, pp. 18 and 97).

15+ On "divination," "clairvoyance," and "pre-vision" in some African tribes, see P. A. Talbot, *The Peoples of Southern Nigeria*, v. 2, pp. 183-192; on "witchcraft" see *ibid.* 200-227. On the "presages" among the primitives, on their "divining practices," see H. Lévy-Bruhl, *La mentalité primitive* (Paris 1922) 124-243.

18* In its restricted technical sense "Indo-Aryan" applies to the remains of Aryan language in the Near East. Useful information and bibliography (1884-1965) on Indo-Aryans is offered by M. Mayrhofer, *Die Indo-Arier im Alten Vorderasien. Mit einer analytischen Bibliographie* (Wiesbaden 1966). See also P. L. Bhargava, "The Original Home of the Aryans and Indo-Iranian Migrations," *Annals of the Bhandarkar Oriental Research Institute* 48-49 (Poona 1968), pp. 219-226; W. Havers, "Die Religion der Urindogermanen im Lichte der Sprache" in F. König, ed., *Christus und die Religionen der Erde*, v. 2 (Vienna, 1951), pp. 697-748; on "priesthood," pp. 740-743, where the term *amphipolos*, with probable Indo-European connections is also studied (see *infra*, p. 39).

18** When Sanskrit ceased to be a spoken language—it survives somewhat in the vernacular Marathi—it became a purely religious language (Vedic Sanskrit). On Sanscrit language and literature see the documentation offered by the art. "Sanscrit" in EncBrit, v. 19 (1964) 954-971.

18*** For an English edition of the Vedic hymns see *The Sacred Books of the East*, M. Müller, ed., v. 32 and 46 (Oxford 1891 and 1897), respectively tr. by M. Müller (Pt. 1) and H. Oldenberg (Pt. 2). For a selection see A. C. Bose, *Hymns from the Vedas* (London 1968). A good edition in German is that of F. K. G. Geldner, *Der Rig-Veda*1-3 (HarvOr-

Ser 33-35; Cambridge, Mass., 1951). See also the older work: H. Oldenberg, *Die Religion des Veda* (3rd/4th edit., Stuttgart and Berlin 1923).

18+ *Rigveda* means knowledge (*veda*) of the laudative stanzas (*ṛc*). The term *veda* is related to the Greek root *Fid* of *eidon*, "I saw," and *oida*, "I know" (cf. Latin *videre*, "to see"). W. N. Brown writes of *Rigveda*: "Our oldest literary records of India lie in the Rig Veda, composed in an archaic form of Sanskrit by Aryans who entered India from the northwest probably between 1500 and 1200 B.C. This work was presumably compiled by 1000 B.C. and consists of 1208 hymns by various priestly authors for use in the public Vedic sacrifice, through which the Aryan gods were gratified and strengthened and in return aided the patron of the sacrifice to achieve his legitimate aims. In this way men and gods collaborated to keep the universe operating smoothly and thwart the machinations of demons and their misguided human allies" ("Mythology of India," in S. N. Kramer, ed., *Mythologies* ... 281). Cf. S. S. Bhawe, *The Soma-Hymns of the Rigveda*, Pts 1-3 (Baroda 1957-62).

20* *Brahman* is the supreme reality that upholds the (objective) universe. *Brahmā* (masc.) is the creator-god, first member of the Hindu Trinity, the others being *Vishnu* and *Shiva*. When in the Epic period these two deities became the object of popular worship, the importance of *Brahmā* declined. The authors of the Upanishads posited *Ātman* (the soul or self; cf. Hebrew *nefesh*, and Germ. *atmen*, "to breathe") as the source-principle of the subjective universe. Finally *Brahmā* was identified with *Ātman* and *Brahmā-Ātman* is described as "that from whence these beings are born, that by which, when born, they live, that into which they enter at their death" (*Taittiriyaka-Upanishad* 3, M. Müller ed., v. 15, p. 64). One celestial deity is called *Dyaus* (cf. Gr. *Zeus*), a term related to the Latin *Deus*, "God" (cf. Fr.: "Dieu") and *divus*, "divine". In Indian mythology, *deva*, the name for "god," was applied to Dawn *Ushas*, children of Sky and Earth (cf. W. N. Brown in S. N. Kramer, ed., *Mythologies* ... 283). See on *diēus* and derivatives: J. Pokorny, *Indogermanisches etymologisches Wörterbuch*, v. 1 (Bern 1959) 184-186. The most conspicuous of the "terrestrial" gods was *Agni*. Although fundamentally related to "fire" (cf. Lat. "ignis," and "to ignite"), *Agni* belonged to the three orders of nature: the sky, the water and the earth.

20** "The power of the sacrifice, writes W. N. Brown, is indeed considered by some late Rigvedic sages to be supreme, and the final word respecting it in that work appears in the celebrated *Purushasukta* (X, 90). There the gods effect creation by celebrating the first sacrifice with all the unordered elements of the cosmos being contained within the body of the sacrificial victim conceived as a gigantic anthropomorphic male (*puruṣa*), who encompasses all the universe which we know and extends beyond it" (in S. N. Kramer, ed., *Mythologies* ... 287).

21* *Soma* was an intoxicating drink, also called *madhu* ("Sweet") in the *Rigveda*. *Indra*, the highest of the atmospheric gods, and the main national deity of Vedic Indra, was a great drinker of *soma*, from which he drew new energy for his vast enterprises. See R. Gordon-Wasson, "The Soma of the Rig Veda: What Was It ?," JAOS 91 (1971) 169-191.

22* The term *Atharvaveda* has to do with "knowledge of fire magic" and is related to *Athravan* (*skr ātharwan*), the term for "priest".

23* Among a multitude of studies on Hinduism the following can be mentioned: B. Griffiths, art. "Hinduism," in NCE, v. 6, pp. 1123-1136; Sri Swami Sivananda, *All About Hinduism* (rev. ed., Sivanandanaga, 1961); J. Gonda, *Les religions de l'Inde*, vol. 1: "Védisme et Hindouïsme ancien," vol. 2, "l'Hindouïsme récent," both translated from the German (Paris 1962 and 1965), with bibliog.; C. Regamey, "Die Religionen

Indiens," in F. König, ed., *Christus und die Religionen der Erde*, v. 3 (Wien 1951), pp. 73-228; P. Masson-Oursel, "Les religions de l'Inde," in M. Gorce-R. Mortier, *Histoire générale des religions*, v. 3 (Paris 1945), pp. 5-30; P. Johanns, *La pensée religieuse de l'Inde* (Namur 1952); *id.*, *A Synopsis of Christ through the Vedanta* (Calcutta 1930-1932; *vedanta* being a philosophical system). A systematic and annotated bibliography can be found in *Studia Missionalia*, XIII (Pont. Univ. Greg., 1963), pp. 225-246.

23** An English translation of the *Upanishads* has been published by M. Müller in *The Sacred Books of the East*, v. 1 and 15 (Oxford 1879 and 1884).

24* It is not the priestly office, L. S. S. O'Malley notes, but his birthright which makes the Brahman, and he does not lose the right to receive reverence from others because he holds a non-priestly office" (*Popular Hinduism. The Religion of the Masses*, Cambridge 1933, p. 188). See pp. 187-213 on "Brahmans, Priests and Holy men." The hereditary character of the institution appears in the name itself *brahmaṇa*, "descendant of a brahman" (cf. A. B. Keith, Hastings ERE, v. 10, p. 312).

25* The Iranian of the Avesta is the sister language of Sanskrit. Our word "paradise" comes from Iranian: "Besides hunting in the wide plain, the king had certain places, called 'paradises,' derived from the Avestan *pairi daeza*, 'enclosure,' specially set apart for the purpose of lighter chase" (M. N. Dhalla, *Zoroastrian Civilization*, New York 1922, p. 263). For an annotated bibliography on recent studies in Old Iranian see J. Duchesne-Guillemin, in *Kratylos* 7 (1962) 1-44.

26* On Zoroaster and his doctrine see also J. Duchesne-Guillemin, *La religion de l'Iran ancien*, in "*Mana*," Introd. à l'hist. des religions, I; Les anciennes religions orientales, 3 (Paris 1962), pp. 384-399, "Histoire des études" (annotated bibliography); A. V. W. Jackson, *Zoroaster, the Prophet of Ancient Iran* (New York 1919); M. N. Dhalla, *Zoroastrian Theology* (New York 1914); J. Duchesne-Guillemin, *Symbols in Zoroastrianism* (New York 1966); F. König, "Die Religion des Zarathustra," in *Christus und die Religionen der Erde*, v. 2 (Wien 1951), pp. 607-664; Mary Boyce, "Zoroaster the Priest," *Bulletin of the School of Oriental and African Studies* 33 (1970) 22-38.

27* The Parsi tradition enumerates 21 books supposedly to have constituted the original Avesta; see the titles and arguments of each in C. De Harlez, *Introduction*, pp. 51-53. The extant text of the Avesta is published in English in M. Müller, ed., *The Sacred Books of the East*, v. 4, 23, and 31 (Oxford 1898, 1883, 1887): "The Zend-Avesta," tr. by J. Darmesteter and L. H. Mills.

27** Included in this term is the word *daeva*, which came to mean "demon" or "evil spirit" in Persian, but its Indian equivalent meant "god," as mentioned above. Of the original 21 books of the Zoroastrian corpus, *Vidēvdāt* (often called *Vendidad*: in *pehlevi* or middle Persian) is the only one to have survived in its entirety.

27+ *Haoma* is the personified sacrificial plant offered with water and milk in the ceremony of the Yasna. The *haoma* is the Iranian equivalent of the Indian *soma*.

28* In the earlier sources, adds Nyberg, the dualistic conception is ethical rather than physical and naturalistic (p. 22). See also J. Bidez-F. Cumont, *Les Mages hellénisés. Zoroastre, Ostanès et Hystaspe d'après la tradition grecque*, 2 v. (Paris 1938); U. Bianchi, *Zamān i Ōhrmazd. Lo Zoroastrismo nelle sue origine e nella sua essenza* (Torino 1958); M. Molé, *Culte, mythe et cosmologie dans l'Iran ancien. Le problème zoroastrien et la tradition mazdéenne* (Paris 1966), bibliogr., p. XVII-XXXI; J. Varenne, *Zarathustra et la tradition mazdéenne* (Paris 1966); G. G. Cameron, "Zoroaster the Herdsman," *Indo-Iranian Journal* 10 (1968) 261-281.

Mani, born in Persia in the 3rd cent. A.D., founder of an eclectic religion called Manichaeism, took from Zoroastrianism the principles of his main teaching, the struggle between Good and Evil. "To the Manichean theologian the present status of man is the unfortunate result of a state of mixture between, what may be called in different terms, Mind and Matter or Good and Evil or Light and Darkness" (M. J. Dresden, "Mythology of Ancient Iran," p. 341). I. J. S. Taraporella described the monastic orders founded by Mani as early examples of "an unwalled monasticism" ("Manichaeism," in V. Ferm, ed., *Forgotten Religions*, New York 1950, p. 222). On Manichaeism, see W. Widengren, *Mani and Manichaeism* (London 1965). See also L. J. R. Ort, *Mani. A Religio-Historical Description of His Personality* (Brill, Leiden 1967), with a bibliography pp. 261-277).

28** During the first years of the reign of Darius the Great (521-486), Magus Gaumata seized power. But Darius returning from Egypt put him and several other magi to death, and resumed control (cf. NCE 9:60).

28+ To the writers of Greece and Rome, notes A. V. W. Jackson, Zoroaster was the archrepresentative of the Magi (*Zoroaster, the Prophet of Ancient Iran*, New York 1919, p. 6). The view, however, that Zoroaster was a *magus* is "open to the serious objection that the term *magu*, 'magus,' is not attested at all in the *Gāthās* and only once in a late passage of the Avesta. However, the *Gāthās* have the word *magavan*, which may be related. It seems to mean 'sharing in the alliance, in the mystic gift.' The existence of this term undoubtedly made the appropriation of Zoroastrianism easier for the Magi. In the Arsacid period [3rd cent. B.C.-3rd cent. A.D.] the heads of the religious hierarchy did not yet have the title *magupat*, 'chief of the magi,' which they acquired under the Sassanids [3rd-7th cent. A.D.], and which they have retained under the form *mobed* to the present time" (J. Duchesne-Guillemin, "Magi," NCE, v. 9, p. 60). On the meaning of "*maga-*, *magavan-*, *magu-*, *moγu*," see G. Messina, *Der Ursprung der Magier und die Zarathustrische Religion* (Roma 1930) 67-75.

29* Cf. art. "Magos," in Kittel ThW (Eng), v. 4, pp. 356-359: in Mt 2, *magos* "means the 'possessor of special (secret) wisdom,' especially concerning the meaning of the course of the stars and its interconnection with world events" (p. 358). See also P. Gaechter, "Die Magierpericope (Mt 2,1-12)," ZKathTh 90 (1968) 257-295. On oneirology see M. Eliade, *Myths, Dreams and Mysteries. The encounter between contemporary faiths and archaic realities* (New York 1960); G. E. von Grunebaum and R. Callois, ed., *The Dream and Human Societies* (Berkeley and Los Angeles 1966), esp. A. L. Oppenheim, "Mantic Dreams in the Ancient Near East," pp. 341-350. On possible connections between the culture of Ancient Iran and the Judaeo-Christian tradition see J. Duchesne-Guillemin, *La religion de l'Iran ancien* (Paris 1962), pp. 257-264, and J. H. Moulton, *art. cit.*, p. 243. There may be an anti-dualist polemic implied in Is 45:7, "I form light and create darkness, I make weal and create woe, I am the Lord, who do all these things." If this is so, then the "Rab-Mag" mentioned in connection with the fall of Jerusalem (Jer 39:3,13) could well be a sort of *archimagos*. The notation of Ez 8:17 that the idol worshipers "put the branch to their nose" is sometimes referred to the Iranian use of the *barsom*, "a bunch of tamarisk twigs held by the priest before his face in worship" (J. H. Moulton, *art. cit.*, p. 243). "Even if Iranian dualism is the source of the myth of the two spirits in the (Qumran) *Manual of Discipline* and in late Jewish pseudepigraphical writings, it has there been transformed so as to preserve the paramount sovereignty of God and to assign a subordinate role to the Devil" (J. P. De Menasce, in NCE, v. 11, p. 166). Indirect influence of Iranian conceptions on St. Paul's or St. John's dualism of light and darkness (cf. 2 Cor 6:14; Jn 1:5; 1 Jn 1:5 etc.) could also be plausibly claimed. See also F. König, *Zarathustras Jenseitsvorstellung und das Alte Testament* (Vienna 1964).

32* "Buddha," in Sanskrit "the Enlightened One," is the honorific title of the founder of Buddhism, the North Indian prince Siddhārtha Guatama. According to tradition he was born c. 563 B.C. at Lumbinī in the Nepal valley. His family name was *Sākya* and he is also known as Sākyamuni, the Sage, or Saint of the Sākyas. For the legends on Buddha's birth and life see W. E. Soothill, *The Three Religions of China* (3rd ed., Oxford 1929), pp. 79-86. The book deals with Confucianism, Taoism, and Buddhism.

33* See E. Conze, "Buddhist Saviours," in S. G. F. Brandon, ed., *The Saviour God. Comparative Studies in the Concept of Salvation presented to E. O. James* ... (Manchester 1963), pp. 67-82. See also S. G. F. Brandon, *Man and his Destiny in the Great Religions* (Manchester 1962), pp. 335-352; C. Humphreys, *Buddhism* (Penguin Books, 1954): a popular but serious presentation. For a bibliography on Buddhist topics see *Supplement to the Buddhist Yearly* (Buddhist Centre, Halle 1966), 71 pp. There is also Shinsho Hanayama, *Bibliography on Buddhism* (Tokyo 1961), 870 pp. See also H. Härtel *et al.*, "Buddha-Buddhismus" RGG[3], I (1957) c. 1469-1491; C. H. Hamilton, *Buddhism in India, Ceylon, China and Japan: a Reading Guide* (Chicago 1931); "Buddhism," in EncBrit, v. 4, pp. 354-362.

33** In founding respectively Jainism and Buddhism, Mahavira and Guatama intended also to refute radically the hereditary claims of Brahmin superiority and to reject the traditional caste system. See E. O. James, *The Nature and Function of Priesthood* (London 1955), p. 288.

33*** A. S. Rosso, *art. cit.*, p. 848. See also E. Conze, *Buddhism. Its Essence and Development* (New York 1959) 53-59 ("monastic Buddhism"). Poverty, celibacy, and inoffensiveness, he writes, were the true essentials of monastic life. On the same subject: N. Dutt, *Early Monastic Buddhism* (Calcutta 1941). In present-day Burma, it is reported, the monks must observe 227 monastic rules and in the lenten season make their annual retreat (see NCE, v. 2, p. 851).

36* "Demarch" is an anglicised *dēmarchos*, the chief official of a *dēmos*, "district." Aristotle mentions as one of three functions performed by a certain category of kings "the religious function of offering such sacrifices as did not require a priest" (*Politics* III, 14, § 12:1285b, tr. of E. Barker). He also writes of ancestral (*patrioi*) sacrifices which have the distinction of being celebrated on the city's common hearth, and, as such, are not legally assigned to the priests (*Politics*, VI, 8, § 19:1322b). In the Homeric world, notes L. Campbell, the king sacrifices, not as combining priestly with regal functions, but as the natural head of his family and clan, or of the army he leads (*Religion in Greek Literature* 55).

36** See Ph.-E. Legrand, "Sacerdoce (*hiereus*)," DictAntGrRom, 4, 2, pp. 934-942, and also on Greek priesthood: J. Martha, *Les sacerdoces athéniens* (Paris 1882), whom Legrand repeatedly quotes; G. Plaumann, "*Hiereis*," in Pauly-Wissowa, ed., *Real-Encyclopädie*, v. 8 (1913) c. 1411-1457; P. Stengel, *Die griechischen Kultusaltertümer*, Hdb der klassischen Altertums-Wissenschaft, V, 3 (2nd ed., Munich 1898) 30-50; E. des Places, *La religion grecque* (Paris 1969) 143-144.

37* See Pausanias, *The Description of Greece* 2, 33, § 2 and 7, 25, § 13. At the sanctuary of Artemis Hymnia in the territory of Orchomenus, he also writes, lived a priestess and a priest: "It is the custom for these to live their whole lives in purity, not only sexual but in all respects, and they neither wash nor spend their lives as do ordinary people, nor do they enter the home of a private man. I know that the 'entertainers' of the Ephesian Artemis live in similar fashion, but for a year only, the Ephesians calling them Essenes" (8, 13, § 1, tr. by W. H. S. Jones in The Loeb Classical Library edit.). On the custom regarding the hierophants, or initiating priests in the mystery cults see id. 2, 14, § 1. At Troezen there is, he reports, a holy sanctuary of Poseidon, and it is served by a maiden priestess until she reaches an age fit for marriage (2, 33, § 2). Drinking the blood of a bull was one of the lie detector tests which candidate priestesses had to pass regarding their marital status (cf. Pausanias 7, 25, § 13).

39* On the purchase of priesthoods in Greece see W. Otto's remarks in *Hermes* 44 (1909) 594-599 and H. Herbrecht, *De sacerdotii apud Graecos emptione venditione* (Strassburg 1885). According to some inscriptions the time and price of the sale was fixed by public edict (see L. Campbell, *op. cit.*, 304).

39** Also in the septuagint *poiein* is commonly used in connection with the offering of a sacrifice: cf. Ex 29:36; Num 6:11,16; Ezek 43:25; 45:22,23,25.

40* It seems that the term *archiereus* occurs in writing for the first time in (5th cent. B.C.) Herodotus (cf. II, 143). *Hieropolos* is also sometimes used with the meaning "chief priest." On *archiereus* see also P. Stengel in Pauly-Wiss RE, 1st ser., v. 2 (1896) 471-483, and W. Otto, *Priester und Tempel im hellenistischen Aegypten*, v. 1 (Leipzig 1905), pp. 134-137.

40** According to T. Mommsen a sharp distinction was made under the republic between magistrature and priesthood (see *Römisches Staatsrecht*, v. 2, Leipzig 1874-75, pp. 16-19). Later, however, the emperors assumed the title *Summus Pontifex* and presided the *collegium pontificum*. On the role of the Roman emperors as "priests" and "pontiffs," see T. Mommsen, *op. cit.*, 16-69 and 1102-1113.

41* The *Salii* were priests of Mars Gradivus forming a corporation. See Titus-Livius, I, 20; Dionysius II, 70, and Cicero, *The Republic*, II, 14. The foundation of the *Salii* has been attributed to Numa Pompilius, Rome's second legendary king (715-672 B.C.), like most of the Roman religious institutions having a claim to a certain antiquity.

41** They retained their priestly character even when sent into exile or when taken prisoners: see Plutarch, *op. cit.* 99, and Pliny the Elder (Gaius Plinius Secundus), *Natural History* XVIII, 2. The author of the *Letters* is Pliny the Younger (Gaius Plinius Caecilius Secundus), nephew of the first (1st cent. A.D.).

41*** Or adolescence: see Titus-Livius, *History of Rome* XLII, 8 and Plutarch, *Life of Tib. Gracchus*, 4.

42* *Pons Sublicius*, "the wooden bridge," built by King Ancus Martius (640-616 B.C.), tradition says, subsequently repaired by the *Pontifices*, from which fact, Varro suggests, they derived their name (*De Lingua Latina* 5, 83).

42** The three major priests at Rome were the *flamines* of Jupiter, Mars, and Quirinus, "the archaic triad" in G. Dumézil's theory: *La religion romaine archaique* ... Paris 1966). See C. S. Littleton, *The New Comparative Mythology: an Anthropological Assessment of the Theories of Georges Dumézil* (Berkeley and Los Angeles 1966). On the Vestals see Pliny the Younger, Letters IV, 11; Dionysius, Roman Antiquities II, 67; III, 67; Plutarch, *Moralia, Roman Questions*, 44; Pliny the Elder, *Natural History* XXVI, 27, 14 (they keep the eternal flame burning). On the priesthood of ancient Rome see also J. Toutain, "Sacerdos (Rome)," in DictAntGrRom IV, 2, pp. 942-946; *id.*, *Les cultes paiens dans l'empire romain*, v. 1 (Paris 1907), pp. 127-180; G. Wissowa, *Religion und Kultus der Römer*. Hdb der klassischen Altertums-Wissenschaft V, 4 (2nd ed., Munich 1912), pp. 479-566; P. Riewald, "*Sacerdotes*," in Pauly-Wiss. RE, 2nd ser., v. 1 (1920), c. 1631-1653; G. J. Laing, "Priest, Priesthood (Roman)," *ERE* X

(1918), pp. 325-335; C. Bardt, *Die Priester der vier grossen Collegien aus römisch-republikanischer Zeit* (Berlin 1871). See also the studies of A. Gemoll, L. Mercklin, and G. Schwede (Bibliogr.).

43* On the Sibylline oracles and the Sibylline books, see E. O. James, *The Nature and Function of Priesthood* (London 1955) 45-48. The origin and the use of the books are briefly explained by Dionysius, *Roman Antiquities*, IV, 62. On the *Quindecimviri sacris faciundis* and the *Haruspices*, see G. Wissowa, *Religion und Kultus der Römer* 534-550.

43+ In *Annales* (III, 64) Tacitus speaks of supplications to the gods and of great plays which the *pontifices*, the *augures*, and the *quindecimviri* were ordered by the Senate to celebrate in association with the *septemviri* and the *sodales Augustales*. Caesar refused to let also the *fetiales* preside the ceremonies. The *fetiales* were the special guardians of the public faith. See Varro, *De Lingua Latina*, V, 38, and Titus Livius, *History of Rome*, XXXVI, 3).

44* The Biblical story about the "tower of Babel" has a demonstrable source in cuneiform literature: see E. A. Speiser, *Genesis* (Anchor Bible; New York, 1964), pp. 75-76; cf. esp. a text of *Enūma eliš*, VI:60-62 (Pritchard ANET, p. 69). "Ziggurats" or "temple towers" are often mentioned in Assyrian texts. See art. "*Ziqquratu*": *The Assyrian Dictionary* (Chicago; henceforth: CAD), Z: 129-132. On the ziggurat of Ur see S. N. Kramer, in V. Ferm, ed., *Forgotten Religions* (New York 1950), pp. 51-52. For "reconstruction" drawings of this ziggurat (from L. Woolley) and that of Babylon see C. F. Pfeiffer, ed., *The Biblical World* (Grand Rapids, 1966), 598 and 125.

45* The Hebrew *'ur kaśdim* (Gen 11:28,31), "Ur of the Chaldeans" is rendered in the LXX by *chôra tôn Chaldaiôn*, "region of the Chaldeans." In the Book of Daniel (2nd cent. B.C.) we read that at the Babylonian court young Hebrews were to be taught "the language and literature of the Chaldaeans" (1:4). In fact Chaldea (from Akk. *Kaldu*) was "the land of aggressive Semitic Aramean nomads who gradually wandered into South Babylonia and, aided by the Medes, conquered Assur in 614 B.C. The line of Chaldean rulers included Nabopolassar, founder of the New Babylonian or Chaldean Kingdom, and his son Nebuchadnezzar (cf. 2 Kg 25:5)" (BBD 96). Older lexicographers call Aramaic "Chaldee." In Jdt 5:6 the Ammonite Achior tells Holofernes of the Israelites: "This people is descended from the Chaldeans" (*apogonoi Chaldaiôn*).

45** The term "Amorites," L. Oppenheim writes, "refers as a rule to one or more ethnic groups speaking Semitic but not Akkadian languages, within Mesopotamia and to the west of it. The Akkadian designation *amurrū* (Sum. *m a r.t u*) denoted in the course of the second millennium B.C. not only an ethnic group but also a language and a geographical and political unit in Upper Syria" (*Ancient Mesopotamia* 390). See also G. Buccellati, *The Amorites of the Ur III Period* (Naples 1966); H. B. Huffmon, *Amorite Personal Names in the Mari Texts: a Structural and Lexical Study* (Baltimore 1965), with an extensive bibliog. (pp. 281-299). More generally, on the early history of Mesopotamia, see S. Moscati, *The Semites in Ancient History* (Cardiff 1959), pp. 44-75 and I. J. Gelb, "The Early History of the West Semitic Peoples," JCunSt 15 (1961), pp. 27-47 (prefers the term "Amorite" to "Hanean," adopted by some authors). J. R. Kupper has extensively treated of both "the Haneans" and "the Amorites," *Les nomades en Mésopotamie au temps des rois de Mari* (Paris 1957), respectively pp. 1-46 and 147-247.

46* Similarities include the building of a house-boat caulked with pitch, according to specific dimensions, on which also the Babylonian Noah loaded his possessions, his family, and the "seed of life of all kinds" and thus escaped the consequences of the

Deluge. In the Babylonian epic a raven and a dove are sent out twice to help determine the safe moment for disembarking. For recent archeological and other discussion of the Deluge, see M. E. L. Mallowan, "Noah's Flood reconsidered," *Iraq* 26 (1964) 62-82, with a "table indicating floods related to archaeological sequences," especially drawn from the excavation finds at Shuruppak (Fara) in Mesopotamia. See also R. L. Raikes in *Iraq* 28 (1966) 52-63.

47* In Egypt, "*Re*ʿ the creator headed the lists of the kings of Egypt as the first ruler of the land who had been succeeded by other gods until Horus, perpetually reincarnated in successive Pharaohs, had assumed the legacy of Osiris" [H. Frankfort, *Kingship and the Gods* (Chicago 1948) 231]. No such process is attested in Mesopotamia.

47** See on the deification of sovereigns: M. J. Seux, *Épithètes royales akkadiennes et sumériennes* (Paris 1967), 107-109, n. 12; W. H. Ph. Römer, *Sumerische 'Königshymnen' der Isin-Zeit* (Leiden 1965), pp. 55-57.

48* It seems that the Enlil shrine at Nippur held in early Dynastic Mesopotamia a position similar to that of the Delphi sanctuary of Apollo among the Greek states. See H. Frankfort, *Kingship and the Gods* (Chicago 1948) 217. In the Sumerian "amphictyony" of the Ur III period, W. W. Hallo explains, the lesser shrines made monthly livestock contributions to Nippur, in turn, as determined by the *b a l a* ("term of office of a certain but not uniform length of time") of the *e n s i*, *s a b r a*, or *s a n g a*, i.e. of city governors ("A Sumerian Amphictyony," JCuneiformS 14, 1960, 90-95). The term *b a l a* (Old Babyl.: *BAL*) becomes *palû* in Akk., to designate in the Assyrian inscriptions the king's "reign" or "a year of reign." See H. Tadmor in JCuneiformS 12 (1958) 26. The *s a n g a* (Akk. *šangu*) performs no distinctively sacerdotal function, according to the texts of Ur III. He is the chief official in the management of the temple property (see N. Schneider, JCuneiformS 1, 1947, 122-142).

48** See A. Falkenstein, "La cité-temple sumérienne," *Cahiers d'histoire mondiale* 1 (1954) 795. Gudea, prince of Lagaš (2143-2124), was *e n s i* of Ningursu, the city god, whose temple was Eninnu (Pritchard ANET 165; cf. 268-269 for a Gudea text, and *Id.* ANEP 430-431 for Gudea statues). See also A. Falkenstein, *Die Inschriften Gudea von Lagaš* (AnalOr 30; Rome 1966) 1-54. On *iss(i)akku* (Akk.) = *e n s i* (Sum.), "régent, vicaire," see M.-J. Seux, *op. cit.* 110-115, who also notes (p. 267) that Salmanassar III (Assyria: 858-824) bore the title *šabru*, "intendant" (of god Assur). See also *ibid.* (p. 287-288) the list of references attesting the use by the Mesopotamian kings of the title *šangu*, "priest," *šangû ellu*, "sacred priest," *šangu ṣi-nu*, "august priest." On *šangu* = *iššakku*. cf. A. Schott in OrLitz 33 (1930) 883. On *iššakku* see especially CAD: I/J, pp. 262-266, The literary material presented covers the two meanings of the term: "territorial ruler" and "member of a class of privileged farmers (from Hammurabi on)." See also W. W. Hallo, *Early Mesopotamian Royal Titles: a Philologic and Historical Analysis* (New Haven 1957) 34-48. On Gudea see also ReallexAssyr III, 9 (Berlin 1971) 676-687.

48*** See A. Falkenstein, *art. cit.*, 795-796, who observes that in the historical period the *e n*-priestesses came from the ruling house; the *e n*-priest and the *e n*-priestess were considered as the spouses of the deity they served.

48**** R. Labat apparently oversimplified when he described the Sumerian monarch as "the high-priest of the temple, who officiates in the cult assisted by a numerous clergy" (*Le caractère religieux de la royauté assyro-babylonienne*, Paris 1938, p. 2. See also, pp. 1-25 and 361-370).

49* His usual title was "Sargon, king of Agade [= Akkad], overseer of Ishtar, king of Kish, 'anointed priest' of Anu, king of the country, great ensi of Enlil" (Pritchard

ANET, p. 267). The inscriptions read, it is true, *PAB.ŠEŠ AN*, lit. "the great elder brother," but the title is generally interpreted as *pašišu an*, "anointed priest of Anu" [cf. H. Hirsch in ArchOr 20 (Graz 1963), p. 34]. M.-J. Seux observes that the *pašišu* (Sum.: *g u d a*) was an "anointed priest" of an inferior rank entrusted with the offerings in the temples (*op. cit.*, p. 222, n. 76).

49** See J. Van Dijk, "Les contacts ethniques dans la Mésopotamie et les syncrétismes de la religion sumérienne," in Sven S. Hartmann, ed., *Syncretism*. Scripta Instituti Donneriani Aboensis III (Stockholm 1969) 171-206.

49*** The Elamites, Eastern neighbors of the Babylonians, occupied a stretch of land north of the Persian Gulf at the foot and on the slopes of the Zagros mountains. They may have been part of the non-Semitic pre-Sumerian population of Babylonia. For reasons geographical, not ethnical, Elam is listed by Gen 10:22 and 1 Chr 1:17 as "son of Shem." In the Elamite capital, Susa (= Shûshan: Neh 1:1; Est 1:2; Dan 8:2; cf. Jer 49:35-39), the priceless Code of Hammurabi stele was found, deposited there by Elamite raiders. The Akkadian texts describe the people of Elam ("highland") as adversaries of the Mesopotamians. On Elam see R. Labat, in *Cambridge Ancient History*, rev. ed., nn. 16 and 23 (London 1963-64), with bibliogr.

50* Hammurabi was the 6th of 11 kings in the Old Babylonian (Amorite) dynasty. The more probable dates of his reign are 1728-1686. He is best known today as the sponsor of "the Code of Hammurabi," which scholars have compared with the Hebrew Code of the Covenant. See its text in Pritchard ANET, pp. 163-180. See also on recent discussion C. J. Gadd, *Hammurabi and the end of his Dynasty*. CAH^2, n. 35. New evidence tends to reduce somewhat the stature of H. as a conquering dynast and even, although in a lesser degree, as a lawgiver.

50** H. Frankfort translates *šar kiššati* "King of the Universe," equivalent, he writes, to "King of the Four Quarters" (*op. cit.* 228). On this title see J. Lewy, HebUCAnn 19 (1945-46) 466-489 and M.-J. Seux, RevAssyr 59 (1965) 1-11.

50*** See C. J. Gadd, "The Harran Inscriptions of Nabonidus," AnatSt 8 (1958) 35-92.

50**** See Pritchard ANEP n. 536. Although there is no inscription to identify him the god in the disk was probably Aššur. See E. D. van Buren, *Symbols of the Gods in Mesopotamian Art*. AnalOr 23 (Rome 1945) 95-96. On the "Winged Disk" as a divine symbol see *id.* 94-104.

50+ On *rubū* (Akk.), "prince, grand" = *n u n* (Sum.), "prince," see M.-J. Seux, *Épithètes royales akkadiennes et sumériennes* 251-253 and 432. Other sovereigns bore the title of *šatammu*, "pontiff" (p. 321). See on "Das Amt des *šatammu*," B. Landsberger, *Brief des Bischofs von Esagila an König Asarhaddon* (Amsterdam 1965) 58-63: the term applies to a function equivalent to that of "high-priest" or "bishop."

53* The relevance of the Babylonian New Year festival in respect to the Israelite Year feast is a much debated question, especially in connection with the so-called "enthronement psalms" and the formula *Yhwh mālak*, "The Lord reigns" in Ps 47:8; 93:1; 96:10; 97:1. See H. Cazelles in DBSuppl, v. 6, c. 597-645.

53** On Sumer and the Sumerians see J. J. van Dijk's art. in H. Haag, ed., *Bibel-Lexicon* (2nd ed., Einsiedeln 1968) c. 1654-1664; S. N. Kramer, "Sumerian Literature and the Bible," in *Studia Biblica et Orientalia*, v. 3 (AnalOr 10, Rome, 1959) pp. 185-204; *id.*, "Sumerian Literature. A General Survey," in G. E. Wright, ed., *The Bible in the Ancient Near East* (New York 1961), pp. 249-266; *id.*, *The Sumerians* ... (Chicago 1963).

54* According to Th. Jacobsen the most important of the Mesopotamian cult dramas were (1) the ritual hierogramy of the king personifying god Dumuzi, (2) the battle drama at New Year in Babylon, where the king symbolically fought and won as embodiment of Marduk the battle against chaos, (3) the dramatic lament for the dead god Dumuzi (in G. E. Wright, ed., *The Bible in the Ancient Near East* 272).

54+ The Hebrew name of Akk. *Uruk*, excavated at the mounds of Warka, 50 miles NW of Ur. See R. North, "Status of the Warka Excavation," *Orientalia* 26 (1957) 185-256. Some of the bricks used for temple building at Erech are stamped with this inscription: "To [goddess] *I n n i n*, his Lady: Ur-Nammu, the mighty man, the king of Ur, the king of Sumer and Akkad: her house he has built for her."

55* See L. Woolley, *Ur Excavations*, vol. 5: *The Ziggurat and its Surroundings* (Oxford 1939); *id.*, *Ur of the Chaldees* (Pelikan Books 1950).

55+ The Sumero-Akkadian vegetation god. Ezekiel saw in his prophetic vision "women weeping for Tammuz" (8:14), for his descent, that is, into the underworld, coinciding with the decline of vegetation. What follows (Ezek 8:16-18) may reflect the Egyptian worship of the sun-god, who was thought to bring forth all vegetation, or the worship of Tammuz-Adonis (cf. OAB). The symbolic rites of the Tammuz-Ishtar, Dumuzi-Inaana cult included in Babylonia life-giving and season renewal hierogamy. See O. R. Gurney, "Tammuz Reconsidered: Some Recent Developments," JSemitSt 7 (1962) 147-160; Th. Jacobsen, "Toward the Image of Tammuz," HistRel 1 (1961-62) 189-213; E. M. Yamauchi, "Tammuz and the Bible," JBiblLit 84 (1965) 283-290. On "Mesopotamian Gods and Pantheons," see T. Jacobsen, in W. L. Moran, ed., *Toward the Image of Tammuz and Other Essays on Mesopotamian History and Culture.* Harvard Semitic Studies 21 (Cambridge, Mass. 1970) 16-38; on Tammuz-Dumuzi, the "Quickener of the Child," see *ibid.* 73-103

56* This epic is a prototype of the standard Babylonian account of man's creation, which should be looked for in the *Atrahasis* epic, not in *Enūma Eliš* (also called "Epic of Creation"). On the *Atrahasis* epic see J. Laessoe, "The Atrahasīs Epic: a Babylonian History of Mankind," BiblOr 13 (1956) 90-102.

57* See the fifty entries of words compounded with *s a n g a* in A. Deimel, *Die Inschriften von Fara*, II, "Schultexte aus Fara" (Leipzig 1923) 6*-7*. According to T. Fish the *s a n g a* were not "priests," BullJRylLibr 34 (1951) 37-43. On *šangum*, Akkadian for *s a n g a*, see J. Renger, *art. cit.* P. 2, pp. 114-119, who notes that each temple had, as a rule, a *šangum* to preside over it. See also C. Frank, *Studien zur Babylonischen Religion*, v. 1 (Strassburg 1911) 5-6. The Akkadian term *pašišum* (Sum. *g u d u*) seems to be a general designation for a category of cult officials, who offered communion sacrifices (involving no shedding of blood) and were concerned with the management of temples (see Renger, pt. 2, pp. 143-172).

57** Cf. Sum. *E n - l i l*, meaning "god of the highest rank," like Akk. *Illilu*. *E n* is usually rendered in Akk. by *bēlu*, "master, ruler, owner" (cf. *bēltu*, "lady, mistress"), also used as a divine title; compare *buʿulu*, "to make somebody a ruler, an owner," and Heb. *bāʿal*, "master."

58* See CAD: I-J, 242-243 and CAD: A, pt. 2: 431-435; E. K. Ritter, "Magical-Expert (= *ašipu*) and Physician (= *asū*). Notes on two Complementary Professions in Babylonian Medicine," *Studies in Honor of Benno Landsberger*. AssyrSt v. 16 (Chicago 1965) 299-321. One of the royal titles in Mesopotamia was *i-šip-pu naʿdu*, "the exalted purification priest." The general meaning of *ašipu* is "exorcist."

59* On Assyro-Babylonian religion see Th. Jacobsen, "Early Mesopotamian Religion: the central Concerns," ProcAmPhilS 107 (1963) 473-484; *Id.* EncBrit v. 2 (1964)

972-978. L. Oppenheim explained why, in his view, it is hardly possible to speak of a "Mesopotamian religion": *Ancient Mesopotamia* (Chicago 1964) 172-183.

59+ No such god is known from the Assyrian inscriptions. Perhaps the name should be *Nusku*, the fire-god, mentioned in Akkadian texts: cf. Pritchard, ANET 298-300, 337-340 and *id.* ANEP, n. 576.

59++ As early as 1849-1853 appeared the first reports on the excavations of Nineveh (A. H. Layard). See also R. Campbell-Thompson in *Iraq* 1 (1934), pp. 95-104; M. Rutten in *DBSuppl*, v. 6 (1960), c. 480-498, with bibliogr., and A. Parrot, *Nineveh and the Old Testament*, tr. by B. E. Hooke. Studies in Biblical Arch. 3 (New York 1955).

60* See Lamgi-Mari represented on Pl. XXV [= *ANEP*, n. 429]. He wears the typical *kaunakès*-skirt. The Grecized term *kaunakès* (or *gaunakès*, from old Iranian, meaning "hairy") refers to a thick cloak of Persian or Babylonian make. See also in the same volume of Parrot, Pl. XXIX, *kaunakès*-dressed worshippers.

60+ One early 2nd millennium ziggurat is a Dagan-temple (cf. A. Parrot in *Syria* 39, 1962, 169 and 41, 1964, 5). The palace, of the same period, comprised at least 300 rooms (cf. *Id.*, *Mission* ..., v. 2, Pts I-II, Paris 1958). The *Archives royales de Mari* are in course of publication by the Imprimerie Nationale (Paris) since 1950. In the palace was also found one more statue of a fertility "goddess with a flowing vase," one among other representations, of "living water" deities. The goddess holds against her body a vase so constructed that water from a reservoir could flow into it and make it overflow (cf. A. Parrot, in *Syria* 18, 1937, Pl. XIII and pp. 78-80; G. A. Mendenhall in Bibl-Archeol 11, 1948, p. 13, *ANEP*, n. 516; *Bible et Terre Sainte* n. 101, pp. 4-5). "Possibly this was one of the contrivances sometimes used in pagan temples to impress the worshippers with what would appear to them to be a miracle. In the Gospel of John, of course, what we have is a bit of ancient symbolism used with a new meaning: 'He that believeth in me, as the scripture has said, out of his belly shall flow rivers of living water' " (M. Burrows, *What Mean these Stones?*, New Haven 1941, p. 264). See also Ezek 47:1-12 and Pr 18:4 (cf. BiblZ 9, 1965, 84-91). A. Parrot, for his part, writes: "What is most striking to us is that the passage ... is an extraordinary and impressive reminiscence of Mesopotamian iconography: monuments from the 3rd, 2nd, and 1st millennia often have representations of male or female deities holding waist-high, in both hands, a vase from which water flows. Rivers literally flow from the heart of the personage represented" [*Land of Christ* (Philadelphia 1968) 102]. See also E. D. Van Buren, *The Flowing Vase and the God with Streams* (Berlin 1933), esp. pp. 1-3. R. Bultmann was apparently the first who made the connection of the ancient symbol with Jn 7:38 (*Das Evangelium des Johannes*, Göttingen 1939, p. 229, note 2). On the water-god Ea, "the god with the spouting vase" and other similar representations see L. Heuzey, "Le sceau de Goudéa," *Revue d'Assyrologie* ... 5 (1903) 129-139 and H. W. Ward, *The Seal Cylinders of Western Asia* (Washington 1910) 213-218; cf. *ANEP* n. 687, 693 and C. F. Jean, *La religion sumérienne* (Paris 1931) p. 223 and fig. 59.

60++ Whether there is any connection at all between this Amorite tribe and the later Israelite tribe of Benjamin is a question that remains open. G. E. Mendenhall (BiblArchaeol 11, 1948, pp. 16-17) points out, however, that the description of the Amorite tribe as sheep raiders (in a letter of king Zimri-Lim) agrees remarkably with the description of Gen 49.27: "Benjamin is a marauding wolf; in the morning he devours the prey, and in the evening he divides the spoil" (cf. Jg 2:16 and 1 Chr 12:2).

61* Details on these six gods can be read in S. H. Hooke, *op. cit.* 12-38. See also on the Assyro-Babylonian pantheon: B. Meissner, *Babylonien und Assyrien*, v. 2 (Heidelberg 1925) 1-51; H. Zimmern, ZAssyr NF 5 (1930) 275-276; J. Renger, "Götternamen in der altbabylonischen Zeit," in *Heidelberger Studien zum Alten Testament. Fs. Adam Falkenstein* (Wiesbaden 1967) 137-171. On the Sumerian pantheon: J. J. van Dijk in H. Haag, Bibel-Lexikon (1968) 1658-62. On the Storm-gods (Wettergötter) see D. O. Edzard, in H. W. Haussig, ed., *Wörterbuch der Mythologie* v. 1 (Stuttgart 1965) 208-213.

63* On Assyro-Babylonian priesthood see also M. Jastrow, *Die Religion Babyloniens und Assyriens,* v. 1-3 (Giessen 1905-1912), *passim*; B. Meissner, *Babylonien und Assyrien,* v. 2 (Heidelberg 1925), pp. 52-101 (the priests and the cult); C. Frank, *Studien zur babylonischen Religion,* v. 1 (Strassburg i.E. 1911), pp. 1-37; H. W. F. Saggs, *The Greatness that was Babylon* (New York 1962), pp. 345-354; and of course J. Renger, quoted in n. 28. On "the personel of the temple of Aššur" see G. Van Driel, *The Cult of Aššur.* Studia semitica Neerlandica 13 (Assen 1969) 179-182.

64* On the *ašuppu* and *bâru,* whom he identifies respectively as exorcists and diviners, see also C. Frank, *Studien zur babylonischen Religion,* v. I (Strasbourg 1911), pp. 23-33. Other categories of Babylonian priests studied in Frank include the *nāru,* singer-musicians, the *ša'ilu,* dream interpreters, the *mušlahhu,* snake-expellers, the *urigallu* (or *šeš-gal-lu,* "elder brother"), seemingly chief priests of the temples, particularly connected with the Babylonian New Year festival. According to Frank, about 30 categories of priests and 20 of priestesses can be identified from the known Babylonian texts. On *išippum* and *bārūm* in the Old-Babylonian texts see J. Renger, *art. cit.,* pt.2, pp. 122-126 and 203-223. The *bārūm* practised divination mainly by means of the sacrificial rite called *nepešti bārim* (see *id.* 208-213). Another name for "exorcist," *wašippum* ("Beschwörer"), occurs frequently in the Old-Babylonian texts (see Renger 223-230).

64** The Babylonian *lilū* or the female demon *lilitu* of Assyria is alluded to in Is 34.14. The OT *šēdim,* demons (Dt 32:17: Ps 106:37) have their equivalent in Ass. *šêdu.*

64*** These "seers" can be compared to the clairvoyants or diviners of Israel's early history, called *ḥôzim* (cf. 1 Sam 9.9-11). On the *bâru* see A. Haldar, *Associations of Cult Prophets among the Ancient Semites* (Uppsala 1945) 1-21, and (more important) *La divination en Mésopotamie ancienne* ... (see n. 16). With the *bâru-* priests are often mentioned the *šā'ilu*-priests, whose primary function was the interpretation of dreams. See L. Oppenheim, *The Interpretation of Dreams in the Ancient Near East.* Transactions of the AmerPhSoc, v. 46 (Philadelphia 1956); *Sources Orientales II, Les songes et leur interprétation: Égypte, Babylonie, Hittites, Israël* (Paris 1959).

66* See the list of the main works published on Ugarit and related problems in A. Herdner, *Corpus des Tablettes en cunéiformes alphabétiques découvertes à Ras Shamra-Ugarit de 1929 à 1939.* Mission de Ras Shamra X (Paris 1963), pp. 295-339.

68* J. Gray, *The Legacy* ..., p. 155. Cf. W. Schmidt, *Königtum Gottes in Ugarit und Israel. BZAW* 80, (2nd edit., Berlin 1966), 58-64. *El* is also called *tr 'el,* "the Bull, *EL.*" This may refer to his strength or possibly to his procreative vigor. "It is remarkable, adds J. Gray, that the God of Jacob is spoken of as *'abir* (Gen 49:24:J), which also means 'a bull' " (*op. cit.,* 158). It is reasonably suspected that the Massoretes changed the punctuation (wrote *abir*) to avoid association of ideas with *abbir* "bull," "the idolatrous emblem of Yahwe in N Israel" (J. Skinner, Genesis *ICC,* 1910, p. 531). But this or similar reasonings seem unconvincing to A. Alt, *Essays on Old Testament History and Religion,* tr. by R. A. Wilson (Oxford 1966), pp. 25-26. See ch. IV, nn. 27 and 188. According to J. Gray, "Dt 32.8-9 represents a stage in the assimilation of the particularist Yahweh-cult to the cult of the universalistic god *El Elyon* in the settled land" (*op. cit.,*

182). It can be noted here that *El* was in fact pronounced *ilu* among the Canaanites and *ba'al* was pronounced *ba'lu*, and *Asherath* was *Ashratu* (T. H. Gaster, in *Forgotten Religions*, p. 141, n. 9). On the gods of Canaan see also M. Dahood, "Ancient Semitic Deities in Syria and Palestine," in S. Moscati, ed., *Studi semitici* 1. *Le antiche divinità semitiche* (Rome 1958) 65-94; M. H. Pope, *El in the Ugaritic Texts* (Leiden 1955).

69* What was said of Baal (e.g. 1 Aqht: 43-44) is applied to God in Ps 68.5: *rōkēb ba'arabôt*, "the Rider of the Clouds." Cf. also Ps 18.10; 68.34; Dt 33.26; Is 19.1; Hab 3.8. On "Baal and the Ugaritic Pantheon," see also Leah Bronner, *The Stories of Elijah and Elisha as Polemics against Baal Worship*. Pretoria Oriental Series, vol. VI (Brill, Leiden 1968) 35-49; U. Oldenburg, *The Conflict Between El and Ba'al in Canaanite Religion* (Brill, Leiden 1969), esp. 46-100.

69** On "the Cult" and the "cultic personnel," see J. Gray, *The Legacy* ..., pp. 192-217; A. S. Kapelrud, *The Ras Shamra Discoveries and the Old Testament* (Oxford 1965), pp. 65-79; A. D. de Guglielmo, "Sacrifice in the Ugaritic Texts," CBQ 17 (1955), pp. 196-216. More generally on "Canaanite religion," see J. Gray, *The Canaanites* (London 1964), pp. 119-138.

70* Baal, conquered and taken to the underworld by *Môt*, is saved by Anath who destroys *Môt*. Alternative names for *Môt*, more popular in actual cult and attested especially in Egyptian sources, were Resheph, "the Ravager" (cf. Dt 32:24; Hab 3:5; Job 5:7) and *Hôron*, "He of the Pit" (cf. T. H. Gaster, in *Forgotten Religions* 122f.).

71* In the OT *qedēšah* designates a prostitute and *qādeš* a sodomite (Dt 23:18; 2 Kg 23:7 etc.; cf. Zorell, LexHebr, p. 712). The OT sometimes calls the idolatrous priests *Kemārim* (2 Kg 23:5; Zeph 1:4; Os 10:5), the term also used by modern Israelis to denote all non-Jewish priests. But the OT also calls pagan priests *Kohanim*: cf. Gen 41:45; 47:22; 1 Sam 5:5; 6:2.

72* See on the Hittites A. Goetze, *Kleinasien. Kulturgeschichte des Alten Orients*, III, 1: *Handbuch der Altertumswissenschaft* III, 1, 3, 3, 1 (2nd ed., Leipzig 1957), pp. 82-183; L. Delaporte, in *DBSuppl*, v. 1, c. 60-78; G. Walser, ed., *Neuere Hethiterforschung* (Wiesbaden 1964); F. Imparati, *Le leggi ittite* (Rome 1964); O. R. Gurney, *The Hittites* (Pelican Book, 1953); *id.*, *Anatolia, c. 1600-1380 B.C., The Cambridge Ancient History*, n. 44 (Cambridge 1966), pp. 26-29 (bibliography).

73* Boghazköy, the site of Hattusa, the ancient Hittite capital, is not far to the East of Ankara, capital of modern Turkey.

73** See O. R. Gurney, *The Hittites*, 216. The cuneiform documents of the Assyrian merchant colony at Kültepe show that Indo-European Hittites were already established in that area by 1900 B.C. (cf. *NCE* v. 7, p. 39). Much later, around 1370, the Hittites reduced to a minor role the *Mitanni*, this Indo-Iranian people who had invaded North Mesopotamia about the time of the Babylonian king Hammurabi (1728-1686 B.C.). On the Hurrians and Mitanni, see A. Kammenhuber, *Die Arier im Vorderen Orient* (Heidelberg 1968) 62-86 and *passim*.

73*** Hieroglyphic Hittite derives from the second millennium B.C. Luwian dialect. See a specimen of the language in *NCE* v. 7, p. 38. On the Hittite languages see L. Delaporte in *DBSuppl*, IV, c. 91-98. After the destruction of the Hittite empire (*c.* 1200 B.C.) there remained in the region of Ugarit a Hittite population which spoke a Luwian language and wrote in Hittite hieroglyphs. See A. Kammenhuber, *Hethitisch, Palaisch, Luwisch und Hieroglyphenluwisch*. Hdb der Orientalistik, Abt. I, v. 2, Sect. 1/2, Fasc. 2 (Heidelberg 1968) 122 (cf. pp. 161-163).

73**** Hurrian is a non-Indo-European language of north Mesopotamia and north

Syria. Hurrian influence on the Hittite institutions was especially felt during the New Kingdom, when the dynasty, it seems, and certainly many scribes, were of Hurrian background.

74* As is now well known the Hittite treaty formulary has provided a better understanding of the important OT concept of covenant. See the bibliography of D. J. McCarthy, *Treaty and Covenant. A Study in Form in the Ancient Oriental Documents and in the Old Testament*. Anal. Bibl. 21 (Rome 1963), pp. XIII-XXIV; *Id.* in CBQ 27, 1965, pp. 219-225; J. Coppens in EphThLov 43 (1967), p. 196, n. 35; D. R. Hillers, *Covenant: The History of a Biblical Idea* (The Johns Hopkins Press 1969). These and other authors speak of ancient Near Eastern "vassal treaties," "suzerainty treatises," "parity treatises."

74+ Rivers and springs are mentioned in the texts as goddesses, whereas mountains are gods. Mountain deities of the Hurrian pantheon were adopted by the Hittites in connection with the cult of their storm-god. The most famous are *Mount Hazzi*, the later *Mons Cassius* at the seashore near the mouth of the Orontes, and *Mount Namni*, whose location is still unknown. Cf. H. G. Güterbock, "Hittite Religion," in V. Ferm, ed., *Forgotten Religions*, p. 89. All the names of the gods contained in the Hittite texts are listed according to their ethnical appurtenance in E. Laroche, *Recherches sur les noms des dieux hittites* (Paris 1947) = *Revue Hittite et Asianique*, VII, f. 46 (1946-1947); see also DBSuppl., v. 4, c. 60-70. On the religion of the Hittites see A. Kammenhuber in *Kindler Literatur Lexikon*, v. 3 (Münich 1968) 1731-1752 + *ibid.* 2267-2274 on the Hurrian myths.

75* At Ras Shamra (Ugarit), *Hadad*, another Weather-God, was considered as "the Rider of the Clouds." See A. Vanel, "Deux dieux de l'orage sur les reliefs de la 'porte des lions' de Malatya en Anatolie" in *L'iconographie du dieu de l'orage dans le Proche-Orient ancien jusqu'au VIIe siècle av.J.C.*, Cahiers de la Revue Biblique (Paris 1965) 119-130; cf. M. Riemschneider, *Die Welt der Hethiter* (Stuttgart 1954), pl. 51, where the Weather-God is seen on his chariot drawn by two horses. Psalm 68 applies to the Lord also the epithet "Rider of the clouds" (v. 5) and adds: "The chariots of God are myriad ..." (v. 18), and we read in Ps 104,3: "You make the clouds your chariot" (cf. Ezek 1:15-21; 2 Kg 2:11-12). The Hittite storm-god corresponds to the Hurrian god *Teshub*, who in turn reminds one of Zeus (Jupiter), the Greek king of the gods. Within the official religion there was a tendency to identify Hebat (consort of Hurrian *Teshub*) with the sun-goddess of Arinna, and *Teshub* with *Taru* (Protohattic name of the Hittite storm-god). On the Hurrian Pantheon at Ras Shamra, see E. Laroche in C. F. A. Schaeffer, ed., *Ugaritica* V (Paris 1968), pp. 518-527.

75+ In "The Song of Ullikurnmi," an epic of the Kumarbi cycle, *Ishtar* joins her two brothers Teshub and Tashmishu to ascend Mount Hazzi, the Semitic Zaphon. Ishtar is the West-Semitic *Astarte* or *'Anat*, related to the Biblical *Asherâh* (1 Kg 16:33), "queen of heaven" (Jer 7:18) and to *Inanna*, the Sumerian goddess of love, whose husband is Dumuzi, the Biblical Tammuz (Ezek 8:14).

77* See on Hittite divination A. Boissier, *Mantique babylonienne et mantique hittite* (Paris 1935); E. Laroche, "Éléments d'haruspicine hittite," RevHistRel 54 (1952), pp. 19-48; J. Nougayrol, "Textes hépatoscopiques d'époque ancienne conservés au Musée du Louvre III," RevAssyr 44 (1950), pp. 1-44.

78* "Egypt" is the Greek form (*Aiguptos*) of the Egyptian *ḥt-k'-ptḥ*, "house of the god Ptah," one of the names of the city of Memphis (near Cairo). The Egyptians themselves called their land *km.t*, "the black."

78** The Egyptians are classed as Hamitic in the Genesis table of peoples (Gen 10.6). The language of ancient Egypt is related to the Hamitic-Semitic group. The situation is thus presented by J. H. Breasted: "The forefathers of the Egyptians were related to the Libyans or north Africans on the one hand, and on the other to the peoples of eastern Africa, now known as the Galla, Somali, Bega and other tribes. An invasion of the Nile valley by Semitic nomads of Asia stamped its essential character unmistakably upon the language of the African people there. The earliest strata of the Egyptian language accessible to us betray clearly this composite origin. While still coloured by its African antecedents, the language is in structure Semitic" (*A History of Egypt. From the Earliest Times to the Persian Conquest* (2nd ed., London 1912, p. 25).

80* This French word "cartouche" means in the present context an ornamental tablet of stone, wood, or metal destined to receive an inscription; the original Egyptian word, *šnw*, comes from a verb-stem meaning "encircle."

80** See on the Egyptian pantheon E. Drioton and J. Vandier, *Les peuples de l'Orient Méditerranéen*, v. 2, *L'Égypte* (4th enl. ed., Paris 1962), pp. 66-83; J. Vandier, *La religion égyptienne* (Paris 1949), pp. 11-31; S. Morenz, *La religion égyptienne*, tr. from German by L. Jospin (Paris 1962), pp. 37-67; 330-338. For representations of the Egyptian gods and their emblems, see Pritchard, ANEP nn. 542-573; E. Drioton, *Pages d'Égyptologie* (Cairo 1957), pp. 86-92.

83* Besides Sauneron, see on Egyptian priesthood: A. Erman, *Die Religion der Ägypter. Ihr Werden und Vergehen im vier Jahrtausenden* (Berlin und Leipzig 1934), pp. 187-191; H. Gauthier, *Le personel du dieu Min* (Cairo 1931); G. Lefebvre, *Histoire des grands prêtres d'Amon de Karnak jusqu'à la XXI*e *Dynastie* (Paris 1929); H. Kees, *Die Hohenpriester des Amon von Karnak von Herihor bis zum Ende der Äthiopenzeit* (Probleme der Ägyptologie IV, Leiden 1964). In the first volume of the same collection Kees had published a valuable monograph on the Egyptian priesthood: *Das Priestertum in Ägyptischen Staat, vom Neuen Reich bis zur Spätzeit* (Leiden 1953), esp. pp. 10-29. In his *Die Hohenpriester* ... Kees has inserted tables of the high priests' genealogies comparable with those of the biblical Chronicler. See besides the bibliographical notes on the Egyptian cult in E. Drioton and S. Vandier, *op. cit.* 118-121.

83** Sauneron would rather speak of the "purified" as belonging to the "low clergy" entrusted with the most varied functions (*op. cit.*, p. 70). He also describes the role of the so-called "funerary priests" or "priests of the dead" who performed the rites at the burials (p. 108). On these priests see also H. Kees, *Das Priestertum* ..., pp. 69-78.

86* The pictorial monumental script of the ancient Egyptians was termed by the Greeks "hieroglyphics," "sacred carving." Later the simplified "hieratic" form was used, while from the 8th century B.C. a shortened and cursive script, called "demotic" ("popular"), was developed for ordinary purposes. The cumbersome hieroglyphic systems remained in vogue until the ancient Egyptian language was supplanted by Coptic in the Christian era. On Egyptian language and writing, see A. Gardiner, *Egypt of the Pharaos. An Introduction* (Oxford 1961), pp. 19-26.

89* A notable priestly accomplishment in Egypt was the transcription and compilation of sacred texts and inscriptions. Prominent among these are the "Pyramid Texts" collected in the 3rd millenium B.C. From the Middle Kingdom there are the "Coffin Texts," written on the inner surface of coffins and setting forth the claims of the deceased to righteousness and justification before the gods.

91* Manetho, a Hellenized priest, in the last half of the 3rd cent. B.C. wrote a history of Egypt which is informative, but also at times misleading. It is edited by W. G. Wedell in The Loeb Classical Library (2nd ed., 1948).

91** Such a repertory exists at the temple of Edfu. See also J. Vandier, *Le papyrus Jumilhac* (Paris, n.d.). On the Egyptian feasts see E. Drioton, *Pages d'Egyptologie*, 133-158; J. Vandier, *La religion égyptienne*, 179-194; 200-203, esp. the feast of god *Min*, the feast of *Opet* (when Amon visited his Luxor "harem"), and the feast of the Valley (when Amon visited the gods and the dead Pharaohs of the "valley" of the kings across the Nile).

95* The most important source for the biography of the prophet Muhammad is also a source of information on the religion of the pre-Islamic Arabs. See A. Guillaume, *The Life of Muhammad. A Translation of Isḥāq's Sīrat Rasūl Allāh* (London 1955). Biographer *Isḥāq* died c. 768; his complete work is known through the recension of Ibn Hishām, who died in 834. There is also Hishām ibn al-Kalbi's *Book of Idols*, published in English in 1952 by N. A. Faris (Princeton OrSt 14). I have used the German edition: R. Klinke-Rosenberger, *Das Götzenbuch Kitāb Al-Asnâm des Ibn Al-Kalbî* (Leipzig 1941). Ibn Al-Kalbi died *c.* 819.

96* See A. Fischer, art. "Kāhin," *Enzyklopaedie des Islam*, v. 2 (1927), p. 669. The uses of *Kāhin* in the ancient Arabic texts are listed in *Wörterbuch der klassischen Arabischen Sprache*, M. Ullmann, ed., Lief. 7 (Wiesbaden 1965), pp. 417-418. It gives the term the following meanings: seer, soothsayer, magician, wizard, priest. There is the abstract form *kihāna* meaning "divination," and the feminine *kāhina*, "woman-diviner."

96** M.-J. Lagrange has suggested that the term *kāhin* applies to a category of priests turned diviners after degenerating from their previous character [*Études sur les religions sémitiques* (2nd ed., Paris 1905) 218-219]. See also W. R. Smith in *Journal of Philology* 13 (1885) 278. E. Dhorme would firmly relate *kōhēn* to West Semitic *khn* (see RevHistRel 108, 1933, 115-118). On the etymology of *kōhēn* see A. Cody, *op. cit.*, 26-29.

96+ Several authors are tempted to equate sadins with kahins because individual persons are known to have been both; see e.g. J. Wellhausen, *Reste arabischen Heidentums gesammelt und erläutert* (2nd ed., Berlin 1897) 134. See *id.*, 130-140, on sacred persons among the Arabs. Yet from the fact that sadins were occasionally also kahins it cannot be concluded that to be *sādin* was about the same as being *kāhin*. The following statement then would have to be qualified: "There is clear evidence that the kahins occasionally exercised priestly functions and belonged to the temple staff, The Arabian kahin was seer, prophet, priest, and even judge in the same person" ([J. Lindblom, *Prophecy in Ancient Israel* (Oxford 1962) 86-87]. Likewise, in the primitive societies, the priest can be unduly confused with other specialists of religion (see ch. I). F. Klinke-Rosenberger disapproves of Wellhausen for translating *sādin* by "priest"; for, she writes, the sādin's function was to watch over the idols (*op. cit.* 92, n. 116).

96++ The noun *istiqsām* is formed from the 10th conjug. (reflexive) of Ar. verb *qasama*, "to divide, to distribute." When the prophet's grandfather, 'Abdu'l Muṭṭalib, wanted to know whom of his ten sons he had to sacrifice to accomphish his vow, he cast lots with arrows before the idol of god Hubal in Mecca. See the whole story in A. Guillaume, *The Life of Muhammad*, pp. 66-68; §§ 97-100. Drawing lots with headless arrows was also part of a secular game of chance called *maisir* (see *Enzyklopaedie des Islām*, v. 3, p. 168).

99* The expression "to serve me as priest" (RSV) or "to be priest in my service"

(JB) often occurs in Yahweh's oracles: Ex 28:1,3,4,41; 29:1,44; 30:30,40; 13:5; Ezek 44:14; Hos 4:6.

99** See in C. H. Gordon, *Ugaritic Textbook* (Rome 1965), glossary n. 1209, the references to the texts where *khn* and *khnm*, "priest(s)," occur in Ugaritic literature. The Nabateans occupied ancient Edom territory from the 4th cent. B.C. to the 2nd cent. A.D. The capital of this North-Arabian people was Petra (see BiblArchaeol 23, 1960, 29-32).

99*** In Semitic languages *kōmēr* means "an ecstatic eunuch priest of a pagan deity" (EncDictBibl 1913). See also P. Haupt, "Assyr. *ramku*, 'priest' = Heb. *kōmēr*," AmJSemLang 32 (1915) 64-75; J. Lewy, ZAssyr 38 (1928-29) 242-246; H. Hirsch, *Untersuchungen zur altassyrischen Religion* (Archiv für Orientforschung 13/14; Graz 1961) 55-56. C. Hauret believes that the ancient Hebrews called their cult ministrant *lēvî*. Later they adopted the Canaanite term *kōhēn*. One could say as in 1 Sam 9:9 modified: "For he who is now called priest was formerly called Levite" ("Moïse était-il prêtre?" in *Studia Biblica et Orientalia*. AnalBibl 10, Rome 1959, p. 386).

101* LXX and Vulg.; Heb. has "ordain yourselves" (lit. "fill your hands"). The Priestly tradition also bases the rights of the Aaron-Phinehas priesthood on an act of zeal for Yahweh (Num 25.13).

102* In 1878, J. Wellhausen devoted a chapter of the first volume of *History of Israel* to the priests and the Levites. In 1883 this volume was published separately and has appeared in English as *Prolegomena to the History of Ancient Israel* (Cleveland 1957). W's study (see pp. 121-151) has influenced subsequent writers on many important points.

103* The Levite was Jonathan, son of Gershom, "son of Moses" (Jg 18.30). "There is no reason to doubt the truth of this detail in such an ancient story, though it scandalized the Massoretes so much that they added a letter to make the text read 'Manasses' instead of 'Moses' " (VAI, p. 362; cf. p. 371).

104* The text is much older than Dt in which it is inserted. In its final form, it could be as early as 800 or even go back to the first years of the monarchy, reflecting slightly earlier tribal circumstances.

107* In his art. "Ark and bull-figure" (ZATWiss 58, 1940-41, 190-215), O. Eissfeldt states that both were *Führersymbole*, but one was accepted by later theology, the other not. He also refers to the leader-standard used at Mari: a miniature bull perched on a staff. See A. Parrot, *Mission archéologique de Mari*, vol. 1, *Le temple d'Ishtar* (Paris 1956) 141-142 and pl. LVI-LVII; also *Syria* 16 (1935) 134. On the representation of Canaanite El as a bull see C. F. A. Schaeffer in *Syria* 43 (1966) 1-19 and pl. I-IV; cf. N. Lohfink in *Stimmen der Zeit* 179 (1967) 62-64, and K. Galling in ZATWiss 79 (1967) 106 (authenticity of the object debated).

107+ Another explanation could be that the formula "referred originally to a central sanctuary in the Northern kingdom (where Dt originated), such as Shechem or Bethel, whose servants wanted to make it the only sanctuary in Israel" (*VAI* 338f.).

108* J. A. Emerton examined especially G. E. Wright's view (see VetTest 4, 1954, 325-330) that, when Dt refers to "priests," it always means "altar-priests" (while "Levites" refers to members of the tribe of Levi whose function was instruction). To a more precise question, "does Dt recognize an impassable and hereditary distinction between altar-priests and ordinary Levites?", Emerton answers negatively, and cannot see how Wright's theory can be reconciled with the correct understanding of Dt 18. 1-8.The evidence, Emerton concludes, favors the view that all Levites were thought to possess the priestly status and that Levites were usually connected with sanctuaries before the policy of centralization was enforced ... The closing of the local sanctuaries created a class of client-Levites, but Dt still recognizes their right to act as priests when they come to the central sanctuary (VetTest 12, 1962, 129-138).

109* Gunneweg reads in Dt a graduated demonstration of the priestly rights of all the Levites in the one *ideal* amphictyonic sanctuary. It reaches its speak with the identity formula "priests-Levites," meaning: "all priests should be Levites; all Levi is a priestly tribe." When "the Levites within your towns," the Levites who pass to the central sanctuary, and the priests-Levites are mentioned, the reference, he thinks, is not to different juxtaposed categories of Levites but to successive stages in the carrying out of the Deuteronomic programme (pp. 128-136).

110* No lasting change of residence is contemplated, rather the possibility for a Levite to go up to Jerusalem whenever he wishes and to officiate there with the other Levites. The reference is not to "the priests of high places," since Deuteronomy could not have granted them such a privilege. On Dt 18:1-8 see also A. Deissler, *Der Priesterliche Dienst,* v. 1. Quaestiones Disputatae 46, Freiburg i. Br. 1970, pp. 32-42.

111* Ezekiel's book has affinities with the priestly tradition, just as that of Jeremiah follows the deuteronomic trend (cf. JB 1130). Ezek 44 is more likely an independent literary parallel of Num 16-18. The Zadokite program certainly presupposes a form of cult personnel organization corresponding to that of P.

111** It is true that Ezekiel uses the expression "the priests, the Levites" (44:15), as in Dt (e.g. 17:9), but he does so only once, and "the priests, the Levites" occurs elsewhere (e.g. Jos 3:3,8; Jer 33:18).

111+ It is difficult to decide who of Ezekiel or of P has first introduced or legalized the distinction between priests and Levites (see Gunneweg 197f.). The passing notice of Ezek 40:45 (cf. 42:13) confirms that the members of Ezekiel's *clerus minor* can be described as "priests" of an inferior degree, or "temple-priests," while the Zadokites are "altar-priests." The Levites are never called "priests" in P, where all the priests are understood to be Aaronites (see Gunneweg 196).

111++ This prohibition seems to imply that they could do so previously (Gunneweg 195), that "they also possessed the highest priestly privilege of *qrb*" ("approaching": Ezek 40:46; 43:19; 44:15; Kraus, *op. cit.* 99). In connection with Ezek 44:13, D. M. G. Stalker writes: "Ezekiel thus occupies a position between that of Dt and that of P. He followed ancient usage in regarding the Levites as legitimate priests, but regards their loss of status after Josiah's reform as punishment for their 'idolatry'—i.e. ministering at shrines other than the temple ... P. adopts Ezekiel's innovation, but regards the distinction in status between Zadokites and Levites as one which had existed from the beginning" [*Ezekiel* (Torch Bible Comm.; London 1968) 296-297].

111+++ *Mišmeret* is in P a technical term denoting the Levitical service. This service which in P concerns mainly the tent of meeting and its holy objects (cf. Num 4.29-32) applies in Ezek 44 to (all) the holy objects and to the temple.

112* The expression "my table" refers to the right of serving at the altar and of eating the offerings thereof. "The altar is only rarely referred to as the table of Yahweh (Ezek 44:16; Mal 1:7, 12), and never in ancient texts" (VAI, p. 413). As compared to 40:46a, where the priests are described simply as those "in charge of the altar," Ezek 44:15-16 extends the area proper to them and speaks rather of "sanctuary service," to fill the gap created by the prohibition imposed on the Levites: "They shall not come near to me, to serve me as priest, nor come near any of my sacred things and the things that are most sacred" (44:13).

113* (OAB *in loc.*). For T. E. Fretheim, however, "the tabernacle of P must be seen not as a projection of the temple back into the Mosaic period, but as an impermanent sanctuary which was programmatically set forth by the Priestly writers as the dwelling place of Yahweh for the post-exilic community" (VetTest 18, 1968, 329).

116* The work of a P editorial hand can be suspected where it is reported that, following David's request, "the priests and the Levites sanctified themselves to bring up the ark of the Lord" (1 Chr 15.14). In 1 Sam 6.15, a later editor, perhaps Deuteronomic, writes that "the Levites took down the ark of the Lord" from the Philistine cart, to make the procedure conform to later requirements. But in the narrative of the ark's transfer to Jerusalem in 2 Sam 6, the Levites are not mentioned. They did not exist as a special class in the time of the historical David (OAB, p. 512).

116** For Gunneweg "priests-Levites" is the correct reading, because specifically priestly functions are involved in the two verses (p. 207). One of the Chronicler's inconsistencies concerns the Korahites, described as "gatekeepers" in 1 Chr 9:17-19 and as "singers" in 1 Chr 6:22,31. But 1 Chr 1-9 and 23-27 are additions to the original work (cf. *VAI* 390, 393). On the Levites in the Chronicler's work see R. Meyer, "Die Mosesagen und die Lewiten," in *Die Israeliten und ihre Nachbarstämme* (Halle 1906) 1-99; G. von Rad, *Das Geschichtsbild des chronistischen Werkes*. BWANT 54 (Stuttgart 1930) 80-118; *id.* "Die Levitische Predigt in den Büchern der Chronik," *Fs. Otto Procksch* (Leipzig 1934) 113-124.

118* On Gen 49:5-7 and Gen 34 see E. Nielsen, *Shechem* (Copenhagen 1955) 241-282; B. Vawter in CathBiblQuart 17 (1955) 1-18. S. Lehming believes that the names of Simeon and Levi were introduced in the third stage of the composition of Gen 34, as a reinterpretation of the existing narrative (ZATWiss 70, 1958, 244). Gen 49 suggested this literary device. For Gunneweg no vanished (secular) Levi tribe has ever existed (p. 220; other references in W. Eichrodt, *Theology of the Old Testament*, v. 1, p. 394, n. 2). The joint mention of Simeon and Levi (Gen 34:25,30) may not belong to the original version of the Dinah episode.

119* The story of Micah's Levite illustrates the way in which the Levites spread over the country from Judah (cf. Jg 17:7-9). "When the document which forms the basis of the list of Levitical towns in Jos 21 was first edited, the Levites were already scattered through all the tribes of Israel" (VAI, p. 371). This would require an explanation if W. Eichrodt is right when he notes "that, according to the scheme of the twelve tribes employed in Gen 49, which comes in fact from the period of the Judges, the secular tribe of Levi must have been in existence after the settlement in Canaan" and that "it would seem impossible[3] to reconcile this twelvefold system with a separation of the tribe of Levi so early as the time of Moses" (*Theology of the Old Testament*, v. 1, pp. 393-394).

121* Perhaps one should not confuse *Gershon*, son of Levi (1 Chr 6:1 = 5:27; Num 3:17), with *Gershom*, son of Moses (1 Chr 23:15; Ex 2:21; Jg 18:30). But the son of Levi is also called Gershom (1 Chr 15:7). According to Gunneweg (p. 169), eponym Gershon is very likely the same name as that of Moses' son (Gershom). On the "Mushite Levites" see L. Waterman, JAmOrSoc 57 (1937) 375-380.

121** According to E. Jacob, all the functions that are in the OT distinctive of priesthood, in the earliest texts are performed by Moses: he communicates God's oracles (Ex 33:7), he pours out the blood of sacrifice (Ex 24:6), he intercedes for the guilty people (Ex 32:20): *Théologie de l'Ancien Testament* (2nd ed., Neuchâtel 1968), p. 200.

122* On Aaron and the Aaronites see B. D. Eerdmans, "Die Aaronidischen Priester," in *Alttestamentliche Studien* IV (Giessen 1912) 41-51; G. Westphal, "Aaron und die Aaroniden," ZATWiss 26 (1906) 201-230. E. Schürer describes as "ein dogmatisches Postulat" the genealogical derivation of the priests from Aaron. P's "sons of Aaron," he notes, represents a wider concept than Ezek's "sons of Zadok," since the former includes the descendants of both Eleazar and Ithamar, while the "sons of Zadok" represent only Eleazar's line, cf. 1 Chr 5:30-41 (see *Geschichte des jüdischen Volkes im Zeitalter Jesu Christi*, v. 2, 4th edit., Leipzig 1907, p. 293, n. 50).

124* This does not mean that de Vaux would easily accept the theory that "sons of Aaron" is a name for the priests who served the sanctuary at Bethel, with the implication that this sanctuary took on a new lease of life after the reform of Josiah (2 Kg 23:15; VAI, p. 395).

126* This in spite of three texts, Dt 10:6; Jos 24:33; Jg 20:26-28, which indicate that the two ancestors had been active in the Northern kingdom. The passages may not be as old as their contexts would suggests.

127* On the eponyms Gershom, Kahath, Merari, see A. Gunneweg, *Leviten und Priester*, pp. 168-170. It is impossible to determine if they represent the heads of *real* families of Levites or not. There is evidence that their lineage set up and the description of their activities reflect in part the interests of real Levitical groups. In fact the three eponyms are names of priestly clans whose members had always occupied an inferior rank or had been demoted to the *clerus minor* status in the post-Josiah reorganization. See Jos 21:4-7; Num 3:17-37; 4:24-45.

129* It is sometimes suggested that in one of its layers P must have spoken of a layman's revolt against priesthood, this layman having been made Levite only later and called Korah. The theory is debatable and unnecessary. It is true that 1 Chr 23 does not mention Korah, but this does not prove that Korah, first a layman, later became a Levite (see Gunneweg 174). L. Leloir suggests that the sin of Korah, Dathan, and Abiram consisted in their denying the distinction between the universal priesthood of the people and the particular priesthood of those consecrated to that office ("Valeurs permanentes du sacerdoce lévitique," NRT 92, 1970, pp. 263ff.).

130* In the sense that the texts critically studied do not draw a firm picture of historical persons called Levi and Aaron. In Gunneweg's view Levi is nothing else but an eponym; Aaron may have been an historical person, but his name occurs only as eponym (*Leviten und Priester*, p. 98, n. 3).

131* Ps 110 seems to express the bestowal upon an Israelite king, possibly David, of both the royal and the priestly powers. See Gunneweg, *op. cit.*, p. 102, who rejects H. H. Rowley's suggestion that in the psalm vv. 1-3 are the words of Zadok and v. 4 the words of David to Zadok (*Fs. A. Bertholet* 461-472).

132* For C. E. Hanes, Zadok was indeed "a Jebusite priest of Jerusalem who, for reasons unknown, went over to the side of David prior to the capture of Jerusalem by the Hebrew army": "Who was Zadok?" (JBiblLit 82 [1963]), p. 94. J. Mauchline has collected much evidence in support of the hypothesis that Gibeon was a very important sanctuary and that Zadok was the priest there. "Aaronite and Zadokite Priests: Some Reflections on an Old Problem," TrGlUnOrSoc 21 (1965-66; ed. 1967), pp. 1-11.

133* There exists really no compelling reason to identify Ahijah and Ahimelech (cf. Gunneweg 106), although this identification is generally taken for granted.

133** According to H. J. Judge "the Aaronite priests who replaced the exiled

Zadokites enjoyed no ancient connexion with Abiathar; Abiathar and the house of Eli, although possibly Aaronic, had not known Ithamar as an ancestor; Zadok was quite independent of the line of Aaron and, *a fortiori*, Eleazar" (JThSt 7, 1956, 74).

134* Nadab and Abihu are, like Hur (Ex 17:10,12; 24:14) eponyms of vanished priestly families. Their disappearance is explained in Lev 10:1-2 as a divine punishment for a ritual offense (see Gunneweg 86-87).

134** In the Chronicler's work the priests are given a Levi ancestry by the following lineage: Levi-Kohath-Amran-Aaron-Eleazar-Phinehas (1 Chr 6:1-4). They are not, however, priests as being of Levi, but as being of Aaron. In Ezekiel, "the sons of Zadok" are priests because they descend from Levi. See Ezek 40-46.

135* Besides Levitehood, three autonomous "priesthoods" existed *de facto* in Israel: the Elids, the Aaronites and the Zadokites. They are distinct by their history, their importance, and the places with which they are associated (See A. Gunneweg, *Leviten und Priester*, p. 114). F. S. North finds in Zech 7:1-3; 8:18-19 confirmation of a theory which he proposes anew. After the fall of Jerusalem in 587, Bethel, served by Aaronic priests, became the national shrine. When the Zadokites returned from exile they represented themselves as Aaronic, to regain the religious leadership of the nation, and claimed that they descended from Levi through Aaron (ZATWiss 66, 1954, pp. 191-199). On the priestly genealogies of Ezra-Nehemiah and Chronicles see M. D. Johnson, *The Purpose of the Biblical Genealogies* .... Soc. for NT Studies, Monograph series 8 (London 1969) 37-76.

136* See VAI 346. De Vaux observes that when the Spirit of God descends upon Zachary, a priest's son, it is to make him a prophet, not to raise him to priesthood (2 Chr 24:20).

137* See also Ex 29:9,29,35; 32:29; Num 3:3 and Lev 8:33 ("ordination"). The full expression seems to be "to fill the hands for Yahweh," as in Ex 32:29; 2 Chr 29:31.

138* The "wave offering" refers to the act of moving the sacrifice toward and away from the altar, to symbolize presenting the gift to God and receiving it back as a portion (OAB 106).

138+ See OAB 106 and VAI 347. On the technical meaning of "to fill the hand" see also P. Joüon, *Biblica* 3 (1922) 64-66. The expression has a pre-history in Accadian texts related to investiture ceremonies (cf. *mullū qātā* or *mallu-u qātū'a*, "to fill the hand"). See the references in W. von Soden, *Akkadisches Handwörterbuch* (Wiesbaden 1966), p. 598 (§ 8e). Considering "that the most important function of the priest was divination," R. Arnold believes, the phrase *millē' yad* "will probably refer to his induction into office by 'filling his hand' with the sacred lots" (*Ephod and Ark* ..., 134).

140* That is clean which is considered worthy to approach God, unclean, whatever makes a person unfit for ritual worship. Purity regulations affect what concerns birth, sexual life, and death, because "all these are the mysterious province of God, the master of life" (JB, p. 143).

140** They are not therefore mentioned in Ex 29 and Lev 8. In postbiblical times, the Jews installed their "doctors" with the *s^emikah*, recalling that Moses laid his hands on Joshua (Num 27.15-23), and presuming that he had done the same for the 70 elders of Israel (Num 11.16-17; cf. VAI, p. 347). According to B. J. van der Merwe the laying on of hands merely strengthened the spoken word which effected the transference of office, as in Num 27:18 and Dt 34:9 ("The Laying on of Hands in the Old Testament," OTWerkgemeenskapSA 5, 1962, 41).

140+ See Ex 29:12; 30:10. The horns, the most sacred parts of the altar (cf. 1 Kg

1:50), were rubbed with blood, also peculiarly sacred to God, as the seat of the mystery of life (Lev 17:11,14).

140++ Ex 28:41, 30:30, 40:13,15 mention the instruction to anoint Aaron and his sons, while Lev 7:36 and Num 3:3 recall that they are anointed. In Lev 10:7 Moses reminds Aaron and his sons Eleazar and Ithamar not to leave the tent of meeting (to attend funerals), because "the anointing oil of the Lord is upon you" (see also Lev 21:12, for the cheif priest). On priestly anointing see E. Cothenet, DBSuppl, v. 6:722-726. Ex 29:21 = Lev 8:30, he thinks, was added later to extend the consecration to the priests' vestments. Also secondary and late are the texts which concern the anointing of the priests: Ex 30:30, 40:15; Lev 7:35-36; Num 3:3. The anointing of the high priest is first mentioned in Zech 4:14. In 2 Macc 1:10 "the race of the anointed priests" refers to the high priests not to the priests in general.

141* Compare with the Greek *chitôn* (Jn 19:23), the Latin *tunica,* not to mention our "cotton." According to Vulg, Tamar wore a *tunica talaris,* an "ankle-length tunic" (2 Sam 13:18,19), of the type also mentioned as worn by Joseph, Jacob's son (Gen 37:3,23: "*Tunica talaris et polymita*").

141** *Nezer* basically means "consecration," and can be rendered "sign of consecration," thinks de Vaux, who rejects as inaccurate the usual translation "diadem" (VAI, pp. 399 and 465). Ex 39:30 can be read: "And they made of pure gold the flower of the holy sign of consecration, and wrote upon it an inscription, like the engravement of a signet, HOLY TO THE LORD." J. E. Hogg understands Ex 28:36 to mean: "Thou shalt inscribe on it (the head-dress) a sacred symbol signifying 'Yhwh,' i.e. the tetragrammation itself and nothing more" (JThSt 26, 1924-25, p. 75, and 28, 1927, pp. 287f.).

141*** Heb. *Yāṣiṣ*. This confirms, notes de Vaux, that *nezer* is an equivalent of *ṣiṣ* (VAI 400). A. De Buck attempts to relate the golden flower (*ṣiṣ*) of the high priest's turban (Ex 28:36; 39:30; Lev 8:9; Sir 40:4) with the flower, symbol of life, in the religious conceptions of ancient Egypt (OudtestStud 9, 1951, 18-29).

141+ Cf. Sir 11:5; 40:4,46 (Hebrew text).

142* For various sorts of royal or pontifical *pectoralia* see the Plates in H. Thiersch, *Ependytes und Ephod* (Stuttgart 1936).

142** Cf. Lev 6:10 [Heb 6:3]; 16:4; Ezek 44:18; Sir 45:8 (the high priest).

142*** Cf. 44:19; Lev 16:23. Garment washing and removal is also prescribed to ward off the danger of ritual uncleanness, contagious, like holiness (see Num 19:19; Lev 16:28, and also Num 16:38 = Heb 17:3; Lev 10:6,7). On the supposed magic meaning of vestment in Israel see A. Jirku, ZATWiss 37 (1917-18) 109-125.

143* Cf. Ex 31:10; Lev 7:34; 13:2; Num 3:6,32; 33:38. In the Chronicler's work Eliashib and Shelemiah are called "the priests" (Neh 13:4,13), while Ezra himself is called "the priest, the scribe" (Ezra 7:11-12).

144* In Jer 29:24-29 Zephaniah's office is described as *pāqîd* (MT: plural) *bᵉbêt Yhwh,* "superintendent of the house of the Lord," and he seems to have been responsible for policing the sanctuary (cf. VAI 379).

144** Num 35 (P) belongs to a late redaction of the Pentateuch and concerns the ruling on cities of refuge. Read probably "high priest" in v. 32, with the LXX and other ancient versions; MT has only "the priest." In the Law of Holiness (Lev 17-26), the oldest part of Lev, the head of the priesthood is called *hakkōhēn haggādôl mē'eḥāw,* "the greatest priest among his brethren" (Lev 21.10), but this formula is a description rather than a title, and the rest of the phrase is an addition (cf. VAI, p. 397).

144+ On the island called Elephantine, near Aswan (first Nile cataract), lived Jewish colonists who were settled there in the 5th century B.C. as mercenary soldiers in the Persian army. They worshipped Yahweh in their own temple.

146* See the references in *VAI* 103-106, where it is also explained that Elisha's "anointing" (1 Kg 19:16) must be understood metaphorically (cf. Is 61:1 and Ps 105:15 = 1 Chr 16:22). For E. Kutsch the anointing of the high priest belonged to a category of consecration different from that of the king and cannot be said therefore to have replaced it (*Salbung* ... 22-27). According to E. Kaufmann royal anointing followed sacerdotal anointing, from which it borrowed the rite (*The Religion of Israel* 186).

146** The high priesthood remained in the Zadokite family until the death of Onias III (cf. 2 Macc 4:30-38). On the high priests of that period and until Herod the great see W. F. Smith, *A Study of Zadokite High Priesthood with the Graeco-Roman Age: from Simeon the Just to the High Priests appointed by Herod the Great* (Diss. Harvard, n.d.; see HarvThRev 54, 1961, p. 303).

147* There has been much dispute among scholars concerning the role of the king in the cult. Bartlett insistently presents the Israelite king as "the chief cultic person" (pp. 9 and 11), who delegated the care of the temple administration to the leading priest. J. De Fraine, on the other hand, refused to consider the king as "a functionary of the cult," although it is true that he was credited with a right to supervise the cult (*Sacra Pagina,* v. 1, pp. 537-547).

148* This does not correspond to the orientation of Bartlett's argumentation, who calls "the house of Zadok" in 2 Chr 31:10 "a misleading and artificial phrase. There was no house of Zadok of any importance that we know of from Solomon's time onward. The only Zadokites we know of are those people gathered by the Chronicler or by some near predecessor of his into a list of priests of Jerusalem arbitrarily made to descend from Zadok." (J. R. Bartlett, "Zadok ..." JThSt 19, 1968, p. 16).

149* The names of Heman's last nine sons (v. 4) when put together, form a little poem, a fragment of a psalm (VAI, p. 392). Some of the other names (see vv. 25-31) also seem artificial, being formed from words often used in prayer: "be gracious," "I magnify," "I exalt."

150* See 1 Chr 9:26; 23:28; 26:20; 2 Chr 24:6,11; 29:34; 31:11-15; 35:11. On the Levites as exegetes, editors, and Masoretes, see M. Gertner, "The Masorah and the Levites," VetTest 10 (1960) 241-284.

150** In Ex 5:6,10,14,15,19 the *šōṭerîm* appear as "foremen" (RSV) or "overseers" (JB). Other distinctive contexts include Jos 1:10; Dt 1:15; Num 11:16. To the question, "were there any women employed in the temple?", the answer is negative, and this is confirmed by the fact that Hebrew has no feminine noun corresponding to *kōhēn* or *lēwy*. Even Ex 38:8 is no indication that women had an office to perform in public worship. But the function of these "ministering women who ministered at the door of the tent of meeting" (RSV) has not yet been adequately clarified.

151* The *teraphim* of Gen 31:19-42 quite certainly designate household idols, while probably in Jg 17:5, 18:17-20, Hos 3:4, certainly in Ezek 21:26, Zech 10:2, the term refers to some kind of oracular instruments (see EncDictBibl 1039).

152* The gold ephod, weighing about 60 pounds, which Gideon made out of the spoil of the Midianites, appears to have been an idolatrous emblem. On ephod as an encased idol, see T. H. Gaster, in V. Ferm, ed., *Forgotten Religions* (New York 1950), p. 141, n. 3.

152** See 1 Sam 23:9-10; 30:7. We do not know what the ephod, as receptacle, looked like. It was not necessarily a box (OAB 348, 361), even though Goliath's sword could be concealed behind it (1 Sam 21:9). In 1 Kg 2:26 some authors read *'arōn*, "ark," instead of "ephod." Solomon would have told Abiathar: "I will not at this time put you to death, because you bore the ephod (not the "ark") of the Lord God before David my father" (see J. Gray, *I and II Kings*, London 1964, p. 106).

152+ Read this verse as restored in accordance with the ancient versions (also in JB and RSV). In 1 Sam 14:18 it is proposed to read with the LXX "ephod" instead of "ark": "Saul then said to Ahijah, 'bring the ephod'; for it was he who carried the ephod in the presence of Israel" (JB). W. R. Arnold, however, argues that "ark" was originally read, for "the specific instrument of priestly divination among the ancient Hebrews was the ark" (*Ephod and Ark*, 16-17). He also believes that the reading "ephod," whenever in the OT it stands for a solid object, has been deliberately substituted by Jewish scribes for a more troublesome word" (p. 10), that is for *'arōn*, "ark." The passages involved are, besides 1 Sam 14:18: Jg 8:27; Jg 17-18 *passim*; 1 Sam 2:28, 14:3, 21:10, 22:18, 23:6,9, 30:7. The purpose of the alteration was to avoid making an oracular device of "the most sacred object in the cult of Yahwe." Perhaps more convincingly K. Budde sustained that wherever it stands for a solid object the term *ephod* replaces an original *'abbîr*, (God) the Bull (cf. Gen 49:24; Is 49:26, 60:16; Ps 132:2,5). What Gideon (Jg 8:27) and Micah (Jg 17:5) had made was not an ephod, but an *'abbîr*, a silver or golden calf to represent Yhwh, "the Bull." It is probable that were Budde writing now he would find his explanation confirmed by the evidence from Mari concerning the use there of the bull-standard (see note to p. 68).

153* In *Syria* 15 (1934) 305-309 C. Virolleaud published a text on the death of Baal, in which the words *'epd* and *ttrp* occur together. Introducing his commentary of the text W. F. Albright writes: "We shall see that the word *ttrp* has nothing whatever to do with the teraphim, except perhaps etymologically, and that the ephod is here still a simple garment, worn by women as well as by men, just as was presumably true of the old Assyrian *epâdâtum* ..." (BASOR n. 83, 1941, 39). For other references to the Ugaritic *'epd* and studies on it, see W. Baumgartner in ThRu 13 (1941) 168-169; C. H. Gordon, *Ugaritic Textbook*, p. 364.

153** See Ex 28:30; Lev 8:8; Num 27:21; Dt 33:8. The term *'ūrîm* occurs, without *tummîm*, in Num 27:21 and 1 Sam 28:6, "no doubt as an abbreviation of the full term" (EncDictBibl, *s.v.*). The ending *îm* in the term may not be a plural but a formation with the enclitic *mem* (*Biblica* 34, 1953, 79-80). *Urim* and *Tummim*, E. Robertson thinks (VetTest 14, 1964, 67-74), represent the first and last letters of the Hebrew alphabet. They would appear combined in Qumran's *'wrtwm* to mean "fulness," as the Alpha-Omega of Rev 22:13. The term *'wrtwm* occurs at Qumran in the *Hodayot* (4.23; 18.29; cf. 4.6; 7.25; 18.3). A. L. Sukenik believed that the term is a singular of *'ūrîm-tummîm* and means "a light of perfectness." But others read *ôrtayim* (dual), translated "point du jour." See more references and suggestions in M. Mansoor, *The Thanksgiving Hymns* (Leiden 1961) 122-123.

153+ According to the Mishnah "when the First Prophets died, Urim and Thummim ceased" (Sotah 9, 12). According to Gemara 48b, all the prophets except Haggai, Zechariah, and Malachi are meant. It is also stated there: "When the first temple was destroyed ... the Urim and Tummim ceased." The three prophets mentioned, it is said, made use of the *Bath Qol* (a voice from heaven, regarded as a lower grade of prophecy).

153++ With no consonantal change it is possible to read *tôrōt*, "laws," or "instructions," instead of the singular. The plural is used, e.g., in Gen 26:5, Ex 16:25, Ezek 43:11; Ps 105:45, Neh 9:13.

153+++ It is less probable that *tôrâh* comes from *yārâh*, meaning "to shoot" (arrows: cf. 1 Sam 20:36-37) or "to cast" (lots: Jos 18:6), although these contexts offer a certain similarity with pre-Israelite oracular divination.

154* Like the *sadin* among the ancient Arabs, the Israelite priest was, in the beginning at least, chosen and installed to serve a sanctuary. The Danites who had migrated had Jonathan the Levite to look after their sanctuary at Laish-Dan, and the family of Eli was responsible for that of Shiloh (1 Sam 1-2). In the later periods, the Israelite priest performed his duties in the temple at Jerusalem. Describing the "tribal (Israelite), priest," R. J. Sklba writes that the fact of being the guardian (of the *zikᵉrôn*, sacred memorial) was the *sine qua non* of his priesthood, but not the essence which was rather his teaching function (*The Teaching Function of the Pre-Exilic Israelite Priesthood*, Rome 1965, p. 31). On this function see also G. Couturier, "Le prêtre et l'enseignement en Israël," in *Le prêtre, hier, aujourd'hui, demain*. Cogitatio Fidei 5 (Ottowa-Paris 1970) 44-45. On "the priest as imparter of *Tōrā*," see B. Osborn, *Tōrā in the Old Testament. A Semantic Study* (Lund 1945) 89-111.

154+ The Israelite priesthood played the principal role in collecting and re-editing the sacred writings during and after the Exile, "subjecting all references to the cultus to a thorough and deliberate rearrangement" (G. Schrenk in Kittel ThW [Eng], III, 261).

155* According to the Chronicler, king Jehoshaphat sent a delegation of five princes, nine Levites and (only) two priests to teach the people the law of God (2 Chr 17:7-9). Of the Levites it is also said that their "understanding was at the disposal of all Israel" (JB, closer to the Heb than RSV). The Levites helped the people to understand the law ... they taught the people (Neh 8:7,9). See also G. W. Anderson, *The History and Religion of Israel* (Oxford 1966) 77.

In the light of what can be learned from Ezekiel's role and writings E. Haag assigns three main functions to OT priesthood: soteriological (covenant mediation), ecclesial (proclamation of God's word), eschatological (pointing to the new covenant), in "Priestertum und Altes Testament," TrierThZ 80 (1971) 20-42. See also O. Schilling, " 'Nicht schwindet vom Priester die Weisung' (Jer 18,18). Der alttestamentliche Priester als Träger der Verkündigung," *Hengsbach-Festschrift* (Essen 1970) 11-38; A. Deissler, *Der Priesterliche Dienst. I: Ursprung und Geschichte*. Quaestiones Disputatae 46 (Freiburg i. Br. 1970) 61-67 (the contribution of priesthood to the OT revelation and theology).

155+ In the story of Eli, 1 Sam 2:27-36 is another formulation of this privilege, but the passage is a later insertion. J. Scharbert notes that only one pre-Deuteronomic text, Ex 18:12 (E), expressly attributes to a priest the offering of a sacrifice, and this priest is not an Israelite but the Midianite Jethro, Moses' father-in-law: J. Scharbert, *Heilsmittler im alten Testament und im alten Orient* (Freiburg im Breisgau 1964), p. 269.

156* F. Michaeli translates: "Aaron was set apart to sanctify the holy of holies," that is, to perform the rites of sanctification in the very holy place. But, he adds, "holy of holies" could designate Aaron himself: "He was consecrated as holy of holies" (*Les livres des Chroniques, d'Esdras et de Néhémie*, Neuchâtel 1967, p. 119). In 1 Sam 9:13 it is said of Samuel that "he must bless the sacrifice."

158* Taken broadly the term "Judaism" embraces the life, worship, and faith of the Jewish people of all times. More precisely, it refers to the Jewish religion as it developed after the Babylonian Exile. On "Judaism" in this latter meaning see the art. of J. M. Oesterreicher, in NCE, v. 8, 3-13, with a bibliog. On "Judaism at the end of the Old Testament period," see J. Bright, *A History of Israel* (Philadelphia, 1959), 413-446.

The conceptions and aspirations in Judaism, although centered on the law, found varying expression among the apocalypticists, the nationalists, and the legalists (see *ibid.*, p. 451). Rabbinic Judaism fully developed only after the destruction of the second temple.

159* Even if *hiereis* (not *archiereis*) is read in Acts 4:1, the reference is again to the priestly aristocratic faction, dominated by the Sadducees, as distinct from the pious and popular party of the Pharisees (see JB and Acts 23.9).

160* Hence the Greek term *ephēmeria,* describing Zechariah's "division" (Lk 1:5, 8) and translating *maḥalōqet* "division" or "course" in 1 Chr 28.13 and elsewhere. The word *ephēmeria* has two meanings: "service for a term of days" (Neh 13:30; 1 Chr 25:8; 2 Chr 13:10) and "a course of priests who were on duty for a term of days" (1 Chr 23:6; 28:13). These courses were also called *diaireseis,* and by Josephus *patriai* and *ephēmerides* (cf. Ant 7.14, § 366; 12.6.1 § 265.

160** Referring to 1 Chr 24:3 Josephus writes: David "after separating the priests from the rest of the (Levi) tribes, found that of these there were twenty-four families (*patriai*) ... and further arranged that one family should minister to God each week from Sabbath to Sabbath ... He also divided the tribe (*phylē*) of Levites into twenty-four parts (*merē*), and, according to the order in which the lots were drawn, they were chosen for a week, in the same manner as the priestly courses (*ephēmerides*)." The weekly alternation, not mentioned in Scripture, represents the arrangement in use in Josephus' time, as is also attested in the *Mishnah*: see Taanith, "Days of fasting," IV, 2. The *Jerusalem Talmud* commentary of this passage suggests explanations for the division into twenty-four classes (see M. Schwab, *Le Talmud de Jérusalem*, vol. 6, Paris 1853, pp. 177-178).

160+ Josephus's ancestors were priests, he writes (*Life* 1), who belonged to the first course (*ephēmeris*), and to the most eminent of its constituent clans (*phylai*). Josephus Flavius, whose Jewish name was Joseph ben Matthias, produced his four main works in Rome: *Jewish War* (75-79), *Antiquities* (93-94), *Life* (autobiography), and *Against Apîon* (very probably after 100). This last title, not the authors's, is misleading, since Apion is only one of the adversaries meant in the work, which is a reply to criticisms on the *Antiquities*, a refutation of current prejudices, and an apology of Judaism. The full title of the first work is *History of the Jewish War against the Romans*. Our quotations in English are borrowed from the Loeb Classical Library edition. See 1 Chr 24:4,6 and the Mishnah treatise *Yoma* ("Day of Atonement"), III, 9. On the "courses" of the priests and of the Levites, see E. Schürer, *Geschichte des jüdischen Volkes im Zeitalter Jesu Christi*, v. 2 (4th edit., Leipzig 1907) 286-296.

160++ See Neh 13:30 and 2 Chr 31:16, where the LXX has *eis leitourgian ephēmeriais diatexeôs autôn.*

161* For *bêt 'abôt* see also *Taanith* II, 6-7 and for "elders" and "eldest" in the priesthood see *Yoma* I, 5 and *Middôt* ("Measurements") I, 8.

161** The division of the Levites into twenty-four classes is well attested in the postbiblical period. Besides *Ant* VII, 14, 7, see *Taanith* IV, 2: "Therefore the First Prophets [David and Solomon] ordained twenty-four Courses, and for every Course there was a *Maamad* in Jerusalem, made up of priests, Levites and Israelites," tr. H. Danby, *The Mishnah* (Oxford 1933) 199; see also *Sukkah* ("Tabernacles") V: 6-8; *ib.* 180-181. The *maamad* ("station") ordinarily means a group of representatives from outlying districts, corresponding to the twenty-four "courses of priests" (see *Taanith* IV, 1-4 and Danby's note, p. 794).

161*** On the officials and other members of the Jewish priesthood at the time of Jesus, see E. Schürer, *op. cit.*, 317-336; A. Edersheim, *The Temple, its Ministry and Services, as they were at the Time of Jesus Christ* (London 1874) 59-76; J. Jeremias, *Jerusalem in the Time of Jesus. An Investigation into Economic and Social Conditions during the NT Period* (Philadelphia 1969) 147-221; A. Büchler, *Die Priester und der Cultus im letzten Jahrzehnt des Jerusalemischen Tempels* (Wien 1895) 90-118.

163* If a high priest and a nazirite travelling together found a neglected corpse, the one to defile himself by burying it was the nazirite, not the high priest: "Let the nazirite contract uncleanness, for his sanctity is not a lifelong sanctity, and let not the priest contract uncleanness, for his sanctity is a *lifelong sanctity* (*qᵉdūšat ʿôlam: Nazir* 7.1; Danby 289).

164* The term occurs as *sāgān* in the OT to designate prefects who governed provinces of oriental empires (cf. Is 41:25; Jer 51:23,28,57; Ezek 23:6,12-23), and also Israelite chief officials in the rapatriated communities (Ezra 9:2; Neh 2:16; 4:8,13; 5:8,17; 7:5; 12:40; 13:11; Greek: *stratēgos*). A. Büchler feels certain, however, that *sāgān* in the OT means "army chief" (*op. cit.* 115).

164** See *Yoma* 3.9; 4.1; *Tamid* 7.3. The *ro'š bêt ab*, chief of the father's house, mentioned in these texts, was the head of the daily priestly courses.

164*** See *Bikkurim* ("first fruits"), 3.3; *Ant* 15.11.4, § 408. In *Ant* 18.4.3, § 91 the "custodian of the vestments" (*phylax tēs stolēs*) is mentioned.

164⁺ See *Ant* 14.7.1, § 107; 15.11.4, § 408; 18.4.3, § 91, as compared to 1 Chr 9:28-29; 26:20-28. According to Neh 13:13 it seems that the treasurers had a priest at their head. When the *Mishnah* says there must be at least three *gizbārim* (see next note) it likely speaks of the chief treasurers only, not of all the treasury personnel needed.

164⁺⁺ In *Shekalim* 5.2 it is stated: "There were never less than three treasurers (*gizbarim*) and seven supervisors (*'ammarkᵉlîn*, with aramaic plural). According to S. Zeitlin, "officers, called *'ammarkᵉlîn*, had authority over the entire economy of the Temple. Later, two other officers, each called *catholicos*, were appointed, to supervise the general financial arrangement of the Temple" (*The Rise and Fall of the Judaean State*, v. 1 (Philadelphia 1962, 261-262).

164⁺⁺⁺ *The Jewish Encyclopedia*, v. 1 (1901), proposes for the word *amarkol* (*sic*) two etymologies: the Persian *amarkir* and the Armenian *hamarakar*, meaning "master of finance," and explains *amarkol* as "a title applied to a Temple trustee superintending the cashiers." While the cashiers (*gizbarim*), it adds, handled all the money that flowed into the temple treasury, "the *amarkolim* (*sic*), seven in number, held the seven keys to the seven gates of the temple hall (*ʿazarah*), none opening his gate before all the others had assembled" (*Tosephta Shek.* 2.15). The term *'ammarkāl* occurs also elsewhere in the Talmud and in Targ. Is 22:23. J. Jeremias rejects, however, any *direct* connection of the *'ammarkᵉlîn* (*sic*) with the treasury and proposes rather to identify them with the *sᵉganîm* or *stratēgoi*, and claims that among these is to be included "the one appointed" (*hamūnnâh*) to assign the tasks by lot and to direct the daily morning and evening service (*Jerusalem in the Time of Jesus*, tr. from German, London 1969 165ff.). It is also possible that the *'ammarkᵉlîn* were these temple officers, who, according to *Against Apion*, 2.8, § 108, each day handed the keys of the temple and the vessels to the succeeding ministers (see A. Büchler, *op. cit.* 96).

164⁺⁺⁺⁺ See *Jer. Talmud* on *Shekalim* 5.2 (in M. Schwab's edit., v. 5, p. 295). The Greek term *katholikos* has in some classical texts the meaning of "supervisor of accounts":

see Liddell-Scott, *Greek-English Lexikon,* v. 1 (Oxford 1940) 855. This would explain the mention of *qatôliqîn* with the *'ammarkelîn* and the *gizbarim.*

165* See *Jewish War* 6.2.2, § 114, and in the Mishnah: *Ketubôth* ("Marriage Deeds"), 13.1-2; *Ohaloth* ("The Tents"), 17.5. In *Ketubôth* 1.5, is mentioned "the court of the Priests," whom Danby equates with the "Sons of the High Priests" in *Ohaloth* 17.5: "The reference is probably to a Sanhedrin dominated by Sadducaic or highpriestly influences, as opposed to the Pharisaic school of thought, represented by Hillel" (*The Mishnah,* p. 245, n. 14). J. Jeremias believes, however, that "sons of the high priests" in *Ket.* and *Ohal.* means the high priests themselves, as in 1 Kg 20:35 the "sons of the prophets" are the prophets themselves. But this interpretation can hardly apply to Jewish War 6.2, 2: "Among those [who went over to the Romans] were the *archiereis* Joseph and Jesus and certain sons of chief priests ..." (§ 114).

165+ The *stratēgoi,* "captains" or "prefects," mentioned with *archiereis* in Lk 22: 4,52, are probably priestly assistants to the chief *stratēgos* (cf. Acts 5:26). See U. Holzmeister, *Historia aetatis Novi Testamenti* (2nd edit., Rome 1938) 206.

166* See Lev 21:17-24. Maimonides finds 140 blemishes which rendered priests unfit for service, either temporarily or permanently: see *The Code of Maimonides* VIII, treatise 3, ch. 7-8 (pp. 110-119 in M. Lewitte's edition).

166+ See the *gemara* of *Kiddushin* ("Betrothals") 4.6-7, § 77-78 (pp. 393-404) in the Soncino edition of *The Babylonian Talmud.*

167* *Ḥullin* 24b (Soncino edit., p. 121, quoting Ezra 3:8). Perhaps the same rule was observed as for the Levites, for whom it varies; from 30-50 years (Num 4:3; cf. 1 Chr 23:3); from 25 years and upward: Num 8:23-26; from 20 years and upward: Ezra 3:8; 1 Chr 23:24; 2 Chr 31:17.

167** K. Hruby has recently written on "ordination" in Judaism. He notes the the *semikhah,* "hand imposition," may have coexisted with the other rite of "ordination," the conferring of the title of "rabbi." First transmitted directly from teacher to disciple the Jewish "ordination" later required the consent of the *nassi,* the head of the sanhedrin, and even of the sanhedrin itself; see his "La notion d'ordination dans la tradition juive," *Maison-Dieu* 102 (1970) 30-56. In this article Hruby also discusses the meaning of Num 11:16-18: the conferring of Moses' spirit on the seventy "elders of Israel."

168* Wernberg-Møller (see footnote 33) reads *bny hṣdyq* in 1 QS IX,14 (p. 137), whereas the common reading is *bny hṣdwq* (vocalized *benê haṣṣadôq*). G. Vermes proposed to excise the article, while conceding that *benê haṣṣedeq* remains possible, with the meaning "sons of righteousness" (*Les manuscrits du désert de Juda,* 2nd edit., Tournai 1954, p. 152). W. H. Browlee reads *bny hṣdwq,* "sons of Zadok," but adds: "Yet there is good ground for the proposed emendation of H. L. Ginsberg *bny hṣdq* (as in III,20.22), "sons of righteousness": *The Dead Sea Manual of Discipline.* Translation and Notes. BASOR Suppl. Stud. 10-12 (New Haven 1951), p. 37. Wernberg-Møller believes that 1 QS IX,14 depends directly of Job 31:6a, "our author having seen in the biblical *bm'zny ṣdq* an allusion to *bny ṣdq.*" See also R. North, "The Qumrân 'Sadducees' ", CathBiblQuart 17 (1955) 168.

168+ The Damascus Document, discovered by S. Schechter in the Cairo (hence CD) genizah, was first edited by him in 1910 and called Fragments of a Zadokite work.

169* *The Rule of the Congregation* (*serek ha 'ēdâh*), called *The Messianic Rule* by Vermes, is a short independent work which was originally included in the same scroll as *The Community Rule.* The original edition is in D. Barthélemy, J. T. Milik *et al., Discoveries in the Judaean Desert* I, Qumran Cave I (Oxford 1955), pp. 108-118.

171* The term *m^e^baqqēr* (cf. CD 13,11-13), translated "Guardian" by Vermes (see p. 19) refers likely to the same office as *pāqîd* (cf. 1 QS 6,14). See A. R. C. Leaney, *The Rule of Qumran and its Meaning* (London 1966) 230. *M^e^baqqēr* and *pāqîd* can be translated "overseer," as the Greek *epimelētēs* (Jos., *Jewish War* II,8,6, § 134; cf. 1 Tim 3:5) and *episkopos* often used in the NT: Acts 20:28; Phil 1:1; 1 Tim 3:2; Tit 1:7; 1 Pet 2:25. "The term *episkopos,* writes H. H. Rowley, closely corresponds in meaning with the Qumran term Overseer, and it may well be that the Church owed something to Qumran for the adoption of the term, though the total organization of the Church was very different from that of the sect" (*From Moses to Qumran,* London 1963, p. 257). In a recent, well documented analysis of Christian ministry terminology in the NT A. Lemaire recognizes presently no basis for making the organization of the Church dependent on that of the Essenian community. It remains also very doubtful if the Qumran function terminology, including *m^e^baqqēr,* has influenced that used by the Church more than a generation later. On "the organization of Qumran and the 'ministers' of the Church," see then A. Lemaire, *Les ministères aux origines de l'Église, Naissance de la triple hiérarchie: évêques, presbytres, diacres.* Lectio Divina 68 (Paris 1971) 203-217, and also his extensibe bibliography, pp. 219-236.

172* For R. B. Laurin "the theory of two Messiahs in the Qumran Scrolls is really built on a tenuous interpretation of one text: *Rule of the Community* IX, 11. The overwhelming evidence elsewhere ... indicates that the messianic hope of the Scrolls was for a Davidic Messiah and a high priestly companion" (RQum 4, 1963, p. 52). On "the Origin of the Idea of the Levitical Messiah," see M. D. Johnson, *The Purpose of Biblical Genealogies ...* (London 1969) 131-138.

173* A. J. B. Higgins observes "that nowhere do we find the title 'the Messiah of Aaron.' This title is simply inferred from the expression 'the Messiah of Aaron and Israel' by those who maintain that it refers to two figures" (NTS 13, 1966-67, p. 216).

174* M. De Jonge finds in *Test. Jud.* 21.1-5 "no Christian alterations and additions," which, however, are very evident in *Test. Neph.* 8.2, stating that the salvation for Israel will come from Judah alone. If kingship, De Jonge adds, is subordinated to priesthood it could be simply that it deals with things on earth, while priesthood's concerns are heavenly (*The Testaments of the Twelve Patriarchs,* Assen 1953, p. 87).

175* It has been suggested that the substitution purposely toned down, if not the priesthood of the Jerusalemite king, at least the liturgical aspect of his offering (H. Lignée, "L'Apocryphe de la Genèse," in J. Carmignac *et al., Les Textes de Qumran,* v. 2, Paris 1963, p. 239).

176* See P. Heinisch, *Theology of the Old Testament,* English edition by W. Heidt (Collegeville 1950) 318, and *Id., Das Buch Genesis* (Bonn 1930) 222-223. Concluding his articles, "Melchisedech, rex Salem, proferens panem et vinum," VerbDom 18, 1938, 208-214, 235-243, A. Vaccari writes: "Although Gen 14:18 does not expressly say that Melchizedek offered bread and wine to God, this can be assumed and is even required by the action as a whole. And this provides a firm basis for the later exegetical tradition (Jewish and Christian) which reads in the passage a sacrifice of bread and wine offered by Melchisedech" (p. 243). And he quotes approvingly (p. 214) Bellarmine's statement: "We do not deny that the bread and the wine were offered to Abraham and his men as refection, but we say that first these (food and drink) had been offered to God and consecrated, then given to the men that they might participate in the sacrifice" (*Controversiarum, de sacramento Eucharistiae,* Lib. V, C. VI).

176** We read in Gen 14:18: "And Melchizedek king of Salem *hoṣî' leḥem wāyāyin* *wehū' kōhēn le'ēl 'elyôn.*" The conjunction *we*, "and," can certainly be translated here by "for" or "since." The context suggests that it should. In a passage syntactically very similar RSV renders the same particule by "for": "*For* I continue childless" (Gen 15:2); "*For* she is a man's wife" (Gen 20:3; cf. 24:31). See also J. F. X. Sheehan, "Melchisedech in Christian Consciousness," ScEccl 18 (1966) 129-130. Others connect 18b with 19. "Blessing" was not, however, at this early period, a distinctively priestly action, at least not as much as offering a sacrifice was.

176+ Bread and wine can constitute an ordinary food supply (cf. Jg 19:19; 1 Sam 25:18), although this is generally represented by bread and water: see Gen 21:14; Ex 23:25, 34:28 (Dt 9:18); 1 Sam 30:12; Ezek 4:17. Wine did not constitute a sacrificial offering by itself but was added to the burnt offering (e.g. Num 15:5). In Num 15:10 the wine oblation is called "a fire-offering" (*'iššēh*). But the word is perhaps intrusive (cf. v. 7). If original, writes G. B. Gray, "it is best taken as loosely referring to the whole accompanying offerings (vv. 9-10) (*Numbers*. ICC, Edinburgh 1903, p. 175).

176++ In Ps 16:4 wine libation appears as an idolatrous rite (cf. Ps 50:13). Although the term *nesek,* "libation" (cf. Num 15:5), is used in only one early passage (Gen 35:14) of a libation offered to Yahweh, "other allusions (Hos 9:4; 1 Sam 1:24; 10:3) prove that it was a customary form of offering in the early worship of Yahweh as in other cults (Jer 7:18; Ps 16:4). In early times (independent) libations occasionally consisted of water (1 Sam 7:6; 2 Sam 23:16). It is possible that (in P) wine libations arose in part as a surrogate for blood" (G. B. Gray, *Numbers*. ICC, Edinburgh 1903, p. 174).

177* On these "holy ones" in the Bible and the Jewish writings, including Qumran, see C. H. W. Brekelmans, "The Saints of the Most High and their Kingdom," *Oudtestamentische Studien* 14 (1965) 305-329. According to J. A. Emerton, Melchizedek is called *elohim* in the Qumran text probably as a result of being identified with the archangel Michael ("Melchizedek and the Gods: Fresh Evidence for the Jewish Background of John X.34-36," JThSt 17, 1966, p. 401.

178* Others translate "... for it is blood that atones for a life" (JB). To this statement Heb 9:22 is often compared. When in the NT, and specifically in Heb (cf. 9:12, 14; 10:19, 29; 13:20), mention is made of Christ's redemptive blood (cf. Eph 1:17; Acts 20:28) the reference is to the costly life he laid down for men, to his atoning sacrifice (cf. Heb 10:10, 12), not to blood as an expiating or purifying substance, as in the ritual of OT sacrifices. In Heb, W. Stott explains, "blood" (of Christ) refers to "blood shed" NTSt 9 (1962-63) pp. 64-65.

179* In a recent study H. Zimmermann has attempted to show, especially from assumed primitive hymnic elements in Heb (cf. 5:7-10; 7:1-3; 7:26), that the Author of Heb has taken over the confession (*homologia*) of Christ (cf. 3:1; 4:14) as High Priest from a firmly existing tradition. The Author's (of Heb) distinctive contribution would have been the paranetic framework given to the traditional material and the insistence on the entry of Jesus in heaven as our Forerunner, through his Passion, which, it is supposed, the community did not easily understand or accept (*Die Hohepriester-Christologie des Hebräerbriefes*, Paderborn 1964, esp. pp. 26-33). The thesis seems overstated in regard to the evidence produced.

179** It must be recorded here that only 30 years ago a Biblical student in his seriously done doctoral dissertation, expressed a strong personal conviction "that Paul, the Vessel of Election, is in a very full sense the author of the Epistle to the Hebrews. Not only the conception of the letter, under the inspiration of the Holy Ghost, but also the logical arrangement and all the substantial constituents of the literary form are the fruit of his great Apostolic mind and heart" (W. Leonard, *Authorship of the Epistle to the Hebrews*, Vatican City 1939, 357). He has, however, to admit that "the essential redemptive work of offering sacrifice is in Heb surrounded with a wealth of sacerdotal details which is only very slightly paralleled in the Pauline epistles" (p. 66). On the Epistle and its doctrinal contents see also Vanhoye's art. of DictSpirAscMyst, v. 7 (Paris 1968) c. 111-126, with classified bibliog. A previous bibliography of Heb (1938-1963) was published by E. Grässer in ThRu 30 (1964) 138-236. On the theology of the Epistle can be consulted J. Moffatt, *Epistle to the Hebrews* (ICC, Edinburgh 1929) XXX-LV and O. Kuss, *Gesammelte Aufsätze*, v. 1 (Munich 1963) 281-328 = MünchThZ 7 (1956) 233-271. Many other studies will be mentioned in the following notes and in our bibliography. Add the more systematic and dogmatic study of J. Alfaro, "Christus der Hohepriester," in J. Feiner and M. Löhrer, *Mysterium Salutis*. Das Christusereignis III/1 (Einsiedeln 1970) 659-705.

179+ The similarities are such, Spicq thinks, that the minimal conclusion is that the author of Heb had studied the works of Philo and may have been trained by him (v. 1, p. 89). For H. Chadwick, "the analogies are so near as to make a relationship of direct dependence much the simplest and most probable hypothesis" ("St. Paul and Philo of Alexandria," Bull JRylLibr 48, 1965-66, p. 290). It is S. G. Sowers' conviction "that the writer of Heb has come from the same school of Alexandrian Judaism as Philo, and that Philo's writings still offer us the best single body of *religionsgeschichtlich* material we have for this N.T. document" (*The Hermeneutics of Philo and Hebrews. Basel Studies of Theology*, N. 1, Zurich 1965, p. 66; see pp. 64-74). Still Heb is fundamentally different from Philo in outlook and thought. Whereas Philo, for example, treats the OT allegorically, Heb interprets it with meticulous literalness and understands it as Messianic. See H. Montefiore, *A Commentary on the Epistle to the Hebrews* (London 1964), pp. 6-9. To show even further how scholars can differ on the interpretation of given data we can hear from R. Williamson, *Philo and the Epistle to the Hebrews* (Brill, Leiden 1970). According to him the evidence points to the conclusion that "the Writer of Hebrews had never been a Philonist, had never read Philo's work, had never come under the influence of Philo directly or indirectly" (p. 579).

180* Among the more recent studies in English can be recalled: I. Hunt, "Recent Melkizedek Study," in *The Bible in Current Catholic Thought*. Fs. Gruenthaner (New York 1962) 21-33; L. R. Fisher, "Abraham and his Priest-King," JBiblLit 81 (1962) 264-270; R. H. Smith, "Abram and Melchizedek (Gen 14:18-20)," ZATWiss 77 (1965) 129-153; M. De Jonge and A. S. Van der Woude, "11Q Melchizedek and the New Testament," NTSt 12 (1965-66) 301-326; A. R. Johnson, *Sacral Kingship in Ancient Israel* (2nd rev. ed., Cardiff 1967) 35-53. For a full recent bibliography on Melchizedek and the sacrifice he offered see S. Lyonnet-L. Sabourin, *Sin, Redemption, and Sacrifice. A Biblical and Patristic Study* (AnalBibl 48, Rome 1970) 310-312. See also R. Williamson, "Melchizedek in Philo and Hebrews," in *op. cit.* 434-449.

According to G. von Rad, the most important thing in the purpose of the Genesis story is that Abraham received the blessing of the precursor to David and the Davidic dynasty, that even Abraham had recognized his duty toward Jerusalem and its king, in the person of Melchizedek (*Genesis*, tr. J. H. Marks, 2nd rev. edit., London 1963, p. 176). For J. Skinner the monarchy and hierarchy of Jerusalem based their dynastic and priestly rights on the Melchizedek tradition (Genesis, ICC, Edinburgh 1910, p. 270).

183* Of Melchizedek, Philo writes: *hiereus gar esti logos* (*Alleg. Interp.* 3.26, § 82), a statement diversely understood: "For he is the Priest-logos" (C. Mondésert) or "For he is a priest, even Reason" (F. H. Colson). Josephus interprets "Melchizedek" as *basileus dikaios*, "Righteous King" (*Jewish War*, b. 10, § 438), although the name's original meaning was apparently "my king is Zedek," Zedek being the name of a Canaanite deity.

In Philo the Logos is identified with the High Priest: (a) in contexts allegorizing the Levitical High Priest: *On Flight and Finding* 20, § 108; *On the Special Laws* I.42, § 230; *On the Giants* 11, § 52; *On the Migration of Abraham* 18, § 102; (b) in passages which identify the logos-high priest with Melchizedek: *Alleg. Interp.* III, 25-26, § 79-82; *On Mating with Prelim. Studies* 18, § 99; *On Abraham* 40, § 235. See R. H. Fuller, *The Foundations of New Testament Christology* (London 1965) 78-81; W. A. Meeks, *The Prophet-King. Moses Traditions and the Johannine Christology* (Brill, Leiden 1967), "Moses as High Priest and Mystagogue" in Philo (pp. 117-125). On the expectation of "a messianic ideal priest" by priestly circles in Judaism, also reflected in the literature of Qumran, see J. R. Schaeffer, "The Relationship between priestly and servant Messianism in the Epistle to the Hebrews," CBQ 30 (1968) 361-368, and J. Gnilka in RevQum 2 (1960) 395-426.

183+ The Author of Heb also avoids allegorizing in the manner, e.g., of Philo, who writes: "For there are, as is evident, two temples of God: one of them this universe, in which there is also as High Priest His First-born, the divine Word (*Logos*), and the other the rational soul, whose Priest is the real Man" (*On Dreams* I, 37, § 215: The Loeb Classical Library tr.).

183++ J. Daniélou sees in the mention of Melchizedek's sacrifice in the canon of the Roman Mass an attestation that not only the sacrifices of the Israelite temple, but also those of the pagan world are reassumed in the sacrifice of the eternal High Priest (*The Holy Pagans of the Old Testament*, Baltimore 1957, p. 110). Spicq notes, however, that the Author of Heb never considers the case of the pagans or the value of any cult other than that of the revealed religion, Jewish or Christian (v. 1, p. 14).

185* *Katharizein*, "to purify," means to remove what contradicts legal purity or moral holiness (cf. 1 Jn 1:7-9; Tit 2:14; 2 Cor 7:1; Eph 5:26). In Heb 9:23 the purification of the heavenly things refers, it seems, to Christ's liberation from the likeness of sinful flesh (Rom 8:3; 1 Tim 3:16).

187* In connection with Heb 3:1-6 S. Aalen writes: "The motif of the faithful Son who is the builder of God's house and is in God's house is exactly that which we find in Targum II Sam 7:12-14. Heb has thereby interpreted the word 'house' in v. 14 as the people or congregation of God (v. 6)" (" 'Reign' and 'House' in the Kingdom of God in the Gospels," NTSt 8, 1961-62, p. 237).

189* Grammatically "for all time" can also be referred to "sat down." Thus Vanhoye's translation has: "à perpétuité s'assit à droite de Dieu," which finds support in the contrast with what the priests do according to 10:1.

189+ The formula in Rom 8.3, *kai peri hamartias*, is more commonly translated "and for sin," but *peri hamartias*, being, so to speak, a technical expression for "sin offering" (cf. Lev 16:5, 6, 9, 11; Heb 10:6, 8), it should be understood thus also when the reference is to the sacrifice of Christ. St. Augustine, having quoted Rom 8:3 and 2 Cor 5:21 (God made him "sin" = "sin offering"), states: "The flesh having the likeness of sinful flesh was called 'sin,' as destined to be 'sacrifice for sin' " (Serm. 134, IV, 5). On the whole question see S. Lyonnet-L. Sabourin, *Sin Redemption and Sacrifice*. AnalBibl 48 (Rome 1970) 248-253. To say that Christ offered for his own sins in the qualified sense proposed is not, I believe, contradicted by the decree of the Council of Ephesus: Denz 261.

190* Although the composition is not ordinary prose there is no need to consider it as a hymn coming from a primitive Christian tradition, as G. Friedrich believes (ThZ 18, 1962, pp. 95-115). Reminiscences of OT texts may have been in the Author's mind, esp. Pss 22:2,3,25; 31:23; 39:13; 69:4 and Ps 116 (LXX 114-115); cf. A. Strobel in ZNTWiss 45 (1954) 252-266. The Greek words corresponding to "petitions and supplications" occur in Job (LXX) 40:22 (= 41:3). In Targum Jonathan Is 53:7 becomes in Aramaic: "He prayed and he was heard."

191* *Teleioun*: Ex 29:9,29,33,35; Lev 8:33; the ram of the *teleiōsis*: Ex 29:26,27, 31,34; Lev 8:22,29. Used alone *teleiōsis* in these contexts means the victim offered at the priestly installation (Ex 29:22; Lev 7:37). In Lev 4:5 the Aaronic "anointed" high priest is described as *teteleiōmenos*, "come to fulfilment," like Christ in Heb 7:28. But see in Lev 21:10 the fuller expression: *teteleiōmenos tas cheiras*, "fulfilled with respect to the hands." On *teleioun* see also M. Dibelius, *Botschaft und Geschichte*, v. 2 (Tübingen 1956) 166-172.

192* According to theologian M. de la Taille, Christ by the rites of the Last Supper made his oblation, which constitutes, he writes, with the immolation of the Cross one redemptive sacrifice: see his *Mysterium Fidei* (Paris 1921) 50 and 76. For him each Mass is an oblation of the once immolated Christ, now permanently in the state of victimhood. Perhaps it is better to say with the main course of tradition that the Mass, like the Last Supper, is the sacrament of Jesus' sacrifice offered once-for-all.

192** By combining two Messianic texts Jesus claimed for himself a divine prerogative, the sitting at the right hand of God, not only metaphorical (as in Ps 110:1) but also real, in heaven (cf. Dan 13:7; Mk 16:19). This is one of the explanations proposed of Christ's "blasphemy": see P. Lamarche in RechScRel 50 (1962) 74-85.

192+ See Mk 16:19; Rom 8:34; Eph 1:20; Col 3:1; Acts 2:34. In 1 Cor 15:25 and Acts 2:35 the second half of Ps 110:1 is quoted: "till I make your enemies a footstool" (cf. 1 Pet 3:22).

194* On "Eternity of Salvation in Heb," see A. Cody, *Heavenly Sanctuary and Liturgy in the Epistle to the Hebrews* (St Meinrad, Ind. 1960) 131-144; he analyzes Heb 2:5; 5:9; 6:2,5; 9:11,12,14,15; 10:1; 11:20; 13:14,20.

195* This is evidenced, for example, by the Aorist use of the verbs in 5:7; 7:27; 8:3; 9:28; 10:12. See A. Vanhoye in VerbDom 37 (1959) 32-36 and W. Stott, "The Conception of 'Offering' in the Epistle to the Hebrews," NTSt 9 (1962-63) p. 65.

196* M.-J. Leenhardt (*L'épître de Saint Paul aux Romains*, 135) finds in Rom 8:34 the suggestion that Jesus pleads for the victims of Satan, as the angel did in support of high priest Joshua (Zech 3:3-10). Several early Christian writers have read in Zech 3 a prophecy of Christ's priesthood (see J. Lécuyer, RechScRel 43, 1955, p. 103). Could not the same context be related to Heb 9:23? By the exercise of his priesthood Jesus passed from the sinners' condition (cf. Rom 8:3) to that of the heavenly perfection.

197* In his commentary of Heb 8-9 (Rome 1966, pp. 55-56) Vanhoye explains that *hypodeigma* should not be translated "copy," but "exemplar" (model) or "figure." Cf. Jn 13:15; Jas 5:15; 2 Pet 2:6; Heb 4:11. H. Montefiore translates: "These priests are serving that which is a model and shadow of the heavenly place."

198* For this reading and interpretation of Heb 9:9-10, see M. Zerwick, *Analysis philologica Novi Testamenti Graeci*, p. 507. *Dikaiōmata latreias* (9:1, 10) literally means "regulations for worship." This meaning can be retained in both places; then in 9:10

dikaiōmata latreias would not be a parallel to "gifts and sacrifices" of 9:9b but the resumption in shortened form of 9:9a.

200* See *Biblica* 46 (1965) 1-28. J. Swetnam finds in Heb and elsewhere evidence for expanding Vanhoye's interpretation: "The greater tent" would be the Eucharistic Body of Christ (*Biblica* 47, 1966, 91-106). At the opposite extreme F. Schröger claims that the Epistle cannot be interpreted Eucharistically and that in the community it represents the celebration of the Eucharist apparently did not take place: MünchThZ 19 (1968) 161-181 (esp. 180). In the beginning of the 17th cent. Cornelius à Lapide proposed to see in "the greater tent" the mystery of the Church. It is simply not true, however, that Christ entered heaven by or through the Church. It is rather the Church which enters through Christ.

201* Westcott correctly states: "The outer Sanctuary was not merely a portal to the Holy of Holies but the appointed place of priestly service" (*The Epistle to the Hebrews*, p. 258).

201+ The author probably "is not interested in distinguishing the different parts of the heavenly tent" (Montefiore, p. 152), and what counts is the comparison of two liturgies represented by "tents." Yet since the "sanctuary" (heaven) corresponds to the Holy of Holies (cf. 6:19), "the greater tent" would have its earthly counterpart rather in the first tent, the "holy," the place of the sacrifice which supplied the blood for Aaron (cf. Lev 16), and was the way to the sanctuary (in Christ's liturgy the way to God: see Heb 9:8). To understand how an object, "the tent," can symbolize a liturgy involving action and movement, it is useful to read carefully 9:6-8 and to compare 9:8, "the way of the sanctuary has not yet been made manifest (*pephanerōthai*)," with 9:26: Christ has been made manifest (*pephanerōtai*) through the sacrifice of himself (see Heb 10:19-20).

202* This "eternal spirit" is the Holy Spirit animating Christ in his sacrificial oblation and effecting the sacrificial transformation of his humanity, his *teleiōsis* (cf. analogically 2 Cor 5:17; Eph 4:24). Of Christ it is elsewhere said that he was "made alive in the Spirit" (1 Pet 3:18), "justified in the Spirit" (1 Tim 3:16). See on the argument A. Vanhoye, *Heb 5-9*, pp. 154-159; J. J. McGrath, "*Through the Eternal Spirit.*" *An Historical Study of the Exegesis of Hebrews 9:13-14* (Rome, 1961).

202** It is grammatically possible to read "for the removal of sin by the sacrifice of himself." That this last phrase should also be related to "he has been made manifest" is strongly suggested by the use of "once" (*hapax*), so often connected with the mention of Jesus' sacrifice: 7:27; 9:12,28; 10:10. See also J. Swetnam in CathBiblQuart 30 (1968) 227-234.

203* In *The Interpretation of the Epistle to the Hebrews and of the Epistle James* (Columbus 1946), R. C. H. Lenski writes about Heb 8:2 that our Ministrant of the Holy Place *sits* because he is both High Priest and King, but he apparently nowhere explains what his ministry in heaven consists of. In "The Perpetuity of Christ's Sacrifice in the Epistle to the Hebrews," JBL 89 (1970) 205-214, W. E. Brooks ably presents viewpoints with which we have to disagree. Lenski and others do not distinguish "the tent" and "the sanctuary" in Heb 8:2a, mainly, it seems, because they have no clear idea of what "the greater tent" is in 9:11.

205* The Greek *tetuchen*, which Vanhoye translates "lui est échu" or "sortitus est" is also correctly rendered by *The New English Bible* by "has fallen to him." Also in Heb's use of *tetuchen* the meaning of the Perfect tense is respected: "The Greek Perfect designates a past action considered both as finished and as abiding in the present in its effect" (M. Zerwick, *Graecitas Biblica*, Rome 1966, p. 97). The effects of Christ's *leitourgia* are permanent, eternal, as is the covenant in which he has mediated. Besides, Christ remains the One-Who-Has-Entered-The-Sanctuary for ever. In somewhat the same way he who has saved us remains for ever our Savior.

205+ The use of *diathēkē* in 9:15-18 in its double acceptation of "covenant" and "testament" raises several problems which are discussed by J. Swetnam in CathBibl-Quart 27 (1965), pp. 373-390. He reads in 9:16 an allusion to the death of the animals at the inauguration of the Sinai covenant. More probably the statement merely recalls a general principle. In 9:15 only "the transgressions of the first disposition" are explicitly mentioned to underline the inefficacy of the old liturgy in removing sin, while in the new dispensation the reign of sin is abolished: cf. Rom 6:1-14; 1 Pet 4:1; 1 Jn 3:9. Christ's perfect oblation is both an expiatory and a covenant sacrifice. On the two covenants compared, the old and the new, see Spicq, v. 2, pp. 285-299.

214* Reading *'emet śām 'āšām napšô* (see VerbDom 41, 1963, p. 161). Perhaps the NT writers read as in the TM: "If Thou [God] makest him [lit.: "his soul"] an offering for sin," which is closer to 2 Cor 5:21.

215* A priestly ministry is not necessarily implied in Rom 15:16, where Paul writes of himself: the grace was given me by God "to be a minister (*leitourgos*) of Christ Jesus to the Gentiles, presenting Him as a sacrifice (*hierourgōn*) (the preaching of) God's gospel, so that the Gentiles might become an acceptable offering" (English adaptation of C. Wiener's translation in *Studiorum Paulinorum* ..., AnalBibl 17-18, v. 2, p. 404). In Josephus and Philo *hierourgein* means "to offer sacrifice," not necessarily to officiate as a priest. In *Jewish War*, 5.3, § 16, Josephus mentions the *hiereis*, "priests" and the *hierourgoi* as two distinct categories. The *hierourgoi* may have been those (perhaps Levites) who immolated the victims; the intervention of the priests would still be required for the sacrificial offering proper. In 1 Cor 9:13-14 Paul seems to compare those "who proclaim the gospel" with those "who serve at the altar." But this is insufficient to deny a break of continuity between the old priesthood and the new ministry.

216* Both the expression and the context suggest that *prosagein* in 1 Pet 3:18 has a cultic meaning (see Kittel, ThW, Eng, v. 1, p. 131): in LXX Ex, Lev, Num, it usually occurs as translating *hiqrîb*, "to bring near" (mainly the victims of sacrifice: cf. Ex 29:10; Lev 1:3; 3:3). *Prosagein* is also used of the priests and Levites "brought near" for their purification (cf. Ex 29:4,8; 40:12,14; Lev 8:24; Num 8:9,10). From this O. Moe argues that in 1 Pet 3:18 it is said of Christ *as High Priest* that he "brings to God" Christians, considered as purified "priests" (ThLitz 72, 1947, c. 337). According to T. F. Torrance "in Christ our sonship and priesthood are the same" (ScJTh 11, 1958, p. 230). On the offering of "the Christian sacrifices" through Jesus Christ see A. Richardson, *An Introduction to the Theology of the New Testament* (London 1958) 297-301.

218* The influence of Sir 50 is also admitted by W. Schenk, *Der Segen im Neuen Testament* (Berlin 1967) 54-58. On the priestly blessing in the OT see C. Westermann, *Der Segen in der Bibel und im Handeln der Kirche* (München 1968) 45-47.

219* See Josephus, *Jewish War* 2:8.3, § 123, and W. Grundmann, *Das Evangelium nach Markus* (2nd ed., Berlin 1959) 181, who suggests that in Mk 9:2 and Mt 17:1 the cultic term *anapherein*, "lead up" (cf. Heb 7:27; 9:28; 13:15) is also a priestly connotation of the Transfiguration account.

219+ See also Josephus, *Ant* 3.7.2, § 153 and 3.7.4, § 159. Compare Rev 1:13 with 15:6, where the motif "a golden girdle round his breast" occurs without the mention of *podērēs*. In 1 Macc 10:89; 11:58 wearing "the golden buckle" appears as a royal prerogative.

219++ "But this tunic (*chitōn*) is not composed of two pieces ... it is one long woven cloth with a slit for the neck" (*Ant* 3.7.4, § 161). The verbal coincidences suggest, do not prove, that John had a high priestly robe in mind. Gnilka favors the view that both Jn 19:23 and Apoc 1:13 allude to high priestly vestments (RevQum 2, 1960, 423 and 425). See also J. Colson, *Ministre de Jésus-Christ, ou le sacerdoce de l'Évangile* (Paris 1966), p. 96 (ch. III, pp. 79-110, deals with the priesthood of Christ). On the views of the Church Fathers see M. Aubineau, "La tunique sans couture du Christ. Exégèse patristique de Jean 19,23-24," in *Kyriakon*. Fs. Johannes Quasten (Münster 1970), c. 1, pp. 100-127.

220* As edited and translated by J. B. Lightfoot, v. 2 (London 1890): Gr.: p. 111; Engl.: p. 290; For *Cor* 61, respectively p. 180 f. and 304. The Ignatius text, in J. B. Lightfoot (London 1889), v. 2. pp. 274 and 565. The account of Polycarp's death, contained in a letter sent by the Church of Smyrna (A.D. 156) to the Christian community of Philomenium in Greater Phrygia, contains an early Christian prayer with the following words addressed to God: "I bless you, I glorify you through the eternal and heavenly High Priest Jesus Christ, your beloved Son ..." (see J. Quasten, *Patrology*, v. 1, p. 79).

220+ See J. Lécuyer, "Jésus, fils de Josédec, et le sacerdoce du Christ," RechScRel 43 (1955) 82-103.

228* See Heb 7:11-19, 8:1-6. Institutionalization had its negative aspects in Israel also. The priesthood gradually lost what charismatic character it enjoyed in the beginning and its members became more and more administrators of given regulations, primarily interested in preserving a tradition, and inclined to impose an exclusive form of worship. See W. Eichrodt, *Theology*, v. 1, pp. 403-404.

BIBLIOGRAPHY

Allon, O., "On the History of the High-Priesthood at the Close of the Second Temple," *Tarbiz* 13 (1941-42) 1-24 [in Hebrew].

Ancessi, V., *L'Égypte et Moïse. Première Partie : Les vêtements du Grand Prêtre et des Lévites* (Paris 1875).

Arnold, W.R., *Ephod and Ark, a Study in the Records and Religion of the Ancient Hebrews.* HarvThStud 3 (Cambridge, Mass. 1917).

Auerbach, "Der Aufstieg der Priesterschaft zur Macht im alten Israel," *Congress Volume.* VetTestSuppl (Brill, Leiden 1963) 236-249.

Bähr, C., *Symbolik des mosaischen Cultus,* v. 2 (Heidelberg 1839) 61-165 (on priestly vestments).

Bailey, J.W., "The Usage in the Post Restoration Period of Terms descriptive of the Priest and High Priest," JBiblLit 70 (1951) 217-225.

Bartlett, J.R., "Zadok and His Successors at Jerusalem, "JThSt 19 (1968) 1-18.

Baudissin, E., *Die Geschichte des Alttestamentlichen Priesterthums untersucht* (Leipzig 1889).

Baudissin, W., "Priests and Levites," Hastings DB 4 (1902) 67-97.

Begrich, J., "Das priesterliche Heilsorakel," ZATWiss 52 (1934) 81-92.

Begrich, J., "Die priesterliche Tora," *Werden und Wesen des Alten Testaments.* Beih-ZATWiss 66 (Berlin 1936) 63-88.

Bentzen, A., *Studier over det Zadokidiske Praesteskabs historie* (Copenhage 1931). See also *Id.* in ZATWiss 51 (1933) 173-176.

Berry, G.R., "Priests and Levites," JBiblLit 42 (1923) 227-238.

Bertetto, D., "La natura del sacerdozio secondo Hebr. 5 :1-4 e le sue realizzazioni nel Nuovo Testamento," *Salesianum* 26 (1964) 395-440.

Bertholet, A., "Weibliches Priestertum," *Beiträge zur Gesellungs- und Völkerwissenschaft. Fs. Prof. Dr. Richard Thurnwald* (Berlin 1950) 42-53.

Blackman, A.M., "Priest, Priesthood (Egyptian)," Hastings ERE 10 (1918) 292-302.

Bolewski, H., *Christos Archiereus. Über die Entstehung des hohenpriesterlichen Würdenamens Christi* (Diss. Hall 1939).

Bourgin, C., "Le Christ-Prêtre et la purification des péchés selon l' Épître aux Hébreux," LumetVie 7 (1958) 67-90.

Bowman, J., "Ezekiel and the Zadolite Priesthood," GlasgowUnivOrSocTransactions 16 (1955-56) 1-14.

Boyce, Mary, "Zoroaster the Priest," BullSchOrAfrSt 33 (1970) 22-38.

Braun, J., "De sanctitate summi pontificis," in B. Ugolinus, ed., ThesAntSacr 12 (Venice 1751) c. 157-218.

A. Büchler, *Die Priester und der Cultus im letzten Jahrzehnt des jerusalemischen Tempels* (Vienna 1895).

Budde, K. "Ephod und Lade," ZATWiss 39 (1921) 1-42. Discusses Arnold's thesis.

Budde, K., "Die Herfunft *Ṣadoḳ*'s," ZATWiss 52 (1934) 42-50.

Buxtorf, J., "Historia Urim et Thummim," in B. Ugolinus, ed., ThesAntSacr 12 (Venice 1751) c. 375-438.

Capmany, J., *et al.*, *Teología del Sacerdocio,* v. 1, "Orientaciones metodológicas" (Burgos 1969).

Cerfaux, L., "Le sacre du grand prêtre (selon Hébr. 5,5-10," BiblVieChr n. 21 (1958) 54-58.

Chapot, V., Toutain, J., "Sacerdos (Rome)," DictAntGrRom IV ,2 (1877-1919) 942-951.

Cheyne, T.K., "The Priesthood of David's Sons," *Expositor* ser. 5, v. IX (1899) 453-457.

Clarkson, Mary, E., "The Antecedents of the High-Priest Theme in Hebrews," AnglThRev (1947) 89-95.

Cody, A., "*Heavenly Sanctuary and Liturgy in the Epistle to the Hebrews* " (St. Meinrad, Ind. 1960).

Cody, A., *A History of Old Testament Priesthood.* AnalBibl 35 (Rome 1969).

Cohen, M.A., "The Role of the Shilonite Priesthood in the United Monarchy of Ancient Israel," HebUCAnn 36 (1965) 59-98.

Colson, J., "Le sacerdoce du Christ," in *Ministre de Jésus-Christ, ou le sacerdoce de l' Evangile.* Théologie historique 4 (Paris 1966).

Congar, Y., "L' Évangile, le sacerdoce Aaronique et les sacerdoces païens," *Evangéliser* 13 (1958-59) 288-304.

Contenau, G., *La Magie chez les Assyriens et les Babyloniens* (Paris 1947). Deals generally with priests, magicians, and exorcists of Mesopotamia.

Coppens, J., *Le messianisme royal. Ses origines, son développement, son accomplissement.* Lectio Divina 5 (Paris 1968).

Cornitescu, E., "Priesthood in (the writings of) the Prophets," *Studie Teologie* 19 (1967) 482-491 [in Rumanian].

Couturier, G., "Le prêtre et l'enseignement en Israël," in *Le prêtre, hier, aujourd'hui, demain.* Cogitatio Fidei 5 (Ottawa-Paris 1970) 44-55.

Cox, W.L.P., *The Heavenly Priesthood of our Lord* (Oxford 1929 and 1938).

Cullmann, O., *The Christology of the New Testament*, tr. S.C. Guthrie and C.A.M. Hall (2nd ed., Philadelphia 1963).

Curtiss, S.I., *The Levitical Priests. A Contribution to the Criticism of the Pentateuch* (Edinburgh 1877).

Darwin, R.C., *Die Entwicklung des Priestertums und der Priesterreiche* (Leipzig 1929). An unscientific diatribe (see ThLitz 55, 1930, c, 481f).

De Groot, J.J.M., "The Priesthood of Animism," in *The Religious System of China*, v. 6 (Leyden 1892; repr; Taipei 1964) 1187-1341.

Deissler, A., *Der Priesterliche Dienst.* I : *Ursprung und Geschichte.* QuaestDisp 46 (Freiburg i. Br. 1970) 9-80 (OT priesthood).

Delcor, M., "Le sacerdoce, les lieux de culte, les rites et les fêtes dans les documents de Khirbet Qumrân," RevHistRel 144 (1953) 5-41.

Dhorme, E., "Le personnel sacré," in *La religion des Hébreux nomades* (Bruxelles 1937) 221-246.

Dillenschneider, C., *Christ the one Priest and we his Priests*, tr. Sister M. Renell, 2 vols (St. Louis, Miss. 1964-65). Ch. I-III treat of the priesthood of Christ.

Dodd, W.H., "Toward a Theology of Priesthood," ThSt 28 (1967) 683-705.

Eberharter, A., "Der israelitische Levitismus in der vorexilischen Zeit," ZKathTh 52 (1928) 492-518.

Edersheim, A., *The Temple, its Ministry and Services, as they were at the Time of Jesus* (London 1874) 58-78.

Edsman, C.-M., ed., *Studies in Shamanism.* Scripta Instituti Donneriani Aboensis, I (Stockholm 1967).

Eliade, M., "Specialists of the Sacred : from Medicine Men to Mystics and Founders of Religions," in *From Primitives to Zen. A Thematic Sourcebook of the History of Religions* (London 1967) 201-228.

Eliade, M., "The Medicine Men and their Supernatural Models," *History of Religions* 7 (1967) 157-183.

Elliger, K., "Ephod und Choschen. Ein Beitrag zur Entwicklungsgeschichte des hohepriesterlichen Ornats," VetTest 8 (1958) 19-35.

Elliot, J.H., *The Elect and the Holy. An exegetical Examination of 1 Peter 2 :4-10 and the phrase basileion hierateuma.* SupplNT 12 (Brill, Leiden 1966).

Emerton, J.A., "Priests and Levites in Deuteronomy. An Examination of Dr. G.E. Wright's Theory," VetTest 12 (1962) 129-138.

Engnell, I., *Studies in Divine Kingship in the Ancient Near East* (2nd ed., Oxford 1967).

Erman, A., *Die Religion der Ägypter, ihr werden und vergehen in vier Jahrtausenden* (Berlin 1934), esp. 187-192, 200-206.

Esteve, H.M., *De coelesti mediatione sacerdotali Christi juxta Hebr. VIII 3-4* (Madrid 1949).

Fisher, L., "Abraham and his Priest-King," JBiblLit 81 (1962) 264-270.

Frank, C., *Studien zur Babylonischen Religion*, v. 1 (Strassburg i.E. 1911) 1-37.

Friedrich, A., *Afrikanische Priestertümer. Vorstudien zu einer Untersuchung...* Studien zur Kulturkunde 6 (Stuttgart 1939).

Friedrich, G., "Beobachtungen zur messianischen Hohepriestererwartung in den Synoptikern," ZTheolKirche 53 (1956) 265-311.

Friedrich, G., "Das Lied vom Hohenpriester in Zusammenhang von Hebr 4,14-5,10," ThZ 18 (1962) 95-115.

Friedrich, I., *Ephod und Choschen im Lichte des Alten Orient.* Wiener Beiträge zur Theologie 20 (Freiburg i. Br. 1968).

Fruin, R., "Eli de priester te Silo," *Nieuw Theologisch Tijdschrift* 20 (1931) 108-113.

Gabriel, J., *Untersuchungen über das alttestamentliche Hohepriestertum, mit besonderer Berücksichtigung des hohepriesterlichen Ornates* (Wien 1933).

Garrigou-Lagrange, R., "La sacerdoce du Christ," VieSpirit 14 (1926) 469-490.

Gates, O.H., "The Relation of Priests to Sacrifice before the Exile," JBiblLit 27 (1908) 67-92.

Gayford, S.C., *Sacrifice and Priesthood, Jewish and Christian* (London 1924 and 1953).

Geden, A.S., "Priest, Priesthood (Buddhist)," Hastings ERE 10 (1918) 288-290.

Gelin, A., "Le sacerdoce de l' ancienne alliance," in *La tradition sacerdotale : Études sur le sacerdoce.* BiblFacCatThLyon 7 (Le Puy 1959) 27-60.

Gelin, A., "The Priesthood of Christ in the Epistle to the Hebrews," in *The Sacrament of Holy Orders* (Collegeville, Minn. 1962) 30-59.

Gnilka, J., "Die Erwartung des Messianischen Hohenpriesters in den Schriften von Qumran und im Neuen Testament," RevQum 2 (1960) 395-426.

Goetze, A., "The Priestly Dress of the Hittite King," JCunSt 1 (1947) 176-185.

González Nuñez, A., *Profetas, sacerdotes y reyes en el Antiguo Israel : problemas de adaptación del yahvismo en Canaán* .Monografías 1 (Madrid 1962).

Gordon, P., *Le sacerdoce à travers les âges* (Paris 1950). Attempts to verify in different religions his metaphysical conception of priesthood.

Graf, K.H., "Zur Geschichte des Stammes Levi," *Archiv für wissenschaftliche Erforschung des Alten Testamentes*, v. 1 (Hall 1867-69) 68-106, 208-236.

Grässer, E., "Der Hebräerbrief 1938-1963," ThRu 30 (1964) 138-236.

Gray, G.B., "The Hebrew Priesthood : its Origin, History, and Functions," in *Sacrifice in the Old Testament. Its Theory and Practice* (Oxford 1925) 179-270.

Gray, J., "Sacral Kingship in Ugarit," *Ugaritica* VI (Paris 1969) 289-302.

Grelot, P., *Le ministère de la Nouvelle Alliance.* Foi vivante 37 (Paris 1967).

Grimme, H., "Der südarabische Levitismus und sein Verhältnis zum Levitismus in Israel, *Muséon* 37 (1924) 169-199.

Guillaume, A., *Prophecy and Divination among the Hebrews and other Semites* (London 1938).

Gunneweg, A.H.J., *Leviten und Priester. Hauptlinien der Traditionsbildung und Geschichte des israelitisch-jüdischen Kultpersonals.* FRLANT 89 (Göttingen 1965).

Gyllenberg, R., "Die Christologie des Hebräerbriefes," ZSystTh 11 (1934) 662-690. Holds that Christ is Priest only in Heaven.

Haag, E., "Priestertum und Altes Testament," TrierThZ 80 (1971) 20-42.

Haekel, J., "Priester, Priestertum (Religionsgeschichtlich)," LexThK² 8 (1963) 735-741.

Haldeman, I.M., *The Tabernacle, Priesthood and Offerings* (New York 1926).

Hansen, M.B., "Den Historiske og den himmelske ypperstepraest i Hebraeerbrevet," *Dansk Teologisk Tidsskrift* 26 (1963) 1-22. The representation of the heavenly High Priest would be connected with the *Anthrōpos* Mytn.

Hanson, A.T., "Christ in the Old Testament according to Hebrews," *Studia Evangelica,* v. 2 = *Texte und Untersuchungen* 87 (Berlin 1964). Foı Heb Melchizedek was Christ pre-incarnate.

Harris, J.S., "The Stones of the High Priest's Breastplate," AnnLeedsUnivOr Soc 5 (1963-65) 40-62.

Hauer, C.E., Jr., *The Priests of Qumran* (Diss. Vanderbilt Univ. 1959, in microfilm).... See RevQum 2 (1959-60) 300 or 303.

Hauer, C.E. Jr., "Who was Zadok ?," JBiblLit 82 (1963) 89-94.

Haupt, P., "Heb. *kôhen* und *qahál,*" JAmOrSoc 42 (1922) 372-375. See also *Id.* in AmJSemLang 32 (1915) 64-65 (on *ramku=kōmēr*).

Hauret, C., "Aux origines du sacerdoce danite : à propos de Jud. 18 :30-31," *Mélanges bibliques rédigés en l'honneur de André Robert* (Paris 1957) 105-113.

Hauret, C., "Moïse était-il prêtre ?" in *Studia Biblica et Orientalia* = AnalBibl 10 (Rome 1959).

Higgins, J.B., "The Priestly Messiah," NTSt 13 (1966-67) 211-239. See also VetTest 3 (1953) 321-336.

Höfner, M., "War der sabäische Mukarıib ein 'Priesterfürst' "? *Wiener Zeitschrift für die Kunde des Morgenlandes* 54 (1957) 77-85.

Hölscher, G., "Levi," Pauly-Wiss RE 12 (1916) c. 2155-2208,

Hölscher, G., *Die Hohenpriesterliste bei Josephus und die evangelische Chronologie* (Heidelberg 1940).

Hooke, S.H., *Prophets and Priests.* Interpreter Series 3 (London 1938).

Horneffer, A., *Der Priester. Seine Vergangenheit und seine Zukunft,* 2 vols (Jena 1912).

Hoschander, J., *The Priests and Prophets* (New York 1938).

Hruby, K., "La notion d'ordination dans la tradition juive," *Maison-Dieu* 102 (1970) 30-56.

Hummelauer, F. von, *Das vormosaische Priestertum in Israel. Vergleichende Studie zu Exodus und 1 Chron. 2-8* (Freiburg i. Br. 1899).

Hydon, P.V., *The Priesthood of Jesus as presented by the Epistle to the Hebrews* (Boston 1941).

Idiart, P., "The Priest, Pagan and Christian," in *The Sacrament of Holy Orders,* tr. from French [1957] (Collegeville, Minn. 1962) 259-291.

James, E.O., *The Nature and Function of Priesthood : a Comparative and Anthropological Study* (New York 1955).

Jansen, A., *Schwäche und Vollkommenheit des Hohepriesters Christus. Ein Beitrag zur Christologie des Hebräerbriefes* (Diss. Univ. Greg., Rome 1957).

Janssens, A., "De sacerdotio et sacrificio Christi," 34 (1931) 376-386.

Jean, Ch.-F., *La religion sumérienne, d'après les documents antérieurs à la dynastie d'Isin (-2186)* (Paris 1931). On Sumerian priesthood : 197-212.

Johnson, A.R., "The Rôle of the king in the Jerusalem Cultus," in S.H. Hooke, ed., *The Labyrinth* (London 1935) 71-111.

Kees, H., *Das Priestertum im ägyptischen Staat vom neuen Reich bis zur Spätzeit.* Probleme der Ägyptologie 1 (Brill, Leiden 1953 and 1958).

Kees, H., *Die Hohenpriester des Amun von Karnak von Herihor bis zum Ende der Äthiopienzeit.* Probleme der Ägyptologie 4 (Brill, Leiden 1964).

Keith, A.B., "Priest, Priesthood (Hindu)," Hastings ERE 10 (1918) 311-319.

Kennedy, G.T., *St. Paul's Conception of the Priesthood of Melchisedech: an historico-exegetical investigation* (Washington, C.U.A. Press 1951).

Kennett, R.H., "The Origin of the Aaronite Priesthood," JThSt 6 (1904-05) 161-186.

Kuenen, A., *Die Geschichte des Jahwepriestertums und das Alter des Priestergesetzes*, tr. K. Budde (Freiburg i. Br. 1894). Translated from the Dutch ThTijd (1890) 1-42.

Kutsch, E., "Salbung des Hohenpriesters im nachexilischen Judentum," in *Salbung als Rechtsakt im Alten Testament und im Alten Orient.* BeihZATWiss 87 (Berlin 1963). 22-27.

Labat, R., Le caractère religieux de la royauté assyro-babylonienne (Paris 1939).

Laing, G.J., "Priest, Priesthood (Roman)," Hastings ERE 10 (1918) 325-335.

Landersdorfer, S., "Das Priesterkönigtum von Salem," JSocOrRes 9 (1925) 203-216.

Landersdorfer, S., "Das Problem der Priestersalbung im Gesetze," ThQdchr 107 (1926) 185-197.

Landtman, G., *The Origin of Priesthood* (Ekenaes, Finland 1905). A good collection of facts, but does not sufficiently distinguish priests from other specialists.

Landtman, G., "Priest, Priesthood (primitive)," Hastings ERE (1918) 325-335.

Langevin, P.-E., "Le sacerdoce du Christ dans le Nouveau Testament," in *Le prêtre, hier, aujoud'hui, demain.* Cogitatio Fidei 51 (Ottawa-Paris 1970) 63-79.

Leclant, J., *Enquêtes sur les sacerdoces et les sanctuaires égyptiens à l'époque dite "ethiopienne"* (XXVe Dyn.) (Cairo 1954).

Lécuyer, J., "Jésus fils de Josédec et le sacerdoce du Christ (Zach 3)," RechScRel 43 (1955) 82-103.

Lécuyer, J., "L'unique vrai prêtre et l'unique vrai sacrifice," in *Le sacerdoce dans le mystère du Christ.* Lex Orandi 24 (Paris 1957) 9-62.

Lefebvre, G., *Histoire des grands prêtres d'Amon de Karnak jusqu'à la XXIe Dynastie* (Paris 1929).

Lefebvre, G., *Inscriptions concernant les grands prêtres d'Amon Romê-Roÿ et Amenhotep* (Paris 1929).

Lefebvre, G., "Prêtres de Sekhmet," *Archiv Orientální* 20 (1952) 57-64.

Legrand, P.-E., "Sacerdos (Hiereus, Grèce)," DictAntGrRom IV, 2 (1877-1919) 934-942.

Leloir, L., "Valeurs permanentes du sacerdoce lévitique," NouvRevTh 92 (1970) 246-266.

Lippert, J., *Allgemeine Geschichte des Priestertums*, 2 vols (Berlin 1883-84). Studies the phenomena of priesthood in the preliterate and literate societies.

Liver, J., "The 'Sons of Zadok the Priests' in the Dead Sea Sect," RevQum 6 (1967) 3-30.

Liver, J., *Chapters in the History of the Priests and Levites. Studies in the Lists of Chronicles and Nehemiah* (Jerusalem 1968). [in Hebrew]

Lundius, J., *Die alten jüdischen Heiligtümer, Gottesdienste und Gewohnheiten, für Augen gestellet, in einer ausführlichen Beschreibung des ganzen Levitischen Priesterthums...* (Hamburg 1738), esp. 409-734.

Magnien, V., "Initiation sacerdotale," *Les mystères d'Eleusis* (Paris 1950) 280-306.

Maier, J., "Urim und Tummim. Recht und Bund in der Spannung zwischen Königtum und Priestertum im Alten Israel," *Kairos* 11 (1969) 22-38.

Manson, T.W., *Ministry and Priesthood: Christ's and Ours* (John Knox Press, Richmond, Va 1959).

Martha, J., *Les sacerdoces athéniens* (Paris 1882).

Mauchline, J., "Aaronite and Zadokite Priests : Some Reflections on an Old Problem," GlasgowUnivOrSocTransactions 21 (1965-66) 1-11.

Maybaum, S., *Die Entwickelung des altisraelitischen Priesterthums. Ein Beitrag zur Kritik der mittleren Bücher des Pentateuchs* (Breslau 1880).

Maystre, C., "Sur les grands prêtres de Ptah," JNEastSt 8 (1949) 84-89.

Mazar, B., "The Cities of the Priests and the Levites," *Congress Volume.* VetTestSuppl 7 (Brill, Leiden 1960).

McNeile, A.H., "The Origin of the Aaronite Priesthood," JThSt 7 (1905-06) 1-9.

Meek, T.J., "Aaronites and Zadokites," AmJSemLang 45 (1928-29) 149-166. See also AmJSemLang 56 (1939) 113-120.

Meeks, W.A., "Moses as High Priest and Mystagogue," *The Prophet-King. Moses Traditions and the Johannine Christology* (Brill, Leiden 1967) 117-125.

Meyer, R., "Levitische Emancipazionsbestrebungen in nachexilischer Zeit," OrLitz 41 (1938) 721-728.

Meyer, R., "Die Mosesagen und die Lewiten," in *Die Israeliten und ihre Nachbarstämme* (Halle 1906) 1-99.

Milligan, A., *The Ascension and Heavenly Priesthood of our Lord* (London 1908) 61-165.

Moe, O., "Das Priestertum Christi im Neuen Testament ausserhalb Hebräerbrief," ThLitz 72 (1947) 335-338.

Mohler, J.A., *The Origin and Evolution of the Priesthood. A Return to the Sources* (Alba House, New York 1970). Has nine pages on "Jewish presbyters," the rest has to do with the Christian ministry.

Montet, P., "Études sur quelques prêtres et fonctionnaires du dieu Min," JNEastSt 9 (1950) 18-27.

Morgenstern, J., "A Chapter in the History of High-Priesthood," AmJSemLang 55 (1938) 1-24, 183-197, 360-377.

Morison, E.F., "The Relation of Priest and Prophet in the History of Israel before the Exile," JThSt 11 (1910) 211-245.

Mouterde, P., "Les mots *hiereus*, sacerdos, et *presbyteros*, presbyter," MélUnSJos 38 (1962) 164-172.

Murmelstein, B., "Adam. Ein Beitrag zur Messiaslehre," WienerZKundeMgl 35 (1928) 242-275, 36 (1929) 51-86. Discusses the priesthood of Adam in the Jewish Haggada.

Nielsen, E., "The Levites in Ancient Israel," AnnSwedThInst 3 (1964) 16-27....

Nomoto, S., "Herkunft und Struktur der Hohenpriestervorstellung im Hebräerbrief,",- NovTest 10 (1968) 10-25.

North, F.S., "Aaron's Rise in Prestige," ZATWiss 66 (1954) 191-199.

North, R., "The Qumrân 'Sadducees'," CathBiblQuart 17 (1955) 164-168.

Nowack, W., "Die heilige Personen," in *Lehrbuch der hebräischen Archäologie,* v. 2 (3rd ed., Freiburg i. Br. 1894).

Olsen, M., "Le prêtre-magicien et le dieu-magicien dans la Norvège ancienne," RevHist-Rel 111 (1935) 177-221, 112 (1935) 5-49.

Orrieux, L.-M., "Problèmes bibliques du sacerdoce," LumetVie 15 (1966) 127-146.

Otto, W., "Kauf und Verkauf von Priestertümern bei den Griechen," *Hermes* 44 (1909) 594-599.

Otto, W., *Priester und Tempel im hellenistischen Ägypten*, 2 vols (Leipzig 1905-08).

Palmer, P.F., "Priest and Priesthood, Christian," NCE 11 (1967) 768-772.

Parente, P., "Teologia del sacerdozio di G. Cristo," in G. Cacciatore, ed., *Enciclopedia del sacerdozio* (Firenze 1953) 581-602.

Paton, L.B., "The Use of the Word *Kōhēn* in the Old Testament," JBiblLit 12 (1893) 1-14.

Pedersen, J., "The Priest," *Israel, its Life and Culture III-IV* (Copenhagen 1940) 150-198.

Piepenbring, C., "Histoire des lieux de culte et du sacerdoce en Israël," RevHistRel 24 (1891) 1-60, 133-186.

Pinches, T.G., "Priest, Priesthood (Babylonian)," Hastings ERE 10 (1918) 284-288.

Plaumann, G., "Hiereis," Pauly-Wiss RE 8 (1913) c. 1424-57.

Plöger, O., "Priester und Prophet," ZATWiss 63 (1951) 157-192.

Porteous, N.W., "Prophet and Priest in Israel," ExposTimes 62 (1950-51) 4-9.

Procksch, O., "Fürst und Priester bei Hesekiel," ZATWiss 58 (1940-41) 99-133.

Quandt, J.J., "De pontificis maximi suffraganeo," in B. Ugolinus, ed., ThesAntSacr 12 (Venice 1751) c. 963-1028.

Rabanos, R., *El sacerdocio de Christo según San Pablo* (Madrid 1942).

Rawlinson, J., "Priesthood and Sacrifice in Judaism and Christianity," ExposTimes 60 (1949) 116-121.

Rehm, M.D., *Studies in the History of Pre-Exilic Levites* (Diss. Harvard, Cambridge, Mass. 1967f). See HarvTR 61 (1968) 648f.

Renger, J., "Untersuchungen zum Priestertum in der altbabylonischen Zeit," Pt. 1 and 2, ZAssyr NF 24 (1967) 110-188, 25 (1969) 104-230.

Riewald, P., "Sacerdotes," Pauly-Wiss RE IA, 2 (1930) c. 1631-53.

Ringgren, H., "The Cultic Functionaries," in *Israelite Religion*, tr. David Green (S.P.C.K., London 1966) 204-219.

Robertson, E., "The *'Ūrīm* and *Thummīm;* what were they ?," VetTest 14 (1964) 67-74.

Rodriguez Molero, F.X., "El sacerdocio celeste de Christo," EstBibl 22 (1963) 69-77. Is mostly concerned with Cody's book.

Romaniuk, C., "Le sacerdoce du Christ," in *Le sacerdoce dans le Nouveau Testament* (Le Puy 1966) 14-42.

Rowley, H.H., "Melchisedek and Zadok (Gen 14 and Ps 110)," *Fs .Alfred Bertholet* (Tübingen 1950) 461-472.

Sabourin, L., " 'Liturge du sanctuaire et de la tente véritable' (Héb. VIII. 2)," NTSt 18 (1971) 87-90.

Salaün, R.-Marcus, E., *Qu'est-ce qu'un prêtre ?* (Paris 1965), esp. 77-98, where a comparison is made between the Christian priest and the Levitical priest.

Salguero, J., "Sacerdocio Levítico y sacerdocio real en el Antiguo Testamento," *Ciencia Tomista* 93 (1966) 341-366.

Sanday, E., ed., *Different Conceptions of Priesthood and Sacrifice. A Report of a Conference held at Oxford December 13 and 14, 1899* (London 1900).

Saubert, J., "De sacerdotibus et sacris Ebraeorum personis," in B. Ugolinus, ed., Thes-AntSacr 12 (Venice 1751) c. 2-80.

Sauneron, S., "Le prêtre-astronome du temple d'Esna," *Kèmi* 15 (1959) 36-41.

Sauneron, S., *The Priests of Ancient Egypt*, tr. A. Morrissett (Pelican, London 1960).

Sauneron, S., "Les conditions d'accès à la fonction sacerdotale à l'époque gréco-romaine," ZIFAO 61 (1962) 55-57. Concerns Egypt.

Schaefer, J.R., "The Relationship between Priestly and Servant Messianism in the Epistle to the Hebrews," CathBiblQuart 30 (1968) 359-385.

Scharbert, J., *Heilsmittler im alten Testament und im alten Orient*. QuaestDisp 23/24 (Freiburg i. Br. 1964) 268-280.

Scheller, E.J., *Das Priestertum Christi im Anschluss an den Hl. Thomas von Aquin* (Paderborn 1934).

Schiller, G., "Erwägungen zur Hohepriesterlehre des Hebräerbriefes," ZTWiss 46 (1955) 81-109.

Schilling, O., " 'Nicht schwindet vom Priester die Weisung' (Jr 18,18). Der alttestamentliche Priester als Träger der Verkündigung," in *Hengsbach-Festschrift* (Essen 1970) 11-38.

Schindler, B., *Das Priestertum im alten China*, I: *Königtum und Priestertum* (Diss., Leipzig 1918).

Schrank, W., *Babylonische Sühnriten, besonders mit Rücksicht auf Priester und Büsser untersucht* (Leipzig 1908).

Schrenk, G., "Hiereus, Archireus," Kittel ThW (Eng) 3 (1965) 257-283.

Schürer, E., *Geschichte des jüdischen Volkes im Zeitalter Jesu Christi*, v. 2 (4th ed., Leipzig 1907).

Scott, R.B.Y., "Priesthood, Prophecy, Wisdom and the Knowledge of God," JBiblLit 80 (1961) 1-15.

Scott, W.M.F., "Priesthood in the New Testament," ScotJTh 10 (1957) 399-415.

Serina, A., *La figura di Melchisedec nel salmo CX. 4* (Trapani 1971).

Sklba, R.J., *The Teaching Function of the Pre-exilic Israelite Priesthood* (Rome 1965).

Smith, H.P., "Priest, Priesthood (Hebrew)," Hastings ERE 10 (1918) 307-311.

Smith, J., *A Priest for Ever. A Study of Typology and Eschatology in Hebrews* (London 1969).

Smith, W.F., *A Study of Zadokite High Priesthood within the Graeco-Roman Age: from Simeon the Just to the High Priests appointed by Herod the Great* (diss. Harvard, Cambridge, Mass., n. d.). See HarvThRev 54 (1961) 303.

Smith, E.R., Bertholet, A., "Levites," "Priests," EncBibl 3 (1902) 2770-76, 3837-47.

Spicq, C., "L'origine johannique de la conception du Christ-Prêtre dans l'Épître aux Hébreux," in *Aux sources de la tradition chrétienne. Mélanges Goguel* (Neuchâtel-Paris 1950) 258-269.

Spicq, C., "Prêtre et sacrifice," in *L'Épître aux Hébreux*, v. 2 (Paris 1953) 119-139.

Stewart, R.A., "The Sinless High-Priest," NTSt 14 (1967) 126-135.

Strauss, H., *Untersuchungen zu den Überlieferungen der vorexilischen Leviten* (Diss., Bonn 1960). See Gunneweg, *op. cit.*, p. 12, and passim.

Strunk, H., "Das alttestamentliche Oberpriestertum," ThStKrit 81 (1908) 1-26.

Strunk, H., *Die hohepriesterliche Theorie im Alten Testamente* (Halle 1906).

Stummer, F., "Gedanken über die Stellung des Hohenpriesters in der alttestamentlichen Gemeinde," *Episcopus. Fs. Kard. M. von Faulhaber* (Regensburg 1949) 19-48.

Szlechter, E., "Le prêter dans l'Ancien Testament et dans les codes Mésopotamiens d'avant Hammurabi," RevHistPhilRel 35 (1955) 16-25.

Teodorico Da Castel S. Pietro, "Il Sacerdozio celeste di Christo nella lettera agli Ebrei," Greg 39 (1958) 319-334.

Thiersch, H., *Ependytes und Ephod. Gottesbild und Priesterkleid im alten Vorderasien* (Stuttgart 1936).

Toepffer, H.A., "De tiara summi pontificis," in B. Ugolinus, ed., ThesentSacr 12 (Venice 1751) c. 811-852.

Torrance, T.F., "The Royal Priest," in *Royal Priesthood.* ScotJTh Occasional Papers 3 (Edinburgh 1955) 1-21.

Ugolinus, B., "Sacerdotium Hebraicum," in ThesAntSacr 12 (Venice 1751) c. 135-1156. See also *id.,ibid.* c. 1051-1102 ("de sacerdote castrensi").

Ungeheuer, J., *Der grosse Priester über dem Hause Gottes. Die Christologie des Hebräerbriefes* (Würzburg 1939).

Urie, D.M.L., "Officials of the Cult at Ugarit," PalExplQ 80 (1948) 42-47.

Vallejo, A., *Melquisedek o el sacerdocio real* (Buenos Aires 1959).

Van Dijk, J.J., "Sumerer," in H. Haag, ed., Bibel-Lexikon (Einsiedeln 1968) 1654-64.

Van Dijk, J.J., "Les contacts ethniques dans la Mésopotamie et les syncrétismes de la religion sumérienne," in Sven S. Hartmann, ed., *Syncretism.* Scripta Instituti Donneriani Aboensis III (Stockholm 1969) 171-206.

Van Hoonacker, A., "Les prêtres et les lévites dans le livre d'Ézéchiel," RevBibl 8 (1899) 175-205; see *id.* in ExposTimes 12 (1900-01) 494-498.

Van Hoonacker, A., *Le sacerdoce lévitique dans le loi et dans l'histoire* (London 1899). Well informed but weak in its critical approach.

Vanhoye, A., *Epistolae ad Hebraeos textus de sacerdotio Christi* and *Lectiones de sacerdotio in Heb.7* (ad usum auditorum Rome, 1969 and 1970).

Vaux, R. de, " 'Lévites" minéens et lévites israélites," *Lex tua Veritas Fs. für Hubert Junker* (Trier 1961) 265-273 = *Bible et Orient* 277-287.

Vaux, R. de, *Israel, Its Life and Institutions*, tr. J. McHugh (2nd ed., London 1965) 345-405.

Vaux, R. de, "Le sacerdoce en Israël," in *Populus Dei*, v. 1, *Studi in onore del Card. Alfredo Ottaviani* (Roma 1969) 113-168.

Vawter, B., "Levitical Messianism and the New Testament," in J.L. McKenzie, ed., *The Bible in Current Catholic Throught* (New York 1962) 83-99.

Vigouroux, F., "Les prêtres de Baal (III Reg., XVIII, 23-28) et leurs successeurs dans l'antiquité et dans le temps présent," RevBibl 5 (1896) 227-240.

Vogelstein, H., *Der Kampf zwischen Priestern und Leviten seit den Tagen Ezechiels. Eine historisch-kritische Untersuchung* (Stettin 1899).

Wambacq, B.N., "De ministris sacris," *Instituta Biblica*, v. 1 (Roma 1965) 113-184.

Welch, A.C., *Prophet and Priest in Old Israel* (London 1936).

Wellhausen, J., *Prolegomena to the History of Ancient Israel*, tr. from German by J.S. Black and A. Menzies (Cleveland 1957). This is the "Meridian Book" edition of the translation published at Edinburgh in 1885. See esp. pp. 121-167.

Wenschkewitz, H., *Die Spiritualisierung der Kultusbegriffe Tempel, Priester und Opfer im Neuen Testament.* Angelos 4 (Leipzig 1932) 70-230.

Westphal, G., "Aaron und die Aaroniden," ZATWiss 26 (1906) 201-230.

Wiener, H.M., "Priests and Levites : the Fourth Chapter of Wellhausen's Prolegomena," BiblSacra 67 (1910) 486-539.

Wikander, S., *Feuer-Priestertum im Klein-Asien und Iran* (Lund 1946).

Williamson, R., "The Logos and the High Priest in Philo and Hebrews," in *Philo and the*

Epistle to the Hebrews. Arbeiten zur Literatur und Geschichte des hellenistischen Judentums IV (Brill, Leiden 1970) 409-434.

Wissowa, G., *Religion und Kultus der Römer*. Hdb der kl. Altertums-Wissenschaft V, 4 (2nd ed., Munich 1912). 479-566.

Witzel, M., "Dienstinstructionen an das hethitische Tempelpersonal," in *Misc llanea biblica et orientalia R.P.A. Miller oblata*. Studia Anselmiana 27-28 (Rome 1951) 476-485.

Woodhouse, W.J., "Priest, Priesthood (Greek), "Hastings ERE 10 (1918) 302-307.

Wright, G.E., "The Levites in Deuteronomy," VetTest 4 (1954) 325-330.

Zeitlin, S., "The Titles High Priest and the Nasi of the Sanhedrin," JewishQuartRev 48 (1957-58) 1-5.

Zimmermann, H., *Die Hohepriester-Christologie des Hebräerbriefes* (Paderborn (1964).

INDEX OF SUBJECTS